W9-AZC-995

# www.wadsworth.com

*wadsworth.com* is the World Wide Web site for Wadsworth and is your direct source to dozens of online resources.

At *wadsworth.com* you can find out about supplements, demonstration software, and student resources. You can also send email to many of our authors and preview new publications and exciting new technologies.

**wadsworth.com**
Changing the way the world learns®

David W. Martin is professor and head of the Department of Psychology at North Carolina State University. Previously he was professor and department head at New Mexico State University. He has a bachelor's degree from Hanover College, where he majored in psychology and physics. He also has a master's degree and Ph.D. from The Ohio State University, where he majored in engineering psychology. His teaching interests include experimental methods, introductory psychology, human performance, and attention. He has won teaching awards at both NC State and NMSU.

Dr. Martin has published in a number of research journals in the areas of attention, decision making, and memory. He is a member of the American Psychological Association, American Psychological Society, Human Factors and Ergonomics Society, and Psychonomic Society. He has also served as president of the Rocky Mountain Psychological Association.

In his leisure hours, Dr. Martin enjoys running, scuba diving, singing, and playing at the beach with his wife and two young sons. For 12 years he raced dirt-track stockcars and was known as "Dangerous David, the Racing Professor."

# Doing Psychology Experiments

## FIFTH EDITION

**David W. Martin**
*North Carolina State University*

**Wadsworth**
Thomson Learning™

Australia • Canada • Denmark • Japan • Mexico • New Zealand • Philippines • Puerto Rico
Singapore • South Africa • Spain • United Kingdom • United States

Psychology Editor: *Vicki Knight*
Editorial Assistant: *Rachael Bruckman*
Marketing Manager: *Jenna Opp*
Project Editor: *Tanya Nigh*
Print Buyer: *April Reynolds*
Permissions Editor: *Bob Kauser*

Production Service: *Scratchgravel Publishing Services*
Copy Editor: *Jamie Fuller*
Cover Designer: *Roger Knox*
Compositor: *Scratchgravel Publishing Services*
Printing and Binding: *Malloy Lithographing, Inc.*

COPYRIGHT © 2000, 1996, 1991, 1985, 1977 by Wadsworth, a division of Thomson Learning

All rights reserved. No part of this work covered by the copyright hereon may be reproduced or used in any form or by any means—graphic, electronic, or mechanical, including photocopying, recording, taping, or information storage and retrieval systems—without the written permission of the publisher.

Printed in the United States of America
2  3  4  5  6  7  03  02  01  00

For permission to use material from this text, contact us:
  **Web:** www.thomsonrights.com
  **Fax:** 1-800-730-2215
  **Phone:** 1-800-730-2214

**Wadsworth/Thomson Learning**
**10 Davis Drive**
**Belmont, CA 94002-3098**
**USA**
**www.wadsworth.com**

**International Headquarters**
Thomson Learning
290 Harbor Drive, 2nd Floor
Stamford, CT 06902-7477
USA

**UK/Europe/Middle East**
Thomson Learning
Berkshire House
168-173 High Holborn
London WC1V 7AA
United Kingdom

**Asia**
Thomson Learning
60 Albert Street #15-01
Albert Complex
Singapore 189969

**Canada**
Nelson/Thomson Learning
1120 Birchmount Road
Scarborough, Ontario M1K 5G4
Canada

**Library of Congress**
**Cataloging-in-Publication Data**
Martin, David W., 1943–
   Doing psychology experiments / David W. Martin. — 5th ed.
   p.  cm.
Includes bibliographical references and index.
ISBN 0-534-24871-3 (pbk. : alk. paper)
1. Psychology, Experimental.   2. Psychology—Research.   I. Title.
BF181.M315   2000
150'.7'24—dc21

                                                    99-16474

*This book is printed on recycled paper.*

*This book is dedicated to:*

*My father, the late Daniel W. Martin,*
*who taught me logical thinking,*

*My high school teacher, Doris Mitchell,*
*who showed me that teachers can care,*

*My undergraduate professor, Harve E. Rawson,*
*who introduced me to psychology,*

*My graduate professor, the late George E. Briggs,*
*who best demonstrated experimental rigor,*

*And all of my students,*
*from whom I am continually learning to teach.*

# CONTENTS

# PREFACE

*Doing Psychology Experiments* has now been on the market for nearly 25 years, and it still seems to be fulfilling its original function: to teach students with little or no background in experimentation how to do simple experiments in psychology. Throughout the five editions of the book I have tried to keep the writing style informal and friendly. Although scientific results are usually reported in an objective, impersonal style, I believe that doing experimentation is a highly personal experience. The experimenter reviews the literature and forms a view of the body of knowledge. The experimenter creates the theories and hypotheses for testing. The experimenter decides which variables to manipulate and which to measure. The experimenter interprets the results and determines how the body of knowledge has been advanced. The experimenter is personally involved in the process of experimentation, and I believe that the best way to teach new experimenters about this process is through a personal book.

Now a few words about what this book does and does not do. It provides enough information so that a student with no experimental background will be able to design, execute, interpret, and report simple psychological experiments. Although the book has most often been used for undergraduate courses in experimental methods, it has also been used with other books for other purposes. Several colleges use it for the laboratory section of introductory psychology courses. It is sometimes used in conjunction with a statistics book or a content book for experimental courses with those orientations. It is frequently adopted for undergraduate content courses (ranging from deviant behavior to consumer psychology) when the instructor requires experiments to be done and the students have little experimental background. I have talked with many users, both instructors and students. They report that the book can be used successfully as a stand-alone text and as a supplement. In fact, in my own experimental methods course, I assign chapters before lecturing on the material, give a little quiz to encourage the students to read the material before class, and then spend lecture time clarifying points where necessary, but mostly discussing experimental proposals and problems. The book does a good job of bringing a diverse set of students up to the same level so that class time can be used for more creative interaction.

Although the book is often used as a supplemental text and may appear physically smaller than some others on the market, it nevertheless does discuss most of the important concepts from experimental methods. I have attempted to provide comprehensive coverage of the area, and some research indicates that the attempt has been successful.* Authors of textbooks representing many areas of psychology were asked to rate the importance of terms and concepts from their subfields. Of the top 100 ranked terms in the methods/statistics area, 33 emphasized statistics or psychometric testing. Of the remaining 67 that emphasized methods, this book discusses all but 6. Four of those terms are discussed at a conceptual level but using alternative terminology. Only two terms, both ranking in the 90s, are not represented in this book. I believe that this evidence confirms the claim that this book provides comprehensive coverage of experimental methods.

What this book does not do is teach students much about the content and current findings in the various areas of experimental psychology. Many of the examples I use are contrived; they illustrate the methods being discussed, but they are not real and certainly will not give students a representative coverage of the content of experimental psychology. The book also does not teach students much about the intricacies of complex experimental design and statistical analysis. I have tried to keep it simple. Although I discuss the rationale behind descriptive and inferential statistics, the actual statistical operations presented in Appendix A are admittedly cookbookish.

The fifth edition has several new and different features. The first chapter, *How to Make Orderly Observations*, has been reduced in size. Over the first four editions I had added material on qualitative designs, surveys, and archival research as well as keeping considerable detail about experimentation. In this edition I moved the material on surveys into Chapter 10, now titled *How to Design Nontraditional Research*. Thus, Chapter 1 has become more of an overview of various research techniques used in psychology. The second chapter is now *How to Do Experiments*. It includes material moved from Chapter 1. In addition, Chapter 2 now includes the discussion of external and internal validity and the various threats to internal validity. Threats to internal validity are relevant to experiments as well as to quasi-experiments, and this discussion should help students better understand confounding variables.

Chapter 3, *How to Get an Experimental Idea*, includes new material to help students adapt an existing study they have found into a new study, one that will be their own. The biggest change in Chapter 4, *How to Be Fair with Participants*, is a rewrite of the section on animal subjects. I updated some of the material and tried to give more emphasis to the benefits that have been derived from animal research. I also underscore the strict standards required of labs doing such research. I added some material on the use of deception in human research based upon recent debates in *American*

*Boneau, C. A. (1990). Psychological literacy: A first approximation. *American Psychologist, 45,* 891–900.

*Psychologist.* In Chapter 5, *How to Be Fair with Science,* I have changed the terminology used to describe unacceptable and acceptable behavior. Some reviewers objected to the term "accepted cheating," so in this chapter I now talk about dirty tricks, questionable tricks, and neat tricks. These terms better reflect the acceptability of the various behaviors.

I have changed Chapter 6, *How to Find Out What Has Been Done,* to emphasize electronic searches rather than paper searches. Nearly all libraries now have either *PsycINFO* or *PsycLIT,* and many have discontinued *Psychological Abstracts.* So I have greatly reduced the discussion of *Abstracts* and, instead, lead the reader through an electronic search. I also discuss some of the advantages and pitfalls of using the Internet as an information source. Chapter 7 now includes a discussion of brain-imaging techniques. In Chapter 8, because it is a more logical order, I moved the presentation of between-subjects designs ahead of within-subject designs.

Chapter 9 is the combination of what had been Chapters 8 and 9 and is called *How to Plan Single-Variable, Multiple-Variable, and Converging-Series Experiments.* The material on single-subject and small-*N* baseline designs has been moved to Chapter 10, which is now called *How to Design Nontraditional Research.* This chapter also contains expanded material on how to do a survey, as well as quasi-experimentation. Chapter 13, *How to Report Experimental Reports,* includes an expanded discussion to help students prepare a poster presentation. It also compares APA style to styles used in other disciplines so students will not feel blind-sided when their previously learned rules don't work in psychology. In addition, all the references have been moved from the ends of the chapters to a single section at the end of the book.

An added feature of the fifth edition is the use of InfoTrac® College Edition. When students purchase the text, they automatically get access to this database for the duration of the course. The database contains recent newspaper, magazine, and journal articles that can be searched using key terms, authors' names, and so forth. Of particular interest for students using this book is access to journal articles and review articles. In writing this book, I have used contrived examples to illustrate most of the points. I have done so because I believe such examples drive home the point without students having to digest many superfluous details contained in real experiments. The problem with this approach is that students may leave the course never having been exposed to actual journal articles and real research results. For that reason, at the end of each chapter in this fifth edition I have included various exercises that encourage students to search the InfoTrac College Edition database to find journal articles illustrating issues raised in that chapter. If they carry out these exercises, by the end of the course students will have considerable experience reading journal articles. Instructors should review students' work to make sure they are indeed using legitimate journal articles rather than magazine or newspaper articles disguised as original research. The InfoTrac College Edition feature should provide a valuable aid for instructors who want to expose their students to the scientific body of knowledge that is psychology.

With all of these changes, the length of this new edition has only marginally increased. To those who have used previous editions, I hope you like the changes. To new users, I hope you like the book.

## ACKNOWLEDGMENTS

I would like to thank North Carolina State University for providing me with the time and resources to write. My editor at Brooks/Cole, Vicki Knight, pushed me gently to write a new edition and helped see the process through. I would also like to thank Carline Haga, Laurie Jackson, Kathy Joneson, Dorothy Kormos, Gay Meixel, Margaret Parks, Kelly Shoemaker, and Bill Waller for additional editorial and design assistance. In addition, I am grateful to the following manuscript reviewers: Gregory Burton, Seton Hall University; Joanna Harris, East Central Oklahoma University; Walter T. Herbranson, University of Utah; Deana Julka, University of Portland; Wolfgang Lutz, Northwestern University; Thomas Palmeri, Vanderbilt University; Kerri Pickel, Ball State University; Annette Taylor, University of San Diego; Benjamin Wallace, Cleveland State University; David Washburn, Georgia State University; Davin Youngclarke, California State University at Fresno; and Todd Zakrajsek, Southern Oregon State College.

Finally, I would like to thank the students in my classes who, by their performance, have told me where I have succeeded (and failed) and the many students from around the country who recognize me at meetings and let me know they like the book.

*David W. Martin*
david_martin@ncsu.edu

# 1

# How to Make Orderly Observations

Direct, intuitive observation, accompanied by questioning, imagination, or creative intervention, is a limited and misleading prescientific technique.

C. F. MONTE (1975)

The perversity of animate subjects has, of necessity, whelped a remarkable degree of experimental sophistication in the behavioral sciences.

S. N. ROSCOE (1980)

This book is meant to teach you how to do experiments in the science of psychology. Aside from the fact that learning to do this is required of psychology majors at many colleges, why would you want to know how to do psychological experimentation? One reason could be because you plan to become a psychologist, a scientist studying human and, sometimes, animal behavior. The experimental method is one of the major research tools for collecting data to build the scientific body of knowledge in psychology. I will briefly discuss some of the other tools in this book, but most of the book is concerned with how to do experiments.

Even if you do not plan to become a psychologist, learning about the use of experimentation in psychology can help you become a well-educated person and can provide you with useful skills that generalize to a number of careers. For example, suppose you go into the banking business and work your way up to being a vice president. Obviously, some of what you learn in psychology courses can help you succeed because you know something about human relations. However, what you know about experimentation can also help. Your boss calls you in and says: "As you know, we've just installed all these automatic tellers in our banks. We spent a lot of money on these newfangled machines, but for some reason the customers don't like to use them. I want you to figure out why and make whatever changes are necessary to get them to use the machines."

You will see as you read this book that carrying out such an assignment, while not a formal experiment, requires most of the skills needed for doing a psychology experiment. First, you must form several hypotheses

1

about why the automatic tellers are not being used: Do the customers feel depersonalized interacting with a machine? Are they intimidated? Do they not know how to use them? Do they feel less safe carrying their money around without the security of another person present? As a second step, some sort of data must be collected to narrow down the possible hypotheses, perhaps by doing interviews or using a questionnaire. Then you would probably want to make a manipulation to see whether you can change the customers' behavior: perhaps offering an educational program, if knowledge is a problem; perhaps giving prizes, if motivation is a problem; perhaps increasing privacy, if security is a problem. Finally, you would want to measure customers' behavior to see whether it changes with your manipulation and to determine whether any such change is meaningful. Although your boss did not ask you to do a psychology experiment, you have carried out most of the steps required to do one. Most jobs require the solving of people problems, and the skills you learn from this book should make you a better people-problem solver.

If you do wish to become a psychologist, the reasons for learning about research and experimentation are probably obvious. Certainly if you want to be an experimental psychologist, then doing experiments will be your main activity and you will repeatedly use the techniques taught in this book. But even if you plan on becoming a clinician or a counselor, at the very least you should know how psychological research is done; ideally, you should be able to do it. One of the major characteristics that distinguish clinical psychologists from others who do therapy, such as social workers and psychiatrists, is how closely tied to behavioral data they are. Early in the history of clinical training, some 50 years ago, educators got together and decided that clinical psychology students should be trained first as scientists and then as therapists, that without the science they would just be guessing about which therapeutic techniques work and which do not. That is why most clinical psychologists get a Ph.D. (doctor of philosophy), a research degree. It is true that today about a quarter of clinical psychologists get a Psy. D. (doctor of psychology) rather than a Ph.D. However, the curriculum for this degree still requires students to be thoroughly versed in research methods. Clinicians must be able to understand research and experimentation or they will not be able to determine the effectiveness of various treatments and to evaluate new interventions as they are introduced. Learning about experimentation is extremely important for future clinicians.

Over and above these practical reasons for learning to do psychology experiments, I hope that part of the reason you want to learn these skills is just because it's fun! We are all curious about the world around us. We want to know why things happen as they do. Humans invented science in order to better understand their world.[1] Science is an attempt to approach this discovery process in an orderly way. Early in life I found out that, for

---

[1]And, in the case of astronomy, other worlds as well.

me, experimentation was the most intriguing tool of science because it leads to the discovery of relationships that have never been known. Then when I learned about the science of psychology, I further discovered that this powerful tool could be used to understand what I considered to be the most interesting subject of all, human behavior.

Most people are very curious about their own behavior and the behavior of others. That is why we watch soap operas, gossip behind people's backs, fantasize, and read the *National Enquirer* in the grocery line—to speculate about human behavior. The use of experimentation in psychology allows us to check our speculations. What a thrill it was during my first course in experimental psychology to find scientific relationships that nobody else had ever seen. Even after years of doing experiments, my heart beats a little stronger when I get that first look at the results of a new experiment. My colleagues probably get tired of my running to their offices to show them the exciting discoveries as they unfold in my lab. I hope that you feel the same excitement when you do your research. Although there are more serious reasons for doing the science of psychology, may you always continue to appreciate the fun of experimentation.

## Psychology as a Science

Psychologists go about their business much like scientists do in other scientific fields. In their search for an understanding of human behavior, psychologists attempt to (1) establish relationships between circumstances and behaviors and (2) fit these relationships into an orderly body of knowledge. In this book we will deal primarily with the first activity, although we will touch on the second activity in Chapters 3 and 13.

What kind of relationship is acceptable to us as scientists? When we can demonstrate that one event is related to a second event in some predictable way, we have a statement that will fit into the scientific body of knowledge. At least one of these events must be a measurable behavior. Here we can make a distinction among the sciences. The behavior of major concern to us as psychologists is human behavior (and sometimes animal behavior). And this is where we run into one of our first problems, a problem that haunts psychologists but not physical scientists. Humans and animals are variable. We humans often cannot repeat a response precisely even if we wish to, and in some cases we may not wish to. In terms of variability, physical scientists typically have it easier than psychologists.

A physicist measuring the coefficient of friction for a wooden block might measure the time it takes the block to slide down an inclined plane. Although the times might vary from trial to trial, such variability would be relatively small. The physicist would not be making too great an error if he or she considered the variability a minor nuisance and measured the time for only one trial. However, a psychologist who wanted to measure the time it takes a human to press a button in response to a light would

be making a considerably greater error by ignoring human variability. Although it is unlikely that our physicist's block will be a little slow on certain trials because it has its mind on other things, isn't ready, or is blinking or asleep, a human can experience these and many other problems.

In addition to variability among trials, variability among humans must also be taken into account by psychologists. Our physicist could construct another block of the same size, weight, and surface finish as the original and repeat the experiment. The psychologist, however, cannot re-create humans. Humans seldom have exactly the same genetic background (identical twins being an exception), and they never have exactly the same environmental background. For this reason, in responding to the light, typically one individual's fastest response is considerably slower than another individual's slowest response. Thus, as psychologists we have to deal not only with one person's variability from trial to trial but also with the variability among humans.[2]

One way to handle variability is to use statistical techniques. Many psychology students learn to do this by taking a statistics class early in their course work. Because this is not a statistics text, we will not spend much time considering statistical solutions. The topic is briefly mentioned in Chapter 12, where interpreting the results of experiments is discussed, and in Appendix A, where simple statistical operations are demonstrated. A second way to handle variability is to control it as much as possible in the

---

[2] You can see why some psychologists decide to use animals in experiments. Whereas psychologists can breed animals with similar genetic characteristics and rear them in similar environments, it would be frowned upon if they tried to do the same thing with humans. Your friends may say, "All men are animals" or "All women are alike," but don't believe them!

design of your research. This book is written to help you do good research, which is a simple way of saying, "Know where the variability is, and be able to account for it."

Psychologists and other social scientists use a variety of research techniques to make orderly observations in an attempt to account for variability. In this chapter I will give you an overview of the various techniques. Then in the next chapter and in most of the rest of the book I will expand on experimentation because that is the main technique emphasized in this book. In Chapter 10 I will also go into more detail about several less traditional techniques: questionnaires, single-subject designs, and quasi-experimental designs.

The most widely used research techniques are sometimes called **quantitative designs,** those in which events can be quantified so that the data end up being numbers. These designs include experiments and correlational observations. In order to give you a complete picture of the research techniques available, in this chapter we will also briefly look at **qualitative designs,** in which the events being studied are not easily converted into numbers.

## Quantitative Designs

### THE EXPERIMENTAL METHOD

We as scientists establish relationships between events, but these events are not always behaviors. In fact, when we do an experiment, or use the **experimental method,** the relationship of interest is between a set of circumstances and a behavior. A physicist wants to know the time it takes a block to slide down a plane when the plane is at a particular angle, has a particular surface, and has a particular temperature. A psychologist, on the other hand, may want to study students' behavior in a classroom. Both scientists are attempting to establish relationships between a set of circumstances and a behavior, the behavior of a physical object or a human. These relationships are scientific facts, the building blocks with which we build our science.

Unfortunately, designing an experiment to establish such a relationship is not always easy. Ideally, we would like to specify exhaustively and precisely a particular set of circumstances and then measure all the behaviors taking place under those circumstances. We could then say that whenever this set of circumstances recurred, the same behaviors would result. However, if we could list *all* the circumstances, we would have a unique set. Again if we wanted to study students in a classroom, what circumstances would interest us? Perhaps we would like to know the effect of the teacher's sex, or perhaps the type of clothes the teacher wears, or perhaps the effect of class size, or perhaps the use of computers in the classroom, or perhaps what time of day the class meets. As you can see, there are many circumstances we might like to investigate. In fact, there is an infinite number of circumstances, and these form a unique set that would never be repeated.

As is the case with the physicist, the psychologist wants to relate circumstances to behaviors, and here a similar problem arises. Which behaviors do we want to investigate? Perhaps how attentive the students are. Or perhaps how many notes the students are taking. Or perhaps how many questions the students ask. Or perhaps class attendance. Or even what type of brainwave activity students are producing. Again, as with the circumstances, there is an infinite number of behaviors that we might choose to measure.

Thus, we are caught in a dilemma. On one hand, we want to build our science on statements of precise relationships between circumstances and behaviors. On the other hand, if we did that, we would end up with an infinite number of statements, one for each unique set of circumstances paired with each of an infinite number of behaviors. Although we would have precise statements about the relationship between circumstances and behaviors, we would never be able to predict future behavior from circumstances because we would never again find those particular circumstances paired with a particular behavior. How do we resolve this paradox?

Scientists have had to make a compromise. They choose only a few circumstances to investigate at any one time and let the other circumstances form a general set of circumstances. That means that the circumstance (or circumstances) of most interest is precisely specified, whereas the other circumstances form a general set. In this way the circumstances no longer form a unique set but rather a general set that can recur repeatedly.

In using the experimental method the scientist manipulates at least one of the circumstances and measures at least one behavior. For example, suppose we were interested in finding out whether words that occur more frequently in the English language are easier to remember. We might make up lists of high-frequency words like *automobile, tree, house,* and *hand* and another set of lists having low-frequency words like *cucumber, hammock, chime,* and *bonnet.* We could then present these lists to people and find out how many trials it takes them to learn each type of list. So we have chosen one circumstance to manipulate—word frequency; set it at two levels—high and low; and measured trials to learn. In this way, when we have done our experiment, we should be able to make a clear statement about whether word frequency has any effect on learning ability. It is true that we cannot just ignore all the other circumstances. As we will see in the next chapter, we have to consider carefully how to handle the circumstances we are not manipulating. However, when an experiment is done correctly, it is possible to make a clear statement that any change in the measured behavior that occurs when the circumstance of interest is manipulated is caused by that manipulation. The reason that the experimental method is so widely used in science is that no other method allows us to make such a strong causal statement. As you will see when we discuss the other scientific methods in this chapter, they all fall a little short of the ideal, being able to say unequivocally that the change in the circumstance *caused* the change in the behavior.

## CORRELATIONAL OBSERVATION

In establishing relationships that add to our knowledge of human behavior, it is not always possible to conduct an experiment. In such cases, **correlational observation** is often appropriate. In correlational observation we try to determine whether two variables are related without attempting to manipulate either one experimentally. Suppose, for example, we were interested in finding the relationship between parental discipline and rate of juvenile delinquency. To fit this problem into the experimental model, we would have to make parental discipline a circumstance we can manipulate and force the parents of a cross section of newborn infants to discipline their children at a particular level of strictness or leniency. When the children reached age 18, we might count the number of appearances before juvenile court for each child. Obviously, few parents would agree to such an experiment, nor would our society smile on our sincere effort to do good research. Rather than give up on what might be an important question, however, we could consider using a correlational observation.

In making such an observation, we could choose a number of children randomly and send their parents questionnaires asking such questions as "How often do you spank your child?" "Does your child have a specific bedtime?" and so on. Based on the answers to these questions, we could assign each set of parents a number on a scale from strict to lenient. Then we could survey court records to determine the number of offenses for each child and determine if a relationship might exist.

Data[3] from correlational observations are typically pictured in a **scatterplot,** in which each variable is represented on an axis and each point represents a single measurement. For example, hypothetical data from our parental-discipline study are plotted in Figure 1-1. In this case, each point represents the parental-discipline score and the number of court appearances for each child. For example, the upper right point in the graph represents a child having four court appearances and a lenient parental-discipline score; the lower left point, a child with no court appearances and a strict parental-discipline score. This scatterplot shows that there is a moderate relationship between parental discipline and court appearances in our fictitious example. The data points tend to cluster about an imaginary line running from the lower left to the upper right of the graph. In this hypothetical example children whose parents are strict tend to have fewer court appearances.

[3] Every good experimenter must remember that *data* is a plural word; a datum is, but data are. If you chant to yourself "these data are" three times every morning when you wake up, you'll probably still forget!

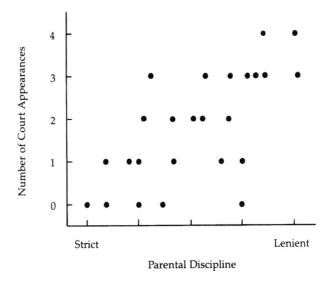

**FIGURE 1-1** Fictitious data showing the relationship between parental discipline and the number of court appearances for children

We agreed at the beginning of this chapter that the business of scientists is establishing relationships between events; why then is this result not as good as the result of an experiment? Remember from our discussion of the experimental method that when we have conducted a good experiment, we can say that the change in the circumstance we manipulated caused a change in the behavior we measured. From a correlational observation, however, the best we can do is conclude that one *variable is related* to a second variable.

Why can't we say that leniency *causes* juvenile delinquency? Basically because we have not manipulated any circumstance; all we have done is measure two behaviors. Only if we had set up an experiment in which we manipulated leniency, perhaps by training one set of parents to be more lenient and one set to be less lenient, would we have been able to make a causal statement. Instead, what we did was allow parents to choose how they would discipline their child. Thus type of discipline was a behavior rather than a manipulated circumstance, and the strong causal conclusion we could make for experimentation no longer applies. Why?

For correlational observation it may be that one of the behaviors is causing the other, but even if this is the case we do not know which behavior is doing the causing and which is being caused. This problem is sometimes referred to as the **directionality problem.** For instance, in our example it may be that as juveniles become more delinquent, parents become more afraid of using strict discipline. In other words, delinquency may cause lenient discipline. From a correlational study we are unable to know the causal direction even if one behavior did cause the other.

It may also be the case that neither behavior directly caused the other even though there is a relationship. Some third variable may have caused both behaviors—cleverly known as the **third variable problem.** Perhaps the following example will illustrate why it is difficult to make casual statements based on correlational observation. The U.S. Army conducted a study of motorcycle accidents, attempting to correlate their number with other variables such as socioeconomic level and age. The best predictor was found to be the number of tattoos the rider had! It would be a ridiculous error to conclude that tattoos cause motorcycle accidents or, for that matter, that motorcycle accidents cause tattoos. Obviously, a third variable is related to both—perhaps preference for risk. A person who is willing to take risks likes to be tattooed and also takes more chances on a motorcycle.

I am sure you are aware of the historical debate between the tobacco industry and the government on the health consequences of smoking. The dilemma faced by the U.S. Surgeon General a decade or so ago is a good illustration of the difficulty in making causal statements based on correlational data. Although it had been known for some time that a positive correlation exists between the number of cigarettes smoked and the incidence of lung cancer and other health problems, the Surgeon General was reluctant to say that smoking caused lung cancer. Some of this reluctance may have been politically motivated. However, much of it was justifiable scientific caution, for there could have been a third variable that caused the cancer but also influenced smoking. For example, people who are nervous might produce a chemical that keeps the body in an irritated state, producing irritated cells that are prone to malignancy. It might also be true that nervous people smoke more cigarettes. Nervousness, then, could have caused the change in both variables.

Thus, the Surgeon General's office would have had to perform an experiment to say definitively from one study that smoking causes lung cancer. Such an experiment might require 1000 people to smoke 40 cigarettes a day, another 1000 people to smoke 30 a day, and so on. In this design, experimenters could determine the probability that an individual in each group would have gotten lung cancer during his or her lifetime. Assuming that the experiment was done properly, any real difference in the incidence of cancer between the groups could be said to be caused by the cigarettes. However, our society requires that a person's preference be honored, so ethically such an experiment could not be and was not conducted.

How, then, did cigarette packs come to have the following warning printed on them: "SURGEON GENERAL'S WARNING: Smoking causes lung cancer, heart disease, emphysema, and may complicate pregnancy"?[4] In this case, correlations were determined for many of the other variables that could have been related to health problems and smoking. As more and more of these variables were eliminated, it became increasingly likely that cigarette smoking was the cause. The Surgeon General apparently felt that all the logically possible third variables had finally been eliminated. That fact, in combination with animal experiments that did show a causal relationship, convinced him that such a statement could be made.

The point, then, is that sometimes we must collect correlational data to establish important psychological relationships. However, we must consider these data carefully to avoid the common error of interpreting the results of a correlational observation as a causal relationship.

As was the case in the example I used earlier in this section, one of the techniques frequently used to collect data for correlational observations is a survey, which can be in the form of a questionnaire or interview. Because students taking a research course and using this book often do a course project that uses a questionnaire, I will discuss the use of questionnaires in more detail in Chapter 10. Here let me just give a quick overview of surveys.

## SURVEYS

**Surveys** typically ask people about their behavior or their opinions. You have probably participated in many surveys yourself, in some cases perhaps without realizing it. For example, in my school graduating seniors are mailed a survey asking them about their experiences at the university: effectiveness of professors, access to health care, availability of career counseling, tastiness of food service meals, etc. Or perhaps you have answered

---

[4] There are actually several statements that warn of the dire consequences of smoking, but they all imply that it is smoking that *causes* health problems.

the phone and been asked questions by a political party regarding your feelings about issues and candidates. On the Internet when you subscribe to some services you have to answer questions about who you are and what your preferences are. Even this is a type of survey.

Surveys include questionnaires that may be in paper-and-pencil form and administered in person either individually or to groups of participants (usually called respondents). Questionnaires can also be mailed or even sent out over the Internet. Surveys also include interviews that can be done face-to-face or over the telephone. Each of these methods has advantages and disadvantages that will be discussed further in Chapter 10.

There are several general advantages to doing survey research. One is that you can directly ask respondents about their opinions, attitudes, and motivations rather than having to infer these from their behaviors. For example, we might do an experiment by changing the way merchandise is displayed at a store and discover customers buy more. However, although we know customers are buying more, we really do not know why. Perhaps they feel more positive toward the store, or perhaps they can find what they are looking for more easily. A survey would allow us to determine why they buy more, or at least why they think they buy more. A second advantage is that it is relatively easy to collect large amounts of data quickly. I watched the president's state of the union address last night, and a TV network presented the results of a viewer survey just a few minutes after it was over.

There are also some disadvantages to surveys. While you may think that people are giving you factual information about their behavior or opinions, what they say may differ from the truth. For example, the Gallup Organization has been asking people about church attendance for 60 years, and about 40% of respondents typically say they attend a worship service once a week. This figure is far higher than in other Western nations, and many churches report a drop in membership in recent years. What is the truth? C. Kirk Hadaway and Penny Long Marler (1998) decided to consult pastors and do head counts. They found attendance at closer to 20% rather than to 40%. Why are all these good church people lying? Perhaps some decide that even if they didn't go the week before, they usually do go so it's okay to answer yes. Or perhaps they think that good people should go to church and they want to be identified as good people. Whatever the reason, we know that in surveys people tend to exaggerate how often they vote or give to charities and underestimate how often they use drugs or the office copier for personal use. So as a researcher you must remember that the biggest problem with surveys is that they can tell you only how people *say* they behave or what they think, not how they actually behave or what they actually think.

Another disadvantage of surveys is the same as one of the advantages —they give you so much data. One problem is that collecting these data requires a lot of respondents, and in some settings the number of respondents is limited. In my university, for instance, researchers who do large surveys using the pool of introductory psychology students as respondents must sometimes wait until other researchers have completed their research or else the whole pool could be exhausted by a few surveys. A more serious difficulty for the researcher is that the large amount of data collected are difficult to interpret. I have read many reports of survey research written by students in which they list the results of a survey they have done but then do not know what more to say. Because survey research is seldom driven by theory, the results do not support or refute some theory, as experiments usually do. In addition, to do detailed analysis of survey results often requires using complex statistical techniques, such as factor analysis, that are beyond the training of beginning researchers. Some of the other advantages and disadvantages of surveys will be discussed in Chapter 10, where I go into much greater detail about questionnaires.

## ARCHIVAL RESEARCH

Another form of correlational observation is archival research. In this case other people have done you a favor by recording your observations for you. That is, there may be public or private records containing information that is useful to you. When you examine these records for research purposes and attempt to organize and interpret the information to find relationships, you are doing **archival research.** I include this under quantitative research because most of these records can be quantified and turned into numbers. However, when the records consist of interviews, case histories, and the like, this research could be characterized as qualitative research. Just some of the records of interest to psychologists are census data, court records, newspapers, hospital files, accident reports, crime reports, clinical files, government agency records, salary listings of public officials, telephone directories, and corporate sales figures.

As an example of research using archival data, Doug Kenrick and a colleague at Arizona State University examined the marriage listings of a number of newspapers (Kenrick & Keefe, 1992). They were testing a sociobiological theory of personal attraction. This theory says that one of the major reasons that a woman finds a man attractive is because of his potential to provide resources for his children. A man, on the other hand, finds a woman attractive, at least in part, because of her potential to give birth to many children. If these statements are true, the theory predicts, women should in general be attracted to and marry older men who have already accumulated resources, and men should marry younger women who have many childbearing years remaining. To investigate this hypothesis Kenrick and his researchers simply read the section of newspapers that lists people getting married and their ages. As the theory predicts, he did find that, up to a point, the grooms were older than their brides. Of course, there are other possible explanations for this age difference, and these reasons have been discussed at length (Kenrick & Keefe, 1992). Nevertheless, this study illustrates nicely that archival data available to all of us, even in our daily newspaper, can form the basis for significant psychological research.

One of the most extensive examples of archival research formed the basis of *Homicide,* a book by Martin Daly and Margo Wilson (1988). These researchers were also investigating predictions made by the theory of sociobiology, also sometimes called selection thinking. In this case the archival data they examined were police reports of homicides. The theory predicts that in general, if people are going to kill other people, they should kill those who contribute least to their probability of reproductive success. The people they should be least likely to kill are their biological children, who carry their genetic material, and other people who contribute to the success of those children or future children, such as their faithful mates. So, for example, the theory predicts that parents are more likely to kill their stepchildren than their biological children and that men are most likely to kill their mates for suspicion of infidelity than for any other reason. The researchers carefully reviewed the homicide reports in police files for the city of Detroit and the country of Canada and discovered that nearly all of their predictions were confirmed. Children were 40 to 100 times more likely to be killed by stepparents than biological parents! Sexual jealousy was the motive in a large majority of cases in which men murdered their mates. Even some predictions that seem to run counter to common sense were supported by the data. For example, for adult children of a given age, those having older parents were more likely to kill them than those having younger parents. Sociobiological theory would predict this finding because the older parents are less likely to have children, who carry the family's genetic material, but the finding runs counter to several other theories of psychology. In Daly and Wilson's study, the archival records were so extensive that it was possible to code most of the data and turn them into numbers so that quantitative statistical analysis could be done.

There are several advantages of archival research. If you can find appropriate existing records, you do not have to spend time and effort collecting your own data. Also, in some cases the records provide data that are much more extensive than you would be able to collect. Finally, some data available in the records would be impossible to collect by doing your own research. Psychologists are not allowed to provoke people into killing each other, or even encourage people to marry each other! Of course, there are some disadvantages. As is the case with both correlational observations and naturalistic observations, no variable has been independently manipulated, so only relationships, not causes, can be found. Additionally, in most cases the information contained in the records was not collected by trained scientists, so its reliability is probably unknown and perhaps suspect. Sometimes the records are also difficult to find or obtain, and even if they are available, they may be difficult to organize in a systematic way. Finally, in most cases there is simply no available record that will provide the information you need.

# Qualitative Designs

The vast majority of research in psychology uses quantitative designs, such as experiments or correlational observations, because during the early history of psychology the scientific side of psychology fashioned itself in the image of the so-called hard sciences, such as physics and chemistry. The first fleeting attempts by the early introspectionists to use verbal reports as data rather than numerically measurable behavior were beaten down by the behaviorists, not to appear again for many decades. However, in recent years, some psychologists, particularly those in areas such as educational, clinical, and social psychology, have felt too constrained by these strict rules. They looked around for methods that would allow them to use verbal reports as data while maintaining some scientific rigor. What they found and adopted were some methods from anthropology and, more recently, sociology called qualitative research. Qualitative researchers use descriptive data: written descriptions of people, including opinions and attitudes, and of events and environments.

## ETHNOGRAPHY

Imagine a cultural anthropologist who has traveled to a distant land wishing to investigate an exotic culture. How would the anthropologist proceed? So little would be known about this strange culture that setting up an experiment would certainly be out of the question. Even developing a questionnaire or a consistent set of interview questions would be difficult until some basic facts about the people were known. The initial goal of the anthropologist would probably be to talk to the people and describe them and their setting so that the culture would stop seeming strange and seem familiar. Those who do a type of qualitative research called **ethnography** are sometimes said to do the reverse, to study familiar cultures in order to make them strange (Erickson, 1973). For example, suppose we were interested in studying the dynamics of a particular type of teaching technique in an elementary school. We have all been to elementary school, so we are pretty familiar with what goes on there. If we wanted to learn something new about the type of class we are studying, ethnographers would tell us, we should approach the task as if we had arrived from outer space and had seen a classroom for the first time, to train ourselves to view everything as strange.

We would probably begin by sitting down to interview the children and the teachers, trying to approach them with a completely open mind without having formed any hypotheses that might bias us about what happens in the class. These interviews would not be conducted in a haphazard way. Rather than relying on our memory, we would probably record the interviews and transcribe them verbatim into a written text. We might also take extensive notes about the behavior of the individuals in the class, the events that took place, and the setting or context within which the events occurred. Because ethnographers usually try to avoid interpreting their data, we would simply attempt to describe as accurately as possible the things the children and teachers said and did and the classroom environment. Ethnographers also sometimes act as participant observers. For example, in the classroom example, a teacher might be doing the research as a participant observer. The participant observer typically would be as unobtrusive as possible to avoid biasing the other participants' behavior—for example, by writing notes only during breaks.

The classroom example that we have been considering is also a case of naturalistic observation, a design that we will be examining next. However, not all ethnography or qualitative research has to occur in a natural setting. I have a colleague who is interested in the relationship between mothers and their daughters and in how mother–daughter relationships have changed from the past to the present. Her method of collecting data is to conduct extensive interviews in her laboratory with both mothers and daughters, record these interviews on tape, and then transcribe the tapes into written text. She is also interested in interpreting the data, rather than just describing them as a pure ethnographer would. Although the interviews are structured so that similar topics are discussed in each interview, she does not have a required set of questions that her interviewers must ask in a specific order. The interview is designed to allow some flexibility rather than simply being an oral questionnaire. Qualitative researchers claim that this flexibility is one of the strengths of their method, that the interaction with participants must allow the participants to describe their experiences, feelings, and attitudes in their own ways. These researchers believe that the experimental method, in which an experimenter is testing a limited hypothesis and collecting highly structured data, is so artificial and constrained that very little of the vast amount of available data is tapped. In fact, some qualitative researchers believe at a basic philosophical level that qualitative research is preferable because it has a humanistic orientation; it treats the participants as human beings and fully taps into their humanity, whereas experiments treat participants as if they were objects (subjects) to be experimented on.

## NATURALISTIC OBSERVATION

As noted in the previous section, some psychologists believe that research is best done by studying behavior in its natural setting, that the act of filling out a questionnaire or reporting for an experiment could distort the behavior of a participant. Suppose we were interested in whether consumption of alcohol was related to social aggressiveness. We could set up an experiment in which groups of research participants drank measured amounts of alcohol. They would then interact while the experimenter sat in the room and noted the amount of aggressive activity. How aggressive do you think the drinkers would be in this situation? They would probably resemble a church congregation more than a bar crowd.

To get an effective answer to our question, we would probably have to go to a bar and observe its customers. This technique in psychological research is called **naturalistic observation** because researchers observe behaviors under the conditions in which they naturally occur.[5] Naturalistic observations are required when we wish to investigate any behavior that we feel might be distorted by the artificiality of an experimental situation. Children, for instance, are typically inhibited by the presence of adults, particularly strangers. We would expect the behavior of children playing at home with their own toys to be far different from their behavior in a psychology lab with unfamiliar toys and a strange-looking psychologist present.

For a long time, comparative psychologists[6] and ethologists wondered whether any animal other than humans used tools, and naturalistic observation provided them with the beginnings of an answer. Initially, data collected by observing chimpanzees in zoos supported the general belief that other animals did not use tools. After a while, however, these researchers began to wonder whether zoo chimpanzees were not using tools because no tools were available in the zoo. They gave them tools like pliers and screwdrivers, but the chimps still didn't use them. Finally, a particularly bright investigator named Jane Goodall moved into the forest with the chimps. She lived with them and constantly observed their behavior for several years. One day she noticed that a particular chimp would take a branch, peel off the leaves to make it smooth, trim it to length, and dip it

---

[5] Naturalistic observations are also sometimes called field studies because the investigator goes into the field to collect data. (If I bite my tongue, maybe I can avoid the old saw about the farmer who was outstanding in his. . . .)

[6] A comparative psychologist is not someone who makes television commercials in which Brand X loses out to Brand Y. A comparative psychologist compares the behavior of animals, including humans, across species. Comparative psychologists contend that the rest of us are far too egocentric in our research; humans form only a small part of the animal kingdom.

into a termite hill and lick off the termites that were clinging to the stick. Although the stick is not as sophisticated as a human's tools, some investigators consider it an appropriate chimpanzee tool, and more recent laboratory work has confirmed the use of tools. Without naturalistic observation, researchers would still be sitting around watching zoo animals not using tools.

Some sciences other than psychology use naturalistic observation as their primary tool because they cannot achieve control over the variables they are investigating. Astronomers, for example, must pretty well investigate the universe as it occurs naturally. The same is usually true for archaeologists, paleontologists, ethnologists, and anthropologists. This limitation has not prevented these scientists from discovering important phenomena such as evolution. Because of problems with control, naturalistic observation in psychology is often used to suggest hypotheses that can later be more carefully investigated through experimentation in the laboratory. Used in this way, naturalistic observation can be a valuable research tool.

The major problem with naturalistic observation as a research technique may be obvious to you. Because investigators have no control over any of the variables they are observing, one variable may be changing systematically along with the primary one being observed. In the bar example, for instance, an investigator might observe that the more alcohol the customers drink, the more aggressive their social interactions become. However, the observer may not notice that as the evening wears on and more drinks are consumed, the number of bar patrons also increases. Maybe aggressiveness is related to crowding. Or perhaps the bartender is getting tired and brings the drinks at a slower rate. Maybe aggressiveness is related to frustration.

Thus, although naturalistic observation has an advantage in realism, it also has disadvantages in its lack of control. As with correlational observations, experimenters must be aware of potential confounding variables and must avoid making causal statements.

## CASE HISTORY

A final research technique available to psychologists is another qualitative design called a **case history**. A case history is a detailed account of the events in a case; the case is usually a person's life, but it can be an incident such as the shutdown of a nuclear plant. Many of the data in clinical psychology come from case studies, dating back to Freud's reports of clinical cases. As is typical of qualitative designs, data for case histories are usually verbal. Suppose you were a therapist with a pair of conjoined ("Siamese") twins having multiple personalities as patients. You might be interested in exploring why Siamese twins develop dual personalities. You would immediately realize that trying to conduct an experiment to answer the question would be futile. Even if you could find enough Siamese twins to do an experiment, it is considered unethical to make Siamese twins mentally ill; it is also unethical to make non-Siamese twins mentally ill!

You might consider a correlational observation next. Perhaps you could correlate the number of personalities in Siamese twins with degree of childhood stress. Again, you would need to find a number of Siamese twins who had dual personalities. Because this task is virtually impossible and a correlational observation based on one data point is meaningless,[7] you would have to abandon this approach also.

The only option left would seem to be a case history outlining the factors in the lives of the Siamese twins that have contributed to their development. First, you would spend many hours interviewing the twins to establish a history of their life from birth to present. In addition, you would talk with their relatives and friends and examine any school, medical, and psychological records that were available. Because all this information would require far too much space to report, you would select what you felt were the most important aspects.

The case-history technique has built into it all the dangers that have been mentioned for the other methods, including unknown confounding variables and inability to establish causality. This method also has additional pitfalls. For one thing, the investigator is generally trying to reconstruct past events from the subjective reports of those who were associated with those events, and research has shown that people are terrible at recalling the past. One investigator found that mothers were inaccurate about recalling the details of their pregnancy and the birth of their child six months to a year after the experience. You can imagine the problems involved when the memories are 20 years old!

A second possible pitfall of the case-history method is the investigator's bias in selecting events to be reported. In a psychology course, I was once required to support a particular personality theory using events from the

---

[7] It is pretty difficult to establish a relationship between two variables with a single point. It is not difficult to establish a relationship with two points, however, because only one straight line can be drawn between them. Reporting a relationship based on two points is a lot like bragging. It's easy to do but no one pays any attention.

life of the major character in the novel *Crime and Punishment*. It was easy to select events that offered convincing support for my theory. However, I discovered that the other students in the class had used the same book to support three other personality theories, also in a convincing way. They had either chosen different events or given a different interpretation to the same events I had chosen. Even with the limited set of events described in a single book, bias was extremely important in determining the relationships we established. Is it any wonder that investigators can find support for their own pet theories from the nearly unlimited set of events in a person's life?

A number of books have been written that analyze the lives and personalities of famous historical figures, such as Richard Nixon, John Kennedy, and Sigmund Freud. Although they may make interesting speculative reading, these so-called **psychohistories** are subject to all the dangers inherent in a case history. In addition, most of the events the authors use as support for their theories are based on secondhand reporting in the public media. Thus, they are one more step away from the objective truth. (For example, one author concluded that Nixon was psychotic; another concluded that he was neurotic.)

A case-history approach has also been used in applied experimental settings for investigating infrequently occurring events. For example, it is basically impossible for a psychologist interested in the causes of aircraft accidents to set up appropriate experiments. What these investigators often do is reconstruct the events preceding an accident in as much detail as possible. By collecting enough of these critical incidents describing accidents and near-accidents, they hope to establish a pattern that will allow them to hypothesize the causes. These hypotheses can then be more thoroughly investigated under controlled experimental conditions.

One of the most defensible uses of the case study approach is in neuropsychology. Neuropsychologists and neuroscientists are interested in determining the function of various structures of the brain. One of the major ways to find out what a part of the brain does is to destroy it and find out how behavior changes. In humans there are obvious ethical problems with destroying brain tissue. Because brain tissue does not grow back, any such procedure would be permanently debilitating. One solution would be to find some unfortunate soul who has had brain tissue destroyed through accident or disease. From an introductory psychology course you may remember the case of Phineas Gage, a fellow who had a metal rod driven through his brain in a mining accident. This was one of the first cases that researchers used to understand the workings of the brain. Today there are many patients with various neurological problems whose behaviors have been extensively documented. These cases are used along with other data, such as data from animal research, to help us understand the functioning of the human brain. However, we should keep in mind that data from even these well-documented case studies do not come from experiments, so establishing causal relationships between these circumstances and behaviors should be done with extreme care.

The obvious advantage of the case-history approach is that it can be used when only one or very few cases can be examined. Some would also argue that an advantage is that behavior can be studied in all of its complexity in a natural context, whereas experiments study artificially simple behaviors in artificial settings. However, because it has the disadvantages mentioned earlier, including, in some cases, relying on potentially biased subjective reports retrieved from somebody's long-term memory, we should remain skeptical of conclusions drawn solely from a single case history.

## Quantitative versus Qualitative Designs

Unfortunately, many investigators who have been trained exclusively in either quantitative research or qualitative research consider those who use the other approach to be misguided. Quantitative researchers argue that unless data can be converted into numbers, they can never be organized into the building blocks necessary for the construction of a scientific body of knowledge, that science cannot advance unless we can build theories that help us understand behavior. Such theories require a knowledge of the causes of behavior, and without experimentation—and to some extent correlational observation—no causation can be established. On top of these problems is the problem of the reliability of the data collected. Without being able to repeat research, we will never know whether our data are reliable. Some experimenters would say that qualitative researchers such as ethnographers do nothing but write descriptions of behaviors, a job for historians and novelists, not scientists.

On the other side of the debate are the qualitative researchers, some of whom would argue that experimentation deals with only tiny bits of unhumanlike behavior, and does so in artificial settings. They say that quantitative researchers will never be able to understand realistic human behavior in a holistic way. In addition, only qualitative research taps into the potential of the individuals being studied, using their insights and creativity to help guide the formation of our science. Some would go so far as to assert that there are ethical problems with experimentation in that it treats the people it claims to study as objects, rather than as humans. In the most extreme camp are qualitative researchers who completely reject traditional science and maintain that those quantitative researchers unwilling to accept qualitative designs are motivated by a desire to maintain political power and silence those who have traditionally been oppressed.[8]

A reasonable and moderate position would seem to be that as scientists we should use whatever type of design is needed to answer our ques-

---

[8] The most extreme qualitative researchers are the poststructuralists, who question the possibility of striving for an objective science. An interesting account of the origins of qualitative research can be found in Chapter 1 of *Ethnography and Qualitative Design in Educational Research,* by Margaret D. LeCompte and Judith Preissle (1993).

tions. At the very least, qualitative methods can be used to help us formulate hypotheses that can be more rigorously tested using quantitative designs. There is also no reason why, in some cases, the methods cannot be used in combination. For example, many surveys have a quantitative section that collects numerical data using a rating scale such as a Likert scale and also a qualitative section that asks open-ended questions. In this case the open-ended questions can be used to help understand and interpret the quantitative responses. The following example also describes a research question that has benefited by the use of a wide combination of methods that we have discussed in this chapter.

## Using Methods in Combination

To illustrate how the various research techniques discussed in this chapter might be used to investigate a research hypothesis, consider the following situation. You are ready to pull your car onto the highway, quickly look both ways, start to step on the gas, and then pull up and say to yourself: "Whoa! There's a motorcycle coming. I almost didn't see it!" Or maybe you have been the motorcycle rider who had a car pull out in front of you as if the driver had never seen you. Why do you suppose this occurs? As we will discuss in Chapter 3, everyday observations and questions like this one can lead to the formation of a hypothesis for psychological research. A first step in forming a hypothesis is to examine the situation logically. What is the major difference between motorcycles and other vehicles such as cars and trucks?[9] Obviously, motorcycles are smaller and so may be less conspicuous than larger vehicles. But we are not the first to have thought of this idea. Once you have read Chapter 6, you will know how to find out if anyone else has investigated this issue. You would discover that many people have. Paul Olson of the University of Michigan Transportation Research Institute has reviewed some of this research and called our hypothesis the *motorcycle conspicuity hypothesis* (Olson, 1989). I will use some of the research he cites to illustrate the research techniques we might use to investigate this hypothesis.

First, although we have seen that the case-history method has many drawbacks, it can be useful in helping us form a hypothesis. In order to study the motorcycle conspicuity hypothesis, although it will be a bit different from the classic case-study method in which a single case is studied intensively, perhaps we can find people who have almost pulled into the path of a motorcycle and ask them what happened to cause their behavior. Is there a way to collect this type of data in a more systematic fashion? Fortunately, somebody has already done some of the work for us, the police. In this case an accident report is a bit like a short case study. If you collected accident reports for motorcycle–car accidents and read them, you

---

[9] I know, motorcycles are a lot more fun. Wrong answer!

would find that drivers who violated motorcyclists' right of way often claim not to have seen them or not to have seen them in time to avoid the collision. This is the kind of statement we would expect if the conspicuity hypothesis were true. In interpreting these findings we should keep in mind the limitations of the case-study approach. Whereas in this instance we have gained some confidence by having many cases, we should remember that the data rely on people's memory, were collected by people not trained in research, and are self-reports by drivers who have just been involved in an accident and for whom the responses may have legal ramifications.

Could we use naturalistic observation to investigate our hypothesis? If we had years to waste, we could sit on a street corner and wait for a motorcycle accident to happen that we could observe. Again, here we are lucky in that accident reports also contain information from people who have observed motorcycle accidents and from police officers, who have observed the consequences of the accidents. We can do archival research and look at the statistical data from various types of motorcycle–car accidents, comparing them with car–car crashes to determine the differences. If we did this we would find that, in general, cars and motorcycles are involved in the same kinds of collisions with about the same relative frequency, except in the case of the motorcycle going straight and the car turning left in front of the motorcycle. We should keep in mind that as in the case of all naturalistic observation, these data are at best correlational observations. An experimenter did not manipulate anything and then measure a change in behavior. Perhaps we could interpret the statistics as support for the conspicuity hypothesis, but it is weak support. Why are motorcycles less conspicuous only under this set of circumstances? Perhaps the automobile drivers would not have seen the motorcycles no matter how conspicuous they were because the drivers were looking left in the direction they were turning instead of forward at the motorcycle.

Would it be possible for us to use the experimental method to investigate our hypothesis? As you will see in Chapter 10, quasi-experimental techniques can be used in some cases where a full-fledged experiment is not possible. One example of such a technique would be to look at accident statistics for each of the years prior to an event that had changed motorcycle conspicuity and then after. Fortunately for us, in 1967 a number of states began requiring daytime use of headlights on motorcycles. If you take measures a number of times before such an event and a number of times after, a quasi-experimental design called an interrupted time-series is created. This design is not as rigorous as an experiment but is certainly more rigorous than a correlational observation. Using such a method, some early investigators estimated the reduction in daytime collisions to range from about 4% to 20%. However, more recent investigators have concluded that the effect of daytime headlight operation on motorcycle crashes is minuscule or nonexistent. It is also the case that when an effect of headlight use on motorcycles has been found, headlight use on cars, for which there was never a claim of conspicuity problems, may be equally effective in reducing crashes. Thus, the headlight data are inconclusive.

It is also possible to do formal experiments to investigate drivers' behavior with respect to motorcycles. In one such study observers estimated when an approaching vehicle would pass in front of them based on a two-second observation when the vehicle was about 100 meters away. There were no differences found for motorcycles, cars, and trucks. Differences were found when observers judged the last moment that they could safely pull out in front of a vehicle; they were willing to accept shorter gaps, on average, for motorcycles. However, no experiments have been done to specifically test the conspicuity hypothesis.

The research reviewed here that was cited by Olson (1989) illustrates nicely the various research techniques that can be used to investigate a single hypothesis. It also illustrates some of the advantages and disadvantages of the various techniques. The case study and naturalistic observation tend to be more realistic but may be lacking in rigor and precision. In contrast, formal experiments may be highly rigorous but can often be criticized as being unrealistic. Table 1-1 lists some of the advantages and disadvantages of the designs that we have examined.

Just so I do not leave you hanging in the air, what does Olson conclude from his review? He thinks that the conspicuity hypothesis lacks support. The most likely alternative would seem to be that because motorcycles are smaller, they are more easily blocked out by objects such as other cars, windshield posts, or trees and shrubs. It may be that drivers often fail to see motorcycles not because they are inconspicuous, but because they are hidden.

## Summary

As scientists of human behavior, psychologists have a number of research designs available to them, all of which aim to establish relationships between events and to fit these relationships into an orderly body of knowledge. Among the **quantitative designs** is the **experimental method,** which

**TABLE 1-1**

A Summary of the Advantages and Disadvantages
of Using Various Research Designs

| Design | Advantages | Disadvantages |
|---|---|---|
| Experimental method | Precise control possible<br>Causal conclusions possible<br>Precise measurement possible<br>Theory testing possible | Artificial setting typical<br>Intrusiveness typically high<br>Complex behaviors difficult to measure<br>Unstructured exploratory research difficult |
| Correlational observation | Relationships between variables can be found<br>Precise measurement usually possible<br>Intrusiveness usually low | Causal conclusions impossible<br>Control of variables difficult<br>Many participants required |
| Questionnaires | Data collection efficient<br>Attitude or opinion can be measured | Causal conclusions impossible<br>Self-reports difficult to verify<br>Unbiased sample selection difficult<br>Response rates low when mailed |
| Archival research | No additional data collection required<br>Rare behaviors can be studied<br>Nonmanipulable events can be studied | Appropriate records often not available<br>Data collected by nonscientists<br>Data usually correlational at best |
| Ethnography | Unfamiliar situations can be described<br>Complex behaviors can be described<br>Intrusiveness low<br>Participants treated humanistically | Control of variables impossible<br>Precise measurement difficult<br>Investigator bias possible<br>Causal conclusions impossible |
| Naturalistic observation | Realistic setting helps generalization<br>Intrusiveness low | Control of variables impossible<br>Data collection inefficient<br>Investigator bias possible<br>Causal conclusions impossible |
| Case history | Rare cases can be studied<br>Complex behavior can be intensively studied | Control of variables impossible<br>Data often based on fallible memories<br>Investigator bias highly likely<br>Causal conclusions impossible |

is the primary focus of this book. It requires that a particular circumstance be manipulated and some aspect of behavior measured. From an experiment it is possible to say that the manipulation of the circumstance *caused* any change found in the behavior.

Sometimes when an experimental approach cannot be used, it is necessary to use **correlational observations,** in which variables are observed and their relationships evaluated. The results of such a study cannot be used to establish causal relationships, because none of the variables is under the control of the investigator. Correlational observations are often carried out using a **survey** in the form of a questionnaire or interview. Correlational data can also be obtained by doing **archival research** using data contained in public or private records, such as census data or court records.

Some investigators are now doing research that employs **qualitative designs.** Qualitative researchers use descriptive data: written descriptions of people, including opinions and attitudes, and of events and environments. **Ethnography** uses interviews and sometimes participatory observations to gather descriptive data. One form of qualitative research uses **naturalistic observation,** in which the data are gathered in realistic settings. A final qualitative design used when the potential number of observations is limited is the **case history,** in which detailed accounts of the events in a person's life or in a historical incident are described and analyzed.

## Find It on InfoTrac College Edition

Chapter 1 gives an overview of many different types of research methods used in psychology. Use InfoTrac College Edition to find examples of these various types of methods: experimental method, correlational observation, surveys (or questionnaires), archival research, ethnography, naturalistic observation, and case history. Try searching the database for these terms and see what kinds of items InfoTrac lists. In some cases you will find very large numbers of items; then you should limit your search in some way, perhaps by using a term that specifies an interest of yours. For example, rather than just entering *survey,* enter *survey and marriage,* which will limit the search to articles that use a survey method to investigate some aspect of marriage. You can customize your search to conform to your specific interests. Write down a reference (author, date, title, journal, and pages) you have found that illustrates each of the methods.

# 2

# How to Do Experiments

During its long history down to the middle of the nineteenth century, psychology was cultivated by able thinkers who did not realize their need of carefully observed facts. . . . Finally psychologists decided that they must follow the lead of physics, chemistry and physiology and transform psychology into an experimental science.

R. S. WOODWORTH (1940)

We must guard against . . . the drawing of a preconceived conclusion from experiments or observations which are so vaguely conditioned that a variety of inferences are as a matter of fact possible.

K. DUNLAP (1920)

In the first chapter we briefly discussed the experimental method. You will recall that the major advantage of doing this type of research is that it allows you to make causal statements, that a circumstance caused a change in behavior. Because this type of statement is so precise, the rules required to support the statement are quite stringent. Most of these rules have to do with being able to account for all of the circumstances that could vary.

By way of example, suppose we were interested in the time it takes a person to press a button in response to a light when the light has a particular intensity. At this point we have chosen a circumstance to manipulate—the intensity of a light—and a behavior to measure—time to press a button. These two variables have formal names.

## Variables

### INDEPENDENT VARIABLES

The circumstance of major interest in an experiment, light intensity in our example, is called an **independent variable.** The best way to remember this name is to recall that the variable is independent of the participant's behavior. As experimenters we manipulate it—that is, choose two or more levels to present—and nothing the participant does can change the levels we have chosen. For example, if our independent variable is light intensity, we might select a high-intensity light and a low-intensity light as our two levels and observe behavior under both circumstances. Without at least two levels, we are not doing an experiment, but we are free to choose many more levels or to have more than one independent variable. Later in the book we will discuss ways of designing these more complex experiments.

## DEPENDENT VARIABLES

Once we have chosen the independent variable, we will want to measure a participant's behavior in response to manipulations of that variable. We call the behavior we choose to measure the **dependent variable** because it is dependent on what the participant does.[1] In the reaction-time experiment, for example, we want to find out whether a relationship exists between light intensity and time to respond. Thus, our dependent variable is the time from the onset of the light until a button is pressed. It is sometimes useful to make a statement about the expected nature of the relationship; such a statement is called a **hypothesis.** In the example, we might hypothesize that the more intense the light, the quicker the response will be. The outcome of the experiment will determine whether the hypothesis is supported and becomes part of the scientific body of knowledge or whether it is refuted.

In some cases the hypothesis is softer and more uncertain, particularly when you simply wonder what would happen to a behavior if the independent variable were manipulated. In this case, the hypothesis is simply the answer to a question. How does crowding affect aggression? Does marking your first guess or thinking longer lead to better grades on multiple-choice tests? Are politicians who smile in their campaign posters more or less likely to be elected than those who don't? Hypothesized answers to questions such as these can also add to the scientific body of knowledge.

## CONTROL VARIABLES

So far, we have chosen one circumstance to manipulate—the independent variable. However, other circumstances in an experiment will need to be accounted for in some way. One possibility is to control them, thus making them into **control variables.** We can control such circumstances by seeing that they do not vary from a single level. For example, in our reaction-time experiment, we might require that the lighting conditions in the room be constant, all participants be right-handed, the temperature be constant, and so on. Ideally, all circumstances other than the independent variable would stay constant throughout an experiment. We would then know that any change in the dependent variable must be due to changes in the independent variable that we had brought about.

---

[1] I believe that it is easier to remember the term this way, although the word *dependent* really refers to the behavior's being potentially dependent on the levels of independent variable.

The concept of control is vital for experimentation and makes the experiment distinct from other forms of research that were discussed in the previous chapter. In the experiments that you do, many of the variables will be set as control variables. As an experimenter, you will want to be sure that you have indeed achieved complete command of the control variables in your experiment. Control is critical to the experimental method. That is why psychologists go to considerable expense to build special environments in which sound, light, and temperature are controlled and to use special equipment to ensure that stimulus characteristics are consistent and that responses are carefully measured.

However, even though many variables in your experiments will be control variables, you should realize that, especially in psychology, not all variables will be assigned as control variables. First, it is impossible to control all the variables. Not only is it impossible to control many genetic and environmental conditions, but it is impossible to force cooperative attitudes, attentional states, metabolic rates, and many other situational factors on our human participants.

Second, we really do not wish to control all the variables in an experiment or else we would create a unique set of circumstances. If we could control all variables while manipulating the independent variable, the relationship established by the experiment would hold in only one case—when all variables were set at exactly the levels established for control. In other words, we could not *generalize* the experimental result to any other situation. As a rule of thumb, the more highly controlled the experiment, the less generally applicable the results.

Suppose, for example, that General Nosedive from the U.S. Air Force came to you and said: "Say, I understand you ran an experiment on reaction time. Tell me how intense I should make the fire-warning light in my fighter planes so that my pilots will respond within half a second." Having conducted a well-controlled experiment, you reply, "Sir, if you can guarantee that the pilot is a 19-year-old college sophomore with an IQ of 115, sitting in an air-conditioned, 10-foot-by-15-foot room, with no distracting sounds and nothing else to do, and if you always give a warning signal one second before the light comes on, then I might be able to give you an answer." You can probably imagine the general's reply. The moral of the story is—if you want to generalize the results of your experiment, do not control all the variables.

The generalizability of an experimental finding has been referred to as **external validity,** how well a causal relationship can be generalized across people, settings, and times. Cook and Campbell (1979) have introduced names for several types of validity. The way they use this term, *validity* refers to whether it is justifiable to draw experimental conclusions about cause. I will introduce other terms for validity at appropriate places in the book. Threats to external validity might occur if you use a limited sample, such as college sophomores, when you wish to generalize to all humans of any age or intelligence (including, as in our example, Air Force pilots). Or you might have done a highly controlled laboratory experiment when you wish to generalize to real-world work settings where it is noisy, hot, and crowded, and the workers are tired and unmotivated but have lots of practice. In general, the more tightly controlled your experiment—that is, the more circumstances you choose to make into control variables—the more likely it is to suffer from threats to external validity.

## RANDOM VARIABLES

Having established that we do not want to control all the circumstances, what can we do with the remaining circumstances in our experiment? One possibility is to let them vary. In what way can we allow the circumstances to vary and still be sure that they will not bias our experiment? One alternative is to permit some of the circumstances to vary randomly. These variables are termed **random variables.**

A random variable is allowed to change levels in an uncontrolled way, but as an experimenter you must be sure that a random process is determining the levels. As long as a random process is allowed to operate many times, it is unlikely that the experiment will become biased. For example, suppose you wish to determine the effects of television violence on aggression in children. You randomly choose 100 6-year-old children to assign the task of watching violent television shows and randomly choose 100 to watch nonviolent shows. Is it possible that most of the first group attend violent schools or eat lots of sugar or come from abusive homes, while few of the second group do? Yes but if the selection was done in a truly random fashion, it is statistically unlikely for such large samples to be biased. Suppose you let the children watch the violent or nonviolent television shows at home. Is it possible that most of one group have large-screen theater-system TVs at home, while most of the second group have small portable TVs? Again, it is possible but not probable; randomness makes this possibility highly unlikely.

There is no particular trick to random selection. Any device that allows each item in a population an equal chance for selection can be used. If two items are in your population, you can flip a coin to select from the population.[2] If there are 6, you can throw a die. If there are 33, you can use 33 equal-sized slips of paper. Most mathematical handbooks and many statistics texts have random-number tables based on a process equivalent to drawing from 10,000 slips of paper. One is included in the back of this book as Appendix C. Using any column or columns in a table of random numbers, you can assign each of your items a number and select the item when that number occurs. Just ignore the extra columns or numbers that are not on your list. If you happen to be a computer buff, you can use the computer to generate random numbers or events.[3]

---

[2] Actually, most coins are slightly biased in favor of heads, but, unless you are running an experiment with over 10,000 trials, don't worry about it.
[3] Computers are also less than perfect at generating random events, but they're much better than coins. For the purpose of assigning events in an experiment, it doesn't make much difference which method you use.

If you have chosen to make a circumstance into a random variable, you must be sure that it varies in a truly random way, because not all events that appear random really are. For instance, if you try to randomize conditions in an experiment by assigning events yourself, you have not randomized! Humans are notoriously bad at producing random events. If you assume that participants will show up for an experiment throughout the day or throughout the semester in a random order, you are wrong! People who are morning volunteers or afternoon volunteers or early-semester or late-semester volunteers have different characteristics. Mistakes in randomization are commonly made by new experimenters. Don't you make them!

The major advantage of using random variables is the generalizability of the results, external validity. As we saw earlier, every time we choose to make a circumstance into a control variable, we can generalize our results only to situations at that level. However, if we make a circumstance into a random variable and randomly select levels from a population, we can generalize the results to that entire population. Thus, randomization can be a powerful experimental tool.

## RANDOMIZATION WITHIN CONSTRAINTS

In some cases you may not wish to make a circumstance into either a random or a control variable. Actually, randomization and control define opposite ends of a continuum. Falling between these two extremes are various degrees of **randomization within constraints.** In this case, you control part of the event assignments and randomize the other part. Suppose in our reaction-time experiment we knew that practice could be an important variable. If we presented all the low-intensity trials first, followed by all the high-intensity trials, we could be accused of biasing the experiment; any difference between response times to low- versus high-intensity light might, in fact, be due to short versus long practice. To avoid this problem, we could decide to control the practice variable and give only one trial to each individual. Or we could assign the low- and high-intensity trials randomly over, say, 12 trials by flipping a coin and presenting a high-intensity light whenever a head occurred and a low-intensity light whenever a tail occurred. This alternative might not be the most attractive, however, because it could result in an inadequate representation of high and low intensities. (The flipping of the coin might result in only three high-intensity trials, for example, and nine low-intensity trials.) To avoid this possibility, we decide to have an equal number of high- and low-intensity trials. Thus, as a solution we establish a constraint on the assignment of trials (an equal number of each type of trial), and we make a random assignment within this constraint. We might write the word high on six slips of paper and the word low on six and draw them out of a hat to determine the order of presentation. This procedure would fulfill the requirement that the conditions be randomly ordered across trials within the constraint that the two intensities be equally represented.

Other constraints, of course, are possible. We might wish to avoid the possibility that too many trials at a particular intensity occurred early in the sequence. We could then **randomize within blocks,** with the block serving as our constraint. Using this alternative, we could choose three blocks of four trials each, ensuring that two high-intensity trials and two low-intensity trials were randomly selected within each block. To describe this procedure, we would say that conditions were randomly assigned to three blocks of four trials each, with the constraint that each intensity be represented an equal number of times within each block.

Many such constraints can be legitimately used as long as they are specified. The more constraints you specify, however, the less random is your selection process, and the less generalizable are your results.

## CONFOUNDING VARIABLES

If we designed our experiment perfectly so that we have chosen an independent variable to manipulate and a dependent variable to measure, and made the rest of the circumstances into control variables, random variables, or variables randomized within constraints, then we would not have to worry about the variable I will discuss next. However, not every experiment is designed perfectly, and in many real-world settings it is impossible to design a perfect experiment. In this case we need to know when a confounding variable rears its ugly head. Any circumstance that changes systematically as the independent variable is manipulated is a **confounding variable.**

Suppose, for example, that we used three different light intensities in our reaction-time experiment: a low-intensity light for the first 20 trials, a medium-intensity light for the next 20, and a high-intensity light for the last 20. If we reported that "people respond more quickly the more intense the light," someone else could say, "No, people respond more quickly after practice." In fact, we could both be correct, or either one of us could be incorrect! The problem is that we have unintentionally *confounded* the experiment with a variable that changes systematically with the independent variable.

An experimenter can record the most sophisticated measurements, do the finest statistical test, and write up the results with the style of Hemingway, yet a confounding variable can make the whole effort worthless. A feud between Coca-Cola and Pepsi-Cola illustrates the type of confusion that can be caused in this manner ("Coke-Pepsi Slugfest," 1976). Pepsi pitted its cola against Coke in a drinkers' test in which tasters who said they were Coke drinkers drank Coke from a glass marked Q and Pepsi from a glass marked M. More than half of the tasters reportedly chose the glass containing Pepsi as their favorite. Coke officials countered by conducting their own preference test—not of colas but of letters. They claimed that more people chose glass M over glass Q not because they preferred the cola in glass M but because they liked the letter M better than they liked Q. This hypothesis was supported when most people tested still claimed to prefer the drink in the M glass when *both* glasses contained Coke.

In this example, the letters were apparently a confounding variable. Because they varied systematically with the colas in the original test, the tasters' preference for the colas could not be distinguished from their preference for the letters.

I mentioned earlier in this chapter that Cook and Campbell (1979) have identified several types of validity. Another type is **internal validity,** which refers to whether the manipulated change in the independent variable caused the change in the dependent variable or whether something else caused the change. If the independent variable didn't cause the change, then a confounding variable must have. So if we want to understand how to avoid confounding variables in our experiments, we need to understand the various possible threats to internal validity. There is no more important task for you as an experimenter than being able to recognize and if possible avoid the threats to internal validity that may introduce confounding variables into your experiments.

## Threats to Internal Validity

### HISTORY

In laboratory experiments, one can usually collect data at all levels of the independent variable over a relatively short time span. In this case, any change in the dependent variable is unlikely to have been due to **history**—that is, to some event that takes place between the testing of the levels of the independent variables.

For example, suppose you wanted to find out whether using computer-generated visuals rather than traditional hand-drawn overhead transparencies in a large introductory psychology class improves grades. Further suppose that this introductory course is taught only once a year. For practical reasons you decide to use the computer-generated visuals this

year and compare the grades of this class to those of last year's class. If you find that the overall grades are better for this year's class, you might be correct in attributing the improvement to the use of the computer visuals. However, some historical event could have caused the change. For example, the school could have tightened admission standards, thereby changing the academic quality of students in the class. Or perhaps the college of engineering decided to require that all senior engineering students take the class, again changing the class composition. Or perhaps the world has undergone an increase in interest for the subject matter being taught, similar to what occurred in computer science courses after personal computers appeared. Or perhaps, at a local level, a fraternity has acquired a copy of last year's test and has made it available to certain students in the class. To have much confidence in the conclusion that the change in grades between the classes was due to the use of computer-generated visuals, you must rule out these historical events as well as any others that might threaten the internal validity of the conclusion.

## MATURATION

**Maturation** is a threat to internal validity caused by participants' growing older or perhaps more experienced. Obviously, maturation is more of a threat with young children than with adults, such as when evaluating the effects of preschool educational programs. However, even for adults, maturation can be a problem in long-term experiments or when participants are undergoing rapid change—for example, when an employee is first assigned managerial duties.

## SELECTION

**Selection** can be a threat whenever participants are assigned nonrandomly, particularly when they are self-selected. If in the previous example the classes chosen for comparison were fall and spring classes, selection could be a problem. My fall introductory psychology class contains lots of first-year students, many of whom are psychology majors. The spring class has many more engineering students who have put off taking this required course until their senior year. Do you think there might be differences between these classes besides the use of computer-generated visuals? Experimenters who use college students as participants are familiar with the potential differences between early-semester volunteers[4] and late-semester volunteers. In general the early-semester volunteers are more eager and motivated and are probably better students or at least better at planning their time. The worst kinds of selection threats are those that are

[4] A *volunteer* in this case is a little like a volunteer in the military. Although some of the students who crowd around experimental sign-up sheets would volunteer even if such service were not a course requirement, most actually volunteer to do this in place of some other requirement, such as writing a paper.

directly linked to the independent variable. For instance, suppose you want to evaluate a new industrial training program. You let workers volunteer to take the new program and then after completing the program you compare the performance of those workers to the performance of workers who did not volunteer for the program. Do you think there might be a difference in the workers who self-selected to be in the two groups? What about the difference between recovery rates of people who choose a new type of therapy and the rates of those who refuse it?

## MORTALITY

When participants drop out of an experiment, **mortality**[5] can also be a threat to internal validity. Fortunately, in most experiments, these individuals die only with respect to their life in the experiment, not with respect to life in general. *Overall* mortality is not really a problem; *differential* mortality is a problem. This occurs when more or different kinds of participants drop out of the groups assigned to various levels of the independent variable. For example, suppose a company decides to try a new training program to inoculate newly promoted middle managers against socially stressful situations. They randomly choose half of their new managers to expose to one hour a day of simulated personal confrontation with employees. The other managers are not exposed to such training. For five years after training, the number of stress-related health complaints of the two groups is counted. It is found that the stress-inoculated group has reported fewer such complaints and the company concludes that the program was a success. Was it?

Among the questions that you should ask is: How many managers dropped out of each group during the training program?[6] It is likely not only that more managers would have dropped out of the stress group, but that these would be the managers who are most sensitive to stress. The success of the training group might have little to do with the inoculation procedure but be due entirely to the fact that mortality changed the characteristics of the groups.

## TESTING

The act of **testing** can change behavior independently of any other manipulation. Testing can be a threat to internal validity when a pretest or multiple-test design is used. Suppose you are interested in whether a new advertising campaign would increase the public's awareness of your company's

---

[5] *Mortality* is the term used by Cook and Campbell (1979). Some experimenters also refer to this as *attrition*.

[6] In addition to the threat to internal validity of mortality, which is being emphasized here, you should be able to find other potential threats. For example, the training program might harbor demand characteristics (see Chapter 4) that bias these managers against reporting stress-related health problems. Or conversely, the training may have sensitized the managers to be more aware of stress-related health problems.

THE THREAT OF
DIFFERENTIAL MORTALITY

brand of shaving cream. You pick a large random sample of consumers and send them a questionnaire. You ask a number of questions about various brands of shaving cream and the commercials associated with the brands. Three months later, after launching a new series of commercials touting your brand, you again send the questionnaire to the same people and discover that they are now much more familiar with your brand of shaving cream. You declare the advertising campaign a success. Are you right?

One problem with the conclusion that the campaign caused a change in awareness is that the pretest itself may have caused the change in awareness. The pretest may have sensitized this particular group of people to noticing shaving cream brands in general. During the following three months, they may have watched all the shaving cream commercials more closely, and now they are able to tell you more about each of the brands regardless of the new advertising campaign.

In addition to sensitizing participants, testing can also inform the participants of the experimenter's topic of interest or even the experimental hypothesis. A pretest can also provide information, increasing the participants' knowledge of a topic so that scores on a posttest will be higher, independent of any experimental manipulation.

## STATISTICAL REGRESSION

Perhaps the most subtle threat to internal validity is **statistical regression.** This term refers to the fact that when participants are chosen on the basis of having scored very high or very low on a particular test, their scores tend to move toward the mean on a second test. It is not immediately obvious why regression toward the mean should occur. Perhaps an example will help.

Suppose you have devised a program that you claim will increase the IQ scores for preschool children who have been classified as mildly retarded (IQ of 53 to 68). You give an IQ test and choose 30 children who score within the mildly retarded range. After one year in your program, the

children are given the test again. You discover that the mean IQ of the group has increased by 7 points and that this change is statistically significant. You declare your program to be a success. Is it?[7]

How could statistical regression have caused or contributed to this result? Imagine that the IQ pretest is composed of two separate components: a "true" IQ that a perfect test would measure and "error." The perfect test yields exactly the same score for a particular child every time you give it. If you could use such a test, statistical regression would pose no problems. But, alas, the IQ that you measure also has an error component.

This error may be due to a number of unpredictable variables. For instance, the child might have been lucky and have guessed the correct answers to several items on the pretest, or might have been unlucky and have guessed fewer correct answers than chance would predict. Or perhaps the child got up on the wrong side of the crib that morning and had a difficult time concentrating on the pretest. Or perhaps the examiner was feeling particularly grouchy that morning and failed to establish good rapport with the child. Because we cannot predict the size or direction of this error component for any particular score,[8] we must treat error as if someone were drawing a random number out of a hat and adding or subtracting it from the true score.

When you chose the mildly retarded group on the basis of a low pretest score, you probably chose many more children who had error working

---

[7] At this point you should be able to identify a number of potential threats to internal validity other than regression. The problem with maturity over a one-year period for preschool children is obvious. Testing could be a problem as well. The IQ pretest was probably the first test of any kind to which these children had been exposed. They might have learned something in general about taking tests. They might also have remembered specific items from the pretest and learned the answers over the year.

[8] If a standardized test is being used, you might be able to get an idea of the general magnitude of the error component for the test, a number that characterizes the reliability of the test. The lower this number, the more we must be concerned with the effects of statistical regression.

against them than children who had error artificially inflating their true score. That is, the true scores of this group were, on the average, not really as low as the ones they received on the pretest. Because you chose only children with low scores, you biased the group toward those with error working against them. However, on the retest one year later, we would expect a less biased error. We would expect as many errors to increase the true scores as to decrease them. There is still an error component, but now it is not biasing the measured score away from the true score.

If you are not yet convinced, try a little demonstration. Pick some true score, say 100. Write the numbers from –10 to +10 on equal-sized slips of paper and put them into a container. Draw a number from the container, add it or subtract it from 100, write down the result, and replace the number. After doing this 30 times, take the lowest five numbers and figure the mean (add the numbers and divide by 5). Now, follow the same procedure, drawing just five numbers and figuring the mean. Is the first mean lower than the second mean? You have just demonstrated statistical regression.

## INTERACTIONS WITH SELECTION

Finally, variables such as maturation and history may have **interactions with selection.** As an example of the possible interaction of selection with history, consider the following study. Stanley Coren and his colleagues studied archival records and found that the distributions of right- and left-handers in age groups ranging from 10-year-olds to 80-year-olds were very different (Coren & Halpern, 1991; Porac & Coren, 1981). From a high of 15% left-handers among the 10-year-olds, the percentage declined until there were 0% in the 80-year-old group. They concluded that left-handers had a "decreased survival fitness" that caused them to die at earlier ages. Obviously, many left-handers, moms of left-handers, and husbands of left-handers were concerned about this conclusion. However, Lauren Harris (1993a) disputes the conclusions and presents evidence that the interaction of selection and history could have caused the change in percentages. Eighty years ago considerable stigma was attached to being left-handed. So parents and teachers strongly encouraged children to be right-handed, forcing them to eat, write, and do other tasks with their right hands. In other words, selection by means of social pressure occurred for right-handedness. But this selection changed with history. Over the years, being left-handed became more acceptable, and fewer truly left-handed children were pressured to become right-handers. So Harris argues that fewer left-handers are in the older groups not because they have died but because there never were many to begin with. The argument is not yet settled (see Halpern & Coren, 1993; Harris, 1993b), but the case of the disappearing left-handers offers an interesting example of the possible interaction of selection with history.

I hope this discussion of threats to internal validity will help you in your search for confounding variables. It might be helpful whenever you are planning an experiment to run over each of these threats to make sure that none of them is a problem for your experiment. In some cases you may have potential threats that are difficult or impossible to eliminate completely, in which case it might be possible for you to use a quasi-experimental design, many of which are discussed in Chapter 10.

## Summary of the Experimental Method

Now that you are familiar with the use of the experimental method, let's try to fit all of the terms we have learned into a schematic framework. Figure 2-1 summarizes the experimental model. On the left all the circumstances that may affect behavior are listed. On the right all the behaviors that could potentially be measured are listed. At the top, on the left, one of the circumstances has been chosen for manipulation, the independent variable. On the right one of the behaviors has been selected for measurement, the dependent variable. The arrow indicates that we are interested in whether the independent variable causes a change in the dependent variable. Although we can ignore the other behaviors, we need to make sure

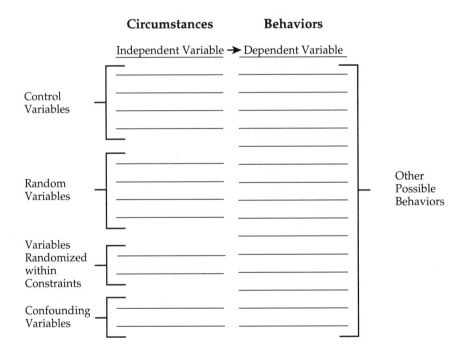

**FIGURE 2-1** A diagram representing an experiment. One of the circumstances has been chosen as the independent variable. The others have been partitioned into control variables, random variables, variables randomized within constraints, and confounding variables. One of the behaviors has also been chosen as a dependent variable.

we can account for all of the circumstances. In the figure these circumstances have been partitioned into control variables, random variables, variables randomized within constraints, and confounding variables. While partitioning the variables, we should keep in mind that a decision to control increases the precision of the results (internal validity) but decreases their generality (external validity). On the other end of the continuum, a decision to randomize decreases the precision but increases the generality.

As a final example to illustrate the types of variables that go into an experiment, I will describe an experiment that two colleagues and I conducted (Grobe, Pettibone, & Martin, 1973) and list some of the variables in a figure like Figure 2-1. We were interested in whether an instructor's lecture pace makes a difference in how attentive the students are. I was teaching introductory psychology to a class of 200 students at the time, so I had the dubious honor of trying to lecture to this class at different speeds. As the independent variable, then, we chose three different lecture paces. I attempted to lecture at each pace for at least five minutes during each lecture. We tape-recorded this portion of each lecture and counted the number of syllables per minute to make sure that my pace was within the allowable range of error. In Figure 2-2 you will see lecture pace listed as the independent variable. The students' attentiveness could have been measured in a number of ways: students could have been videotaped, and judges could have inferred their attentiveness; students could have filled out a questionnaire indicating how attentive they had been to each lecture; and so forth. To get a reliable, quantitative measure, we recorded the background noise level in the room and inferred that when students were quietest, they were most attentive. In Figure 2-2 you will find noise level listed on the behavior side as the dependent variable.

Many variables became control variables and did not change throughout the experiment: the classroom, the instructor, the time of day the lecture was given, the students in the class, and so on. Some of these are listed as control variables in Figure 2-2. Other variables were allowed to vary in an uncontrolled and (we hoped) random way, such as how much sleep I got the night before, the weather outside, the success of the football team each week, how many people in the class had colds (and coughed out loud), and many others. Some of these variables are listed as random variables in the figure. One variable was randomized within constraints. Because we were afraid that attentiveness might be affected by day of the week, we did not want to have all of the slow-paced lectures on Mondays, the medium ones on Wednesdays, and the fast ones on Fridays. So we randomized the day of the week each pace would be used within the constraint that each pace be given the same number of times on each day. Finally, although we tried to minimize confounding variables, we knew that, as in many applied experiments, some would occur. One was, undoubtedly, the average pitch of my voice. I am not a machine, so—as with most people—the faster I talk, the higher my voice becomes. I am sure that vocal pitch was confounded with lecture pace. It is also the case that

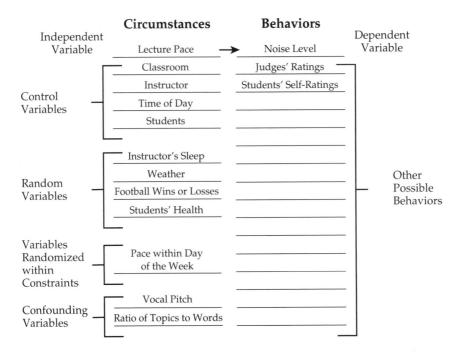

**FIGURE 2-2** Variables from the lecture-pace experiment partitioned into an independent variable, control variables, random variables, a variable randomized within constraint, confounding variables, and a dependent variable

as long as the length of a lecture remained constant, as I talked faster I could either say more words about a particular topic or say the same number of words and have the number of topics I covered vary. I tried to do the former, so the ratio of topics to words was necessarily confounded with lecture pace. These two confounding variables are also listed in Figure 2-2. I hope that this example illustrates how variables can be partitioned into the various types of circumstances and behaviors.[9]

## Summary

The experimental method allows causal statements to be made—that when a circumstance is manipulated it causes a change in behavior. The circumstance that is manipulated is called the **independent variable** and is set by the experimenter to at least two levels. The behavior that is measured is

---

[9] A reader commented that she wanted to know how this experiment came out. Briefly, we found that lecture pace did affect attentiveness. Fortunately, ambient noise levels were lowest for my medium pace. The noise levels were highest for my fast pace. So we infer that a medium pace is best, and it is better to err on the side of going too slow than too fast.

called the **dependent variable** because it may be dependent on the levels of the independent variable. Some of the other circumstances called **control variables** may be set at a particular level and not allowed to vary. Other circumstances called **random variables** may be allowed to vary in a random fashion. Generally, random variables improve the **external validity** of an experiment and allow it to be generalized to other people, settings, and times. Some circumstances called **variables randomized within constraints** may be allowed to vary randomly but within limits imposed by the experimenter. Experimenters should attempt to eliminate or minimize **confounding variables** that change systematically with the independent variable and distort the relationship between the independent and dependent variables.

Confounding variables can cause low **internal validity** and make it difficult to say that only the independent variable caused a change in the dependent variable. Threats to internal validity include **history,** the occurrence of an uncontrolled event during the experiment; **maturation,** the change in age or experience of individuals during experimentation; **selection,** the biased assignment of individuals to groups; **mortality,** the nonrandom loss of individuals from groups; **testing,** the change in participants due to the testing process; **statistical regression,** the movement of scores toward the mean for groups selected on the basis of extreme scores; and **interactions with selection,** the differential effect of a threat on nonequivalent groups.

# Find It on InfoTrac College Edition

Chapter 2 identifies the types of variables found in an experiment: independent variable, dependent variable, control variable, random variable, and confounding variable. Find a journal article that uses the experimental method and, after reading the article, list the independent variable(s) (including the various levels), the dependent variable(s), and the control variables and random variables. It is unlikely that the author will tell you about any confounding variables in the experiment, but look for them anyway. It is probably best to look for articles describing experiments in psychology journals such as *Human Factors*. However, many other journals also describe experiments.

# 3

# How to Get an Experimental Idea

You can observe a lot by just watching.

YOGI BERRA

Perfection is the greatest enemy of a good beginning.

ANONYMOUS

As he was testing hypothesis number one by experimental method a flood of other hypotheses would come to mind, and as he was testing these, some more came to mind, and as he was testing these, still more came to mind until it became painfully evident that as he continued testing hypotheses and eliminating them or confirming them their number did not decrease. It actually *increased* as he went along.

R. M. PIRSIG (1975)

The greater the island of knowledge, the longer the shoreline of the unknown.

JOHN DONNE

We do not know one millionth of one percent about anything.

THOMAS ALVA EDISON

Einstein told me how, since his boyhood, he thought about the man running after the light ray and the man closed in a falling elevator. The picture of the man running after the light ray led to special relativity theory. The picture of the man in a falling elevator led to general relativity theory.

L. INFELD (1950)

[Holmes:] I have no data yet. It is a capital mistake to theorize before one has data. Insensibly one begins to twist facts to suit theories, instead of theories to suit facts.

A. CONAN DOYLE (1891/1989)

was once so bold and foolish as to assign introductory psychology students the task of proposing seven experiments as a course requirement. At first I was puzzled by their reactions to this assignment. Above the din of gnashing teeth, the moaning, and the groaning could be heard the plaintive wail of my stupefied students, "How do we get an idea?" Not only did I find it difficult to understand why getting an idea would pose such a problem, I also found it impossible to answer the question. I have now pondered this pervasive problem and formed an opinion about why it occurs and what can be done to solve it.

I don't believe the problem is that students have no ideas. As small children, we are curious about everything, including human behavior: "Mommy, why is that man so fat?" "How does Jenny eat with her left hand?" "Why can't I spell as good as Betty?" "Why do Tommy's parents spank him so much?" I refuse to believe that this curiosity simply fades away. In fact, the same students who "could not get an idea" seem to have plenty of thoughts about human behavior at parties or bull sessions: "What's the best way to study for my bio exam?" "Should I marry him or just move in with him?" "Am I more creative in the morning?"

For this reason I will refuse to believe you if you tell me you don't have any ideas for an experiment. It's not true that you don't have any ideas, but it may be true that you are afraid something is wrong with the ideas you do have! This fear can paralyze your natural creativity, and after a while, all your ideas seem inadequate to you.

## Fearing Experimental Ideas

Fears about experimental ideas are usually irrational, stemming from a misunderstanding of psychology experiments. Psychologists call irrational fears *phobias*. Because I am a psychologist, I cannot resist the temptation to name the phobias behind our inability to get experimental ideas. The following phobias seem to be the most common.[1]

### GENIEPHOBIA (FEAR OF GENIUSES)

Geniephobia stems from the common belief that anyone doing research must be a genius and that your modest brainpower couldn't possibly measure up. Researchers often do little to counteract this belief, and a few have been known to cultivate it. For years, every time I read a journal article I pictured the author as a wise-looking old man with flowing white locks. It was a shock to find that many experimenters are young, ordinary-looking people who make silly mistakes and say stupid things just like the rest of us.

My own geniephobia is still being cured. The more experimental psychologists I meet, the less I think only geniuses can do this kind of work.[2] So relax. Your ideas are probably as good as theirs were when they were getting started.

---

[1] Any resemblance of these names to accepted psychological terminology is purely coincidental.
[2] I do not mean to imply that experimental psychologists are dumber than other scientists. Biologists and physicists can be dumb, too.

A PREPHOBIC HAVING
LOTS OF IDEAS

## IMITATOPHOBIA (FEAR OF IMITATING)

Those people with imitatophobia are afraid to propose any idea unless it is absolutely original. An imitatophobic who combines this fear with a belief that everything worthwhile has already been thought of often reaches a state of total paralysis. Truly original experiments are few indeed in psychology. Most experiments use variations of somebody else's method to test somebody else's theory. In Chapter 6 you will learn how to find out what other experiments have been done in your area of interest, and you will find out exactly how unoriginal you are. Don't be afraid to move science along in small steps, however. That's what the rest of us do.

## PARAPHERNALIOPHOBIA (FEAR OF APPARATUS) AND MANUPHOBIA (FEAR OF DOING THINGS BY HAND)

If the sum total of your mechanical knowledge of the automobile is that the right pedal makes it go and the left pedal makes it stop, you are a prime candidate for paraphernaliophobia. This malady will scare you away from any experimental idea requiring an apparatus more sophisticated than a deck of cards.

On the other hand, if you will not consider doing any experiment unless it requires sophisticated scientific equipment, you are a victim of the opposite affliction, manuphobia. Everyone knows that the more complex the equipment, the better the research.

Both positions are unfounded, however. Some of the best research uses little or no equipment. Piaget developed a major area of child psychology with no more apparatus than toy blocks, water glasses, and modeling clay. Other areas of psychology, such as verbal learning, concept formation, attitude assessment, and personality, require no more than pencil and paper. An apparatus can help you do research, but it isn't the research itself. And when an apparatus is necessary, someone will be available who can teach you how to use it.

## PARSIMONIOPHOBIA (FEAR OF SIMPLICITY)

Parsimoniophobics think they must come up with grandiose experiments that will change the course of science in one fell swoop. Their motto is: If it's simple, it can't be science. Although there are some advantages to complex experiments, you should generally aim for the simplest experiment that can answer your experimental question. People with parsimoniophobia seldom complete their majestic experiments; when they do, they usually cannot interpret the results. To start with, then, think simple. You can always pursue more complex questions later. (In Chapter 9 I will talk about what I mean by simple and complex experiments.)

## CALCULATOPHOBIA (FEAR OF STATISTICS)

Some people dread having to do any calculations tougher than counting on their fingers. If you can never remember how to figure out your car's gas mileage or how to keep your checkbook straight, you are a potential calculatophobic. If you will consider only those experiments that require the simplest statistical tests, remember that such tests are tools that can help you interpret your results; they should not cause you to throw out good experimental ideas. You can always find someone who enjoys playing with numbers to help you analyze your data. I am not saying that a knowledge of statistics is unimportant, but it is, after all, just a tool used in science, not science itself.

A CALCULATOPHOBIC

## IMPERFECTAPHOBIA (FEAR OF BEING IMPERFECT)

An imperfectaphobic will not tell you about an experimental idea until every tiny detail is perfectly worked out, and his or her proposal looks like the final report. This attitude often stems from having read too many pristinely presented journal articles. As we will see in Chapter 5, journal articles are end products; they seldom reflect the sloppy thinking and general air of confusion that precedes most experiments. Completed experiments are often quite different from the experimenters' original ideas. The original idea for an experiment simply forms the kernel; the experimental procedure will evolve as you set up and conduct the experiment. If you take the plunge and begin talking about your experiment in rough form, others may be able to help you mold it into a perfect experiment. Well, almost perfect.

## PSEUDONONPHONOSCIENTIAPHOBIA
## (FEAR OF NOT SOUNDING SCIENTIFIC)

People with this hideous affliction can recognize a great idea only if it is expressed in *scientific jargonese.*[3] Scientific jargonese is a pseudolanguage that some scientists make up to sound good when they talk with other scientists who do similar research. It helps obscure the research from the general public—and sometimes from other scientists as well. For example, in jargonese an experiment designed to determine whether people remember words better when the words are in groups is described as an investigation into "the effect of taxonomic and categorical clustering on the retention of verbal material." Or a notion that people from ethnic groups live in the same neighborhood because of pressure from their friends is described as an experiment examining "the effect of demographic distribution by ethnic affiliation as a function of peer-group coercion." Jargonese can also be translated into everyday language. If you are interested in "the effect of affiliative preference on the salience of dimensions in person perception," you are actually trying to find out whether people who join certain organizations differ in the way they see other people. Try translating one yourself: "the effects of maternal employment on sibling aggressive tendencies."[4]

As you can guess from the way this book is written, I believe that most pseudoscientific jargonese is nonsense. Good scientists need not hide behind their language. A good idea is a good idea regardless of the words used to express it.

## ERGOPHOBIA (FEAR OF WORK)

Sorry, there is no known cure for this affliction.

Now that we are aware of what fears might block our creativity, let's try to get some experimental ideas. What is the best way to start?

---

[3] I am using *jargonese* to refer to the dictionary definition of *jargon,* meaning "speech or writing characterized by pretensions, complex terminology, and involved syntax," rather than meaning "the language peculiar to a particular trade, profession, or group." The line between jargon and jargonese is thin indeed.

[4] If you came close to "Do working mothers' kids fight more?" you are catching on. Be sure to buy my next book: *Scientific Jargonese for Fun and Profit.*

# Observation

Someone once said that it's easy to write: Just sit at the typewriter and stare at the keyboard until drops of blood appear on your forehead. This also describes the best way to avoid coming up with experimental ideas. Because we are interested in human behavior rather than typewriter behavior, the best thing to do is observe humans, not typewriters!

Getting experimental ideas is simply a matter of noticing what goes on around you. Once you become a good observer, your natural curiosity will provide you with experimentally testable questions. One week of constant observation should provide you with enough experiments to last three careers.

Indeed, some of the classic research in experimental psychology started with a simple observation. If Ekhard Hess's wife had not noticed that his pupils got bigger when he was looking at bird pictures, pupillometrics might never have been created. If Ivan Pavlov had not noticed that his dogs were salivating to stimuli other than meat powder, Igor Nosnoranovitch might have been the father of classical conditioning instead. If Jean Piaget had not noticed that his daughter Jacqueline stopped making gurgling noises when she could no longer see her bottle, he might have become a famous Swiss watchmaker. Most revolutionary experimental ideas have been generated by simple observation.

## PUBLIC OBSERVATION

After reading the next couple of paragraphs, take a paper and pencil, leave the room you are in, and walk outside where there are people to observe. As a training exercise in observation, make notes of possible experimental questions that occur to you as you stroll around.

First I'll go on a stroll to show you what I mean: I wander outside, and I see that the sun is shining.

1. Do people get more or less work done when the weather is nice?

I walk past two workmen laying concrete for a bike rack. One is working; the other is standing and watching.

2. Do workers stand around more when they are unionized?

A couple of joggers run by.

3. Do people who exercise regularly sleep better at night?

A young woman is sitting over there under a tree with a young bearded fellow. They are looking rather amorous, and I feel like a peeping Tom. Better move on.

4. Do women find men with beards more attractive than men without beards?

I see a large group of students filing into a classroom.

    5. Do students in large lecture classes make better grades than those in small classes?

I arrive at a crosswalk. Will that car stop? Yes, it did. Across I go.

    6. Are drivers more likely to give the right of way to pedestrians of the opposite sex?

I stop to watch a sports car zooming down the street.

    7. Do people drive sports cars faster than regular cars?

I head back past the library.

    8. Do students who study in the library retain information better than those who study in the dorm?

I pass the bike rack at the front of my office building and see lots of bikes.

    9. Are mountain bikes easier to ride than road bikes?

I lope upstairs to my office. I am back.

    I just got nine potential ideas for experiments. That's almost one per minute! Now you try it while I wait.

## ME WAITING

    Welcome back. Did you get plenty of ideas? Think about the ideas you could get if you were that observant all the time. Now the problem is "Which idea should I turn into an experiment?" because not all important questions can be answered by experiment. All experimental questions must pass the ROT test: they must be **Repeatable, Observable,** and **Testable.** For example, some supporters of extrasensory perception claim that ESP occurs only under certain conditions and that it is impossible to predict when the conditions are right. In other words, ESP works only some of the time and fails the repeatability test. As long as this basic tenet governs ESP effects, it is impossible to test for the existence of ESP. Other questions fail because they are not observable: "Do dogs think like humans?" "Is my experience of the color red the same as yours?" Finally, some questions fail because they are not testable. For example science cannot answer moral questions, such as "Is abortion wrong?" "Is it proper for women to wear short skirts?" "Are drugs evil?" Although we can certainly use the scientific method to determine people's opinions about these questions, we cannot devise any test that could answer the questions themselves. We must therefore eliminate all such questions from any list of experimental ideas.

Do all the questions in your list of ideas meet the ROT requirements? Take a moment to go through your list and eliminate any that fail to do so.

they are not observable: "Do dogs think like humans?"

After reading Chapter 1, you should also recognize that some questions must be answered by correlational observation rather than by experimentation. For example, if, as in question 7, we want to know whether people who choose to drive sports cars drive at a faster speed than those who drive other types of cars, we must do a correlational observation to answer the question. On the other hand, if we wish to know whether any driver tends to drive faster when driving a sports car, we could design an experiment to answer the question. Take another look at your list of ideas, and label each idea experimental or correlational.

Our little walks have been interesting, but people in public provide us with a limited set of behaviors. Whom else can we observe?

## OBSERVING YOURSELF

Introspection was one of the earliest techniques in experimental psychology. Introspectionists, however, concentrated on looking at their own mental processes rather than at their own behavior. Because a controversy developed about whether a person can know his or her own mental processes, ex-

KNOW THYSELF.

perimental psychologists stopped watching themselves altogether. Rather than follow the dictum "Know thyself," they resolved to "Know not thyself."[5] It is still generally frowned on to do an experiment with yourself as the only participant; nevertheless, you can get some good experimental ideas this way. Not only will you be able to collect many samples of the behavior you are interested in, but you might even have some idea why you did what you did. The former can give you an idea for an experiment, the latter an idea for a theory. We will examine theories later in this chapter.

With a little effort, you can begin to notice your own behavior. It may seem ridiculous to suggest that you do not notice yourself, but it is probably true. When dressing, which arm do you put into your shirt or blouse first? When you brush your teeth, do you brush the left side first or the right? Do you put the key to your house or room into the lock rightside up or upside down? When you cross your legs, do you put your left leg or your right leg on top more often? These are all things you do every day. Do you notice them? Observing yourself can be entertaining[6] as well as a good source of ideas. Write down the ideas as they occur to you.

## OBSERVING YOUR FRIENDS

Your friends are also good sources of experimental ideas. It is important, however, to observe their behavior as unobtrusively as possible. Staring is considered impolite at best and grounds for a fight at worst. People sometimes avoid paying attention to their own behavior because they are not

---

[5] Some experimental psychologists still don't know who they are.
[6] If you develop this skill, you will have to learn to control yourself in public. You may be considered strange if you break into gales of laughter over your own behavior.

particularly fond of the way they behave. Consequently, to avoid losing friends, keep your observations to yourself. Pointing out your insights, no matter how brilliant, will not help you win friends and influence people.

## OBSERVING CHILDREN

Observing children is a necessity if you are interested in doing experiments in the area of developmental psychology, but children can also give you good ideas for other areas of research. If you are not blessed with[7] children, you probably have friends and relatives who would be more than happy to let you watch theirs for a while. Unlike adults, who have learned that their behavior should appear rational, logical, and consistent to an outside observer, children generally behave in ways that are uncomplicated by complex patterns or social inhibitions. Because most kids couldn't care less about adult standards, you will be able to observe relatively uncontaminated behavior patterns in children.

## OBSERVING PETS

Animals are interesting to study in their own right, but much of their behavior can also be generalized to humans. Furthermore, you will find that pets are even less inhibited than children; because they are less capable of highly complex behavior patterns, their behavior is often easier to interpret. In addition, you can manipulate your pet's environment without worrying as much about the moral implications of possible permanent damage (see Chapter 4 for a discussion of the ethics of animal treatment).

OBSERVE YOUR PETS.

# Vicarious Observation

Although you may find it less exciting than direct observation, you can also get experimental ideas by reading other people's research. You might feel that this technique of *vicarious observation* feeds off other people's creativity, but nonetheless this approach has certain practical advantages. For one

[7] Or plagued by (depending on your point of view).

thing, because the broad experimental question you are researching already has a stamp of approval from the author and journal reviewers, you know that the questions being asked are considered important. Second, somebody else has already fit the experimental result into the existing body of knowledge and has probably even proposed a theory, thereby structuring the area of research for you and saving you time and effort. Finally, earlier researchers have devised a method of attack that apparently works and that you may be able to modify and use in your research.

In beginning your search for an idea, you should first identify an area of research that interests you. You will then know what types of journals you should read. Your topic should be as specific as possible: competition in small groups, play therapy in schools, perception of visual illusions, development of arithmetic abilities, and so on. For the more general topics, you can simply scan journals having related articles. For more specific topics, this procedure is rather inefficient, and you will need to do a literature search, as described in Chapter 6.

As you read these articles, try to discover what important questions are left unanswered by the research. The author will sometimes help you discover these questions by suggesting where future research should go. But after you finish reading the article, *you* should also be able to determine where it should go by the questions left unanswered. Usually you wouldn't want simply to replicate the research, but it is certainly appropriate to do something similar.

By way of example, suppose you had read about an experiment asking whether violence on TV causes aggression in children. In the experiment 6-year-old children were exposed to two hours of either violent or nonviolent television 30 minutes each day for a month. Then their behavior was measured by seeing which toys they played with—aggressive toys like guns, knives, and tanks, or nonaggressive toys such as dolls, trucks, and blocks. After reading this article you might decide that you can think of a better way to manipulate the independent variable. Maybe you do not like the way they defined violence and the shows they picked to show the violent and nonviolent groups and you would like to see these defined in a different way. Or you might wish to add a third group that watches a mixture of violent and nonviolent shows, or a more neutral set of shows, or perhaps does not watch TV at all.

Instead of changing the independent variable, you might wish to change the dependent variable. Maybe you think that determining how aggressive children are by looking at what toys they play with is a poor way to measure aggression. Perhaps you think it would be better to have trained judges watch the children playing together and have them rate each child on aggressiveness. Or you might want to interview the children's teachers or their parents.

You might also think that some of the control variables were set at inappropriate levels. Six-year-olds have already been exposed to a lot of television. Perhaps you think it would be better to use younger children or to use several groups of children at various ages. Maybe you think that two hours of TV is too little given that the average watched by children is closer to four hours per day. Or maybe you think that one month is too short a time to show much effect of TV on behavior.

It may be that you think one of the control variables should have been randomized. For example, you think that the investigators were wrong to have the children watch TV in groups of six in a laboratory rather than allowing them to watch it in a family setting in their homes.

An even more interesting reason for doing your own research would be if you thought you had discovered a confounding variable that you could eliminate. For example, it may be that the violent shows were simply louder than the nonviolent shows; maybe loud noises rather than violence make children more aggressive. You can probably think up many more ways that the original experiment could be altered to test the hypothesis in a different way, to elaborate on the hypothesis, or to test a similar but different hypothesis.

So as you read about other people's research, you might find it helpful to go through a similar set of questions: Are there better or different ways of manipulating the independent variable, of measuring the dependent variable, of choosing levels for the control variables, of making control variables into random variables or vice versa, of avoiding confounding variables? To say this another way, can you think of ways to improve the internal or external validity of the research? I believe that if you read the articles carefully and ask yourself these questions, you will think up many excellent ideas for research.

## Expanding on Your Own Research

Once you have done several experiments, you will find that your own research provides many experimental ideas. Every experiment you do will leave a number of questions unanswered. For example, after using several levels of an independent variable in an experiment, you may want to see what happens when you choose other levels. Or you may have controlled a certain variable at a particular level in one experiment and may wonder what would happen if you set it at a different level. Or you may come up with unexpected results and want to find out why the outcome was not as predicted. Each experiment usually brings up more unsolved questions than it answers.

This picture of science as a continual growth of new questions is different from that held by those who think of science as a fixed body of knowledge we need only uncover. This latter outlook views scientific research as leaving fewer and fewer questions unanswered as it proceeds. In reality, however, each experiment actually increases the number of questions to be answered. Instead of working ourselves out of business, we are working ourselves into more business than we can possibly handle.

This open-ended view of science can be discouraging and exciting. It can be discouraging because it is sometimes difficult to chart our progress through an ever-expanding universe in which we sometimes seem to take five steps backward for every step forward. On the other hand, it is exciting because we end up asking better and better questions. Perhaps the goal of science is not to find answers to all possible experimental questions but to answer ever more promising and important questions. In following up on your own research, you will find that your main problem is not "How can I get an experimental idea?" but "Which idea is the most important one to work on?"

## Using Theory to Get Ideas

Now that you have collected a number of observations, how do you put these together into a framework that suggests what kind of experiment you might do? This is usually done in science by proposing a theory. In the most typical case the reason for doing an experiment is to test a theory. So one thing that will help you get an idea for an experiment is to convert some of your observations into a theory and then test that theory with an experiment. Unfortunately, those who do not understand how theory is used in science often have a negative opinion of it. One mistaken belief is that theories are extremely complex and can be understood only by geniuses: "Einstein may have understood what $e = mc^2$ means, but I never could." A second misconception is that a theory is simply somebody's wild guess: "That's only a theory." In fact, a theory can be quite simple to understand, and as evidence is collected supporting a particular theory, we can become ever more certain that it is true—but, as we will see, never entirely certain.

Why do we need theories? The outcomes from experiments and other types of research are facts. But science is more than a loose collection of facts. It is an organized body of knowledge; it has a structure much as a building has a structure. And just as a randomly arranged pile of bricks is not a building, an unstructured collection of facts is not a science. Theory

EXPERIMENTAL PSYCHOLOGISTS DO TWO JOBS.

provides the blueprint that tells us how these facts can be put together into an organized scientific body of knowledge. From my point of view, one of the reasons that experimental psychology is more fun than some of the other sciences is that experimental psychologists can be architects and builders as well as brick makers. Some of the other sciences have imposed a division of labor. For instance, most physicists are either theoretical physicists or experimental physicists, but not both. Experimental psychologists have traditionally done both jobs.

I find it difficult to give a simple understandable definition of theory. If forced to do so, I would say that a **theory** is a statement about the probable relationships among a set of abstract variables. The theoretical statement is only *probable* because it is still subject to testing, and as we will see shortly, theories are easier to disprove by testing than to prove. The relationships are among *abstract* variables because if the variables consisted of directly observable events, all we would have would be a statement of fact, a direct observation rather than theory. The abstract variables in a theory are general categories of circumstances or behaviors rather than specific circumstances or behaviors. For example, the theoretical statement that viewing violence causes aggression is different from an experimental demonstration that after seeing a war movie, children choose to play with guns.

To help you understand the use of theory a little better, I will show how theorizing fits into the planning and interpretation of experiments by using an example. Suppose we have been observing the world around us and have noticed the following things: Children seem to play rougher after watching shoot-'em-up shows on TV. In recent years younger kids seem to have been charged with violent crimes more frequently, and at the same time, violence in the media seems to have increased. Children in war-torn countries take up arms and fight at a very young age. These observations, and perhaps others, might lead us to propose a theory: *The more that children observe violent acts, the more likely they are to display aggressive behavior.*

That theory is pretty easy to understand. Note that it is more abstract, more general, than any of the observations that led to it. We may not realize it, but we came up with this theory through induction. **Induction** is a logical process in which the conclusion contains more information than the observations on which it is based. That is, we would expect from our theory of violence and aggression that it would hold not only for the three observations that led to it but also for all cases of children viewing violence. We could be wrong, of course. Perhaps the theory is true only for the cases we have observed, in which case our induction is in error. But at least once the theory has been stated, it can be further tested through experimentation.

If our theory is any good, it should allow us to make a number of predictions. The logical process by which we make these predictions is deduction. When we use **deduction,** we draw a conclusion from a set of premises, and this conclusion contains no more information than the premises taken collectively. Thus, if the information in the premises is true, the conclusion

must be true. For example, if a horse is a mammal, and all mammals are animals, then by deductive reasoning a horse must be an animal. In our example, if the more that children observe violent acts the more aggressive they become, and if watching detective shows on TV involves observing violent acts, then watching a large number of detective shows on TV must lead to increased aggressive behavior. So from our theory, through deduction, we can predict a number of observations such as this one. Each predicted observation forms a **hypothesis** for an experiment. To test one hypothesis we might set up an experiment in which one group of children watches four hours per day of TV detective shows containing violence and a second group watches four hours of nonviolent TV. After a number of days we observe the children's play behavior to determine how aggressive they are. The hypothesis deduced from our theory is that the group observing the detective shows will display more aggressive behavior. If the theory is true, the hypothesis must be true. Figure 3-1 shows the thought process we have gone through so far. At this point we have used induction to turn our observations into a theory and used the theory to deduce a predicted observation. We are now ready to do the experiment to test this prediction.

Suppose that the experiment confirms the predicted observation. Have we proved the theory? No, confirming a hypothesis does not prove the theory that generated it. It does support the theory, but only through induction, not deduction. In order to conclusively prove a theory, we would need to test every hypothesis that could be deduced from the theory. In our case, we would have to test every possible way that violence could be observed by children and measure every type of aggressive behavior that could be displayed. Short of doing this, all we can say is that the outcome of our experiment supports the theory. As additional experiments are done that support the theory, particularly if they test a wide range of variables, our confidence in the theory will continue to increase, but you can see how difficult it would be to ever say that the theory had been proved.

Suppose, on the other hand, that the experimental outcome disconfirms the predicted observation. Have we disproved the theory? From a logical point of view, we have (again, see Figure 3-1). Even a single dis-

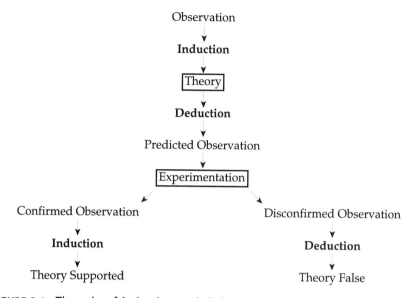

**FIGURE 3-1**  The role of induction and deduction in linking theory to experimentation

confirmed prediction disproves at least one of the premises, because the prediction was arrived at through deduction. Remember the example "a horse is a mammal, all mammals are animals, a horse must be an animal"? If we discovered that a horse was not an animal, it would have to be the case that either all mammals are not animals, or a horse is not a mammal. No other logical possibilities exist. Using the same logic, if viewing four hours of violent TV rather than nonviolent TV does not cause increased aggressive behavior, then either what we were showing the children was not violent, or our theory as stated is wrong. You can see why some have stated that our job as scientists is not to prove theories, but to disprove them (Popper, 1968).

The weakness in the argument that we can logically disprove a theory through experimentation is that the statistics we do to reach our experimental disconfirmation are not deductive. Although we will examine this issue in more detail in Chapter 12, I will give you the basic argument here. In our example, the way we would disconfirm our experimental hypothesis would be to find no difference in aggressiveness between the two viewing groups—that is, to find no statistically significant difference. The problem is that our statistical tests are typically designed to determine whether the levels of the independent variable cause a *difference* in behavior, not a sameness. Yet experimentally disconfirming a hypothesis usually involves showing these levels to be equivalent rather than different, and we do not generally do statistical tests to test this. So we must be very careful in concluding that a hypothesis, and therefore a theory, is false from such an outcome.

Even if we could have disconfirmed the hypothesis by testing in the proper statistical direction (that is, by determining that the hypothesis is false because an effect is statistically significant), we could still be in error. As we will see in Chapter 12, even when used properly, these statistical tests are accurate at only a probabilistic level. We can reach only a certain level of confidence that there is a real difference in the population from the difference on our sample. For instance, we might conclude that our result is statistically significant at the .05 level of significance. That means that we might be wrong up to 5% of the time. So, we know that 1 time out of 20 we could be in error in believing that we have disconfirmed the hypothesis, and thus we would be in error to consider the theory disproved.

There are other reasons, besides the statistical ones just mentioned, why the disconfirmation of a hypothesis would not provide as strong a disproof of a theory as might be expected by deductive logic. For example, there could be problems with the way the theory was implemented in the experiment, with the way violence was manipulated or aggression was measured, or with the control or randomization of variables. So a single experiment is seldom considered to have disproved a theory until a number of contrary results have been found.

I have gone into some detail here about the role of theory in helping us get an idea for an experiment and in helping us interpret the results. It is important for you to understand, in a general way, how theory and experimentation interact. Fortunately, however, you do not have to go through this formal logical process every time you do an experiment. The steps are the same for all experiments. In fact, the process I have been describing is quite natural to humans. In leading our lives we continually make observations, generalize from the observations, and test the generalizations by making additional observations. Although we do not call them theories, we live our lives based on these generalizations. All I have described here is a bit more formal version of the same natural process.

## TYPES OF THEORIES

So far I have given only one example of a theory. But theories can take many forms. Here I will discuss three types of theories[8] and continue to illustrate them using the question "Does violence on television cause aggression?"

### Descriptive Theories

A **descriptive theory** simply attaches names to events without necessarily explaining why or how the events have occurred. For example, Freud, as part of psychoanalytic theory, said that repression occurs when we uncon-

[8] The three types of theories discussed here are similar to those mentioned by Arnoult (1972) in his book *Scientific Method in Psychology,* although some of the names have been changed.

A DESCRIPTIVE THEORY

sciously refuse to admit painful or disagreeable ideas to conscious thought. Although such a theory may help clinicians in their work, the mere naming does little to explain the conditions under which repression occurs or how it might be examined experimentally. In a similar way, for many years psychologists interested in motivation were enraptured with naming instincts. At first the concept of an instinct seemed to be useful, because it appeared that most animal behaviors could be classified as reflecting certain instincts (such as the feeding instinct or the mating instinct). However, eventually psychologists began to accumulate as many names for instincts as there were observable behaviors (such as the "running into a hole when attacked from the front" instinct), and the concept lost its usefulness.

Descriptive theories can be useful if the names are attached to abstract events rather than to directly observable events. For example, we might state that the observation of violence is related to aggressive behavior. If we could carefully define "violence" and "aggressive behavior" as general classes of events, we might have a useful descriptive theory. But even this kind of descriptive theory is of limited value because it does not explain how the relationship works.

### Analogical Theories

**Analogical theories** explain how relationships work by drawing an analogy between a psychological relationship and a physical model so that the physical analog becomes a psychological model of behavior. For example, many of the theories that attempt to explain how humans process information use the computer as a physical analog. Of course, nobody believes that the brain works exactly like a computer, but enough similarities exist for computer modeling to provide some useful analogical theories.

As an example of an analogical theory, let's take the physical properties of momentum as an analog for the relationship between violence and aggression. As you may know, a physical object has momentum in proportion to its speed and mass; the faster it is traveling and the more massive

AN   ANALOGICAL   THEORY

it is, the more momentum it has. This momentum can be overcome by friction. Thus, an analogical theory relating violence and aggression might be stated this way: "The amount of aggression expressed by an observer is like the force exerted by a moving object, where the degree of violence observed is analogous to the mass of the object and the time of observing is analogous to the speed of the object. After exposure to violence, the aggressive tendencies will be high but will decrease over time in the same way that friction overcomes momentum."

This analogical theory is more useful than the descriptive theory proposed in the previous section because it explains some of the complexities of the relationship. We should also be able to test the theory based on our knowledge of how the physical model works. For example, we know that the longer a force is exerted on a physical object, the faster its speed and the greater its momentum. Thus, a longer time is needed for friction to overcome the momentum. By analogy, the longer a person observes violence, the longer it would take the aggressive tendencies to disappear.

Because of its explanatory power, an analogical theory is certainly more useful than a descriptive theory. However, analogical theories are also doomed to failure in the end, for at some point the properties of the physical analog will no longer correspond to the properties of the human. For this reason, you can best use analogical theories as first approximations that help you identify the major variables and outline in a general way how the variables affect one another. But you will find that analogical theories are seldom powerful enough to help you specify the exact mathematical relationships among the variables.

## Quantitative Theories

**Quantitative theories** do attempt to state relationships in mathematical terms. They specify not only the direction of relationships among categories of variables but also how these categories are quantitatively related. Few psychological theories have reached this level of sophistication. Only a few subareas in learning, memory, and cognition have attempted to use quantitative theories.

Quantitative theories have been limited in psychology because psychologists have more difficulty with variability than do physical scientists. For example, in physics the theory of gravity is a quantitative theory expressed in precise mathematical terms. Because gravity affects all physical objects in the same way, a physicist can assume that any variability in experimental results is simply a measurement error. In psychology, however, we cannot predict how all individuals will behave based on one individual's behavior, nor can we predict how the same individual will behave at any given time. Consequently, our quantitative theories must be able to accommodate variability. The best we can do is to predict how probable it is that a behavior will occur,[9] so we must express mathematical relationships in probabilistic terms. (For example, the probability that a particular individual will learn this list of words in five trials is .8.)

Psychologists also face the problem of deciding what scale to use in measuring behaviors. In the physical sciences, the units for measuring speed or mass are not controversial. In psychology, however, we have to find scales by which such concepts as violence or aggression can be measured. For example, consider the following quantitative theory: Humans express a level of aggressiveness in direct proportion to the average level of violence they have observed. Because our proposed theory attempts to establish a mathematical relationship between the scales of violence and aggression, we must first determine how to measure them. As you can see, establishing scales for such concepts is no easy task.

There are several areas of psychology in which quantitative theorizing has grown rapidly in recent years. One of these, *structural equation modeling*, starts with a theory much like a descriptive theory, in which a number of concepts are identified and described. A best guess is then made about how these concepts might relate to one another, and links are drawn among concepts to indicate these possible relationships. Then measurements are made for each of the concepts, and statistics (that are well beyond what you want to know here) are calculated; these give weights to the links indicating which links are the important ones. In this way the investigator learns how the concepts are quantitatively linked together.

A second area in which more quantitative theorizing is being done is *connectionism* (sometimes called *parallel distributed processing*). This type of theorizing begins with an analogical model in which the analog is the human nervous system. At least three levels of units are set up on a computer. These are similar to three levels of neurons and can send signals to one another. As the units experience the world (for example, they might

---

[9] In some areas, physical scientists deal with similar problems. The structure of atoms, for example, is expressed probabilistically. In fact, chaos theory, a theory of dynamical systems based on nonlinear mathematics, has been developed recently in order to deal with probabilistic events in the physical sciences that do not follow the deterministic rules of classical science.

analyze the curves and lines of letters) they send signals to the units at deeper levels and make some of these more or less likely to send their own signals, just as neurons do. After repeatedly experiencing the world, the units start to establish weightings that reflect how the learning has progressed (for example, the deeper units begin to recognize some letters). These quantitative weightings can be considered a theoretical representation of the way a human nervous system works, and the behavior of the resulting theoretical representation can be compared to human behavior in a quantitative way—for example, does the system mistake certain letters for others, as humans do?

With some of these exceptions, most theories in psychology are still descriptive or analogical. However, as psychology becomes more sophisticated and we learn to handle the difficulties caused by variability and scaling, more psychological theories will become quantitative.

## PROPERTIES OF A GOOD THEORY

How do you know a good theory when you see one? I have implied that quantitative theories are better than analogical theories, which in turn are better than descriptive theories. Why is this true?

First, a theory must be able to **account for most of the data** already collected. There is no use proposing a theory if the data do not support it. (You can see why a thorough literature search is so important; it will allow you to eliminate some of the competing theories before collecting any data.) One or two items of disconfirming evidence, however, will usually not destroy a theory unless an alternative theory can account for all the evidence.

A theory must also be **testable.** As we saw earlier in this chapter, science advances by doing research that eliminates some theories and leaves others as still possible. To be testable, then, means that the theory can potentially be disconfirmed. A theory is disconfirmed if the outcome of an experiment is not what the theory predicted it would be. If a theory is so universal that it can account for any experimental result, then disproving it is impossible.[10] One reason a theory might not be testable is that the predicted results are expected to occur only some of the time in an unpredictable manner. For example, Freud's theory of repression is virtually untestable as it is usually stated. How could you disprove repression experimentally? Perhaps you could provide people with an experience they would rather forget. For instance, you might tempt people to cheat and then confront those who succumbed with their dreadful deed.[11] Sometime later you might have a close friend of each person ask that individual whether he or she had ever cheated. If no one reports having cheated, you have support for the theory, because it shows that everyone repressed the

---

[10]For this reason, testability is called *falsifiability* by some. Karl Popper (1968) is well known for suggesting that an idea is testable only if it can be falsified.

[11] Let's ignore for the moment whether this experiment would be considered ethical.

A GOOD THEORY ALLOWS YOU TO PREDICT...

incident. However, if everyone reports having cheated, this result doesn't eliminate the theory, because the theory never claimed that all people repress a particular event, only that some people sometimes repress some events. Thus, your experiment would do little to dislodge the theory. A theory that is so general that no test can be proposed to discredit it is a worthless theory from a scientific point of view.

Although a theory should not be so general that it can account for any behavior, it should also **not be too restrictive.** That is, the fewer directly observable events the theory can account for, the less valuable it is. In the most extreme case, a theory simply restates the relationship between observable events.[12] For example, the statement that "8-year-old children hit a punching bag more after watching a televised Roadrunner cartoon" is less useful than the statement that "watching violence on television causes aggression in children." Even more useful is the statement that "observing violence causes people to be more aggressive." The more general our statements, the more valuable they are because they account for a larger set of observable events.

Finally, a good theory **predicts** the outcome of future experiments. Even descriptive theories specify the relationship between categories of events. Thus, the relationships between directly observable events that are members of these categories are predictable from the theory. Analogical and quantitative theories also allow you to predict the relationships between events, and these predictions are even more precise.

## DOES THEORY ALWAYS PRECEDE DATA?

In this somewhat idealized discussion of the relationship between theories and experiments I have probably led you to believe that you must always have a theory in mind before you do an experiment. However, there are certain types

---

[12] Actually, such a statement would not fit our definition of a theory, but some investigators would call it a theory.

of research in which theory is less important. Some investigators prefer to with-hold theorizing until after they have collected a lot of data. They are like the sleuth Sherlock Holmes: Only after collecting all the clues (data) will they nail the culprit (theory). They feel that, particularly early in a research program, proposing a theory before collecting data is like deciding on the villain and then looking for clues related only to that person's guilt: Both procedures are biased. In fact, B. F. Skinner, the late father of operant conditioning research, maintained that most theories do more harm than good (Skinner, 1950).

Skinner believed that our job as scientists is to account for observable events and that because theories use abstractions rather than events, they do not help us. And because they are abstract, theories also lull us into believing that our research is complete when it is not. We are tempted to use the theories to fill in the holes in our research without really knowing whether the answers the theories give us are true. Finally, Skinner worried that when we let a theory guide our research and then the theory is disproved, we lose much of the research generated by the theory. Skinner's rather extreme position must be understood within the context of behaviorism's general rejection of all mental events and intervening variables that are the basis of many current theories. Most research psychologists today disagree with the position he held and feel that theories are vital to most types of research. However, even these researchers know that there are times when theories should play a smaller role in guiding research.

When a particular research topic is still in its infancy, premature theorizing may cause more problems than it solves. If prior to collecting much data we propose a tenuous theory, then we can spend a lot of time and effort testing that theory when our efforts might be better devoted to collecting additional data that might lead us to a better theory. Particularly at the start of a new research program, there is certainly nothing wrong with doing a number of experiments whose purpose is simply to answer the question, "I wonder what would happen if . . ." rather than testing a theoretical prediction. After a sufficient number of observations have been made so that theorizing is warranted, collecting data in this unstructured exploratory way becomes increasingly less efficient.

Another danger is that playing the theory game can be great intellectual fun. In the beginning a researcher finds an important problem, makes initial observations, and proposes a theory. Others then test this theory, reject it, propose their own, have those rejected, and so on. As theory begets theory, the game takes on a life of its own, and we sometimes forget what the important problem was. We can end up investigating easily testable theories instead of looking for important problems. But because no science has the resources to investigate all problems, we must choose, and we obviously should choose important problems to work on. If, because of theories, we choose to investigate easy but rather unimportant problems instead of more difficult but more important ones, we are misusing our resources.[13] To counteract this trap, I have threatened at times to teach a course entitled *Psy 371*, "Things Psychology Knows Nothing About." The purpose of this course would be to find important areas of human behavior that nobody is currently investigating and to propose how one might begin research in these areas.

A final type of research in which theory is sometimes less important is **applied research.** Applied research is designed to solve a specific problem, as opposed to **basic research,**[14] which is done for the sole purpose of increasing the scientific body of knowledge. Most of the research we have been considering up to this point is basic research. Even though basic research is not designed to solve practical problems, it can help solve such problems. Today's behavior-modification techniques, which provide some of the most powerful procedures for correcting human behavior problems, are based on basic research done in the rat laboratories of yesteryear. Jack Adams (1972) found that many of the military systems of the '70s had been designed using information from basic research done more than 20 years earlier.

Applied research, on the other hand, has as its primary purpose the solution of problems. Perhaps you need to know how humans read handwritten numbers so that you can design a machine to read ZIP codes. Or you may wish to know whether daily quizzes will improve students' classroom performance on major exams. Or you may want to know whether cognitive-behavioral therapy is more effective than psychoanalysis. Many such practical problems need immediate answers that basic researchers might never find. Needing an

---

[13] Kuhn in his book *The Structure of Scientific Revolutions* (1970, p. 37), argues, in fact, that once the scientific community has accepted a paradigm (a set of assumptions, widely accepted model, or global theory), scientists then work only on problems that can be assumed to have solutions within that paradigm: "To a great extent these are the only problems that the community will admit as scientific. . . . A paradigm can, for that matter, even insulate the community from those socially important problems that are not reducible to the puzzle form, because they cannot be stated in terms of the conceptual and instrumental tools the paradigm supplies."

[14] Basic research is sometimes also called pure research, perhaps because one is not supposed to have mixed motives for doing it. Unfortunately, some people who do this kind of research seem to prefer other dictionary definitions of *pure*—for example, untainted with evil or guilt. I have never heard pure scientists defend the position that they are physically chaste, even though I suspect that this is the subconscious reason behind wearing white lab coats.

answer to a practical problem is a perfectly legitimate reason for doing research, and it can be satisfying, especially if your findings have an immediate impact on the world. In many cases it is even possible to test a theory while doing applied research. When this is possible, the research can make an immediate practical contribution and also help build the scientific body of knowledge.

Observation is again the key to getting ideas for applied research. Finding a practical problem is simply a matter of carefully observing human behavior and giving your curiosity free rein. As with the other procedures we have discussed for getting experimental ideas, you will find that more practical problems need to be solved than you can possibly do experiments to solve. As before, the question is not so much "What can I do?" but "What should I do first?"

# Importance of Psychological Research

Before I end this chapter, I want to point out that though I have emphasized having fun with research and doing research to satisfy our curiosity about human behavior, psychological research should also be done because it provides answers to some of life's most important problems. If I were to ask you to name the problems that cause our society the most grief and cost us the most money, which ones would you name? Here are ten I can think of:

1. Our children do not learn enough in school (for example, many can't read, write, do math, etc.).
2. Too many people abuse drugs.
3. People behave in ways that are unhealthy (smoking, sexually transmitting diseases, eating poorly, not exercising, etc.).
4. Human conflicts bring about the possibility of wars.
5. Domestic violence harms family members.
6. Violence causes high crime rates.
7. Too many people are on welfare.
8. Civility in our society is breaking down, as shown, for example, by road rage, littering, impoliteness, and frivolous litigation.
9. Too many people are killed or injured in accidents.
10. Many workers are poorly trained to do their jobs or need retraining.

How many of these problems are problems with human behavior and therefore within the scope of psychology? You are right—all of them! Think of the issues politicians talk about: crime, health, education, drugs, the economy. Problems in these areas come about because of the way people behave. To solve these problems we need to understand human behavior better, and to do that we need research. Thus, the work we do as psychological researchers is not only interesting and fun but also frequently very important. Society needs this research, and the answers we find will help people live better lives.

# Summary

Although we all have natural curiosity about human behavior, many of us develop irrational fears that block our ideas. Some of us fear that all other researchers are geniuses and that our ideas will not be original. Some people are afraid to propose an experiment requiring a complex apparatus, while others are afraid of experiments with a simple apparatus. Others fear that their idea is too simple, that their experiment will require complicated statistics, or that their idea is not perfect when it is proposed. Finally, many people do not believe they have good ideas until they translate them into scientific jargonese.

The major key to getting experimental ideas is to learn to *observe* the world about you. You also need to know which ideas are scientifically appropriate. Ideas must be **repeatable, observable,** and **testable** to be experimental ideas. To get ideas, you can observe yourself, friends, children, and even pets. Although some of the best ideas come from direct observation, you can also get ideas by reading other people's research (vicarious observation) and from following up your own research.

The typical way in which observations are turned into experiments is through a **theory,** a statement about the probable relationships among a set of abstract variables. Observations lead to theory through a process called **induction,** in which a general statement is derived from specific instances. A prediction, called a **hypothesis,** can then be made from the theory through a process called **deduction.** If an experiment testing this hypothesis confirms it, the theory is supported, not proved. If the hypothesis is disconfirmed, according to the rules of logic, the theory is disproved through deduction. However, because the statistical tests used to disconfirm the hypothesis are probabilistic, disproof of the theory is not certain.

A **descriptive theory** attaches names to events and is most useful when the names are attached to abstract but definable events. **Analogical theories** explain how relationships work by drawing an analogy between psychological relationships and a physical model. **Quantitative theories** specify relationships in mathematical terms. Psychology has very few quantitative theories because we are still learning how to account for variability and how to develop precise scales of measurement. A good theory **accounts for most of the data,** is **testable,** is **not too restrictive,** and is **able to predict** the outcome of future experiments.

Skinner held that theories are practically useless because they do not help account for observable events, they lull us into believing that unfinished research is complete, and they cause research to become useless when the theory is overthrown. Although most investigators disagree with this position and believe that theories are useful, theories are not always required to do good research, particularly during the early stages of research, and for **applied research**—which is done to solve a problem—as opposed to **basic research**—which is done to contribute to the scientific body of knowledge.

# Find It on InfoTrac College Edition

Chapter 3 discusses various ways to get an idea for research. Vicarious observation refers to finding a piece of research previously done by somebody else and changing it in some way to make it your own. Using the InfoTrac College Edition database, identify an area of research that interests you and try various search terms to find relevant articles in the database. Once you have found one that is of particular interest, read it very carefully and then suggest ways that you would adapt it to do your own research. Remember from the chapter that you might change the way the independent variable is defined or add levels to it. You might measure a different dependent variable. You might change the settings of control variables or make them into random variables or change random variables to control variables. Or you might try to eliminate a confounding variable. Sketch the design for a new piece of research based on the article you have read.

# How to Be Fair
# with Participants

> Do unto others as you would have them do unto you.
>
> MATTHEW 7:12
>
> Our data show that the social structure of competition and reward is one of the sources of permissive behavior in experimentation with human subjects; the relatively unsuccessful scientist, striving for recognition, was most likely to be permissive.
>
> B. BARBER (1976)
>
> Oh, what a tangled web we weave,
> When first we practice to deceive!
>
> SIR WALTER SCOTT
>
> The human mind has no other means of becoming acquainted with the laws of the organic world except by experiments and observation on living animals.
>
> IVAN P. PAVLOV
>
> From an ethical point of view, we all stand on equal footing—whether we stand on two feet, or four, or none at all.
>
> P. SINGER (1985)

Now that you have an idea for an experiment, you are ready to begin planning it in more detail. First, however, we need to consider the issue of ethics. As experimenters we can be unethical in at least two ways: We can mistreat the people or animals whose behavior we are measuring. We can also mistreat the body of knowledge that we are trying to establish—in other words, treat our science unfairly. In this chapter we will discuss treating participants fairly; in the next chapter we will discuss treating science fairly.

Society as a whole and the scientific community in particular have agreed on a set of rules by which we must do our research. Some of these rules are unwritten, such as the basic rules of courtesy. The assumption is that such rules are so obvious that everybody understands them. Other rules are written, such as *Ethical Principles of Psychologists and Code of Conduct* (American Psychological Association [APA], 1992) and *Ethical Principles in the Conduct of Research with Human Participants* (APA, 1982). These rules are continually revised as society's conception of the role of experimentation and the rights of an individual change. In the first part of this chapter, we will consider the relationship between the person doing the experimenting and the one being experimented on, including some basic courtesies in the relationship. Then we will examine how this relationship can affect the outcome of an experiment. We will also explore alternative experimenter–participant relationships. Finally, we will consider the ethics of treating animals fairly.

## Treating Human Participants Fairly

Because our purpose in doing research in psychology is to understand behavior, we will usually be interacting with humans (and in some cases animals). Traditionally, psychologists have referred to the people who provide the behavior as *subjects.* The early forefathers and foremothers of psychology probably liked this term because it sounded scientific and the subjects of the research were humans. Unfortunately, the term also may imply that people are subject to the experimenter's will, or even worse, subjected to it! Back in the 1930s it was suggested that the term *experimentee* should be used in place of subject, but the suggestion never caught on (Rosenzweig, 1970).

This discussion may seem pretty trivial to you: What's in a word? In this case, the word *subject* reflects the nature of the relationship between this individual and the experimenter and suggests certain ethical considerations. Subjects are passive and react to conditions of an experiment much as chemicals passively react when combined in the laboratory. For these reasons, the accepted terminology has changed in recent years, and those who were formerly called subjects are now usually called **participants.** This term properly acknowledges the help that our participants are giving us by participating on our research and gives them a more equivalent status to the experimenter. As you will see in Chapter 13, in writing research reports it is best to call the participants what they are: students, children, women, and so forth, but the appropriate generic term is *participants.*

In the early history of experimental psychology, nobody worried about what to call the people who were experimented on because the experimenter and the participant were the same person. In those days, most psychologists reported their own internal experiences as the dependent variable in their experiments. Believing that only time and training made it possible to become aware of these internal experiences, experimenters considered themselves their own best participants.

Later in the history of psychology, many experimenters came to feel that verbal reports of internal events were inappropriate data for the science of psychology. Arguing that it is not possible to be objective and subjective at the same time, these experimenters started a revolution in psychology. Some psychologists, overreacting to the revolution, decided that only animals were appropriate for psychology experiments. If you think verbal reports of a participant are not appropriate subject matter, then pick one who cannot talk![1] During this era, the rat became a prime participant for experimentation. Other investigators felt that although experimenters were too experienced to be experimented on, rats were rather unlike most humans. What was needed was a naive human. The naive human chosen was the college student. College students are the participants in 70% to 85% of published research (Schultz, 1969; Smart, 1966) and as much as 90% of research conducted by university psychology departments (Jung, 1969).

In this latest view, the participant is supposed to be a naive, well-motivated observer who will react to experimental manipulations in an uncontaminated way. Yet, as we will see, participants are not uncontaminated observers. They usually have definite ideas about the experiment they are serving in, and they attempt to achieve specific goals that are often different from the experimenter's.

98-POUND PARTICIPANT          SUPER-EXPERIMENTER

Humans (even college students) also have certain legal and moral rights. A physicist can take the block of wood from the inclined-plane experiment and drop it, hammer on it, swear at it, kiss it, or do any number of things with it. Although his colleagues may think he is pretty weird, they would not have him arrested or throw him out of the profession. Psychologists, however, must preserve their participants' rights at all times.

The nature of the experimenter–participant relationship makes participants particularly vulnerable because the experimenter usually has most of the power. For example, many individuals serve in experiments to satisfy part of a psychology class requirement. Under these circumstances, students may feel that their course grade will be affected if they fail to do as the experimenter asks. On the other hand, if people are paid for their services, they may feel that noncooperative behavior will earn them less money. Finally, if

---

[1]OK, I am taking a bit of liberty with history here. I will discuss some better reasons for using animals in research later in this chapter.

individuals volunteer for experiments because they believe they can advance the science of psychology, they may feel that society will benefit from their cooperation. In any of these cases, participants see the experimenter as having the ultimate power to evaluate or manipulate their behavior.

In addition to these academic, monetary, or altruistic motives for cooperating with the experimenter, participants may also share the commonly held opinion that psychologists have a mysterious bag of tricks for determining whether someone is cooperating. The first three sentences between a psychologist and a stranger illustrate this belief: "What do you do for a living?" "I'm a psychologist." "Oh, are you analyzing me?" For some reason, many people believe that psychologists have X-ray vision and can look deep into their minds and find out what they are thinking. They believe they had better cooperate or the experimenter will get 'em! This myth again helps stack the experimenter–participant relationship in favor of the experimenter.

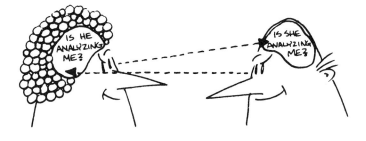

## RULES OF COURTESY

To unstack the relationship a little, experimental psychologists need to follow a code of behavior that treats their participants with respect and dignity. As a new experimenter, you should hang a sign in your experimental room (an imaginary sign is OK) that says "Participants are humans too!" Participants deserve the same courtesies you would give anyone who offered to help you with a project. Some simple rules of courtesy you should follow are:

1. *Be present.* Too often experimenters forget that they have a participant signed up or fail to notify the individual if the equipment has broken down or if the experiment has been delayed or called off for some other reason. Once a person signs up for an experiment, you should make every effort to fulfill your obligation to be present for the experiment.

2. *Be prompt.* A participant's time is valuable too. Don't waste it.

3. *Be prepared.* You should rehearse all phases of the experiment prior to meeting any participant. Not only is it discourteous to do otherwise, but if you stammer over the instructions, tinker with the equipment, and gen-

erally fumble and mumble your way through the experiment, participants may become so confused or disgusted that they perform poorly.

4. *Be polite.* Unless the experiment calls for it, ask your participants to do something; don't order them. Make liberal use of the words "please," "thank you," and "you're welcome."

5. *Be private.* Treat all information that a participant gives you within an experimental context as confidential. Be discreet not only about what the individual tells you but also about how he or she performs on the experimental task. Federally funded grants are specific about what information you may obtain, how you may use that information, and how to code and store it. If possible, eliminate participants' names from data sheets, and use a method that will prevent others from discovering the identity of individuals.

6. *Be professional.* You need not be so sober and stiff that your participants feel uncomfortable, but do not be so casual and flippant that you convince them that you don't care much about the experiment. They won't care either! Nor is an experiment the proper place to make dates, hustle golf partners, sell insurance, or use the experimenter–participant relationship for any purpose other than research.

These rules seem simple enough, but not all ethical issues concerning human participants are so straightforward. More controversial issues, such as "What constitutes informed consent?" and "Should mental stress be permitted?" are discussed at length in *Ethical Principles in the Conduct of Research with Human Participants*. However, no publication can cover all possible ethical issues, and many experiments involve "close calls" where an unbiased opinion is required. For these reasons research-oriented institutions have **institutional review boards.**[2] These boards are made up of experienced researchers and sometimes physicians and other technical experts. All research using human participants should be screened by such a board.[3] Typically, the researcher fills out a form that contains a number of questions, such as "Will participants be asked to give informed consent?" and "Will confidentiality of the data be maintained?" This form also asks

---

[2] The National Institutes of Health require institutional review boards for all research funded by them. They put out a publication, *Protecting Human Research Subjects: Institutional Review Board Guide (NIH Guide,* Volume 22, Number 29, August 13, 1993) that is designed to assist review board members, researchers, and institutional administrators in fulfilling their responsibilities. Copies can be obtained from the U. S. Government Printing Office, Superintendent of Documents, P.O. Box 371954, Pittsburgh, PA 15250 (reference GPO Stock No. 017-040-00525-3).

[3] In some cases for courses that use a book such as the one you are holding, the instructor can convince the institutional review board to let the instructor evaluate classroom experiments for ethical considerations. When this happens, the instructor tends to be very conservative about what will be approved. Although from time to time a course experiment is important enough to publish, the primary purpose of most of them is to train students to do research. In most cases, the students' training can be accomplished as well with a low-risk experiment as with a high-risk experiment. So if you are planning a classroom experiment in which participants take a handful of drugs and then disclose their kinkiest sexual fantasies to an audience . . . forget it!

the researcher to describe briefly the research being proposed. The members of the board pay particular attention to the issue of potential physical or psychological harm to participants. It is unrealistic to expect that the risk of harm can be reduced to zero in any piece of research; a participant may break a leg tripping on the carpet. However, the review board's task is to make sure that the risk of harm is minimized. And when known risks are a necessary part of the research, the board's job is to decide whether the benefits likely to be derived from the research outweigh these risks.

Such review boards certainly help eliminate or improve many potentially unethical investigations. However, review boards in the biomedical field have themselves been the subject of research, for it has been found that a significant minority of people who serve on such boards are poor at balancing the risks and benefits of human research (B. Barber, 1976). A large majority of board members surveyed had received no formal training in research ethics. So although these boards can be very helpful, the primary responsibility for doing ethical research still lies with you, the experimenter.

## INFORMED CONSENT

One of the issues of concern to institutional review boards and to you is **informed consent**. Before they consent to participate, participants are entitled to be informed about the factors that might influence this decision. Once they have been so informed, the researcher must document their consent, usually in writing. Although informing participants and obtaining their consent may seem to be pretty straightforward, a number of factors may cloud the issue—for example, documenting that the information given was understandable, ensuring that participants in a subordinate position are not pressured to participate, or, for some participants, determining whether they are capable of making an informed decision. *Ethical Principles of Psychologists and Code of Conduct* (APA, 1992) goes into some detail about such issues:

6.11  Informed Consent to Research
(a) Psychologists use language that is reasonably understandable to research participants in obtaining their appropriate informed consent (except as provided in Standard 6.12, Dispensing with Informed Consent). Such informed consent is appropriately documented.
(b) Using language that is reasonably understandable to participants, psychologists inform participants of the nature of the research; they explain the foreseeable consequences of declining or withdrawing; they inform participants of significant factors that may be expected to influence their willingness to participate (such as risks, discomfort, adverse effects, or limitations on confidentiality, except as provided in Standard 6.15, Deception in Research); and they explain other aspects about which the prospective participants inquire.
(c) When psychologists conduct research with individuals such as students or subordinates, psychologists take special care to pro-

tect the prospective participants from adverse consequences of declining or withdrawing from participation.

(d) When research participation is a course requirement or opportunity for extra credit, the prospective participant is given the choice of equitable alternative activities.

(e) For persons who are legally incapable of giving informed consent, psychologists nevertheless (1) provide an appropriate explanation, (2) obtain the participant's assent, and (3) obtain appropriate permission from a legally authorized person, if such substitute consent is permitted by law.

6.12 Dispensing with Informed Consent

Before determining that planned research (such as research involving anonymous questionnaires, naturalistic observations, or certain kinds of archival research) does not require the informed consent of research participants, psychologists consider applicable regulations and institutional review board requirements, and they consult with colleagues as appropriate.

Once you are comfortable that you have provided a means for your research participants to give informed consent, you need to consider the nature of the experimenter–participant relationship that will be set up in your experiment. The nature of this relationship is important because it affects not only the participant's rights but also the experimental outcome. Although experimental psychologists like to pretend that participants in psychology experiments are neutral creatures reacting in a sterile, controlled environment, most know that such is not the case. In the next section we'll consider in more detail how the experimental situation can influence the outcome of an experiment.

## DEMAND CHARACTERISTICS

When participants show up for an experiment, they have little idea what they will be required to do, but they are usually interested in the experiment and want to know exactly what it is about. Experimenters in turn are often secretive about their intention, which prompts the participants to try to determine what the experiment is really about from clues the experimenter gives them. The experiment then becomes a problem-solving game.

These clues that influence participants in the experimental situation have been called **demand characteristics** because they demand certain responses (Orne, 1962). Whereas the experimenter provides many such clues, participants also bring demand characteristics with them to the experiment. If they have taken a psychology course, have read about psychology experiments, or have even been told about the experiment by a friend, they may bring such expectations as the following with them: The experimenter is going to shock me. The experimenter is trying to find out how intelligent I am. The experimenter is going to trick me into revealing something nasty about myself.

Sometimes these notions are so overpowering that a participant cannot be swayed from them. A participant in one of my experiments was once required to memorize a set of words presented to him through earphones. Shortly after starting the experiment, he tore off the headset and shouted, "This thing is shocking me!" Thinking he might be right, I carefully measured for any current passing through the headset. The headset was well grounded. I tried to continue the experiment, but this fellow still claimed that he was being shocked. He had made up his mind that I was going to shock him and would not believe otherwise. As a result, his data had to be discarded.

Other demand characteristics come from subtle cues that the participant picks up during the experiment. To minimize such cues, experimenters attempt to standardize all experimental procedures. An experimenter usually reads instructions from a written copy, for example, so that all participants will at least have the same verbal demand characteristics. In some experiments, however, even the way the experimenter reads the instructions can affect the participant's performance. In one experiment, two sets of tape-recorded instructions were made by experimenters who were biased toward opposite experimental outcomes (Adair & Epstein, 1968). The experimenters found significant differences between the performances of those hearing different tapes. Although the experimenters read the same instructions, the subtle differences in their voices apparently produced results consistent with their biases.

Even animals seem to be influenced by subtle cues given by the experimenter. In one of the more famous experiments on experimenter bias, student experimenters trained rats to run a maze (Rosenthal & Fode, 1973). Some of the experimenters were told that their rats had been specially bred to be bright, fast learners; the others were told that their rats had been bred to be dull, slow learners. The supposedly bright rats learned to run the maze in fewer trials, even though they were in fact littermates of the supposedly dull rats. The usual reason given for this result is that the student experimenters must have treated the rats differently, playing with the "bright" rats more and handling them so that they became less fearful of being manipulated. However, other investigators have claimed that the results might be due to student experimenters' cheating with their data (Barber & Silver, 1968). Whatever the reason, experimenter bias was reflected in the outcome of the experiment.

Though my presentation of the concept of demand characteristics makes it sound pretty ominous, it may be less of a problem than I have suggested. Investigators (Weber & Cook, 1972) have reported finding little evidence that experimental participants typically try to confirm what they believe is the experimenter's hypothesis, which they have deduced from cues in the experiment. Instead, these investigators claim that participants try to put their best foot forward; that is, they try to appear competent, normal, and likable. The participants' concern with how they will be judged is far more important than their concern about fulfilling the experimenter's expectancies or confirming the hypothesis.

T. X. Barber (1976), in a book dealing with the pitfalls in human research, reports that many experiments claiming to demonstrate demand characteristics are themselves seriously weakened by other design flaws. He believes that much of the research supporting the concept has been poorly done. However, just because this research may be flawed, we cannot necessarily conclude that demand characteristics can be ignored as a potential problem in our experiments. Anything that we can do to minimize their potential effects should be done to improve our experiments.

## Responses of Participants to Demand Characteristics

If participants do detect the demand characteristics in an experiment, how might they respond?

**Cooperative participants.**    After human participants determine in their own minds what the demand characteristics of the experiment are, they react according to their attitude toward the experiment (Adair, 1973). Most people tend to be *cooperative* and try to fulfill the perceived demands of the experimenter. Some cooperate to an astounding degree. In one experiment testing cooperativeness, the experimenter gave the participant a stack of 2000 sheets of paper and asked him to compute the 224 addition problems on each page. Although this task was obviously impossible, the individual continued to add for five and one-half hours, at which point the experimenter gave up! In a second experiment, the experimenter instructed participants to tear up each sheet into at least 32 pieces after completing the additions. Again, they persisted in the task for several hours without appearing hostile.

To see how this desire to cooperate might be behind a participant's response to demand characteristics, consider the following experiment on group pressure: A person is brought into a room with six other people. The group is asked to judge which of two lines is longer. The first few problems are easy, and everybody agrees. Then two lines are presented, and our participant is sure that the top line is longer, but everybody else says the bottom line is longer. After a long pause, the participant finally agrees that the bottom line is longer. What happened in this experiment?

The experimenter designed the experiment to find out whether group pressure can cause someone to make an obviously incorrect response. The other participants in the room were confederates or stooges trained by the experimenter to lie on the appropriate trial. Because the real participant gave in to the group pressure, the experimenter feels that the hypothesis has been confirmed. But let's read the mind of our participant[4] and see what really happened: "Well, here's another pair of lines. The top line is

---

[4] See, psychologists *do* have mystical powers.

definitely longer. What a dumb experiment this is! Why waste our time having us do such an obviously easy task? And why are we doing it as a group? The experimenter must be trying to see if we can influence each other. Sure enough, everybody else is saying the bottom line is longer. They couldn't possibly really think that. Let's see, I could either give in to these shills and agree or hold my ground. I want to do a good job so I can get out of here. Besides, I'm sure that a group of people can get someone to change his or her mind, so I might as well agree. Besides, the experimenter seems like a nice person and I don't want to mess up the experiment."

If our mind reading is correct, our experimenter's conclusion was wrong. The participant, who is only trying to be cooperative, can cooperate us into drawing an incorrect conclusion! In fact, by the 1970s it became apparent that participants in conformity studies such as the one just described were often highly suspicious, ranging from 50% to 90% indicating suspiciousness (Glinski, Glinski, & Slatin, 1970). However, the effect of suspiciousness on behavior appears to be negligible. In other words, there is little difference between the behavior of suspicious and naive participants (Kimmel, 1996), and where there are effects, the participants tend toward making themselves look good rather than reacting negatively toward the experimenter.

**Defensive participants.**    Some participants are less concerned with making the experimenter look good than with making themselves look good; let's call them *defensive* participants. These individuals search for demand characteristics in the same way that cooperative participants do, but they use them differently. Usually a participant trying to perform as well as possible is an asset to an experiment. But, in some experiments, particularly attitude-assessment experiments, such a person can cause problems.

Suppose we are investigating the difference in the way Hispanics and Anglos view sex-role behavior in children. We post one sign-up sheet requesting volunteers who have Spanish surnames and speak Spanish as a first language and a second sheet requesting Anglos who meet neither of these criteria. Now we show each volunteer pictures of children in traditional sex roles (such as girls playing with dolls) and in nontraditional sex roles (such as boys playing with dolls). We then ask the participants to rate the acceptability of each behavior. Suppose more Hispanics than Anglos report that they find the nontraditional behaviors acceptable. We might conclude that Hispanics are more liberal than Anglos. On the other hand, another interpretation is possible. The members of each group are aware that they were selected on the basis of ethnic origin. Suppose the Hispanics were more concerned with upholding the pride of their ethnic group than were the Anglos. In this case, they might have bent over backward to keep from looking like socially unacceptable chauvinists. In other words, they appropriately perceived the demand characteristics of the experiment and attempted to defend their ethnic group.

In an actual experiment that demonstrated the defensive participant's reaction to demand characteristics, experimenters asked participants to tap a key with their right and then their left index finger (Rosenberg, 1969). Tapping rates are usually faster for the preferred finger, but one group was told that graduate students at Yale and Michigan had been found to tap the key at similar rates with each finger. A second group was not given this information. The difference between tapping rates for the two fingers was significantly smaller for the first group. Again the participants perceived the not-so-subtle demand characteristics of the experiment and tried to make themselves look as good as possible.

**Noncooperative participants.**    Some participants are neither cooperative nor defensive but downright *noncooperative!* The result of such behavior has been picturesquely called the "screw-you-effect" (Masling, 1966). The non-cooperative individual attempts to determine the demand characteristics of an experiment and then behave in such a way as to contradict the experimenter's hypothesis. Such people act out of any number of motives. They may be participating to fulfill a course requirement and resent being coerced. Or they may be opposed to the whole idea of studying human behavior scientifically. Or perhaps they are simply turned off by the experimenter. Whatever the reason, such individuals can be a real nuisance in an experiment. One way to eliminate noncooperative participants is to set some minimal standard of performance so that you may exclude any participant's data that fall below this standard. This standard should be determined prior to the experiment and noted when the experiment is reported. Even this procedure will not eliminate the data of all noncooperative participants, however. Sometimes the best we can do is attempt to give the participants a positive impression of our experiment and hope that they will be cooperative.

## How to Minimize Demand Characteristics

Although we cannot completely eliminate demand characteristics from an experiment, every attempt should be made to minimize those demand characteristics that might become confounding variables by differentially affecting the levels of the independent variable. It is important to know whether a change in behavior is due to the experimenter's manipulation of the independent variable or to the participant's perceived demand characteristics. Confounding caused by demand characteristics can be minimized in several ways.

**Automation.**    Demand characteristics can be controlled by **automating** as much of the experiment as possible. We have already discussed the use of tape-recorded instructions as one type of automation. Experimenters are often rather poor at reading instructions anyway, particularly after reading them aloud 20 or 120 times. You can also ask a person who is unaware of the expected outcome of the experiment to record the instructions if you want to minimize experimenter bias caused by voice inflections.

I have also used videotaped instructions in some of my own experiments. Videotape is particularly effective because it combines visual and aural modes during instruction. If experimental trials involve complicated sequences of events, sample trials can be presented at a slow enough rate for participants to follow, thereby eliminating the need for the experimenter to go back and explain earlier portions of the instructions.

In some laboratories, computers are used to play all or part of the experimenter's role in an experiment. Some investigators program the computer so that the participants never see a human experimenter. The participant shows up at the appointed time. A sign instructs the individual to be seated at the computer terminal and to press a button. The computer then displays the instructions. The individual indicates his or her understanding of the instructions, and the experiment proceeds. The general idea behind this approach is that if participants are not the passive automatons we once thought they were, we can turn experimenters into automatons instead. However, some researchers object to this procedure on the grounds that the artificiality of the situation not only causes participants to feel dehumanized but also decreases the generalizability of the results. This procedure also requires that participants be able to read and understand the instructions, which makes it unsuitable for some participants, such as children and rats (and college sophomores?)

**Blind and double blind.**   A second way of minimizing demand characteristics transmitted by the experimenter is to keep the experimenter from knowing the level of the independent variable being presented. Typically participants are unaware of the level being presented to them. For this reason such experiments are usually called **blind** experiments. However, it is sometimes important that neither the participant nor the experimenter be aware of the manipulations in an experiment. For example, I once did an experiment to determine whether it was possible to "feel" colors with the fingers. Participants were blindfolded and given three cards, two red and one blue. On each trial they were required to put the two cards that were alike in one stack and the one that was different in another. I was concerned that I might unintentionally signal them when they were correct by changing my breathing rate, coughing, or grunting when they had the cards correctly arranged. Some of my ESP-believing friends even suggested that I might be sending ESP messages when they were correct! To avoid such signaling, I sat behind a screen so that I could not observe the participants. I was thus "blind" to the color they were feeling. In fact, this procedure is sometimes called **double blind,** because neither the participant nor the experimenter is aware of which level of the independent variable the participant is exposed to.[5]

---

[5] One of my reviewers points out that this procedure then made me double color blind!

Psychopharmacologists, who investigate the effects of drugs on behavior, often do research using a double-blind design. Suppose a researcher wanted to know whether a drug called Crowzac, which had just been developed, cured people of being depressed whenever they saw crows. The researcher realizes that there may be a problem if she just gives the drug to one group of patients and then tries to determine whether their depression has been relieved. The depression might get better solely because of the patients' expectation that the drug will help them. It is also possible that if the experimenter is evaluating the patients' depression, she might see a phantom improvement because she expects it. To protect against the effects of patient or experimenter expectations, she could use a second, no-drug level of the independent variable with another group, a control group. She would have to treat this control group in exactly the same way she treats the drug group except for actually giving them the drug. She would probably decide to give the control group placebos in place of the drug. Giving a **placebo** involves administering a nonactive substance in the same manner that the active drug is administered. If the drug is taken in pill form, the placebo might be just a sugar pill, or if it is an injection, a saline solution might be the placebo. Even in research on marijuana, placebo cigarettes have been produced that taste like marijuana but do not contain the active ingredient. The purpose of the placebo is to produce a double-blind design; both the experimenter and the participants are blind to whether any individual is receiving the drug or the placebo.

Sometimes it is difficult or impossible to keep participants and the experimenter from knowing the level of the independent variable to which participants are being exposed. If you were an investigator interested in how lighting conditions in an assembly plant affect worker productivity, you might keep one group of workers under existing conditions and put a second group under increased illumination. Now, the workers are obviously aware of the lighting conditions as soon as they step into the room, and nothing you do would prevent that. I use this example because this was the initial experiment done in the 1920s from which the term *Hawthorne effect* came. Hawthorne was the name of the Western Electric Company plant where the experiment was done. The reported outcome was that productivity increased by the same amount for both groups regardless of the lighting conditions. The **Hawthorne effect,** then, refers to a change in behavior that is due simply to the experimenter's paying attention to the participants rather than to the effects of the independent variable. The overall finding from this research was that over a five-year period as changes were made in working conditions such as lighting, rest pauses, and number of hours worked, productivity kept increasing regardless of which condition the workers were under (Roethlisberger, 1977).

The original interpretation of this finding was that the workers' morale kept improving as continuing attention was paid to them during each change in conditions. However, Mac Parsons (1974) reviewed the original research and discovered that over the course of the experiment the workers were given increased access to feedback about their daily productivity. That, combined with changing the way they were paid, could have led to the increased productivity. His claim was that the workers had simply increased their output as a function of increasing reinforcement. So the Hawthorne effect as it is typically interpreted may not have actually caused the results observed at the Hawthorne plant. Nevertheless, it is certainly possible for an experimental manipulation to cause a change in behavior independent of what that manipulation was. So as an experimenter you must attempt to minimize these effects and the effects of participants' knowing to which level of the independent variable they are exposed. If these effects cannot be completely eliminated, at least you should be alert to the possible confounding they might cause.

**Multiple experimenters.**    A third way to deal with experimenter-caused demand characteristics is to use **multiple experimenters.** In this case you do not control the experimenter variable but allow it to vary by using random assignment of the available experimenters to the various levels of the independent variable. Such a procedure increases the generality of your result and decreases the chances that a single, blatantly biased experimenter will influence the outcome.

### Are Demand Characteristics a Problem in Your Experiment?

Even when you have attempted to minimize demand characteristics, they can creep into your experiment. Here are some procedures for detecting them.

**Postexperiment questioning.**    For a number of years after the revolution against subjective verbal reports, experimenters seldom questioned participants about their impressions following the experiment. Fortunately, many experimenters now routinely seek this information. Such information can be valuable not only for uncovering demand characteristics but also for suggesting new hypotheses that can later be tested in a formal experiment.

**Postexperiment questioning** can take many forms, from the experimenter's asking an offhand question to a well-structured written questionnaire. If you want to be sure to uncover demand characteristics, you should plan your questions ahead of time.

In planning your questions, make sure that they do not have demand characteristics built into them. For example, in the group-pressure experiment discussed earlier, a biased question would be "You weren't aware that the other participants weren't real participants, were you?" The question itself demands that the respondent say no. If respondents say yes, they are admitting that they were not the naive, cooperative people they had agreed to be. They also put themselves in the position of telling the experimenter that the experiment was a waste of time because their data cannot be used.

You should also plan your questions so that they go from general, open-ended questions to specific, probing questions. For example, in one experiment designed to determine whether humans could be conditioned without being aware of it, participants were asked to talk about any topic they wished and to continue until asked to stop (Krasner, 1958). Whenever they said a plural noun, the experimenter nodded, said, "Good" or "Uh-huh," and was generally reinforcing. As participants continued to talk, they used plural nouns more frequently. As evidence that the participants were unaware of the conditioning, the experimenters asked the postexperiment question "Did you notice that the experimenter was doing anything peculiar as you talked?" Most reported that they had not. Other investigators, not convinced by this experiment, did a similar experiment but followed the original question with progressively more specific questions, such as "Did you notice that the experimenter would respond when you said certain words?" Although the participants had trouble verbalizing it, most of them were aware that "the experimenter was happier when I talked about certain things, like listing parts to cars." Those who mentioned this awareness were the same ones who had shown the effect of conditioning. Thus, to determine whether participants are influenced by demand characteristics, we should ask questions related to specific demand characteristics as well as more general questions.

**Nonexperiments.**    Another way to determine whether demand characteristics could have affected the experimental outcome is to compare a **nonexperiment control group** with an experimental group (Adair, 1973). The nonexperiment control group is not exposed to manipulation of the independent variable at all. Members are simply told about the experiment, given the instructions, shown any apparatus, and then asked to describe how they think they would perform if put into that situation. If their prediction is similar to the outcome of the experimental group, they may have been able to detect demand characteristics. These characteristics, rather than the independent variable, could have caused the outcome of the experiment. If their prediction is different from the experimental outcome, demand characteristics probably did not cause the observed behavior.

For example, Mitchell and Richman (1980) were suspicious of a finding that supported a "quasi-pictorial" memory representation of mental images. In a typical experiment, participants are asked to memorize a visual stimulus, generate a mental image of it, and then "scan" from one point on the image to another. The usual finding is that there is a direct linear relationship between scan time and physical distance on the stimulus. Mitchell and Richman thought that demand characteristics were possible with this procedure, so they conducted a nonexperiment in which participants were simply asked to predict their scan times. These individuals produced scatterplots that were indistinguishable from those found in the previous experimental work. For this reason, the researchers could not rule out the possibility that the original findings had also been caused by demand characteristics.

**Simulation control groups.** Although asking participants who have not been in the actual experiment how they would have behaved may give you some idea of demand characteristics, it really doesn't tell you how they would actually behave and may mislead you. For example, for a long time people have been curious about whether folks who are hypnotized can be made to perform antisocial acts or to injure themselves. In 1939, Rowland reported an experiment in which hypnotized participants were told that a large diamondback rattlesnake was a rope and were asked to pick it up. One of the two participants immediately attempted to do this, striking his hand on the invisible glass separating him from the poisonous snake. However, 41 of 42 nonhypnotized control participants asked to do the same thing refused. The original finding was again replicated in 1952 by Young (as cited by Kihlstrom, 1995); 7 of 8 hypnotized participants tried to pick up the snake and also were willing to throw a glass of nitric acid at a research assistant, also behind glass. Do these results indicate that hypnotized people are willing to carry out antisocial and harmful actions?

In 1965, Orne and Evans devised a new procedure, the simulation control group, to investigate this topic. A **simulation control group** is exposed to the experimental situation but without a critical manipulation of the independent variable. In this case, an experimental group of highly hypnotizable participants was hypnotized and asked to pick up a snake called an Australian two-step, because that is as far as you get after it bites you! All participants complied, and they were also willing to remove a coin from a beaker of nitric acid and even throw the acid at one of the experimenters, again protected behind glass. However, both a group of participants not susceptible to hypnosis but asked to simulate being hypnotized and a group of nonhypnotized participants also complied without exception. Were these folks really so insensitive that they were willing to hurt themselves and the experimenter? Of course not. When interviewed after the experiment they said they felt perfectly safe in the experiment. They knew that the experimenter would not allow them to be harmed; safety was one of the demand characteristics of the experiment and they knew it. The simulation control group in this case was needed to fully understand how the demand characteristics rather than hypnosis might have dictated behavior.

## ALTERNATIVE EXPERIMENTER–PARTICIPANT RELATIONSHIPS

In the beginning of this chapter was the naive participant. And the naive participant was pleasing in the sight of the experimenter. But not all naive participants are good; most are not even naive. So far we have been considering ways of keeping participants as naive as possible, or at least discovering when they cannot be considered naive. We have another alternative, however. We can give in to the fact that participants are not naive and make use of their problem-solving ability.

### Deception and Role Playing

One way to use this problem-solving ability is to give participants false cues so that their interpretation of the demand characteristics is incorrect. This procedure of **deception,** defined as concealing or camouflaging the real purpose of an experiment, is a controversial topic in psychology, for both moral and practical reasons.

Deception is widely used in psychology, particularly in some areas of social psychology. Indeed, some areas of social psychology could not be investigated experimentally without deception. For example, suppose you are interested in which conditions bias bystanders to give aid to someone who is apparently in trouble. It would obviously be quite inefficient to stand around on a street corner until someone is actually in trouble. Instead you would probably contrive a situation in which a confederate[6] faked being in trouble and then observe bystander behavior. Of course, then you have deceived the bystander, but how could you do the experiment otherwise? Deception runs the gamut from the famous and notorious experiment by Stanley Milgram (1963), who deceived participants into believing they were administering dangerous and perhaps fatal electrical shocks to other participants, to fairly innocuous experiments in cognitive psychology. For example, in an experiment on incidental learning, the participants may be asked to look at a list of words and rate them on some dimension like emotionality. Then at the end of the experiment they are given a memory test and asked to recall the words from the original list. In some respects they have been deceived because they were never informed that they should memorize the words. But it would have been impossible to study incidental learning if they had been informed; the learning would have been purposeful, not incidental.

---

[6] No, not a rebel soldier! In psychology this is what we call people who are trained to help the experimenter by acting in a prescribed way during an experiment.

Whether the use of deception is increasing or decreasing is debatable. As shown by several surveys, it certainly did increase in the 1970s and into the 1980s (Gross & Flemming, 1982). However, more recent surveys indicate that its use has leveled off or even declined (Nicks, Korn, & Mainieri, 1997). It certainly appears to be the case that the kind of deception used has changed in that there are now few studies that blatantly mislead participants and more that simply withhold relevant information.

The argument for using deception goes something like this: Although it is generally wrong to lie, we are justified in temporarily misleading participants because we are contributing to the advancement of science. And as we have discussed, in some areas of psychology it would be impossible to answer many of the most important questions without using deception. Besides, we debrief our participants after the experiment is over and are perfectly honest at that point, thereby wiping out most of the effects of the deception.

The argument against the use of deception goes something like this: You can use a term like "misleading" if you wish, but that is just a nice way of saying "lying." There is enough dishonesty in the world without being dishonest in the name of science. How many of these "scientifically justifiable" experiments have caused great leaps in science? Not many! We can devise alternative ways of doing many of the experiments anyway, such as having participants role-play. It is naive to think that debriefing participants at the end of the experiment wipes out all effects of the deception. As a practical matter there are two additional problems: deception increases future participants' suspiciousness and reduces trust in psychologists, giving the profession a bad name. Deception in psychology is not worth the costs and should be eliminated (Ortmann & Hertwig, 1997).

Research on these first two points has been done (Kimmel, 1996), and it suggests that the effects of participant suspiciousness on research performance are negligible. In addition, this research indicates that deceived participants do not become resentful about having been fooled by researchers and deception does not negatively influence their perceptions about psychology or their attitudes about science in general. For example, Christensen (1988) reviewed studies that assessed research participants' reactions to deception experiments and found that people who participated in deception experiments report that they did not mind being deceived, enjoyed the experience more (than those participating in nondeception experiments), received more educational benefit from it, and did not perceive that their privacy was invaded. In addition, surveys have consistently shown that most individuals in the general population do not have serious objections to deception used in research.

Role playing has been suggested as an alternative procedure to deception. Is it equally effective? Some experimenters have tried to use both deception and role playing under the same conditions and then compared the results. In *role playing* the experimenter asks participants to imagine that they are in a particular situation and to respond as they think they would in a similar real-world situation. If you are interested in bargaining behavior, for example, you might ask one individual to imagine that he is a labor leader, another to pretend that she is the president of a company, and a third to act like an arbitrator. You then operate under the assumption that their responses in some way resemble those of people in the same real-world situation.

Unfortunately, although some experiments do report equivalent results from deception and role playing (Greenberg, 1967), many others do not (Orne, 1970). It is also difficult to specify the conditions under which similar results can be expected from the two methods. In many respects role-playing experiments are much like the simulation control mentioned in the previous section. Perhaps role playing simply reflects the demand characteristics of the experiment, rather than allowing us to predict what behavior would occur in a real-world situation.

The American Psychological Association says the following about deception in its *Ethical Principles of Psychologists and Code of Conduct* (APA, 1992):

6.15  Deception in Research
    (a)  Psychologists do not conduct a study involving deception unless they have determined that the use of deceptive techniques is justified by the study's prospective scientific, educational, or applied value and that equally effective alternative procedures that do not use deception are not feasible.
    (b)  Psychologists never deceive research participants about significant aspects that would affect their willingness to participate, such as physical risks, discomfort, or unpleasant emotional experiences.
    (c)  Any other deception that is an integral feature of the design and conduct of an experiment must be explained to participants as early as is feasible, preferably at the conclusion of their participation, but no later than at the conclusion of the research.

As fledgling psychologists you should take these rules seriously, and if you are considering the use of deception in one of your experiments, you should carefully weigh its costs and benefits.

## Naturalistic Observation

I already mentioned this final alternative to the standard experimenter–participant relationship in Chapter 1. *Naturalistic observation* depends on the experimenter's being an unobtrusive observer. Rather than having participants pretend to be in a bargaining role, for example, the experimenter might go to an actual bargaining situation and observe behavior. We have already discussed the problems associated with this method. Experimenters usually have little control over the variables in the situation. They often have to wait for them to occur naturally, and even then they cannot control potential confounding variables or draw causal conclusions from the correlational data.

In this section we have examined the problems of treating participants as naive, uncontaminated observers. At the least, we should be aware of the problem-solving nature of participants and design our experiments so that the effects of their attempts to solve problems can be evaluated. Where possible, these attempts should work for us rather than against us.

I will give the American Psychological Association the final word (paraphrased) on the investigator's responsibilities for treatment of human participants. Here are the principles the investigator would do well to follow (APA, 1982):

1. Evaluate the ethical acceptability of the experiment.
2. Determine whether participants are at risk.
3. Retain responsibility for ethical procedures.
4. Disclose risks to participants, and obtain informed consent.
5. Determine whether deception is justified and necessary.
6. Respect the freedom of participants to decline participation.
7. Protect participants from discomfort, harm, and danger.
8. Give postexperimental debriefings.
9. Remove any undesirable consequences of participation.
10. Keep individual research information confidential.

If you follow these basic principles and, when in doubt, seek the advice of experienced investigators, you will probably never have problems with the ethics of human participants. Perhaps the best advice concerns your attitude. The participants are doing us a favor. Without their willingness to participate, the science of human behavior comes to an abrupt halt. Treat your human participants with the proper appreciation.

# Treating Animals Fairly

When I ask my introductory psychology students to picture an experimental psychologist, most of them come up with an eggheaded, nerdy guy in a white lab coat running rats in a maze. That picture is a bit deceptive, not only because not all experimental psychologists are eggheaded, or nerdy, or guys, but because only about 7 or 8 percent of psychology studies involve animals. It is true that of those experiments using animals, 90% of those use rats, mice, and birds; very few use dogs, cats, or nonhuman primates.

## WHY PSYCHOLOGISTS DO RESEARCH ON ANIMALS

Although the use of animals in psychological research is small, why is it done at all? Why not always use humans?

### Continuity of Behaviors

As scientists, we take an evolutionary perspective and assume a continuity in the animal kingdom not only of biology but also of behavior. Although primates do not behave just like humans and rats even less so, our nervous systems are built out of the same building blocks, and there are commonalities. Because certain behavioral abilities occurred early in evolutionary history, many of the most basic human behavior patterns are also present in the lower animals. Thus, animal research is based on the assumption that we can investigate certain universal basic behaviors using lower-order animals. We know that during evolution animals kept basic behaviors but also acquired more complex behaviors that tended to override the basic behavior patterns. Thus, if we are interested in studying basic behaviors, such as simple learning or motivation, it may be not only possible but also preferable to use animals that display the basic behaviors unconfounded by the more sophisticated patterns of behavior shown by higher-order animals. However, we must be careful when we attempt to generalize the behavior of a lower-order animal to humans. Humans are obviously much more complex than rats, and no reputable investigator suggests that rat behavior is exactly the same as human behavior. Although some less reputable interpreters of animal research have been known to overgeneralize findings out of ignorance or simple-mindedness, such occasional misuses of animal data do not invalidate the original premise behind using animals.

## Control

In addition to theoretical reasons for using animals in research, there are a number of practical reasons. For one thing, animals are available nearly all the time. For some reason, college students insist on taking weekends and holidays off. Animals can also be used for experiments that take place over a long period. It is also possible and legal to *control* the conditions under which animals exist, both in and out of the experiment. Thus, animal experimenters can investigate such interesting variables as overcrowding, sensory deprivation, wake–sleep cycles, and environmental stressors.

We can control both the heredity and the environment of animals, a task made easier by the fast reproduction and multiple births common to lower animals. In human research, heredity is seldom a controlled or constrained variable, whereas in animal research, it often is. It is not true that "anything goes" with animals, however. We will consider animal ethics shortly.

## Uniqueness

Some animals also have *unique characteristics* that make them more appropriate for certain types of research. For example, fruit flies not only reproduce quickly but also have large, simple chromosomes. Squid have much larger nerve cells than humans and so lend themselves to investigation of nervous-system structure. Similarly, many animals have a larger portion of the central nervous system devoted to the sense of smell or the sense of balance than we do. In such cases, humans are simply not the best participants for research.

### Irreversible Effects

Finally, lower animals are often used when the research could have *irreversible effects* on the structure or function of the animal. Ablation research can be done only with animals, because it requires that a portion of the nervous system be purposely destroyed to observe behavioral consequences. Similarly, humans cannot be used in experiments requiring that electrodes be implanted into the central nervous system. In many cases this type of research also requires that the animal be destroyed and a histology[7] performed to locate the specific structural changes.

Manipulations such as keeping animals socially isolated can also cause irreversible effects. One famous example of this procedure was the work in which infant monkeys were separated from their mothers shortly after birth and then presented with various artificial mothers to determine what the important mothering dimensions were (Harlow, 1958). People frown on using human babies for such research, and some people likewise frown on using animal babies.

### ANIMAL ETHICS

The relationship between humans and animals has been defined in different ways by different cultures throughout history. In the Christian tradition humans have dominion over animals, and animals have been put on earth for the express use of humans. In the Western world this relationship was widely accepted until the time of Charles Darwin, the father of evolution. Darwin's proposition that there was a continuity within the animal kingdom was a double-edged sword. On one hand, animals became an important subject matter for the scientific community because of this continuity.

---

[7] *Histology* usually involves examining the tissue of the nervous system to see what has been destroyed or where the electrodes were placed. The brain is stained and sliced into very thin pieces for microscopic examination.

On the other hand, this continuity removed the human from holding a unique place, superior to that of all other animals. Perhaps, then, it is not surprising that about this time, toward the end of the 1800s, the first animal rights groups, the antivivisectionists, began having a notable effect on people's opinions, particularly in England (see Dewsbury, 1990). By the turn of the century and for several decades thereafter the antivivisectionists were quite active not only in Europe but in the United States. They had a number of run-ins (verbal in nature at that time) with notable psychologists such as William James, Ivan Pavlov, Walter Cannon, and John Watson.

The animal rights movement then waned until spurred on by the civil rights movement and the publication of the book *Animal Liberation* by Peter Singer (1976). You are probably aware of the modern animal rights movement. There are now approximately 7000 animal protection groups in the United States alone (Justice Department, 1993). The largest of these organizations is People for the Ethical Treatment of Animals, or PETA, with approximately 350,000 members, a staff of 70, and a budget of $7 million (Meyers, 1990a). An aspect of the modern movement that was not present with the antivivisectionists is terrorism. The most militant group is the Animal Liberation Front, or ALF, an underground organization that has taken credit for 60% of the terrorism on research laboratories and researchers and has been deemed a terrorist organization by the FBI. Although PETA denies any official connection with ALF, it has agreed to publicize ALF's actions because it believes that breaking into a facility is the way to expose the alleged abusive treatment of animals.

There are those who believe that public interest in animal rights has peaked (Herzog, 1995). The number of articles referenced in a periodical review peaked at about 60 in 1990 and decreased to about 25 by 1994. However, terrorist acts continue. In 1997 a prize-winning researcher on drug abuse at a major university was picketed by a student organization, and later several members of that organization and an individual wearing a black mask and identifying himself as an ALF member showed up at her house, harassed the researcher and her family, and threatened to burn down their home (APA, 1997). It has been reported that there have been a total of 313 acts of terrorism by animal-rights groups, peaking in 1987–88 and declining somewhat since then (Burd, 1993). These incidents and threats of harassment have cost research institutions millions of dollars and have increasingly involved threats on researchers' lives (Mangan, 1990). What is going on here? What is the source of this controversy?

Part of the problem is that the most extreme activists believe that the rights of animals are the same as the rights of humans and, that, therefore, all animal research should be banned. For example, one advocate says, "Today, animals are by far the most oppressed section of the community: their exploitation is as great an evil as were Black slavery, child labour and the degradation of women at the beginning of the last century. It is the great moral blind spot of our age" (Ryder, 1979, p. 14). These animal research abolitionists include the cofounder of PETA, who says she is "working for the day when there will be no animals in cages" (Havemann, 1989). Is this what the general public, psychologists, and students of psychology think?

Unfortunately, there has been no survey of the general public's attitude toward animal use in psychology. In the medical field there is some evidence of a decline in public support. Respondents who were asked if they agreed with the statement "Scientists should be allowed to do research that causes pain and injury to animals like dogs and chimpanzees *if* it produces new information about human health problems" fell from 63% in 1985 to 53% in 1993 (Pifer, Shimizu, & Pifer, 1994, as cited in Plous, 1996a). Negative opinion in Great Britain is even stronger. However, on the positive side, a poll found 88% approval for the use of rats in medical experiments, compared with 55% for dogs (Associated Press, 1985). And several polls have shown that more than three-quarters of the public believe "the use of animals in medical research is necessary for progress in medicine" (American Medical Association, 1989, as cited in Plous, 1996a).

To find out what psychologists and psychology students think about animals in psychology experiments, Plous (1996a, 1996b) conducted two excellent surveys, one of 3982 psychologists and one of 1188 psychology majors. Perhaps surprisingly, about the same proportion of psychologists and students agreed on most issues. When asked their level of support for the use of animals in psychological research, about 80% of psychologists and 72% of psychology majors indicated that they either strongly supported it or supported it. And, of those giving an opinion, 84% of psychologists and 81% of the majors believed that the use of animals in psychological research is necessary for progress in psychology. However, surprising to me was the fact that 47% of the psychologists and 44% of the majors indicated they were not sure whether animals used in psychological research were treated humanely. Let's look at the rules regarding treatment.

For many years the regulations at the federal level concerning the treatment of most research animals, excluding rats, mice, and birds, have been monitored by the U. S. Agriculture Department. Under pressure from the animal-rights groups, amendments were made in 1985 to the Animal Welfare Act, the legislation that regulates the care of dogs, cats, and nonhuman primates. After many hearings a set of rules was passed in 1991: complying with these cost institutions an estimated $537 million (Jaschik, 1991). The rules deal with issues such as exercise for dogs, the establishment of institutional animal-research committees, and special care for young animals. Primates in particular are entitled to care that ensures their psychological as well as physical well-being.[8] Other laws exist that protect animals such as rats, mice, and birds. Over 1000 institutions receiving funds from the U.S. Public Health Service to conduct animal experiments are required to comply with the provisions of the Health Research Extension Act and to follow the recommendations in the Guide for the Humane Care and Use of

---

[8] Ironically, one of the researchers most vilified by the animal-rights radicals, Harry Harlow, did much of the research that forms the basis for these regulations.

Laboratory Animals ("Position Statement," 1993). This guide was prepared to assist researchers in maintaining high-quality care for *all* commonly used laboratory animals. Many other state and local rules and regulations across the country also deal with research animals. In addition, all institutions supported by federal funds that do research using animals are required to have an animal research committee composed of experts including a veterinarian and a member from the general public. This committee must approve all proposed research that uses animals and ensure that the research is done following the rules that we have already discussed.

I have gone into some detail about this topic to convince you that many people, including psychologists, are concerned about the animal-rights issue and are keeping a close watch on it. Because psychologists do use animals for research, the American Psychological Association has not been silent on the issue. *Ethical Principles of Psychologists and Code of Conduct* (APA, 1992) contains the following:

6.20  Care and Use of Animals in Research
  (a) Psychologists who conduct research involving animals treat them humanely.
  (b) Psychologists acquire, care for, use, and dispose of animals in compliance with current federal, state, and local laws and regulations, and with professional standards.
  (c) Psychologists trained in research methods and experienced in the care of laboratory animals supervise all procedures involving animals and are responsible for ensuring appropriate consideration of their comfort, health, and humane treatment.
  (d) Psychologists ensure that all individuals using animals under their supervision have received instruction in research methods and in the care, maintenance, and handling of the species being used, to the extent appropriate to their role.
  (e) Responsibilities and activities of individuals assisting in a research project are consistent with their respective competencies.
  (f) Psychologists make reasonable efforts to minimize the discomfort, infection, illness, and pain of animal subjects.
  (g) A procedure subjecting animals to pain, stress, or privation is used only when an alternative procedure is unavailable and the goal is justified by its prospective scientific, educational, or applied value.
  (h) Surgical procedures are performed under appropriate anesthesia; techniques to avoid infection and minimize pain are followed during and after surgery.
  (i) When it is appropriate that the animal's life be terminated, it is done rapidly, with an effort to minimize pain, and in accordance with accepted procedures.

Why are psychologists so concerned that their right to do research on animals might be taken away? Aside from the fact that most of those who work with animals enjoy doing so and consider themselves animal lovers, they also cite the many advances they have made that have improved human welfare (Miller, 1985), and animal welfare as well. Certainly on the medical front animal research can be cited as leading to the virtual elimination of polio, rabies, cholera, and diphtheria as well as the development of insulin treatment, cataract surgery, and the curing of many cases of lymphatic leukemia in children. In psychology, animal research has led to significant advances in the treatment of mental disorders, pain control, drug abuse, and recovery from strokes. The highly successful behavior therapies are largely founded on animal research of 40 years ago. In some cases, particularly with basic research, it is often difficult to anticipate the exact nature of future benefits. Nevertheless, most researchers feel that the costs in terms of possible animal suffering are more than offset by the potential benefits.

Even most animal advocates occupy a middle ground between the two extreme positions and are willing to approach the issue from an informed and reasonable perspective. Most certainly condemn the extremists who terrorize researchers. If you wish to read more on this topic, the American Psychological Association has published an expanded set of guidelines, *Guidelines for Ethical Conduct in the Care and Use of Animals* (1986). Boyce (1989) has a balanced treatment in the *Journal of the American Veterinary Medical Association,* and Segal (1982) does a nice job of weighing the needs of science against the needs of life. Finally, Dennis Feeney, a psychologist at the University of New Mexico with paraplegia, makes a strong case for animal research in an article in *American Psychologist* (1987). He argues that the discussion of animal rights versus human rights has involved those in science, agriculture, and animal-welfare organizations but has virtually ignored individuals who are disabled. He points to basic behavioral research in biofeedback and stroke recovery that has led to unanticipated therapeutic advances. The following passage captures the essence of his position:

> Those of us who have an incurable disease or have permanently crippling injuries can only hope for a cure through research. Much of this experimental work will require the use of animals, and accordingly, we must find some compromise that defends both human rights and animal welfare. In the determination of a compromise between the reduction of human suffering and the violation of animals' welfare, which at times includes causing pain or discomfort, I unequivocally choose to reduce human suffering. [p. 593]

In the end, you will have to decide for yourself about the ethics of using animals in research. In making your decision, you will have to go back to the very foundations of your beliefs about the relationship of humans and animals. If you are like most people, you will find it difficult to reach an entirely consistent position: Do you eat hamburgers? Would you agree to have your dog or other pet in a medical experiment? Would you condone the sacrifice of 100 dogs to find a cure that would save the life of your child? Do you buy ant and roach spray? Are you willing to adopt all the cats at the local animal shelter? From your answers to these questions, can you determine where you stand and come up with a consistent philosophy?

The issue is not clear-cut. Like most of us, you may simply have to weigh each case and try to determine whether the benefits exceed the costs. Some psychological experiments, by their very nature, will subject animals to stress and pain. In such situations, you should be convinced that the potential scientific gains are worth the costs before starting your research, and you should be able to defend your decision. Although institutions do have committees composed of experts to screen animal research, you should consider these committees as imposing only minimum standards. You must satisfy what should be a more stringent standard of ethics—your own.

## Summary

The ethical and methodological issues of treating human and animal research **participants** fairly were considered in this chapter. Because most of the power in the experimenter–participant relationship lies with the experimenters, it is important that they follow certain basic rules of courtesy. They must be present, prompt, prepared, polite, private, and professional. **Institutional review boards** have been established to screen research proposals and help experimenters make ethical decisions with respect to their treatment of human and animal participants. Among the issues they consider is whether human participants have given **informed consent** prior to participating.

Although we have assumed in the past that human participants are naive and passive, they are in reality problem solvers who are sensitive to the **demand characteristics,** or hidden clues, of the experimental situation. How they react to these demand characteristics depends on whether they are *cooperative, defensive,* or *noncooperative* in the experiment. We can minimize demand characteristics by **automating** much of the experiment, by using a **blind** or **double-blind** design so that the participant or both participant and experimenter are unaware of the specific conditions being responded to, or by using **multiple experimenters.** One form of double-blind design in drug research uses a nonactive **placebo** for the control condition. When it is impossible to make participants blind to the experimental manipulation, the experimenter must be aware that the **Hawthorne effect** may occur: a change in behavior due simply to the attention given to the participants. If unwanted demand characteristics are present in an experiment, we can sometimes detect them through **postexperiment questioning** or by using **nonexperiment** or **simulation control groups.** An alternative to assuming that participants are naive is to use their problem-solving natures and give them false demand characteristics to deceive them about the actual purpose of the experiment. Alternatives to deception are to ask participants to role-play or to observe them in a naturalistic setting.

Psychologists also use animals in experiments because they exhibit continuity, engaging in some of the same basic behavior patterns that humans do in a form unconfounded by more complex behaviors. They also provide an opportunity for greater environmental and genetic control. Some animals possess certain unique characteristics that make them superior for certain types of research. There is a long history of the animal rights movement worldwide. In the past few decades this movement has some advocates who have taken extreme positions and even advocated violence. The general public, as well as psychologists and psychology students, is more favorable toward animal research. In recent years the rules and regulations regarding animal experimentation at the federal, state, and institutional levels have been upgraded so that the possibility of abuse is minimized. Most researchers who do this kind of work believe that the benefits usually outweigh the costs and point to many advances in human welfare due to animal research in psychology, including treatment of mental disorders and drug abuse, pain control, and recovery from strokes.

## Find It on InfoTrac College Edition

In Chapter 4 we discuss several issues with respect to treating participants fairly. Using InfoTrac College Edition find several recent articles that explore these issues in more detail. Here are some terms you might use in your search: *informed consent, institutional review boards, demand characteristics, deception.*

We also discuss the ethics of using animals in research. You can learn more about this issue by searching InfoTrac College Edition for recent articles. Try using search terms such as *animal rights* and *animal welfare.*

# 5

# How to Be Fair with Science

> Science is willingness to accept facts even when they are opposed to wishes.
>
> B. F. SKINNER (1953)

> To obtain a certain result, one must wish to obtain such a particular result: If you want a particular result you will obtain it.
>
> T. D. LYSENKO,
> quoted in I. M. LERNER (1968)

> Fraud in science is not just a matter of rotten apples in the barrel. It has something to do with the barrel itself.
>
> NICHOLAS WADE,
> quoted in K. McDONALD (1983)

> Research is a collegial activity that requires its practitioners to trust the integrity of their colleagues.
>
> ARNOLD S. RELMAN,
> quoted in K. McDONALD (1983)

> Dishonesty has always been perceived in our culture, and in all cultures but the most bizarre, as a central human vice. We should note that this perception is consistent with a certain hesitancy about what constitutes a lie and with the more than sneaking suspicion that there might be a number of contexts in which lying is actually justified.
>
> TONY COADY (AUSTRALIAN PHILOSOPHER)

> . . . living ethically is much more than not living unethically.
>
> MARTIN E. P. SELIGMAN (APA PRESIDENT, 1998)

In this chapter our examination of ethics continues, but here we deal with treating science fairly. In some respects, science has fewer defenses than a research participant does. Animals squirm and yell and sometimes die when mistreated, and the animal-rights groups yell too. Human participants squirm and yell and sometimes sue when mistreated. Science can't even squirm and yell. If you mistreat it long enough, however, your fellow scientists might eventually squirm and yell.

You might wonder how you can be unfair to an inanimate thing like science. In one sense, science *can* be considered animate in that it is a moving, changing, and, we hope, expanding body of knowledge. New research constantly replaces or builds on old findings and theories. Anything you do that retards the expansion of science or causes it to expand in the wrong direction can be considered scientifically unethical.

Science has a few safeguards built into it to ensure that the body of knowledge will continue to expand in a proper direction. For example, before you are allowed to report the outcome of an experiment in the scientific literature, a group of scientists selected for their research accomplishments reviews it. This review establishes whether the research appears to follow the rules of experimentation discussed in this book. Furthermore, the reviewers attempt to determine whether your contribution is sufficient to warrant using the limited number of pages available in the journals. In this way the reviewers and editors of our journals attempt to screen research so that only competent and relevant findings are added to the body of knowledge.[1] Although this reviewing process is not perfect, most psychologists feel that it accomplishes this important screening function rather well.

Although the review system is designed to exclude research that was poorly done or that fails to make a large enough contribution, it is not designed to determine whether an investigator who may be capable of doing good research has lied about his or her research. People who know the rules and say that they have followed them when in fact they have not are cheating science. Such behavior is usually geared toward making personal gains of some sort: "They weren't going to promote me unless I had five publications"; "I had to make our product look good"; or "I had to have a positive result on the experiment to get a passing grade."

Because unethical behavior can be so harmful to our science and because we have so few built-in safeguards to detect it, unethical behavior in science is not tolerated, and a researcher quickly loses the privilege of practicing science when this behavior is detected. I will discuss these clearly unethical and unacceptable behaviors in the first section of this chapter under *dirty tricks*. In the next section I will discuss some behaviors that are frowned upon and that should be guarded against but are not so egregious that a researcher would lose scientific privileges; I will call these *questionable tricks*. Finally, there are times in science when a researcher tells the truth, but not the whole truth, and our science benefits rather than loses from this behavior. This behavior can make our science more efficient and easier to understand and is considered not only acceptable but necessary. I will call these behaviors *neat tricks*.

---

[1] Note here that I am using the term *relevant* differently than many people use it. I mean relevant to science, not relevant to faddish topics. Sometimes topics that are relevant in the latter sense are the least relevant in the former sense.

# Dirty Tricks

## FABRICATING

One form of blatant cheating is to **fabricate results.** Some "experimenters" know that the easiest way to run an experiment is not to run it at all. They do not have to bother with such mundane matters as buying equipment, signing up participants, or learning to do statistics. All they have to do is learn to write up experiments (fabricators had better read Chapter 13). They had also better learn a different profession, because they will not be psychologists for long.

As a student, you may be tempted to fabricate because an assignment is due and you have not completed it. Don't do it! Late assignments cause lowered grades, but contrived results cause class dismissals and terrible letters of recommendation. Professional scientists are totally intolerant of such behavior.

Back in the early 1900s, a biologist named Kammerer attempted to demonstrate that acquired characteristics could be inherited (Ley, 1955), a concept quite different from Darwinian evolution. He claimed that he had kept generations of fire salamanders on black soil. He reported not only that the salamanders, which are normally black with yellow spots, had showed increasingly smaller spots over generations, but also that this reduction had been passed on by inheritance. A second researcher, who doubted these claims, added the time required to bring forth the number of generations Kammerer had reported and found that the total time was considerably longer than Kammerer had been at work. Other scientists also began to demand explanations until, after seven years, two leading scientists were allowed to examine some specimens. They found injections of India ink. Kammerer admitted that his results "had plainly been 'improved' post mortem with India ink." He then promptly committed suicide.

The most dastardly deed in science is to add noise to the body of knowledge. If you do bad research, people can and will ignore it, but if you pretend that you have done good research when you have not, you will retard the expansion of the body of knowledge. Others will come along and attempt to build their research on yours, only to discover eventually that something is wrong. They must then waste time fixing the foundation and possibly rebuilding the whole structure. The longer such cheating goes undetected, the greater the eventual waste of science's resources.

If undetected, the cheating of science can also lead to the cheating of society. In the late 1930s, for example, a Russian named T. D. Lysenko also supported the notion that acquired characteristics could be inherited (Lerner, 1968). He was so adamant about this theory that he falsified a great deal of data. Lysenkoites claimed that they had brought about such miraculous results as transforming wheat into rye, barley, oats, and even

cornflowers; beets into cabbage; pine into fir; a tree of the hornbeam group into forest walnut (using doctored photographs as evidence); and even the hatching of cuckoos from eggs laid by warblers (Lerner, 1968).

Lysenko's grossly unethical behavior hurt not only science but society as well. He was personally responsible for the dismissal, exile, and execution of a number of Russian geneticists. He convinced Stalin and later Khrushchev that his theories were correct and that they should be applied on a large scale in agricultural programs (Medvedev, 1969). When devastating agricultural failures were eventually attributed in part to Lysenko's methods, he fell, Khrushchev fell (though not only for this reason), and Russian society suffered.

When I wrote this section for the first edition of this book, I had to look back into history to find examples of scientific fraud. Unfortunately, finding examples of fraud is much easier today. In several professional and local newspapers I recently found the following headlines: "Allegations of Plagiarism of Scientific Manuscript Raise Concerns About 'Intellectual Theft,'" "Nobel Honoree Faces Misconduct Charges," and "U.S. Enters Lawsuit Accusing Scientist, Institutions of Fraud."

Are dirty tricks new, or is there simply more interest today in discovering them? Apparently even the old-time scientists were not without guilt. The 19th-century geneticist Gregor Mendel stands accused of having been somewhat less than truthful (Fisher, 1936). Even Sir Isaac Newton apparently reported correlations to a degree of precision well beyond his ability to measure (Westfall, 1973).

Closer to psychology and more recently, a prominent ESP researcher discovered that his laboratory manager had fudged data. A suspicious research assistant had concealed himself and observed the manager changing the data to support ESP findings.

The most famous case in psychology concerned Sir Cyril Burt, an eminent British psychologist who had been knighted by King George VI. His research with identical twins was one of the major pillars supporting the argument that IQ is largely inherited. After his death, researchers discovered that the correlations he had reported for identical twins had remained the same to the third decimal place over many years as more twins were added to the study. This seemed a highly unlikely coincidence. Fraud allegations were made in the London *Sunday Times,* and the controversy continues. On one side are researchers who argue that Burt's data should be considered fraudulent and were probably fabricated (McAskie, 1978). Others argue that the case for fraud is weak and that a more probable explanation is simply carelessness (Jensen, 1978). It is also unfortunate that this heated debate is fueled by the politics of elitism versus egalitarianism.

How can we guard against the possibility of dishonesty by researchers? No foolproof system will ever be developed, because both the costs and the loss of intellectual freedom would destroy the scientific enterprise. A number of safeguards are currently in place. The Public Health Service, under which the National Institutes of Health operate, already requires universities to have guidelines for preventing misconduct (Cordes, 1990). The Association of American Universities recommends that institutions establish explicit policies about standards and have administrators to carry out the policies ("AAU Statement," 1983). When the researcher is federally funded, there is even a "whistle-blower" law dating back to the 1800s that allows citizens to file lawsuits against researchers and universities and collect a sizable percentage of any money the government is awarded. Recently, a former technician in a research laboratory filed such a suit against a researcher and his university, alleging that the researcher had falsified results (Cordes, 1990).

One suggestion for minimizing fraud is to establish data archives for the raw data[2] from research (Bryant & Wortman, 1978). Apparently one problem encountered by investigators attempting to validate Burt's research was his incredibly sloppy data storage. The raw test sheets on the twin studies were among papers stuffed into half a dozen tea chests and later destroyed! The data from research could be

---

[2] The individual measurements of your dependent variable prior to combining them for statistical analysis are your *raw data.* Unlike meat, raw data do not spoil—they just take up room.

stored by individual researchers or possibly sent to a centralized location. In this way, research data would be available to the public, which is often not the case. For instance, a graduate student requesting raw data from 37 published authors received only 24% compliance (Wolins, 1962).

The archiving requirement has the following additional benefits: Researchers would probably be more careful in their original data analysis; others could add to the body of knowledge by examining issues not originally addressed; and longitudinal studies in which data are compared over a number of years are possible.

The costs of a formalized central data storage system include the cost of the bureaucratic structure to administer it, the time and money required to duplicate the data or conform to a standardized format, and perhaps the cost to science of a recognized loss of trust in the integrity of scientists. Some feel that the costs of this solution are too great when the problem is relatively small. They believe that the checks and balances provided by the replication process are sufficient to detect most fraud and make the problem of dirty tricks an anomaly rather than a common practice.

Regardless of the formal requirements, you should keep data for a minimum of five years (APA, 1994). Investigators often request data from one another, and with computers, storage and retrieval of raw data are easy. If you make a habit of storing raw data, you are helping to protect science, and you are protecting yourself against false accusations as well.

Some data do indicate that scientific fraud is relatively rare. For example, from 1982 to 1988 the National Institutes of Health, which supports the research of 50,000 scientists, had handled reports of only 15 to 20 allegations of wrongdoing. On the other hand, among scientists at a major research university who responded to a survey, one-third said they had suspected a colleague of plagiarism or falsifying data, but fewer than half took action to verify or report their suspicions (Hostetler, 1988). At this time it appears that unless scientists take more formal steps to find and eliminate scientific misconduct, Congress will impose such steps through legislation. This possibility disturbs the many scientists who believe that regulation by those not trained or experienced in science could lead to undesirable consequences.

The best and most cost-effective way to prevent fraud in our science is to emphasize to new researchers the importance of ethical conduct. That, of course, is the purpose of the chapter you are reading. It is only through an understanding of the way science works that the real motivation for ethical behavior can be established. Researchers must understand that science is built on trust. Unless we can trust our colleagues' research findings, we might as well discontinue the attempt to build the scientific body of knowledge. As part of its effort to inform research psychologists of their responsibilities, the American Psychological Association (1992) states the following in its *Ethical Principles of Psychologists and Code of Conduct:*

6.21 Reporting of Results

(a) Psychologists do not fabricate data or falsify results in their publications.

(b) If psychologists discover significant errors in their published data,
they take reasonable steps to correct such errors in a correction,
retraction, erratum, or other appropriate publication means.

6.22 Plagiarism

Psychologists do not present substantial portions or elements of another's work or data as their own, even if the other work or data
source is cited occasionally.

6.23 Publication Credit

(a) Psychologists take responsibility and credit, including authorship
credit, only for work they have actually performed or to which
they have contributed. . . .

6.24 Duplicate Publication of Data

Psychologists do not publish, as original data, data that have been
previously published. This does not preclude republishing data when
they are accompanied by proper acknowledgment.

6.25 Sharing Data

After research results are published, psychologists do not withhold
the data on which their conclusions are based from other competent
professionals who seek to verify the substantive claims through
reanalysis and who intend to use such data only for that purpose,
provided that the confidentiality of the participants can be protected
and unless legal rights concerning proprietary data preclude their
release.

## FALSIFYING CREDENTIALS

If you were to walk up to a friend and say, "Would you stand on your head
for me?" the response would probably be "Why?" However, if you were to
walk up to another friend and say, "I'm doing an experiment; would you
stand on your head for me?" your friend's response is more likely to be
"How long?" This difference arises from the fact that our society grants scientists a number of privileges not given to the average citizen. We allow
scientists, particularly behavioral scientists, the freedom to experiment
because, as a society, we feel that the gains usually outweigh the costs. We
also grant scientists a certain amount of prestige and generally respond to
them somewhat compliantly.

Scientists not only are allowed to manipulate the lives of those around
them in approved ways but also are sometimes supported in this effort by
our tax money. However, we are also capable of taking away these privileges if we believe that the gains no longer outweigh the costs. Requiring
professional credentials of experimenters is one way we police ourselves.
Consequently, to prove to other scientists that you are a qualified investigator, you must present them with your professional record, usually in the
form of a vita or résumé. A résumé is a piece of paper that shows who you

are professionally; it lists your educational degrees, your job experience, and your published papers and articles. You use it to get into graduate school, to become professionally certified, or to get a job. Perhaps it should go without saying that this document must be totally accurate. I will say it anyway: *Falsifying credentials* is a blatant dirty trick.

Early in my career, I saw a very talented student attempt to get into graduate school using a falsified vita. He had a fine record and great letters of recommendation from his professors, but he listed several papers and articles on his vita that did not exist. When his professors discovered his deception, the student no longer had either a fine record or letters of recommendation, nor is he an experimental psychologist today. Because the agreement between scientists and society is fragile, this type of dishonesty upsets the delicate balance and cannot be tolerated.

I hope that this discussion of dirty tricks was a waste of your time and that you would not have considered doing these in the first place. Yet I believe that such topics must be mentioned early in an experimenter's training. Doing psychology experiments can be fun, but the real purpose of experimentation is building science. Those who are not willing to follow the rules that make this process orderly do not belong in science.

## Questionable Tricks

Those actions that most investigators find unacceptable but that lead to frowning and scolding rather than banishment can be considered questionable tricks. These actions can occur during the design of an experiment, during the experiment itself, during data analysis, or in experimental reporting.

### EXPERIMENTAL DESIGN

In the previous chapter, we discussed experimenter bias as communicated through demand characteristics. If you design your experiment so that the demand characteristics themselves could cause a desired change in the dependent variable and do not attempt to minimize these demand characteristics or even discover them, you are, in a sense, being dishonest. You can also confound an experiment if you claim to have made a particular variable into a control variable when, in fact, this variable systematically changed with your independent variable. In some nonlaboratory experiments such confounding is difficult to control, but in many cases we can legitimately call this situation cheating.

For example, remember the experiment mentioned in Chapter 2 in which I attempted to lecture an introductory psychology class at several different rates to determine whether lecture pace had an effect on the students' attentiveness? On some days I tried to speak at a slow pace, on other days at a moderate pace, and on others at a fast pace. We measured attentiveness by recording the level of background noise. Such an experiment would be easy to bias. I could have changed not only my pace but also the degree of liveliness with which I talked about the topic or perhaps the number of interesting examples I used to illustrate my points. These changes in dimensions other than lecture pace could easily confound the independent variable, whether I intended to or not.

One way to minimize the chance of cheating is to design the experiment so that colleagues with little stake in any given outcome rate each lecture in terms of the possible confounding variables. The experimenter can then collect data only from those lectures with equivalent ratings. Moderate cheating in the form of experimenter bias will not necessarily occur in the first design, of course, but the second design will be more convincing because such bias is less likely to occur.

## COLLECTING DATA

You can also be dishonest when collecting your data, especially if you must use human judgment to determine what response the participant has made. In the experiment just discussed, for example, the experimenter wants to classify the students' behavior as attentive or inattentive to record the percentage of time spent in attentive versus inattentive listening. Suppose one student sits scribbling with her pencil on a piece of paper. Is she taking notes or doodling? Another student has his eyes closed. Is he concentrating or sleeping? We can classify the behaviors differently depending on our bias. If the experimenter who holds the bias is also doing the classifying, the potential problems are obvious.

WHICH STUDENT IS THE ATTENTIVE ONE?

To avoid this form of trickery, the experimenter might construct a standard checklist of attentive and inattentive behaviors and have several judges observe the tapes and independently classify the students' behaviors. It is even possible to keep judges blind to the pace the instructor used for the tape being observed. Such precautions decrease the possibility of cheating, either intentional or unintentional.

Bias can sometimes occur even in experiments in which measurement of responses seems straightforward. An experiment was carried out in which participants moved a stick to line up a marker with a moving target. After every ten-second interval, the experimenter quickly read a pointer on a voltmeter dial and reset it. (The farther the marker was from the target, the more quickly the pointer moved across the dial.) This task was difficult because the needle seldom fell directly on an index line. The experimenter could easily have made biased judgments about the location of the pointer on the dial. In this experiment, experimenters had to read the dial over 15,000 times, giving rise to the possibility that small inconsistencies in reading the instrument would eventually bias experimental results. Thus, whenever biased experimenters must use judgment to interpret a response, they should devise procedures to ensure that the judgment will be made accurately.

## DATA ANALYSIS

You must also avoid trickery in analyzing your data in a biased way. As we will see in Chapter 12, statistical tests are usually computed to determine whether a particular result is likely to be a real effect or whether it is due to chance. These statistical tests can be used only when certain assumptions can be approximated. Using the test when the test assumptions are grossly violated is questionable at best.

For example, the most frequently used statistical tests require that the underlying distribution be approximately normal, a symmetrical bell shape. Although a small violation of this assumption usually does not totally

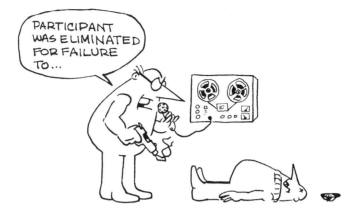

invalidate such a test, some investigators continue to use one of these tests when their distributions in no way resemble a normal distribution. As an experimenter, it is up to you to know what assumptions your statistical test requires and how likely it is that you will make an error if you fail to meet one or more of these assumptions.

When analyzing your data, you may discover that although most of the participants seem to be showing the predicted experimental effect, several do not show the effect. At this point, you can do nothing about these renegades.[3] Obviously, if you could throw out data from all the participants who failed to show an expected result, you would never do an experiment that failed to support your predictions! For this reason, you must be careful about eliminating participants from an analysis on the basis of their performance on the dependent variable. And you should never eliminate them on the basis of their differential responses to the levels of the independent variable.

You can eliminate participants for failing to meet some overall performance level on the dependent variable only if you determine this performance level before collecting the data, if you can logically defend it, and if you specify the performance level in your experimental report. As an illustration, suppose you were interested in the effects of noise on people's ability to perform a typing task. Before starting the experiment, you might decide to exclude data from all participants who fail to type at least ten words per minute in the absence of noise. Your logic might be that these individuals are such poor typists to begin with that even if noise has a detrimental effect on typing, they would not show the effect. Or you might argue that you are interested in the effect of noise on experienced typists and that a speed of less than ten words per minute indicates that the person is not an experienced typist. However, if you do not have a logical argument for eliminating participants on the basis of a predetermined dependent-variable performance level, you should not do it.

---

[3] Unless you are specifically interested in investigating individual differences.

You are much safer in eliminating participants on a basis other than performance on your dependent variable. Again, however, such criteria should be set prior to the experiment and should be specified when you report the results. For example, you might be having participants search through an array of letters to report which letter is printed in red ink. In this case, you might exclude individuals who cannot pass an acuity test or a color-blindness test prior to the experiment.

## REPORTING RESULTS

Suppose you have analyzed your experiment and are now ready to report the results. Usually you will want to put some of your results into a graph. We will discuss some rules to follow in making a graph in Chapter 12. People have written books on how to lie by *distorting graphs* (Campbell, 1974; Huff, 1954). For example, an experimenter could blow up one of the graph's axes to make a tiny effect look like a gigantic effect or possibly distort the scale on one axis so that the function being displayed changes shape. If you are a creative person, you can find all sorts of ways to make crummy results look good. Obviously, such behavior does nothing to advance science and so is considered inappropriate.

One other form of questionable trickery is *piecemeal reporting* of experimental results. Although research must progress one experiment at a time, you should not report research in this way. Many decades ago the typical journal article in psychology reported the results of a single experiment. In recent times, however, the field has grown so much that there has been a literature explosion. So many people are doing so many experiments that the process of keeping current with experimental advances is nearly impossible. For this reason, few journals will accept a report of a single experiment unless it makes an unusually large contribution by itself.

Usually, you should report the results of your experimental research program as an integrated series of experiments. With this procedure, the growth of knowledge becomes much more efficient and orderly, and readers are spared the task of reorienting themselves to the research, rereading introduction and procedure sections with each experiment, and integrating fragmented research into a coherent structure. In today's "publish or perish" world, an investigator can be tempted to do piecemeal reporting to accumulate publications. However, in the end, such behavior does nothing to improve either the investigator's reputation or the body of scientific knowledge.

# Neat Tricks

Although it seems counterintuitive, it is sometimes necessary to "lie" to the reader of a research report to communicate efficiently. Research is usually a sloppy process, yet when you read an experimental report it sounds as if the investigator proceeded in a systematic, orderly fashion at all times.[4] Don't believe it! Rarely does a researcher's mind work in the totally logical manner reflected in the report. Experimenters make many decisions based on hunches or gut-level intuitions. They make false starts based on bad guesses. They do experiments the right way for the wrong reasons or the wrong way for the right reasons.

Unfortunately, many students become turned off to experimental psychology because they think it is dry and unexciting, when in most cases it is actually an exciting, disorderly, haphazard treasure hunt. You know little about experimentation until you try your first experiment.[5]

The most obvious reason for cleaning up an experimental report is to save time and space. Though it might be fun to read about all your colleague's mistakes, you do not have the time and journals do not have the space to allow you the luxury. The experimental report is designed to convey information efficiently, not entertain the reader.[6]

## LEAVING THINGS OUT

One way of cleaning up your experimental report is to *leave out experiments and analyses.*[7] Suppose you had a bad day when you designed the third experiment in a series, you had a bad intuition, or you were temporarily confused. Nobody else is interested in the condition of your life, your viscera, or your head. So you blew the experiment. I don't want to read about it. You don't want to write about it. So don't. Science loses nothing, I lose nothing, and you save face. Be sure, however, that you are not tempted to leave out a perfectly good experiment because the results do not support your favorite hypothesis. Doing this is not a *neat trick!*

Not only is it acceptable to leave out whole experiments if they add nothing to the report, but at times it is also proper to ignore the details of some data analyses. Perhaps there were a number of ways to analyze your data, and you did them all. Although you should probably report that you did the analyses, you need give details of only those that are most representative and convey the most information.[8]

## REORGANIZING

Especially when doing exploratory research, you may find that the outcome of an experiment shows that it should not have been the first experiment in the series. You may find it desirable to back up and do some preliminary

---

[4] A charmingly written article on the sometimes haphazard process of research is B. F. Skinner's "A Case History in Scientific Method" (1959).

[5] It's kind of like making love: Reading about it is a poor substitute for doing it.

[6] A lot of textbook writers think this, too. They never have any fun!

[7] Or else put them in a footnote. Nobody reads footnotes.

[8] Note that I am not endorsing the practice of conducting a multitude of tests and then picking and choosing only those that yield significant results. In this case, you are distorting the level of significance (Chapter 12).

experiments. In such cases, you need not tell the reader that "owing to mis-judgment and lack of foresight on the experimenter's part, the following experiments are out of order." You may report them in the most logical order, whether or not this order matches the order in which you did them. Data are data, and you should report them as efficiently as possible, as long as bending the truth does not bend the science.

### REFORMULATING

Finally, it is generally acceptable to *reformulate the theory* underlying an experiment. Occasionally you do an experiment for some reason and later discover a better reason for having done it. Or perhaps you discover that somebody else has done an experiment that casts a different light on one you are conducting. In this case, you have to determine how your contri-bution to the body of knowledge best fits with the new information. Unfor-tunately, there will be times when your theory does not fit at all, and you will have to go back to the drawing board. Often, however, you will be able to fit your experiment into the revised theory by changing your emphasis or reinterpreting your results. In reporting your results, you need not bur-den the reader with obsolete theory. Again, your major ethical considera-tion should be whether you are adding to the body of knowledge in an effi-cient manner.

In this chapter we have by no means exhausted all the ethical ques-tions that you will face as an experimenter. In some cases, you will find it difficult to decide whether a particular action is fair to science. When a problem comes up, you may wish to discuss it with colleagues, who may be able to raise points and suggest alternatives that you have not consid-ered. In the end, though, the decision is yours. If you apply the principle that ethical actions are those that aid in the efficient growth of the body of knowledge, you will never do dirty tricks and seldom do questionable tricks.

## Summary

Because science is a growing body of knowledge, any action that retards the efficient expansion of that body of knowledge is unethical. We can be less than totally truthful with science in a number of ways. We can engage in dirty tricks by *fabricating results* or by *falsifying our credentials*. We can also engage in questionable tricks—by *failing to control confounding variables* in the design of an experiment, for example, or by *misclassifying responses* and *misreading instruments* during collection of our data. During data analysis, *failing to meet test assumptions* and *inappropriately eliminating participants* are also unacceptable, as are distorting graphs and reporting a series of exper-iments as piecemeal reports. For the sake of efficiency, it is acceptable to write up experimental reports in a form that does not exactly parallel the experiment. For example, we can *leave out experiments and analyses* from a report if they do not add to the report, or we can *reorder experiments* and *reformulate theory* if these actions increase the efficiency of the experimental report.

## Find It on InfoTrac College Edition

As indicated in Chapter 5, ethics in science have been widely discussed in recent years, particularly in light of cases in which these ethics have been violated. You can update your knowledge of the issue and find out what is being suggested to curb these violations. Try searching InfoTrac College Edition with terms such as *scientific fraud* and *plagiarism.*

# 6

# How to Find Out
# What Has Been Done

> *Polonius:* What do you read, my lord?
> *Hamlet:* Words, words, words.
>
> WILLIAM SHAKESPEARE
>
> But why do we have to endure the academics who insist on making verbal mountains out of intellectual molehills?
>
> S. I. HAYAKAWA (1978)
>
> The house of social science research is sadly dilapidated. It is strewn among the scree of a hundred journals and lies about in the unsightly rubble of a million dissertations. Even if it cannot be built into a science, the rubble ought to be sifted and culled for whatever consistency there is in it.
>
> G. V. GLASS, B. McGAW, & M. L. SMITH (1981)

Perhaps while you were reading Chapter 3, about getting an experimental idea, a terrific idea came to you in a blinding flash of inspiration. Or, an idea might have crept in on little cat feet. In any case, I hope that some interesting experimental idea has begun to form and that you are getting eager to start your experiment. However, before you begin serious planning, you should realize that your terrific idea may already have been somebody else's terrific idea.

## Why Search the Literature?

Although psychology is a relatively young science, more than 50,000 references are published in a typical year. Although another investigator probably has not done exactly what you are planning to do, it is likely that out of all the research accumulated over the short history of psychology, somebody has done something quite similar. It would be counterproductive for you to repeat an experiment unless you did not think the results were reliable.

You might also find it helpful to discover how other investigators have attacked similar problems. Perhaps they have used experimental techniques

with which you are unfamiliar. You might also find that other investigators have already discovered a number of pitfalls you would rather not waste your time rediscovering.

Science is an organized body of knowledge, not a haphazard collection of facts built by scientists doing small, isolated experiments. Thus, the most important reason for knowing what research others have done is that you will be required to fit your findings into this existing body of knowledge. When you have completed your research, you will be required to say not only "This is how it came out" but also "This is where it fits in." To know where your work fits in, you obviously have to know what the body of knowledge was like prior to your research. This chapter discusses how to find out what is in that body of knowledge through a **literature search.**[1]

While you are doing a literature search in the library, be sure to keep a record of what you find. Each time you find an article or book that might be useful, make a note of the important points and write down the complete reference. Include the names of the authors,[2] title of the work, name of the journal or book, date, volume number, page numbers, and, for a book, the publisher. You will need all of this information later if you decide to refer to the article in your research report. Some people find it helpful to use an index card for each reference. As I will mention later, one nice

---

[1] Scientists have traditionally called this process a literature search, although you will probably not study this type of literature in your college lit courses.

[2] People who are new to psychology sometimes find it strange that experimental psychologists talk about experiments by author rather than by subject. If you hear your instructors say such things as "The Carothers, Finch, and Finch (1972) findings agree with Peterson, Bergman, and Brill (1971)," they are talking not about law firms but about experimenters.

feature of an automated search is that you will get a full bibliographic record for each reference you find and you can simply print this out. Regardless of how you do it, the more orderly you are the first time through, the less time you will waste later looking for references that you put on the back of a long-lost gum wrapper. If you find several particularly well-written articles, you should be sure to make full copies and hang on to them. You can use them as good models when you are ready to start writing.

Although a literature search is not particularly difficult to do, it can be time-consuming[3] and not particularly inspirational, because it involves lots of paper shuffling. Knowing the literature, however, is an absolute necessity; it is your science! Nothing is more embarrassing when presenting the results of your life's work than to hear someone remark, "You are, of course, familiar with Klip and Klap (1999), who did this same experiment last year?"

## The Timeliness of Sources

If you are completely unfamiliar with the possible research sources in psychology, such as books and articles, you may not know where to begin your literature search. First, you need to get a feel for the sources available and how up-to-date each source is. To do that, let's follow a typical experiment as it is reported to the scientific community. Figure 6-1 summarizes this process on a time line in which zero represents the time a project is started.[4] After collecting data, the investigator might present preliminary results to a small gathering of friends at a local institution. Assuming the researcher isn't laughed out of the room, he or she may decide to attend a professional meeting such as an annual convention and read a paper summarizing the research.[5] Again, assuming that this somewhat more hostile audience offers a little support, the investigator might decide to write a manuscript based on the research and submit it to a journal. If the article is accepted, it will appear in the journal about nine months to a year later. Following journal publication, *Psychological Abstracts* will publish an abstract of the article. If the article is important, it may appear later in the *Annual Review*, be cited in other articles, and perhaps be mentioned

---

[3] One of the most time-consuming and exasperating things that can happen is to uncover references that have been ripped off or ripped out. It's enough to make the most ardent pacifist have fantasies of catching the scalawags and hanging them by their thieving thumbs in the town square.

[4] This figure is based on research that is now a bit old. It is likely that with technological advances in publishing, the time line has been compressed in recent years. However, I know of no more recent research that speaks to this issue. I believe that the order of events is essentially unchanged today and that the figure still provides a useful way to organize our thinking about the publication process.

[5] This is where your professors go when they miss class. And you thought they were on vacation having fun.

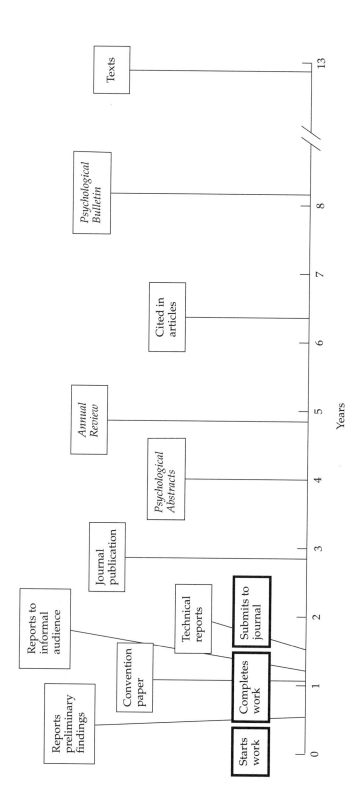

**FIGURE 6-1** The publication history of research from its inception until its appearance in the psychological literature. The boldface boxes indicate when the investigator started and completed the research and submitted it to a journal. The lightface boxes and attached lines indicate the average number of years after the start of the research before it appeared in the various sources.

SOURCE: Adapted from "Scientific Communication: Its Role in the Conduct of Research and Creation of Knowledge," by W. D. Garvey and B. C. Griffith, 1971, *American Psychologist*, 26, 353. Copyright 1971 by the American Psychological Association. Reprinted by permission.

in a publication such as *Psychological Bulletin*. Finally, after several years, a textbook author might mention the research as part of the accepted body of knowledge.

Figure 6-1 points out the **time lag** involved in the scientific communication process. If you use the library, your first access to an experimental result is its appearance as a journal article. As you can see, you have lost considerable time at this point because the research was probably started at least three years before its publication in a journal. If you begin your experiment at this point and go through the same process, the other author will have to wait three more years before your results will be reported in a journal article. (Even the U.S. mail has better turnaround time than this!) Because of the need to avoid such delays, fewer than one in seven research efforts originate from formal sources such as journal articles (Garvey & Griffith, 1971). Most ideas originate from more informal communication among scientists in a given field such as presentations at meetings, discussion lists, and Web pages. However, as a new investigator without the contacts necessary for such informal communication, you might have to be content with the formal sources for the time being. If you continue to work in a particular area of research, you will find out who else works in your area and will get to know your fellow researchers personally. You will then be ahead of the journals and the "new" new investigators.

In the following section we will consider the formal sources in more detail, discuss the advantages and disadvantages of each, and determine how to locate relevant sources. Let's start with books and work our way to more recent sources.

## Formal Sources

### BOOKS

Because books include only research that was begun years earlier, you might think that they would be the worst possible source. However, this enormous time lag makes them in some ways the best source. An important process occurs between the time research is completed and the time it is reported in one of the sources: The research is screened on the basis of importance and quality so that by the time it appears in a book, it has been integrated with other research to form a coherent body of knowledge. Thus, the value of book research lies in the fact that the author thinks it is well done and important and that it fits into the growing body of knowledge. The author has already done much of your work for you; it's just a bit obsolete.

A good place to start your literature search is a recently published book that deals with the general research topic you are interested in. If the author has done a good job, you can have some confidence that you have a good summation of the most important research from the start of psychology up to about 13 years prior to the publication date of the text. Your job is now considerably easier: to find out what has happened during the last 13 years or so.

One problem with this approach is that the author has had to be selective and has not been able to include all the research done on a particular topic since the beginning of psychology. Each book author is biased toward some theoretical or methodological approach and selects research based on this bias. In addition, most books are not subjected to the same level of peer review that journal articles are. Peer review means that several highly respected researchers have read the material and given it their stamp of approval. Most major journals require this of all articles selected for publication, but the process is used less frequently by book publishers. Thus, to be sure you can trust the author's scholarship and bias, try to develop a consensus of several resource books; at the least, try to discover the author's particular bias.

I hope you know how to find books in the library. If you do not, you would be better served asking the reference librarian at your college library how to do this than having me describe it. Most libraries now have an electronic catalog of all the books available in that library. You should start there by typing an author's name, book title, or subject you are interested in. The computer screen will display all the books meeting your requirements. It is even possible now to use a computer on the Internet to search for books at other libraries, although getting those books can be a problem. Interlibrary loans can help here, but be sure you don't wait until the last minute after you have collected data and you are writing up your results. It will be too late to get what you need. Finally, you can find books using one of the computerized search databases I will discuss later in this chapter. In this case you will certainly not be guaranteed that any book you find will be in your local library.

Prior to your library visit, you might also look in an introductory psychology book under your topic. Most basic texts will list some suggested readings to get you started. You might also talk to an instructor in your psychology department who does research in the area. He or she will probably be happy to give you some book references. Finally, the American Psychological Association's *Library Use: A Handbook for Psychology* (Reed & Baxter, 1992) should be helpful to you in learning library skills specific to psychology.

## REVIEW ARTICLES AND BOOKS

Several other sources make an attempt to summarize and integrate research within particular areas of psychology. These sources are more up-to-date than textbooks, and consequently there has been less time for the research to be put into perspective. One such source is a journal published by the

American Psychological Association called *Psychological Bulletin,* which publishes "evaluative and integrative reviews and interpretations of substantive and methodological issues in scientific psychology." Here are some titles from various issues:

"Arousal and the Inverted-U Hypothesis: A Critique of Neiss's 'Reconceptualizing Arousal'"

"Attributions in Marriage: Review and Critique"

"Gender Differences in Mathematics Performance: A Meta-Analysis"

"Effects of Alcohol on Human Aggression: An Interactive Research Review"

"Hindsight: Biased Judgments of Past Events after the Outcomes Are Known"

"Ideas about Causation in Philosophy and Psychology"

"Psychotherapy for the Treatment of Depression: A Comprehensive Review of Controlled Outcome Research"

"Children of Depressed Parents: An Integrative Review"

"Science and Morality: The Role of Values in Science and the Scientific Study of Moral Phenomena"

As you can see, the topics covered in these articles are generally narrower than textbook topics. A *Bulletin* article may also take a previous summary article as its starting point, rather than the beginning of psychology, and fall short of a complete survey. Nevertheless, a recent review article can save you a great deal of search time. And review articles are generally more timely than books.

For those experiments that are similar to the one you are planning, a review article will not go into enough detail for you. In this case, the original sources cited at the back of the article will allow you to quickly find which references are important and to determine how your experiment will fit in with past research.

Another source of research reviews is the *Annual Review of Psychology,* published by Annual Reviews, Inc. The topics vary from year to year depending on the decision of an editorial board. Each chapter is written by an author who is a recognized expert in that field and whose job it is to summarize and integrate the research done since the topic was previously included in the series. The topics are generally broader than *Psychological Bulletin* topics:

"Personality"

"Developmental Psychology"

"Spatial Vision"

However, some topics are a bit narrower:[6]

---

[6] Did you notice the interesting relationship? The broader the topic, the shorter the title.

"Intervention Techniques: Small Groups"
"Social and Cultural Influences on Psychopathology"

In recent years, many edited books have appeared. Some of them summarize the most recent work in a particular area of psychology. Each chapter is usually written by a researcher who gives an up-to-date review of an even more narrowly defined research area. These chapters resemble review articles, and if you can find a chapter that is relevant to your research, you will save search time. For this type of book, in particular, the publication lag is much shorter than for more standard textbooks. Many of them, in fact, are now produced by "desktop publishing," in which the lengthy process of typesetting, editing, and producing a final copy is considerably shortened. In this case some of the research reported may be only a year or two old. However, again, these books have not been peer-reviewed in the same way as journal articles.

## JOURNAL ARTICLES

Psychological journals form the backbone of our science. They are called *primary sources* because they present the basic results as interpreted by the experimenter or experimenters who did the research rather than by third parties, such as those who compile reviews. To do a really thorough literature search, you must use journal articles. As you recall, they are the most up-to-date of the formal sources, following the actual research by only a few years. Thus, although article authors try to integrate their work with the existing body of knowledge, their effort can be only partly successful because they often cannot know about other research being done at the same time. Therefore, you will have to do some integration yourself to make the research form an orderly body of knowledge.

I cannot possibly list all the journals related to psychology here. Many professional organizations publish journals for their members, with a number of publishing companies sponsoring individual journals as well. However, to give you an idea of the kinds of journals available, here is a listing of some journal titles:

*American Journal of Psychology*
*Animal Learning & Behavior*
*Audiology*
*Behavioral and Brain Sciences*
*Behavioral Neuroscience*
*Cognition*
*Cognitive Psychology*
*Developmental Psychology*
*Journal of Abnormal Psychology*
*Journal of Applied Psychology*

*Journal of Comparative Psychology*
*Journal of Experimental Analysis of Behavior*
*Journal of Experimental Psychology: Animal Behavior Processes*
*Journal of Experimental Psychology: General*
*Journal of Experimental Psychology: Human Perception and Performance*
*Journal of Experimental Psychology: Learning, Memory, and Cognition*
*Journal of Memory & Language*
*Journal of Personality and Social Psychology*
*Learning and Motivation*
*Memory & Cognition*
*Motivation and Emotion*
*Perception & Psychophysics*
*Perceptual and Motor Skills*
*Psychological Record*
*Psychological Reports*
*Psychological Review*
*Psychological Science*
*Quarterly Journal of Experimental Psychology: Comparative and Physiological Psychology*
*Quarterly Journal of Experimental Psychology: Human Experimental Psychology*

## TECHNICAL REPORTS

Technical reports are often ignored as a source of psychological literature, but they can be helpful in certain areas of research. When the federal government supports research, particularly Defense Department research, the investigator is usually required to report it in the form of a technical report. This report is similar to a journal article but usually goes into more detail about the procedure and the apparatus, and sometimes it even lists the data. Technical reports are automatically distributed by the supporting governmental agency to other investigators who are doing similar research supported by that agency.

About one author in ten produces these technical reports, and only about one-third of these reports are later published in a journal (Garvey & Griffith, 1971). Most libraries do not routinely order technical reports, because they would quickly fill up the shelves and are difficult for a library to organize and classify systematically. Investigators who are working on defense grants or contracts get a monthly publication listing abstracts of all technical reports. *Psychological Abstracts* also lists many of these reports. Unfortunately, technical reports are often difficult to obtain. To purchase them, you must send to the Defense Documentation Center in Alexandria, Virginia, and you must know the document number and the price of the report you want.

Searching through technical reports is a waste of time for some areas of research. However, if you are working in an area supported by a major government agency, the technical report is a valuable source of information. Some examples of government-supported research are automobile driver safety, personnel training and selection, operator control of complex machines, and human decision making.

## ELECTRONIC PUBLISHING

I am including **electronic publishing** under formal sources even though some might believe I am giving it too much credit at this time. There is a wide range of electronic publishing, from researchers who decide to put the latest draft of an article on their Web page to electronic journals that publish peer-reviewed articles similar in quality to printed journal articles. For this reason, it is sometimes difficult to determine the quality of what one finds. Some have predicted that electronic publishing will become the dominant form of scientific communication and will eventually eliminate paper publishing entirely, but this has not happened yet. The advantages are obvious. The time between completing research and publishing it can be shortened. People can immediately get the article off the Internet and have a hard copy for only the price of printing it. The researcher can post succeeding drafts of the article and revise these on the basis of comments from readers.

However, there are also problems. Who will ensure the quality of articles? Professional associations that publish journals carefully select editors, and those editors send research manuscripts submitted to highly respected peer reviewers. In some cases an average of only 10 to 20 percent of the submissions are chosen for publication and then only after being revised and carefully corrected by a copy editor. On the Internet anybody with access can create a home page and post a research paper. A second problem occurs when there are different drafts of a posted paper. Which is the final version? Publications, particularly journal articles, form the building blocks of our science, and as scientists we have to be able to know that a particular article is the sole block that will be added to the scientific structure. Finally, there is the matter of money. Professional societies have generally been the keepers of the science. They have provided the infrastructure that has allowed the scientific enterprise to expand in an orderly fashion. This infrastructure costs money, which has come largely from subscription fees paid by libraries and individual scientists. If articles are published at no cost on the Internet, where will the money come from to provide the scientific infrastructure?

These are just some of the issues yet to be worked out. For these reasons, the American Psychological Association, the publisher of the largest number of prestigious journals, currently has a policy that it will not consider for publication any manuscript that has been publicly posted on the Internet. It takes the position that if it has been posted, it has already been published. This doesn't mean you cannot send your manuscript by e-mail to selected people for comments. However, you should keep this policy in mind if you expect to eventually publish your research in a standard sci-entific journal.

You should also keep some of these issues in mind when you are doing your literature search. You may find some important articles on the Inter-net. In particular, articles that are posted on the home pages of well-known researchers are probably worth reading and citing in your paper. However, there is a lot of junk on the Internet, too. You should look with skepticism at what you find using nonscientific search engines. There is no mandatory quality control on the Internet, so you will have to do your own quality control. By all means, before you cite information found on the Internet, be sure to check the credentials of the author and get the opinions of others experienced in the field about the information being cited.

## SEARCHING THE FORMAL LITERATURE

At this point your mind is probably boggled by the impossibility of search-ing through this mass of journals and books. I don't blame you; you could spend the rest of your life in the library looking through publications as they come out and you would still fall farther and farther behind. Fortu-nately, the American Psychological Association has come to your rescue. One of their departments is called PsycINFO and is dedicated to creating products to help researchers locate the literature they need. Since 1927 the APA has published *Psychological Abstracts* containing references and abstracts of articles. Until recent years students doing a literature search would go to the many volumes of this publication in the library and man-

LITERATURE SEARCH

ually try to find articles related to their topic by using key terms or author's names. It was a tedious but necessary task.

Today the availability of electronic communication has greatly simplified this task. I addition to the *Abstracts*, APA also produces the *PsycINFO* electronic database and a similar database stored on CD-ROM called *PsycLIT*. Many larger libraries buy a site lease for *PsycINFO* and make it available both on terminals in the library and, in many cases, remotely. For instance, at my university students and faculty can use their personal computers to do a literature search from their dorm rooms or offices. The database contains more than 1.5 million references to psychological literature from 1887 to today, with about 5500 new references added each month. Included are articles, dissertations, reports, English-language book chapters and books, and other scholarly documents. *PsycLIT* is similar to *PsycINFO*, but it is on CD-ROM and has only a subset of the total database. For instance, it does not contain technical reports or dissertations, and it is updated quarterly instead of monthly. However, for most searches it provides an adequate database.

Figure 6-2 shows an example of an entry from the database. The three basic parts are a bibliographic citation, a summary, and standardized subject indexing. The bibliographic citation includes the title, the author or authors, and the source. This is the information you would put in a references section if you were including the entry in a paper you were writing. The summary is usually an abstract, and for journal articles it is the one written by the author. The summary does not evaluate the research; it just

ACCESSION NUMBER: 1997-05223-007
DOCUMENT TYPE: Journal-Article
TITLE: The availability heuristic: Effects of fame and gender on the estimated frequency of male and female names.
AUTHOR: McKelvie,-Stuart-J.
SOURCE: Journal-of-Social-Psychology. 1997 Feb; Vol 137(1): 63-78
ISSN: 0022-4545
PUBLICATION YEAR: 1997
ABSTRACT: In 2 experiments, Canadian undergraduates heard a list of 13 male names and 13 female names; then they estimated how many male and female names there seemed to be. In Exp 1, the list consisted of 26 famous names or 26 nonfamous names. Both male and female participants gave similar estimates for the number of male and female names, contradicting hypotheses of a bias toward males or toward one's own gender. In Exp 2, where the list contained names of famous men and nonfamous women or names of famous women and nonfamous men, participants gave higher estimates for the gender that was famous. This result confirmed A. Tversky and D. Kahneman's (1973) fame availability effect and showed it to be moderate to large in size. ((c) 1997 APA/PsycINFO, all rights reserved)
KEY PHRASE: fame and sex of name, estimated frequency of male and female names, college students, Canada, test of fame availability heuristic
MAJOR DESCRIPTORS: *Estimation-; *Fame-; *Human-Sex-Differences; *Names-
MINOR DESCRIPTORS: Adulthood-

**FIGURE 6-2** A typical entry from *PsycINFO* showing the various data fields.

describes it. The standardized subject indexing is done using key phrases and descriptors. Note that all you get from an entry is a brief description of the research. This is usually enough to tell you whether it is of interest to you, but it does not substitute for reading the original reference. In order to do that you have to obtain the article, book, or chapter from your library. Most larger libraries have a selection of standard journals. If your library does not have the item you are looking for, a librarian should be able to tell you how to get it from interlibrary loan. There are now also full-text document delivery sources that can send articles to you over the Internet— for a fee.

How do you find entries related to your research topic? There are several ways. If you have some idea about the subject matter of the research you are interested in, you can search using key phrases or descriptors. I found the entry in Figure 6-2 that way. I was considering doing an experiment looking at how the availability heuristic might affect people's favorability toward nuclear power generation. The availability heuristic says that our opinions can be influenced by the mental availability of instances related to that opinion. For instance, I might be of the opinion that people die more frequently from shark attacks than from wasp stings because I have more instances available in my memory of shark attacks. Mortality from wasp stings is actually higher. In our experiment we asked people to give us either advantages of nuclear power generation or disadvantages and then asked them to rate how favorable they were toward nuclear power. We expected that just having recalled either the advantages or the disadvantages would make the advantages or disadvantages more available and bias the favorability rating. In this case I was interested in looking at references having to do with the availability heuristic, so that is what I entered into the search.

I got back a message saying that the search had produced about 50 documents. I then began looking through the entries, one of which is shown in Figure 6-2. I read the title and abstract of this particular entry and determined that it was not close enough to my interests to look at the whole article. You can see why the search selected this article: Both the title and the key phrase contain the term *availability heuristic*. This term could have appeared anywhere in the entry and the entry would have been chosen. I could have limited the search by specifying which field to search. Each of the capitalized words indicates a separate field. So, for instance, I could have searched just the KEY PHRASE field. Only 11 search fields are shown in Figure 6-2, but there are actually 89 possible search field values.[7] In this way you can limit your search to journal articles, or English-language references, or adult participants, etc. In that way you would not have to search through so many entries.

---

[7] You can learn more about these fields by going to the following World Wide Web address: www.apa.org/psycinfo/. This address will also go into much more detail about how to conduct an electronic search.

The exact procedures for conducting a search are too detailed to go into here and change frequently. You can learn these from a librarian, from one of a number of booklets, and even on-line from APA (www.apa.org/psycinfo/). However, I will give you a general description of the steps you will go through. First you should compose a narrative of your search question. For example, suppose you wanted to know, "Do people develop anxieties about using computers?" Then identify the separate concepts in the question—for example, *anxiety* and *computer*. Next use the electronic *Thesaurus* available as part of *PsycINFO* or *PsycLIT* to find appropriate descriptors. The *Thesaurus* will allow you to explode or narrow the terms as needed to customize the search for your purposes. You should do that for each of your terms. For example, maybe *anxiety* should include *fear* or *phobia.* Now you need to combine your sets of descriptors using the words AND, OR, and NOT. Be careful when you do this, because these words have very specific meanings. AND means that you want the search to be restrictive in that the entry will have to contain all the concepts—for example, both *anxiety* and *computer.* OR gives a much wider search and means that the entry could have either descriptor. NOT is used if you are sure that you want to exclude all entries having a particular descriptor.

Once the search is complete, the screen will tell you how many entries were found. If there are only a few or none, do not automatically assume that little or no research has been done in the area. You should check what you have done a few ways. If the search has produced a few usable references, look at the descriptors listed in the entries you have found to see if any would be appropriate for your search; add them if they are. Try combining your descriptors in different ways to see what effect this has on the number of entries found. On the other hand, if your search has identified hundreds of entries, scan through some of these to see if there are research areas that are of no interest to you and try to eliminate these entries by using a NOT or by combining descriptors in some other way.

Another way to search the electronic databases is to use authors rather than descriptors. Perhaps you know of an author or several authors who regularly publish in your area of interest, or you have found several such authors while doing your descriptor search. You would probably want to enter these authors' names into a search of the author fields of the database to see what other things they have published. For example, while I was doing my search on the availability heuristic, I knew that the originators of this term, Daniel Kahneman and Amos Tversky, had published other articles, chapters, and books on this topic, so I searched the database using their names and found a few more relevant references, as well as many more irrelevant ones. Be sure to use all the variants of the names, both with and without initials, because names are sometimes listed in a variety of ways.

When you have a reasonable list of entries from your various searches, sort through them on the screen, picking the most appropriate and "marking" them electronically. Later you can print or download all the ones you have marked or send them to yourself via e-mail. This list will provide you with the information necessary to find the original articles, books, or chapters you want to read in full, and later you can select bibliographic entries from the list to produce the references section of your research report.[8]

## "TREEING" BACKWARD THROUGH THE REFERENCES

There is another way to do a literature search that is not nearly so thorough as using *PsycINFO* or *PsycLIT*. However, it is a good way to determine whether you have missed any key research in your previous search. I will refer to this technique as *treeing backward through the references*. The first thing to do is find the most recent article that deals with the topic of interest; this article will form the "trunk" of your research tree. Find the references at the end of the article. Many of these references should also be relevant to your topic. (With any luck most of them are already on your list.) Each of these articles will also have a reference list from which you can select in the same way. Follow each reference list backward through the literature until you have found all the important articles that form a new set of branches on your tree. This method can be helpful, but do not rely on it as your sole technique, since you cannot always assume that every author has done a scholarly job of finding the important references.

TREEING THROUGH THE REFERENCES

---

[8] There are additional electronic databases that I do not have the space to discuss here, such as *ERIC* and *Medline*. If you want to become an expert on such searches, ask your instructor to tell you about them.

## "TREEING" FORWARD THROUGH THE REFERENCES

To be thorough in your literature search, you can tree forward through the references as well as backward. For example, if you find a key article that is several years old and want to find more recent articles that have referenced that article, you can use the *Social Sciences Citation Index*. The SSCI is published quarterly and cumulated annually by the Institute of Scientific Information. It covers nearly 1400 journals from virtually every social science discipline.

The SSCI now comes in both electronic and paper form. In either case you will be using a key article, and you want to find all the articles published since that date that cited the key article. If doing a paper search, you would look through all the yearly volumes published since the key article came out. In each volume the key article would be listed, followed by each of the other articles that cited it. If you are doing an electronic search, you can search all the years at once and, as with other electronic databases, you can electronically mark the citations you are interested in and have them printed out. The electronic database also now allows you to base your search on the subject or location of the article.

You can also recycle yourself by finding each article that cited the original article, then treeing backward using the references for each of these new articles. You may wish to take some of these newly acquired references, use them as key references, and go forward again. You can continue this process until you feel you have covered all the important references.

HOW TO RECYCLE YOURSELF

## REPRINT REQUESTS

A professional courtesy among scientists allows you to get some journal articles free. When authors get articles published, they usually order 100 or so reprints of the article from the journal. As long as these reprints last, the author will send one to you if you ask nicely. The usual way is to send a postcard saying, "I would very much appreciate receiving a reprint of your article entitled _____ that appeared in _____." You might also try sending the author an e-mail rather than a postcard. If you know where the author conducts research, you can probably find an e-mail address. For instance, if the author is a faculty member, simply go the one of the search services that lists colleges, find the faculty member's college Web page, then go to the psychology department Web page or the university directory, and you will usually find an e-mail address to use. While you are communicating with this author, you might also ask for other articles dealing with the same subject if you have a general interest in the area of research. Be sure to include your address. The author will usually send you a copy as a courtesy. Do not be embarrassed to send out these *reprint requests*. Many younger investigators who are trying to become familiar with research in a particular area but do not have the resources to buy their own journals send out reprint requests, and most authors find these requests flattering rather than a nuisance.

## CURRENT RESEARCH

The Smithsonian Science Information Exchange provides a way of finding out what is going on in current research. Their current file contains records for more than 14,000 projects in all areas of the behavioral sciences. All these projects are being supported by a funding agency such as the National Science Foundation. Each listing contains a 200-word description of the work being performed. You can order a package containing the listings for general topic areas such as "insomnia" or "behavior therapy with alcoholics." There is a fee for this service that depends on the number of listings. The disadvantages of this system are the cost and the fact that only funded research is listed. However, it is one of the few means of finding out about ongoing research.

# Informal Sources

## PROFESSIONAL MEETINGS

As I mentioned earlier, to be completely up-to-date on the research in a particular field, you must become familiar with informal sources of communication. About 15 to 18 months prior to journal publication many investigators present their research at a professional meeting by reading a paper. In fact, about one-fifth of the articles published in major psychology journals are based on material previously presented at an APA convention (Garvey & Griffith, 1971). The APA annually sponsors a national meeting and six regional conventions. In addition, many other non-APA professional groups, such as the Psychonomic Society, the Psychometric Society, and the American Psychological Society, sponsor meetings.

Of course, you can't attend every single meeting or convention in your field. Thus, some of the meetings publish papers in a bound volume called a *proceedings*, which is available in most libraries. In addition, just prior to the meetings, members of these organizations receive convention programs. You might be able to find faculty members in your psychology department who belong to these organizations and get programs before the meetings. Once you know that one of these papers is of interest to you, simply send the author a reprint request. You will understand the paper better if you read it than if you listen to it anyway.

The real reason for attending conventions, aside from engaging in superfluous hedonistic activities,[9] is to talk to other researchers doing work in your area of interest. Depending on how defensive they are, you might even find out what they are planning to do in the near future. In this way, you can fill in the information gap between "starts work" and "convention paper" in Figure 6-1.

By the way, if you learn something in one of these discussions that you might wish to quote in an article, be sure to write it down, note the date, and get the person's permission to use it. You can then cite the source in an article as a *personal communication.*

## RESEARCH GROUPS

Once you learn who does research in a particular area of interest to you, you may find that they have set up an informal means of keeping one another informed. In some cases this will be a group whose members send one another preprints of articles and papers as soon as they are finished or, in some cases, when they are in draft form. Today the Internet also offers a way for members of these groups to interact. In some cases the purpose may be to distribute papers. In other cases the members of the group may have research-related discussions via a listserve or a chat room. Sometimes such a group would be willing to have anybody who is interested join in the discussions. Other groups are more restrictive, and you would have to be invited to participate. Once you have established an interest in a particular area of research, be sure to keep an eye out for such groups. They offer a valuable way of staying informed about the latest research information.

## FACULTY MEMBERS

Be sure not to overlook a handy source of informal help with your literature search, the *faculty members* in your psychology department. Students are sometimes reluctant to approach professors, thinking that they will be too busy to help them or even thinking that asking the faculty for help is some form of cheating. To the contrary, most are not only willing to help

---

[9] Havin' fun!

but also flattered to be asked. This kind of help is as much a part of teaching as standing in front of a class lecturing. And real researchers use whatever sources they can find to help them conduct their science. Science is a team effort in which the goal is the creation of the body of knowledge, not a struggle of researcher against researcher or student against teacher. So give it a try. You may be pleasantly surprised not only at the willingness of your professors to help but also at how knowledgeable they are.

Although the written record of our science is maintained by the formal sources, the informal sources also perform a vital service for science. They offer a forum for saying stupid but creative things. Your informal colleagues will chuckle quietly and tell you where you are wrong. Your formal colleagues are forced to guffaw loudly and boisterously tell the world where you have gone wrong. With only the formal sources, few of us would have the courage to try to move science by leaps and bounds, and we would stick with small, conservative steps. The encouragement and friendly discouragement offered by informal contacts are important in shaping our thoughts into a form suitable for the formal literature.

I have tried to make this discussion of searching the literature as complete as possible. I hope that in doing so I haven't made the process sound more complex than it really is. Many new investigators believe that a literature search requires some sort of mystical power and many years of experience. However, if you follow the simple steps outlined in this chapter, you will find that doing a thorough literature search can be a straightforward, satisfying experience.

## Summary

A **literature search** is necessary to find out if your experimental idea has already been investigated, to determine whether similar experiments have been done, and to see how your experiment will fit into the current body of knowledge. To do this search efficiently, you should understand the lines of communication within the scientific community and the *time lag* associated with various sources of information. It is usually most efficient to begin your search in *books* that are relevant to your area of interest. Books describe research from the beginning of psychology up to about 13 years prior to current research. You can then use *review articles* to bring you within five to eight years of current research. *Journal articles* will form the backbone of your literature search. Technical reports can be an important source of information, particularly in applied fields. You can track down relevant articles, books, and book chapters using either descriptor terms or authors by doing an electronic search using *PsycINFO* or *PsycLIT*. You can double-check your search by treeing backward through the references of recent journal articles. The *Social Science Citation Index* also allows you to tree forward through the references by determining which articles have cited a particular earlier article. Informal sources such as *papers read at professional meetings, personal communications, preprints,* and even *faculty members* are a valuable way to learn about current and future research.

# Find It on InfoTrac College Edition

The purpose of Chapter 6 was to introduce you to literature searches. To fully familiarize yourself with literature searches you should visit your library and, if at all possible, try to find the various sources discussed in this chapter, such as PsycINFO, PsycLIT, and the Social Sciences Citation Index. You may also find that these sources are available remotely from a computer lab or from your own personal computer. I encourage you to try your hand at searching these sources for various topics using key words and authors' names.

If you do not have these sources readily available, then try a rudimentary search using InfoTrac College Edition. With this database, you can call up entire original articles rather than just abstracts. However, if you use only this one database, do not be misled into believing that you have done a thorough literature search. InfoTrac College Edition contains literature from only the most recent years. In addition, although it contains a number of useful sources, it certainly does not have an exhaustive set of all the possible formal primary sources as PsycLIT does. So, although you will find many useful references with InfoTrac College Edition, you will miss many additional essential references.

Nevertheless, try your hand at finding references for various topics through InfoTrac College Edition. Here are a few suggestions: violence in high schools, repressed memories, visual imagery, implicit memory. For a few of these topics or for other topics that interest you, find out how many references you can locate. Look at some of the original articles to see what type of research has been done in these areas.

# 7

# How to Decide Which Variables to Manipulate and Measure

> We believe that a concept has no meaning beyond that obtained from the operations on which it is based.
>
> W. R. GARNER, H. W. HAKE, & C. W. ERIKSEN (1956)

We learned about various types of research in Chapter 1, discussed a general model of an experiment in Chapter 2, learned how to get an experimental idea in Chapter 3, and considered ethics in Chapters 4 and 5. In Chapter 6 you probably learned more about doing a literature search than you wished to know. Now it's time we got to work doing what experimental psychologists are supposed to do—experiments.

In this chapter we will consider two decisions that have to be made when planning any psychology experiment, from the simplest to the most complex: We need to choose the independent and dependent variables.

## Choosing an Independent Variable

Recall from Chapter 2 that the independent variable is the one that the experimenter manipulates. Because the whole purpose of any experiment is to find the effect of the independent variable on behavior, choosing this variable is about the most important decision you have to make. At first blush it may seem that the decision should be rather straightforward. And for some experiments it is. For example, if you want to know whether people press a button in response to a light more quickly when a tone is given as a warning signal, the independent variable is rather obvious: the presence or absence of the tone. If, however, you want to find out whether children are more aggressive after exposure to violent versus nonviolent television programs, the independent variable (violence) may be tougher to define. What constitutes violence on television? Is *Monday Night Football* violent? Are Roadrunner cartoons violent? Are rap videos violent? Not everyone would agree on a particular definition of violent television programs.

## DEFINING YOUR INDEPENDENT VARIABLE

The problem here is that there is a difference in precision between what the general public will accept in defining a term and what experimental psychologists will accept. Experimental psychologists require **operational definitions** of the independent and dependent variables. This means that they must specify the operations anyone must go through to set up the independent variable in the same way they did. So an operational definition is a bit like a recipe, except the procedures and ingredients create a variable rather than a cake.

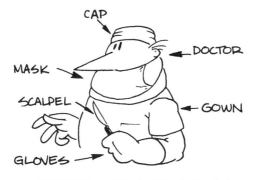

CAP

DOCTOR

MASK

SCALPEL

GOWN

GLOVES

OPERATIONAL DEFINITIONS

In the TV-violence experiment, the operational definition would specify the steps required to determine whether certain shows are violent. For example, you could operationalize the concept of a violent television program by showing each program to a randomly chosen group of 100 people and requiring that 75% of them indicate a program is violent before you operationally define it as violent. Another alternative is to devise a checklist with such items as "Is there physical contact that causes harm to another person?" "Has an illegal act taken place?" and "Did one person act so as to make another feel inferior?" Perhaps you would require that each program have at least two out of ten such items checked "yes" for it to be considered violent. Again, such a procedure would specify exactly what operations any other experimenter must carry out to meet your operational definition of violent television programs.

Psychology researchers have more difficulty agreeing on operational definitions than do physical scientists.[1] Galileo did not have to ponder over a definition for mass before determining whether objects that have different masses fall at the same speed in a vacuum. Yet a great many important psychological questions require complex operational definitions: Do people

---

[1] A physicist first used the term *operational definition*. However, in the physical sciences, operational definitions are usually so widely accepted that physical scientists spend considerably less time agonizing over them than do behavioral scientists.

whose mothers were affectionate make more successful marriage partners? Do students learn more from popular professors? Does a worker's morale affect work output? Does anxiety cause depression? Before doing an experiment to answer any of these questions, you need operational definitions for the terms *affectionate, successful, learn, popular, morale, output, anxiety,* and *depression.* Try making up operational definitions for these terms: You will quickly see the psychology researcher's challenge.

For most concepts that you want to operationally define, you will find from your literature search that other investigators have already been faced with defining these concepts. The good news is that if they did a good job, much of your work has been done for you. The bad news is that if you disagree with their definitions, you may have a difficult time getting a new definition accepted. Science is rather conservative in that it does not like rapid changes. You can imagine the chaos if every investigator insisted on a different operational definition of each important concept. The scientific body of knowledge would resemble the Tower of Babel, because everyone would be speaking a different language. So once a concept gets operationally defined, that definition carries some status, and it is sometimes difficult to convince others that a new one is needed. As you begin trying to operationally define the terms for your experiment, be sure to do a literature search and discover how others have defined the concepts you wish to investigate.

## CHOOSING THE RANGE OF YOUR INDEPENDENT VARIABLE

Once you have defined your independent variable, you still have to choose the **range** of the variable. The range is the difference between the highest and lowest level of the variable you choose. For example, suppose we decided to define violent television programs by using our group of 100 people to classify each program as violent or nonviolent. We could choose to use two levels of violence in our experiment: those programs classified as violent by 100% of the people and those that nobody thought were violent. These two levels of the independent variable give us the largest possible range.

On the other hand, we might have chosen the programs rated violent by over 50% of the people as violent and those rated violent by less than 50% as nonviolent. These levels would obviously create a much smaller range.

How do we determine what the range should be? Unfortunately, I can't give you any hard-and-fast rules for making this decision, for it is as much an art as a science. However, following are some guidelines that you might find useful.

## Be Realistic

First, you should try to choose a range that is *realistic* in that it is similar to the levels found in the situation you will be generalizing to. You should avoid "sledgehammer" effects caused by setting the levels of the independent variable at such extremes that you are certain to find a difference in behavior. Some of the early medical research on marijuana was plagued by sledgehammer effects. In some cases, experimenters gave mice the human equivalent of a truckload of marijuana per day! The experimenters got impressive but impractical results.

## Select a Range That Shows Effect

Within realistic limits, you should have a range that is large enough to show an effect of the independent variable on the dependent variable if such an effect exists. For example, if you were interested in the effect of room temperature on manual dexterity in a sorting task and you chose temperatures of 23°C and 25°C,[2] you might conclude falsely that room temperature had no effect on manual dexterity.

Real-world[3] experimental situations require special attention to choosing a large enough range, because the experimenter does not always have complete control over the levels of the independent variable. You can choose an approximate level, but the actual level may vary from trial to trial. For instance, in the lecture-pace experiment, I attempted to vary my lecture pace by speaking at a slow, medium, or fast rate. The levels I attempted to achieve were 100, 125, and 150 syllables per minute. Because I am not a machine that can be set at a particular speaking rate, I was bound to produce some variability around the desired levels. To determine my

---

[2] For those who refuse to be converted to converting Celsius, 73°F and 77°F.
[3] I use the term *real world* to refer to nonlaboratory experiments designed to find answers to applied problems, not to imply that most people in universities are unreal. People who live in ivory towers shouldn't throw snipes.

actual rate, we recorded the lectures and counted the number of syllables per second. Fortunately, the fastest lecture at the slow pace was still slower than the slowest lecture at the medium pace, so there was no overlap of levels. If I had chosen a smaller range, however, I would have had less chance of producing these reliable differences among the levels of the independent variable. Thus, in some nonlaboratory experiments, you must remember to make the range large enough that differences in the levels of the independent variable are not covered up by the uncontrolled variability of that variable.

## Do a Pilot Experiment

Determining the best range for an experiment is, to some extent, guesswork. In some cases you may find experiments using the same independent variable you are planning to use that can give you an idea about an appropriate range. However, if your experiment is original and nobody else has used an independent variable similar to yours, you may choose to do a **pilot experiment.**[4] A pilot experiment is a small-scale version of the experiment you are planning, done so you can iron out any problems before you proceed. Because you need not report the results of this experiment, you may break some of the rules of experimentation. For example, you might cajole your friends into participating, and you might even serve as a participant yourself. You can also change the levels of your independent variable halfway through a trial, stop the experiment, or do only part of the experiment, depending on what you learn as you proceed.

PARTICIPANT IN A
PILOT EXPERIMENT

When doing a pilot experiment, you will sometimes find that what looked good on paper just does not work. For example, I once discovered during a pilot experiment that a supposedly simple experiment I had designed required at least three experimenters to operate the equipment. The pilot experiment may also help you determine whether the levels of your independent variable are what you expected. Levels that seem realistic during the planning stage of an experiment may seem unrealistic in the laboratory. By having a trial run, you can change an obviously inappropriate range of the independent variable before investing a great amount of time and effort in the experiment.

---

[4] I suppose the term *pilot* in this case is used in the sense of "guiding through unknown places," as when a ship's pilot comes on board to steer a vessel through unknown waters. The pilot experiment becomes the guide for future experiments, leading the experimenter through uncharted waters.

Although searching the literature and doing pilot experiments can give you some idea of an appropriate range for your independent variable, in the end you still have to make your best guess. If you turn out to be right, you can claim good judgment. If you are wrong, you claim bad luck.

## Choosing a Dependent Variable

As we know from Chapter 2, the dependent variable is some measure of behavior. We saw that we could choose an infinite number of things to measure. In selecting our dependent variable, we must decide what we will measure.

### OPERATIONAL DEFINITIONS AGAIN

Let's return to the question "Will violent television shows cause a change in a child's aggressiveness?" In this experiment, we clearly want to measure aggressiveness, but again we need an operational definition of aggressiveness so that we can determine whether a child's behavior changes after viewing violent television shows.

One way to develop an operational definition in this example would be to have a panel of judges watch a movie of each child in a free-play situation and then rate the child's aggressiveness on a seven-point scale. Or we could tell each child several stories about other children in frustrating situations and ask the child what he or she would do in each situation. We could then use the number of "direct-attack" responses as a measure of

A  NONAGGRESSIVE  TOY?

aggressiveness. Another alternative would be to observe children as they played with a selection of toys we had previously classified as aggressive (such as guns, tanks, and knives) or nonaggressive (such as trucks, tools, and dolls). We could then measure the percentage of time that the child played with each type of toy. You can undoubtedly think of many other behaviors that would be an indication of a child's aggressiveness.

Sometimes, even when a dependent variable seems quite straightforward, there can be problems with operationally defining it. For example, two investigators wished to determine whether some predictions from a theory of evolutionary psychology would be supported by homicide figures (Daly & Wilson, 1988). The theory predicts that people are much less likely to kill blood relatives living with them than to kill genetically unrelated people living with them. Now, it would seem to be a pretty simple matter to count homicides within a particular sample. But what exactly is a homicide? In several countries homicide figures include all "murders, attempted murders, and manslaughters." Should attempted murders and manslaughters be counted for this study? For most manslaughters, such as a reckless auto accident, there is no intent to kill. Is intent important? If intent is important, perhaps attempted murders should be treated as murders. Should only the cases in which a conviction was obtained be counted? At first that might seem appropriate; we would not want to include a case if the person were innocent. But counting convictions may be even more misleading. In a sample of homicides committed in Detroit in one year, 20 men were convicted for killing their wives, and 9 women were convicted for killing their husbands. One might conclude that men killed their wives more often. Actually, though, women killed their spouses more often. But homicidal wives had their cases dismissed without trial 75% of the time, whereas homicidal husbands were spared a trial only 20% of the time. As the researchers point out, counting only convictions may say more about the behavior of prosecutors than about the behavior of offenders! Unfortunately, as this example illustrates, operationally defining dependent variables is no easier than doing so for independent variables.

With dependent variables, not only do we have to be concerned with determining an operational definition, but we have to know whether the measurement is reliable and valid.

## RELIABILITY AND VALIDITY

A measuring instrument is perfectly reliable if we get exactly the same result when we repeat the measurement a number of times under comparable conditions. The more variable the results, the less reliable is the measurement instrument. A rubber ruler, for example, would not be very reliable. It might measure a tabletop at 18 inches one time and 31 inches the next time. To find out how reliable the ruler is, we would have to measure a number of objects at least two times and see how the results correlate (Chapter 1). If the result of the first measurement is similar to that of the second, correlation is high, and we can assume that the measurement instrument is reliable. If correlation is low, we know that the instrument is not very reliable.

To use our example of violent television programs, we might show the same set of videotapes of each child's behavior to a second panel of judges and compare the aggressiveness ratings given by the two panels. If the panels gave similar ratings, we could feel more confident that ratings taken from a panel of judges were reliable.

Formally determining **reliability** is particularly important when the dependent variable is the score from a test instrument such as a test of achievement, aptitude, or personality traits. A standardized test will already have had its reliability tested, and a statistic indicating this reliability can be found in the test manual. However, if you use a test or questionnaire that you constructed, you may have to determine its reliability yourself. There are several methods to do this. The most obvious is **test–retest reliability,** in which the same test is simply repeated on the same group at a later time. The reliability is determined by calculating a correlation coefficient using the two scores from each test taker (see Appendix A). However, the score on a second test given to the same person can be contaminated by the previous testing. The events occurring during the passage of time between test administrations can also influence scores. For these reasons, a second way to determine reliability is to use the **alternative-form** method. A second test having items similar to the first is constructed and given to the same people. Again the two scores for each person are correlated. A third way of establishing reliability is to use the **split-half** technique, in which a single test is statistically split into halves (such as using odd versus even questions) and scores for the two halves are correlated. Some of the advantages and disadvantages of using each technique for establishing reliability are listed in Table 7-1. If your dependent variable is not a test score, you may not have to formally determine its reliability. Nevertheless, you should be aware of the necessity of having a reliable measure.

**Validity**[5] refers to whether we are measuring what we want to measure. Suppose we have a wooden ruler marked as 12 inches long, but it is really 24 inches long because each inch on the ruler actually measures 2 inches. In this case, we could measure the tabletop many times, and the ruler would indicate 11 inches every time. We have a reliable measuring instrument, but, of course, the measurement is wrong because we claim that we are measuring in inches when in fact we are not. Thus, we also need to know if our measuring instruments are valid—that is, if they measure in the same units as a standard measuring device known to be valid.

In establishing our operational definition of aggressiveness, for example, suppose we had decided to measure the percentage of time each child spent playing with aggressive versus nonaggressive toys. If our stopwatch were working correctly, this measurement would probably be reliable, because we would get about the same reading when we timed the behavior a second time. However, people might argue that our measure is not a valid

[5] For a more detailed discussion of types of validity, see Chapter 2.

**TABLE 7-1**
Advantages and Disadvantages of Three Methods
of Determining Test Reliability

| Reliability method | Advantages | Disadvantages |
|---|---|---|
| Test–retest | It uses the same test items. It is simple to do. | First testing may contaminate the second. Respondents may change with time. |
| Alternative-form | It minimizes repeat-item contamination. Little time passes before retesting. It is useful for pretest–posttest designs. | Use of different items lowers reliability. |
| Split-half | It minimizes repeat-item contamination. No time passes. It is done in one sitting. | Use of different items lowers reliability. It requires a longer test. |

measure of aggressiveness. They might claim that children tend to play with toys that they already know how to use. Because they have seen guns and tanks and knives used on violent television programs, they choose those toys to play with. Or they might claim that children can use trucks and tools and dolls in aggressive ways as well as nonaggressive ways. To convince them that your measurement is valid, you must compare it with some standard that you both agree is a valid measure of aggressiveness. If your measuring instrument agrees with the standard, you can call it a valid instrument.

When a test score is used as a dependent variable, it is sometimes necessary to more formally establish the test's validity as well as its reliability. The weakest form of validity is **face validity,** which means that, on the surface, it looks as if the test measures what it is supposed to. Obviously, face validity is so subjective that it is not of much scientific use; all investigators think that their tests have high face validity. A more formal and defensible validation procedure is to establish **content validity.** The subject matter covered by the test is carefully analyzed in detail for its content. The test is then constructed so that it contains a representative sample of questions from each content area identified. A third validation procedure is to establish **predictive validity** to see whether the test successfully predicts some specific criterion. For example, the value of the tests that high school students take for entrance to college is that the tests can partially predict the criterion of their college grade-point average. A high correlation between the test score and the GPA would indicate high validity. **Concurrent validity** is also established by comparing the test score with a criterion, but in this case the two measures are taken at the same time. For example, if we were attempting to construct a questionnaire to be filled out by our TV-watching children's parents as a measure of their child's aggressiveness, we might determine its concurrent validity by correlating the questionnaire score for each child with a teacher's numerical rating of aggressiveness. As you can see, measuring a dependent variable's validity is even more difficult than measuring its reliability. Often the best we can do is to simply argue that our measures are valid from a logically defensible position.

## DIRECTLY OBSERVABLE DEPENDENT VARIABLES

The closer you can come to directly observing a behavior, the less controversy there will be over your measure. However, if your interest is in determining the workings of the human mind, you should recognize that all dependent measures are, in a sense, indirect. For example, suppose you are interested in memory and want to compare two ways of presenting material to be remembered. After a week you wish to measure how much your participants remember. What should you measure?

That's easy; just ask them what they remember. But suppose they cannot recall any of the material in either presentation condition. Could you then conclude that they remember nothing? You might have given them a recognition test instead and determined their accuracy at distinguishing previously presented material from new material. Or you could have had them relearn the material and measured the percentage of time saved by having learned it before. Each of these methods might give you different answers to your question: How much do people remember? I hope you can see from this example that dependent variables, even those that at first appear to be directly observable, may be linked only indirectly to the behavior you are interested in.

### Single Dependent Variables

Suppose we want to know whether people respond more quickly to a bright light than to a dim light when signaled to push a button. We would probably start a clock when a light goes on and stop the clock when a button is pressed. We should recognize that only one characteristic of the response is being measured. We could have chosen any number of other characteristics—how people press the button, for example. Does one individual move her finger from the side of the button on one trial and from directly over the button on the next? On one trial, does she miss the button on the first try? On another trial, does she hit the button lightly at first and then mash it down? From this diverse set of responses, we chose to measure only one characteristic of the response: time from light onset to button depression. In other words, we selected a **single dependent variable.**

Any single dependent variable we choose may or may not be the appropriate measure to take. For example, suppose we ask people to use a pencil to trace the outline of a star while looking at the star in a mirror. Because the mirror reverses everything, most people find this task very tough on the first few trials. Suppose we want to measure the improvement

from Trial 1 to Trial 10 on this task. What dependent variable would best reflect this improvement?

The standard dependent variable used in these experiments is the number of times the participant's tracing crosses the outline of the star. Figure 7-1 shows the tracings from two fictitious individuals whom we will sagaciously call Participant 1 and Participant 2. On Trial 1, Participant 1 crossed the boundary 20 times; on Trial 10, 6 times. For this individual, the dependent variable reflects the expected improvement in performance. But look at Participant 2. This individual crossed the outline 14 times on each of the two trials. Our dependent variable indicates that Participant 2 did not improve in mirror-tracing performance. Do you believe this conclusion?

The basic problem is that even when a directly observable dependent variable such as number of border crossings is used, we must be concerned with validity. Border-crossing behavior is only one possible measure of mirror-tracing performance. Is it a valid measure? Other dependent variables might better reflect overall mirror-tracing performance. As an alternative, we could have measured the total length of the tracing and determined what percentage fell within the borders of the star. Or we could have measured the area between the border and the tracing for each trial. Or we could have timed the participants to find out whether they were tracing the star more quickly by the tenth trial.

## Multiple Dependent Variables

One way to improve the chances of using a valid dependent variable is to use **multiple dependent variables.** In fact, in some areas of experimental psychology, it is considered quite inappropriate to report only one dependent measure. For example, many types of research use choice reaction time as a dependent measure. **Choice reaction time** is the time it takes to give one of several responses when one of several stimuli[6] occurs. Naturally, if people wish to make as few errors as possible, they must respond rather slowly.

[6] Because I haven't used the term *stimuli* before, I should point out that *stimulus* is singular and *stimuli* is plural. It is time to expand your chant: "This stimulus is, this datum is; these stimuli are, these data are." Got that?

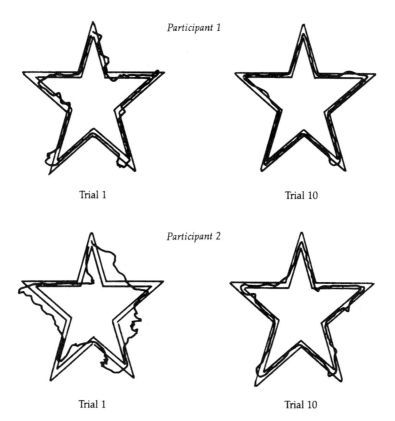

**FIGURE 7-1** Star-tracing performance of two participants on Trials 1 and 10

If they are willing to be less accurate, they can respond more quickly. This speed–accuracy tradeoff makes it necessary that both speed and accuracy be reported as dependent variables. If we are interested in the overall level of performance, one measure is useless without the other. For this reason, the better journals will not accept articles that report only speed or only accuracy of a choice-reaction-time response.

## Composite Dependent Variables

Although it is generally a good idea to report as many aspects of behavior as possible, this practice can make interpreting the results much more difficult. Suppose we have four dependent variables: One measure shows great improvement across conditions, two stay the same, and one decreases slightly. To say anything about the overall change in behavior, we need a way of combining our single dependent variables into a **composite dependent variable** that will give some indication of overall performance.

A number of areas in experimental psychology use composite dependent variables. One area is intelligence testing. The Wechsler Adult Intelligence Scale is an example of a composite dependent variable. The IQ (intelligence quotient) is a composite of two subscales, a verbal scale and a performance scale. The score on each of these is a composite made up of subtests. For example, the verbal score is derived from the scores on the following tests: general information, digit span, vocabulary, arithmetic, comprehension, and similarities. The idea behind intelligence testing is that it is useful to have a single measure that characterizes intelligence in general. Not all psychologists agree that a single number does adequately represent intelligence, of course, but the use of composite dependent variables is traditional in the psychology of testing.[7]

A second type of composite dependent variable combines several instances of a single measure. These instances are taken at different times or under different conditions. **Percent savings** is one such dependent variable used in memory research. Suppose, for example, that one group of people learned to ride a bicycle when they were young and then did not touch a bike again until they were 40 years old. We could have them relearn bike riding, practicing for a number of trials until they could stay on for a minute without touching the ground. Suppose it takes them seven trials to do this. We could compare this number to the number of trials it takes a second group of 40-year-olds who had never ridden a bike to stay on for a minute. Suppose it took this group an average of 14 trials. We could then calculate the percentage of trials saved by having learned to ride at an earlier age:

$$\% \text{ saved} = \frac{\text{Number of trials to learn} - \text{Number of trials to relearn}}{\text{Number of trials to learn}} \times 100$$

In our example:

$$\% \text{ saved} = \frac{14 - 7}{14} \times 100 = 50\%$$

Through this type of composite dependent variable, you can use a single number to show the effect of a change caused by the independent variable (past bike-riding experience).

It may not be clear to you yet how these composite dependent variables are derived or why they are appropriate measures, but you will become familiar with many others if you do research in certain areas of psychology. You may even find yourself making up your own composite variables someday.

## INDIRECT DEPENDENT VARIABLES

It is sometimes impossible to directly observe the behavior you are interested in, yet we know that the ROT (repeatable, observable, testable) test of science requires that the behavior we are studying be publicly observable. How, then, can we do scientific research in such areas as emotion,

---

[7] Stephen Jay Gould (1981) in his book *The Mismeasure of Man* takes the radical position that the use of a single number such as IQ as a measure of a person's worth has been a major misuse of science in this century. He believes that this composite dependent variable has been largely used to maintain social ranks and distinctions.

learning, or intelligence? We need an indirect variable that changes along with the internal behavior we are interested in.

## Physiological Measures

Probably the most popular types of indirect variables are **physiological measures,** which are based on the idea that if the behavior is a private event, such as an emotion, perhaps the physiology of the body will change along with the private event. Because modern technology allows us to observe changes in the physiology of the body, experimenters use these changes to infer what the private event must have been.

Of course, when we use physiological measures to infer internal states, we are assuming that a unique physiological pattern accurately reflects an internal state. For example, a polygraph, or lie detector, measures four physiological processes—respiratory rate, heart rate, blood pressure, and galvanic skin response.[8] The operator uses these measures to determine whether a person is telling the truth. Some people doubt whether the assumption behind using physiological measures is correct. For this reason, the results of a lie-detector test are admissible evidence in most courts only if both the plaintiff and the defendant agree to their use. And recently, federal law has severely restricted the use of polygraph tests in employment screening.

Other physiological measures become popular as researchers claim that they give an indication of some emotional state. They then lose favor as other investigators show that they can get the same type of physiological change with a different internal state. For example, an investigator named Hess at one point claimed that the diameter of a person's pupil increases when he or she is thinking pleasant thoughts and decreases when the person is thinking unpleasant things. For a while, the Madison Avenue advertising tycoons were so impressed that they used pupillary responses to choose magazine advertisements. Other investigators have since found that the diameter of the pupil is perhaps a better indication of the amount of information the person is processing than of the emotions the person is feeling (Johnson, 1971). Pupillometricians are no longer as welcome on Madison Avenue as they once were.

More recently, some investigators have reported that the characteristics of a person's voice can be used for "psychological stress evaluation." By tape-recording a voice, slowing it down, and measuring certain aspects of vocal frequencies, these investigators believe they can tell when people are under great stress, such as they would be when lying. These claims have not been supported by research, and this measure is now considered worthless by many researchers.

---

[8] In case you are not familiar with the term *galvanic skin response,* it is not a rash caused by handling too many garbage cans. It is a measure of how well the skin will carry a small electric current. Although not technically accurate, the reasoning goes something like this: Because wet skin carries electric current better than dry skin, a person who is "in a sweat" has a different galvanic skin response from one who is "cool and calm."

## SOME STIMULI BRING ABOUT
## A CHARACTERISTIC BRAIN WAVE.

In the past several decades, one of the fastest-growing areas of psychology is brain imaging, in which the activity of the brain can be measured as various tasks are being carried out. The early work often involved measuring general brain wave activity in the form of the electroencephalograph (EEG). This general pattern of activity, however, is not very useful other than for determining a person's overall level of arousal. More recently, researchers have been able to present a particular stimulus repeatedly and average the brain-wave activity from either the time of stimulus presentation or the time of response. With these event-related potentials (ERPs), small changes in the characteristic peaks and valleys of the EEG can be analyzed to determine what happens as changes are made in the stimulus presented or in the cognitive processing required by the task.

Even more recently researchers have been able to use physiological techniques to map activity in various locations in the brain as tasks are being carried out. For instance, positron-emission tomography (PET scan) allows researchers to determine blood flow to areas of the brain. For example, suppose I put you in a PET scan machine and had you view a particular word. In one condition I might simply have you read the word. In a second condition I might have you make a judgment about the meaning of the word. In each condition I can get a picture showing blood flow to various areas of the brain, and by subtracting the first picture from the second, I can infer which areas must be used to process the meaning of the word. Researchers have used not only PET scans to do this kind of work but also CAT scans, functional magnetic resonance imaging (fMRIs), and multiple-site EEGs. Great progress has been made in understanding the function of the human brain using these techniques.[9] As we learn more about what these measures can tell us, the use of physiological measures will undoubtedly increase.

---

[9] However, there are researchers who advise caution in the unquestioned acceptance of brain imaging as the royal road to understanding the brain (Van Orden & Paap, 1997).

## Behavioral Measures

Some **behavioral measures** can also be used as indirect dependent variables. As with physiological measures, changes in the way a person performs a behavioral task can reflect the person's internal state.

Indirect behavioral measures are particularly important in some areas of cognitive psychology. Cognitive researchers are interested in determining what goes on in the "black box" of the human mind during cognitive tasks such as reading or problem solving. Because all they really have to work with are the inputs to (stimuli) and outputs from (responses) the box, they have had to devise clever ways to infer what must be happening in the box. Suppose, for example, that we want to know how much information is processed in completing a particular task. If we assume that limited resources are available in the brain for processing cognitive information, one way to determine how much information is being processed is to measure how long it takes to make a response: The more information processed, the longer the response time will be. However, response time would give us only a single measure for the entire task and would tell us little about the processing required of subtasks such as encoding or response selection.

**Dual-task methodology** offers an indirect way of determining the processing requirements of a task while it is being performed. In this case, while the task of primary interest is being performed (the primary task), a second task (the secondary task) is also presented. The participant is instructed to do the primary task as well as possible and to use whatever resources are left over to do the secondary task. We can then measure performance on the secondary task and infer what the processing requirements of the primary task were. The better the performance on the secondary task, the fewer resources the primary task must have required. For example, the primary task might be to read a sentence. While the sentence is being read, tones are presented, and participants are instructed to press a button as quickly as possible whenever they hear a tone. We would infer that the slower the response to the tone, the more processing the sentence must be requiring at that time. With several trials, it would be possible to plot response times to the tones at various times while the sentence was being read and thus get a profile of processing resources required by the sentence (Martin & Kelly, 1974).

As with all indirect behavioral measures, the measure is only as good as the assumptions that underlie it. In the case of dual-task methodology, the primary assumption is that a single pool of processing resources provides resources for all cognitive tasks. Some researchers have questioned this basic assumption (Navon & Gopher, 1979; Wickens, 1984). Indeed, evidence is now pretty good that there are multiple pools of resources and that the type of pool used depends on whether the task is visual or aural, spatial or verbal, and so forth (Wickens, 1984). Even though some of the assumptions of dual-task methodology have been disputed, the technique still seems to provide a good measure of processing resources in many cases and is widely used.

Other indirect behavioral measures do not necessarily make the same assumptions as dual-task methodology. However, in general, the more indirect the measure, the more elaborate the underlying assumptions have to be, and the less confident we can be of our inferences. The advantage of indirect measures is that they do offer a way of investigating experimental questions for which we have no direct measures. As long as we are aware of the assumptions we are making when using indirect measures, they can be a valuable tool for helping us get an idea of the nature of otherwise unobservable events.

## Summary

In choosing an independent variable for your experiment, you must first specify an **operational definition** of the variable so that other experimenters will be able to go through the same operations when they conduct similar experiments. It is also important to choose the levels of your independent variable so that the **range** is large enough to show the experimental effect but small enough to be realistic. A trial run, or **pilot experiment,** will sometimes help you in this decision.

The dependent variable must also be operationally defined. In addition, we must be able to show that the dependent variable is **reliable** and **valid.** It is reliable if the same result is obtained every time a measurement is taken. When using test scores as a dependent variable, reliability of the test can be determined in several ways: **test–retest, alternative-form,** and **split-half.** The dependent variable is valid if it agrees with a commonly accepted standard. There are several ways of establishing the validity of a test: **face validity, content validity, predictive validity,** and **concurrent validity. Directly observable dependent variables** are relatively easy to measure, but deciding which **single dependent variable** to use is sometimes difficult. Some areas of research require that **multiple dependent variables** be reported or that dependent variables be combined to form a **composite dependent variable. Indirect dependent variables** are used when the behavior we are interested in is not publicly observable. **Physiological measures** may provide an indication of internal states, but they are often difficult to interpret. **Behavioral measures** such as **dual-task methodology** also offer the possibility of determining a participant's internal state.

## Find It on InfoTrac College Edition

In Chapter 7 we discuss operational definitions at length. Remember that these are ways of defining the independent and dependent variables by using the specific operations researchers would have to go through to repeat the experiments. Using InfoTrac College Edition, find journal articles describing three different experiments. For each experiment write down the authors' operational definitions for their independent and dependent variables. Do you think the authors did a good job of operationally defining these variables?

# 8

# How to Decide on a Between-Subjects versus Within-Subject Design

> There may be said to be two classes of people in the world: those who constantly divide the people of the world into two classes, and those who do not.
>
> ROBERT BENCHLEY

Now you have chosen an independent variable to manipulate and a dependent variable to measure. If everybody were exactly alike, you would need to take only a single person and do your experiment on that one individual. Fortunately for the sake of having an interesting world, but unfortunately for your task as an experimenter, we are not all alike. Because we are individually different, you will have to use a sample of participants and try to minimize the variability by doing statistical tricks such as taking means. However, you have some choice about what to do with the variability caused by differences among participants, depending on how you choose to assign them to the levels of your independent variable.

There are two basic ways to assign participants: You can expose each individual to only one level of the independent variable, or you can expose each individual to all levels. The first method is called a **between-subjects design** because the variable is manipulated between at least two subjects, or participants;[1] the second is called a **within-subject design** because the independent variable is manipulated within a single subject, or participant.[2] Table 8-1 illustrates the two methods of participant assignment for an experiment that has two levels of an independent variable. In the top case

---

[1] Up to this point in the book I have been following recent APA style changes by referring to those who participate in experiments as participants rather than as subjects. However, in this chapter the terminology gets a little awkward because the names for commonly used designs and statistical tests have not yet changed to keep up with the APA's *Publication Manual*. So I will still refer to the designs and tests by their accepted names (for instance, within-subject) but I will continue to refer to those being experimented on as participants. I hope we can all agree on a common terminology in the near future.

[2] Others have called within-subject designs *Treatment × Subject designs* or *repeated-measures designs* on the same subjects. Between-subjects designs are sometimes called *separate groups* or *independent groups* designs.

**TABLE 8-1**

The Assignment of Participants for a Between-Subjects
Experiment and a Within-Subject Experiment

| Between-subjects | Independent variable | |
| --- | --- | --- |
| | Level 1 | Level 2 |
| | Participant 1 | Participant 11 |
| | Participant 2 | Participant 12 |
| | . | . |
| | . | . |
| | . | . |
| | Participant 10 | Participant 20 |
| Within-subject | Independent variable | |
| | Level 1 | Level 2 |
| | Participant 1 | Participant 1 |
| | Participant 2 | Participant 2 |
| | . | . |
| | . | . |
| | . | . |
| | Participant 10 | Participant 10 |

a different set of ten participants is assigned to each level; in the bottom case each of the ten participants is assigned to both levels.

Suppose we want to do an experiment to determine whether taking rest breaks improves studying for students. In one condition we have students study certain material continuously for two hours. In the other condition students study for a total of two hours but take a five-minute break after every half hour. In either case they take a test at the end of the study period. Now, we could use a between-subjects design and have a different group

BETWEEN-SUBJECTS DESIGN: EACH
PARTICIPANT IS EXPOSED TO ONLY ONE LEVEL.

of randomly selected students assigned to each study condition. Or we could use a within-subject design, in which case the same group of students would study different material under each study condition. If we use different people in the two groups, we have not only individual differences within the groups but also a possible difference between groups. On the other hand, if we use the same students, we know that though there are still individual differences in studying ability between students, there should be no overall difference in studying ability between the groups— they are the same people. However, because we must use different study materials for the two conditions, there may be differences in the difficulty of these materials. Let's consider some of the advantages and disadvantages of the two types of designs in more detail.

# Between-Subjects Experiments

### ADVANTAGES

The biggest advantage of between-subjects designs is that exposure to one of the levels of the independent variable cannot contaminate the participant's behavior under other levels. Because each participant is exposed to only one level, you can effectively ignore the other levels for that participant.

Earlier in the book I described an experiment my students and I did in which we were testing the availability heuristic by having participants list three advantages of nuclear power generation, three disadvantages, or three advantages and three disadvantages. After listing these, participants indicated how favorable they were to nuclear power by marking a scale. This experiment used a between-subjects design, so each participant listed three advantages *or* three disadvantages *or* both. What if we had used a within-subject design? In that case each participant would list three advantages and then give a favorability rating, *and* then list three disadvantages and give a rating, *and* then list three advantages and three disadvantages and give a rating. Would this design accomplish what we wanted? Remember that the reason we expected the favorability rating to be affected by listing advantages or disadvantages is that by making a list, those reasons listed were expected to become more available, more easily accessed in the mind of the participant. But once an advantage has become more available, how long does it take to become less available? Indeed, in this case if we had used a within-subject design, once participants had been exposed to the first two conditions, listing three advantages and three disadvantages, they would already have been exposed to the third condition, listing both.

For many experiments, such as the one just described, it is really logically impossible to use a within-subject design because we cannot reverse the effects of former exposure to other levels of the independent variable. In other cases, it may be logically possible to reverse this exposure, but, as we will discuss later in this chapter, the design can become much more complicated. In the end, even with sophisticated designs we are sometimes not sure that we have completely counteracted the effects of prior exposure. Because between-subjects designs do not have this problem, they are sometimes preferred. There are some additional practical advantages for doing between-subjects experiments.

Because each participant performs under only one level of the independent variable in a between-subjects experiment, we can collect more data at that level during a single experimental session. Because participants are likely to get tired or lose interest in what they are doing, it is easier to keep the total experimental time short for each. You can also avoid bringing participants back for more than one experimental session, which is an advantage because the number of individuals who actually complete an experiment tends to decrease dramatically with each additional session required.

## DISADVANTAGES

The biggest disadvantage of a between-subjects design is that the groups assigned to each level of the independent variable might not be equivalent. Whenever groups are formed with different people, it is *possible* that the groups will be quite different. For example, in the experiment asking whether watching violent TV causes aggression in children, it is possible that all the children assigned to the violent TV group might come from dysfunctional families with a history of abuse, whereas all the children in the nonviolent TV group might come from wonderfully healthy families. But if random assignment of children to groups is done, it is not *probable* that this would happen.

When between-subjects designs are used, participants are usually assigned to the groups in a random fashion. This assignment can be done in a number of ways, such as using slips of paper drawn from a hat, tossing coins, or selecting from random-number tables such as the one in Appendix C. People who have little experience with psychological experimentation or statistics seem to have little confidence in random processes. They often think that randomization is the equivalent of being haphazard or sloppy, and they believe that even with large groups there are likely to be sizable differences in behavior. With experience and an increased understanding of statistical sampling, researchers come to have considerably more confidence in random assignment of participants. For although randomness may seem like the ultimate in lack of orderliness, it is at least unbiased. So it allows you to assign participant variability to the groups in an unbiased fashion. Especially for large groups, the likelihood that the groups are quite different on any behavioral dimension is rather small. On top of that, the statistical tests that you do in analyzing your data take potential differences due to random assignment into account. Random assignment of participants for between-subjects experiments is actually quite effective in removing potential bias among groups.

# Within-Subject Experiments

Although within-subject designs are by no means the best choice for all experiments, they do offer a number of advantages.

## PRACTICAL ADVANTAGES

One practical advantage of a within-subject experiment is immediately obvious from Table 8–1: Fewer participants are required. If $N$ participants[3] are required to give you an adequate number of data points at any level of a within-subject experiment, then $N \times 2$ are required for a two-level between-subjects experiment, $N \times 3$ for a three-level between-subjects experiment, and so on.

In many cases, increasing the number of participants also substantially increases the total time required for an experiment. For example, if your experiment requires that you pretrain individuals to do a basic task before you expose them to the experimental manipulation, you will have to pretrain twice as many in a two-level between-subjects experiment as in a within-subject experiment. Suppose you want to know if requiring people to remember a certain number of words will interfere with their ability to perform a complex tracking task, which in itself takes several hours to learn. If you add levels to your independent variable (number of words presented for memory), you add no more pretraining time in a within-subject experiment. But in a between-subjects experiment, you increase the number of participants and thereby the pretraining time.

It is common to conduct several practice trials at the beginning of an experiment, a practice that also adds time to an experiment the more participants you have. These practice trials are designed to minimize warmup effects—that is, a fast improvement during the first few trials as participants get into a state of general readiness.

In addition to the inconvenience of using a large number of participants for a between-subjects experiment, at times the number of participants available to you will be limited, especially when they must meet certain requirements. For example, you may need pilots, race-car drivers, or ballet dancers for certain experiments. Or you may want participants to be afflicted with some disorder like psychosis, color blindness, or left-handedness.[4] In such cases, you may not be able to find enough people who meet these requirements to use a between-subjects design, and you will need to rely on a within-subject experiment.

---

[3] I am using $N$ here to refer to any given number of participants, such as 10 or 20, for a particular experiment.
[4] Just kidding, lefties. (This was just a *sinister* joke!)

**TABLE 8-2**
Individual Times to Run the 100-Yard Dash for Two Groups
of Randomly Chosen Men

| Men wearing 7-mm spikes | Time (in seconds) | Men wearing 13-mm spikes | Time (in seconds) |
|---|---|---|---|
| Mike | 11.7 | Don | 15.7 |
| Bob | 18.2 | Hector | 13.4 |
| Homer | 12.2 | Ron | 18.0 |
| George | 15.4 | Tom | 12.8 |
| Harry | 15.8 | Steve | 13.6 |
| Gordon | 13.2 | Dale | 19.0 |
| John | 13.7 | Pete | 16.2 |
| Bill | 19.1 | Juan | 11.9 |
| Randy | 12.9 | Dan | 14.6 |
| Tim | 16.0 | Paul | 18.0 |

Mean for 7-mm men = 14.82 sec.          Mean for 13-mm men = 15.32 sec.
Mean difference = 0.5 sec.

## STATISTICAL ADVANTAGES

In addition to their greater efficiency, within-subject designs can be preferable for statistical reasons. We will take a brief look at statistics in Chapter 12, but I will mention a few concepts here.

In an inferential statistical test, experimenters attempt to infer whether any differences they find among the data samples collected at the various levels of the independent variable are due to real differences in behavior of some larger population or due to chance. To make this inference, most of these tests compare the differences between the average performance at the two levels with an estimate of how variable the performance is within each of the levels. A statistical test is more likely to call a difference *real* if the difference between levels is large or if the estimated variability within levels is small. An example will show you how logical this principle is.

Suppose a track-shoe manufacturer wanted to know whether to sell shoes with 7-mm spikes or 13-mm spikes[5] to the 100-yard dash[6] runners on a men's track team. To test these shoes, the manufacturer could randomly choose ten men from a college campus to wear one type of shoe and ten additional men from the same campus to wear the other type. The men in the two groups would probably be variable in their times to run the dash—from the 300-pound, 38-year-old ex-bartender to the 125-pound, 19-year-old halfback. Their scores might look something like those in Table 8–2. If you calculate a mean[7] for the two groups, you find that those

[5] 0.276 in. and 0.512 in.
[6] 91.44 m.
[7] As will be discussed in more detail in Chapter 12 and Appendix A, a mean is the sum of the individual scores divided by the number of scores that were added.

wearing 7-mm spikes average 0.5 seconds faster than those wearing 13-mm spikes. Examining the times for the two groups, would this difference convince you that the shorter spikes were better for running the 100-yard dash?

Now suppose the manufacturer decided to do a second experiment, using members of the men's track team this time, and randomly assigned them to the 7-mm and 13-mm groups. Their scores might look something like those in Table 8-3. Again there is a 0.5-second average advantage for the runners wearing the shorter spikes. Would these data convince you that the shorter spikes were better?

**TABLE 8-3**

Individual Times to Run the 100-Yard Dash for Two Groups of Randomly Chosen Track-Team Members

| Men wearing 7-mm spikes | Time (in seconds) | Men wearing 13-mm spikes | Time (in seconds) |
|---|---|---|---|
| Art | 10.6 | Rob | 10.8 |
| Simon | 10.3 | Frank | 11.0 |
| Nick | 10.3 | Walt | 10.8 |
| Daryl | 10.2 | Gary | 10.6 |
| Ralph | 10.4 | Ken | 10.8 |
| Will | 10.0 | Bryan | 10.7 |
| Reuben | 10.2 | Dick | 10.6 |
| Ed | 10.1 | Stan | 10.7 |
| Fred | 10.3 | Rich | 10.7 |
| Wayne | 10.4 | Mark | 11.1 |

Mean for 7-mm men = 10.28 sec.     Mean for 13-mm men = 10.78 sec.

Mean difference = 0.5 sec.

Undoubtedly, you would be more likely to accept the difference found in the second experiment as being a real difference. Because the scores in the second experiment are less variable, you probably feel that the difference found there is less likely to be due entirely to chance variation.

Most of the variability in the first experiment's scores was apparently due to large individual differences in the men's ability to run the 100-yard dash, regardless of the shoes. In the second experiment, much of the variability due to individual differences among the runners was eliminated by choosing runners who were more alike.

How could we make the participants even more alike in the two groups? By using the same participants, some first, some second! You should be able to see why a within-subject experiment having only one group gives you a statistical advantage here: It is the ultimate way to minimize the individual differences between participants. By using a within-subject design, both you and statistical tests are more likely to be convinced that any differences in performance found between the levels of the independent variable are real differences.[8]

## DISADVANTAGES

Because there are so many practical and statistical advantages to using within-subject designs, why should we ever use between-subjects designs? Unfortunately, the within-subject design also carries some rather serious disadvantages. Although their position is debatable, some experimenters would go so far as to say these disadvantages make within-subject experiments next to worthless: "The day should come then when no reputable psychologist will use a within-subject design, except for a special purpose, without combining it with a separate groups [between-subjects] design" (Poulton, 1973).

As we discussed under advantages of between-subjects designs the basic problem is that once participants are exposed to one level of the independent variable, there is no way to change them back into the individuals they were before being exposed. The exposure has done something irreversible, so we can no longer treat them as pure, uncontaminated, and naive. Because the way participants are changed depends upon the order in which they are exposed to the levels of the independent variable, these are called order effects. An **order effect** in a within-subject experiment occurs when the behavior resulting from a level of the independent variable depends upon the order in which that level was presented. Order effects can be caused by a number of factors.

One way order can affect behavior is through learning. That is, what participants have learned during exposure to an earlier level of the independent variable can affect later behavior. For example, suppose we want to know whether it takes someone longer to type on a standard QWERTY[9] keyboard or on a newly designed keyboard where the more frequently used letter keys are under the fingers when they are in resting position. We decide that because there are likely to be large individual differences in typing ability, we will use a within-subject design. We take ten people and find out how many hours they have to practice to type 30 words per minute on a standard keyboard. We then switch them to the newly designed keyboard and find out how many hours they have to practice to type 30 words per minute on it. We find it takes them an average of 45 hours of practice to

---

[8] If you have a bent toward statistical rigor, you may have shuddered and blanched at my attempt to make the logic of inferential statistics intuitively palatable. I'll be a little more rigorous in Chapter 12. But not much.

[9] The QWERTY keyboard is named after the first six letters in the upper letter row of the standard keyboard. Studies have shown that there are more optimal arrangements for the keys that would make typing a bit faster. However, the effort required to retrain all the typists who already know the QWERTY system makes it highly unlikely that any new system would be widely adopted.

reach criterion on the QWERTY keyboard but only 2 hours on the new keyboard. Can we conclude that using the new keyboard is much easier? Obviously not.

During the first part of the experiment, in addition to learning the specific skill of using a QWERTY keyboard, the participants were also learning a general typing skill. The general skill is confounded with the specific skill. By the time they typed on the new keyboard, their general typing skill was undoubtedly at a higher level than when they started the experiment. Because the QWERTY keyboard always occurred in the first ordered position, it took longer to learn because both a general skill and a specific skill were being learned. Because the new keyboard always occurred in the second ordered position, it took less time to learn because the general skill had already been learned for the most part. Learning is one of the most common order effects. However, there are others, such as fatigue and maturational development. Any time an effect changes systematically during the course of an experiment, we need to be aware that order effects are possible and be careful to keep our independent variable from being confounded by order.

Because of this disadvantage of within-subject designs, they are used far less frequently in some areas of psychology than others. For instance, investigators who study learning, memory, and some areas of social psychology, such as attitude formation, expect to make long-lasting changes in their participants by the very nature of the experiment. You cannot tell someone, "OK, now forget that list of words I just had you memorize for ten trials" and expect them to do so, or, "Change your attitude back to where it was before you read that persuasive bit of propaganda." In these research areas, participants are usually irretrievably contaminated by exposure to a level of the independent variable. However, there are other areas of research in which prior exposure has little effect. For instance, if we were studying people's ability to distinguish between the intensity of two tones, it would be unlikely that exposure to a particular intensity difference would affect their ability to distinguish a second difference. In this case, and for many other experiments in areas such as sensation and perception, within-subject designs are appropriate and are often used.

## COUNTERBALANCING

One way to minimize an order effect like learning is to **counterbalance.** Essentially, when you counterbalance, you admit that a potential confounding order effect is present. You also admit that you cannot control it or randomize it out of existence. So you attempt to distribute an equal amount of the confounding effect to each level of your independent variable. In this way, you hope, the order effect will counterbalance itself and not bias any effect that is due to the independent variable.

To illustrate the concept of counterbalancing, I will use scales as shown in Figure 8–1. For a moment, let us pretend that we are omnipotent and

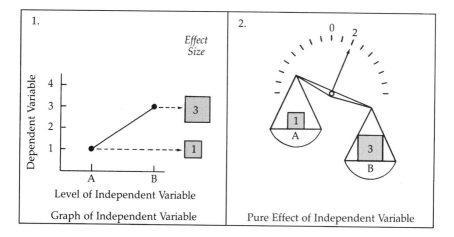

**FIGURE 8-1** The graph in panel 1 shows the effect of the two levels, A and B, of the independent variable on the dependent variable. The scales in panel 2 indicate that the pure unconfounded effect of the independent variable is 2 units.

know the actual size of effects due to the independent variable and the confounding variable. If we carried out a perfect experiment presenting two levels of our independent variable, A and B, we might find the result illustrated in the graph in panel 1 of Figure 8–1. We are assuming that no variables are affecting the result other than the independent variable. The size of the effect on the dependent variable is 1 unit for level A and 3 units for level B. Because these quantities will be put on the scales, I have converted them to weights. By placing the weights on the scales in panel 2, we see that the pure unconfounded effect of the independent variable is 2.

Because we are using a within-subject design and cannot present both levels of the independent variable at the same time, we obviously must have several trials. Suppose that some confounding effect, like learning, increases with each trial, as shown in panel 1 of Figure 8–2. As you can see, on trial 1 the effect of the confounding variable is 1 unit on the dependent variable, and by trial 4, it is 4 units. Again the effect size is converted to weights. What we wish to do is distribute these weights so that the scales are counterbalanced. In this way, the scales will show no bias when the independent variable is added.

One of the more frequently used counterbalancing schemes is called **ABBA counterbalancing.** The A and B, as in our example, stand for the two levels of any independent variable, and the sequence represents how the levels are assigned to trials. Thus, level A would be presented on trial 1, B on trial 2, B on trial 3, and A on trial 4. Each participant receives all trials.

Panel 2 of Figure 8-2 illustrates what happens when the weights for trials 1 and 4 are placed on the A side of the scales and those for trials 2 and

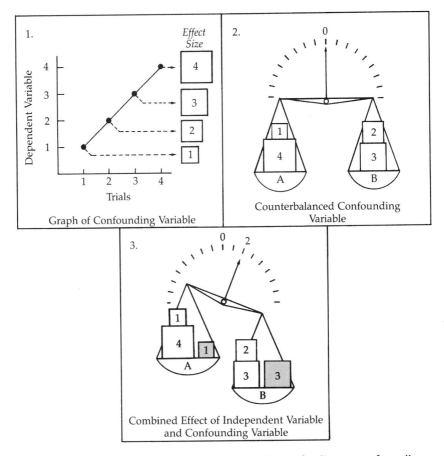

**FIGURE 8-2** The graph in panel 1 shows the effect of a linear confounding variable on the dependent variable. The scales in panel 2 indicate that an ABBA ordering of the independent variable has successfully counterbalanced the confounding variable. When the shaded weights representing the effects of the independent variable are added in panel 3, a correct net effect of 2 units is found.

3 on the B side. The scales are counterbalanced. When we also add the shaded weights representing the effects of the independent variable, the net combined effect is 2, the original pure effect of the independent variable. Basically, this unbiased outcome is what we try to achieve with all counterbalancing schemes.

Before you wax too ecstatic over the beauty of counterbalancing, permit me to tell you that counterbalancing schemes are based on certain assumptions, and when these assumptions are violated, the beauty turns into a beast.

One assumption of ABBA counterbalancing is that the confounding effect is linear, that it forms a straight line. To illustrate what can happen when it is not, let's return to our weights. Suppose the confounding effect

looks like that shown in panel 1 of Figure 8-3. In fact, learning is the most likely candidate for confounding, and most learning curves look a lot like this one; an initial large increase in performance is followed by progressively smaller changes. Converting to weights and stacking the weights according to an ABBA design, we can see in panel 2 that the scales are not counterbalanced. They are biased by 3 units toward the B side. When the weights representing the independent variable are added in panel 3, the net effect is 5 units rather than the 2 units we omnipotently know it should be.

Under certain conditions, ABBA counterbalancing not only fails to correct for a confounding variable but can compound the confounding problem. An example of this is shown in Figure 8-4. The confounding effect first improves performance, then degrades it. Combining the effect of learning with the effect of fatigue could cause such a function. I will let you work out the size of the bias caused by the unbalanced confounding variable.

We have seen that ABBA counterbalancing can eliminate the effects of a confounding variable in within-subject experiments, but only if the confounding effect is linear. If the effect is nonlinear, we must choose a different counterbalancing technique or else design a between-subjects experiment.

An ABBA-counterbalancing technique attempts to counterbalance order effects in a completely within-subject manner: The same participants get both the AB order and the BA order. Other counterbalancing techniques treat order as a between-subjects variable by counterbalancing order across individuals. In the simplest two-level case, one group of participants would receive AB and a second group, BA. The "A" data from groups one and two would be averaged, as would the "B" data from both groups. If you use this method, the confounding effect does not have to be linear. How-

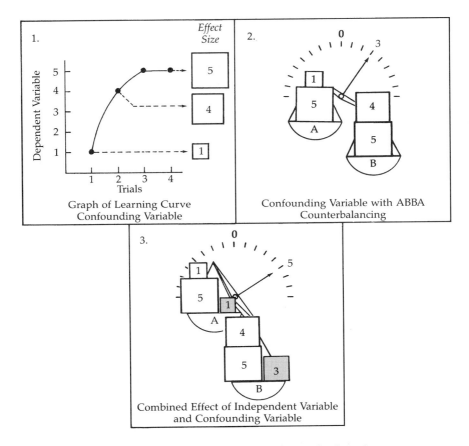

**FIGURE 8-3** The graph in panel 1 shows the effects of a learning curve confounding variable on the dependent variable. The scales in panel 2 indicate that an ABBA ordering has not successfully counterbalanced the confounding variable; the scales are biased 3 units toward B. When the weights representing the effects of the independent variable are added in panel 3, the net effect of 5 units overestimates the effect of the independent variable by 3 units.

ever, you are still making the assumption that the effect of having B follow A is just the reverse of the effect of having A follow B (Poulton & Freeman, 1966). This assumption is sometimes called an assumption of **symmetrical transfer.**[10] When this assumption is violated and you get asymmetrical transfer instead, this type of counterbalancing is not effective.

Consider an experiment in which asymmetrical transfer was found. The investigator was interested in the effect of noise on complex performance (Aldridge, 1978; Poulton, 1979). The people were first given a consonant-vowel-consonant trigram (for example, DOF) to remember for 16 seconds. While doing this memory task, they also listened to a series of "Bs," spoken

---

[10] Sometimes it is called **nondifferential transfer.**

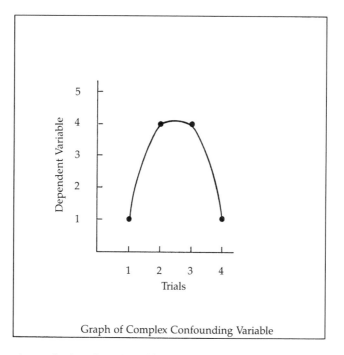

Graph of Complex Confounding Variable

**FIGURE 8-4** A graph showing the effect of a complex confounding variable on a dependent variable. Such a function could be caused by learning and fatigue.

one per second, to detect occasional "Ps." In the noise condition a loud, continuous, hissing noise was also present. To counterbalance for order effects, one group received a block of quiet trials followed by a block of noise trials (AB), while a second group received the reverse order (BA).

You can see the results of the experiment in Figure 8-5. The group members exposed first to the quiet trials did well at remembering the trigrams. However, when transferred to the noise condition, their performance dropped drastically. The other group members performed poorly in noise, as expected. Notice, however, that their performance improved only a little when transferred to quiet. The magnitude of the effect was 31 percentage points for the quiet-first group and 10 percentage points for the noise-first group. We would expect the same size of effect if symmetrical transfer were present. What is the reason for the finding of asymmetrical transfer?

Apparently the two groups learned to do the task in different ways. The quiet-first group probably learned to use an *echoic store* to retain the words. An echoic store is sort of like an echo in the head that automatically reverberates for a short time after the auditory stimulus disappears.[11] But like an echo, a subsequent loud auditory stimulus can cover it up. Although

---

[11] Echoic store is what the husband uses to dredge up a memory when he is reading the paper and his wife says, "Did you hear what I just said?"

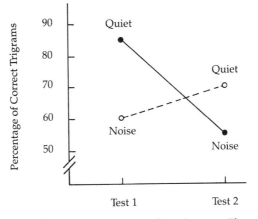

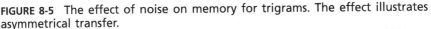

**FIGURE 8-5** The effect of noise on memory for trigrams. The effect illustrates asymmetrical transfer.

source: Adapted from "Levels of Processing in Speech Perception," by J. W. Aldridge, 1978, Experiment 4, *Journal of Experimental Psychology: Human Perception and Performance, 4,* 164–177.

the echoic strategy worked well when it was quiet, the quiet-first group probably had to change to a new strategy when noise was added, using an *articulatory store.* In this case they repeated the trigram to themselves or at least activated the program that moves the muscles required for articulation.[12] Upon switching to this strategy their performance dropped. Members of the noise-first group apparently learned the task using the articulation strategy. When switched to quiet, they probably maintained this less efficient strategy, and their performance improved a bit without the noise. Although this explanation is somewhat speculative, some additional data I am not bothering you with support the speculation.

One additional example might help you understand asymmetrical transfer. Suppose you are interested in the effects of drinking alcohol on complex motor performance, such as driving a race car in a virtual reality video game. You have members of one group consume the equivalent of three drinks during each of the first three, one-hour sessions that they drive the race car. They then switch to racing the car sober for the next three sessions. To control for order, you have a second group do the reverse, going from sober to inebriated. You expect that each group will score fewer points on the video machine when under the influence of alcohol. Depending on the specific racing conditions, you may be amazed to find that members of the alcohol-first group actually drop in performance initially when switching to the sober condition and that they never show as large an effect of the alcohol as those in the other group. Such an outcome would be an example of asymmetrical transfer due to state-dependent learning. When we learn a skill in a particular state (not Idaho, but sober or inebriated) we

---

[12] Essentially, mumbling to yourself.

**TABLE 8-4**

Completely Counterbalanced Design for Two-, Three-,
and Four-Level Independent Variables

| Two levels of independent variable | | Three levels of independent variable | |
|---|---|---|---|
| *Number* | *Order of levels* | *Number* | *Order of levels* |
| 1 | AB* | 1 | ABC |
| 2 | BA | 2 | ACB |
| | | 3 | BCA |
| | | 4 | BAC |
| | | 5 | CAB |
| | | 6 | CBA |

| Four levels of independent variable | | | |
|---|---|---|---|
| *Number* | *Order of levels* | *Number* | *Order of levels* |
| 1 | ABCD | 13 | CABD |
| 2 | ABDC | 14 | CADB |
| 3 | ACBD | 15 | CBAD |
| 4 | ACDB | 16 | CBDA |
| 5 | ADCB | 17 | CDAB |
| 6 | ADBC | 18 | CDBA |
| 7 | BACD | 19 | DABC |
| 8 | BADC | 20 | DACB |
| 9 | BCAD | 21 | DBAC |
| 10 | BCDA | 22 | DBCA |
| 11 | BDAC | 23 | DCAB |
| 12 | BDCA | 24 | DCBA |

*The letters *A, B, C,* and *D* represent the levels.

tend to perform best when put back into that state. Maybe you know someone who shoots pool better after a couple of beers; that's state-dependent
learning. In our experiment, state-dependent learning could cause asymmetrical transfer effects similar to those I have described. When you get
such asymmetrical transfer, no form of counterbalancing can save a within-
subject design.

As you add more levels to your independent variable, you increase the
complexity of a complete counterbalancing procedure. In a completely
counterbalanced design, every level has to occur an equal number of times
and also follow every other level an equal number of times. Table 8-4 shows
completely counterbalanced designs for two-, three-, and four-level experiments. As you can see, **complete counterbalancing** can become a monu-
mental task when you have a large number of levels or many independent
variables. With large experimental designs, it is possible to assign levels
randomly or to randomize within blocks, as described in Chapter 2. You
can also sometimes use a technique called **partial counterbalancing,** in

Order of Presentation

|  | 1st | 2nd | 3rd | 4th |
|---|---|---|---|---|
| Participant 1 | **Chicago** | `Courier` | Geneva | Times |
| Participant 2 | `Courier` | Times | **Chicago** | Geneva |
| Participant 3 | Times | Geneva | `Courier` | **Chicago** |
| Participant 4 | Geneva | **Chicago** | Times | `Courier` |

**FIGURE 8-6** A balanced Latin Square for ordering the presentation of four print fonts to at least four readers

which you choose only some of the orders while making sure that each level occurs the same number of times in each position.

A partial counterbalancing scheme that is often used with independent variables having more than two levels is a **Latin Square.** A Latin Square assures that each level appears at every position in the order equally often. There are many possible Latin Squares for a given number of levels of the independent variable. Perhaps the most useful of these is a balanced Latin Square, in which not only does each level appear at every position in the order equally often but each condition also precedes and follows each of the other conditions equally often. Suppose that we wanted to know how long it took people to read standardized paragraphs presented on a computer screen in four different print fonts: Chicago, Courier, Geneva, and Times, and we were afraid that the order of presentation might confound the experiment. Figure 8-6 illustrates a balanced Latin Square for this experiment. Note that each of the four print fonts appears in each position across the four participants. Taking Courier by way of example, also note, moving down the rows, that it is preceded by Chicago, nothing, Geneva, and Times, and followed by Geneva, Times, Chicago, and nothing. Thus, we have satisfied the requirements of the design. In order for a Latin Square to work, you must have at least as many participants as levels of the independent variable and, generally, some multiple of that number. This form of partial counterbalancing takes care of most of the potential confounding variables due to order or asymmetrical transfer, but it leaves a few possible subtle confounds due to possible interactions between order and asymmetrical transfer. A fully counterbalanced design is still best, but if you have too few participants, a Latin Square does pretty well.

You have seen that a counterbalancing technique is often necessary to minimize the sequential confounding effects found in some within-subject experiments. At this point, you should also be aware of the assumptions underlying the technique you are using and should try to use a counter-balancing technique that allows you to meet the assumptions. However, in some experiments, such as those having asymmetrical transfer, it may be impossible to meet the assumptions, and you will have no choice but to use a between-subjects design. One other potential disadvantage of within-subject designs cannot be corrected by counterbalancing and may force you to use a between-subjects design—**range effects.**

## RANGE EFFECTS

Suppose you are the purchasing agent for a widget factory and you are ordering a new set of working tables for widget assembly. You must choose the height of the tables, and you want to make sure that the tables are the right height to maximize production. You decide to do an experiment to determine the correct height. You take one group of workers, Group A, and have them sit at tables of varying heights while you count how many blocks they can turn over during a three-minute period. The table heights you choose are −10, −6, −2, +2, +6, and +10 inches from elbow height. Having read this book, you realize that you could have a problem with sequential-ordering effects, so you carefully counterbalance the order of table heights.

After you have completed the experiment, your boss suggests that she would like to see you test some tables of even lower height. You design another experiment just like the first, except this time you have Group B use tables of the following heights: −18, −14, −10, −6, −2, and +2 inches from elbow height.

Figure 8-7 shows the actual results of this experiment. The startling thing about the results is that the best table height is different for the two groups. Group A performed best at about elbow height and Group B at 6 inches below elbow height. Why is this? In learning a task like turning over blocks at a table of a given height, people also learn a skill that is useful for other tasks, like turning over blocks on a table of a different height. The more alike the two table heights, the better people can transfer the skill from one height to the other. This is simply a basic principle of learning. So if we consider the block-turning experiment to be a learning experiment, we would expect workers to perform best at the table height that is most like all the other table heights used in the experiment. Table 8-5 shows the average number of inches of difference in height between each table height and the other five heights presented for each group. For example, the dif-ference between the +10 condition for Group A and the −10 condition is 20, between +10 and −6 is 16, and so on. Adding all difference scores between +10 and the other five conditions for Group A and dividing by 5 produces a mean of 12. If we expect the highest rate of work for the task that is most similar to the other conditions presented in each experiment, we could do a fairly good job of predicting Figure 8-7 from Table 8-5. You can now see

**TABLE 8-5**
Average Number of Inches of Difference between Each Table Height
and the Other Five Heights Presented

| | Table Height | | | | | | | |
|---|---|---|---|---|---|---|---|---|
| | −18 | −14 | −10 | −6 | −2 | +2 | +6 | +10 |
| Group A | | | 12 | 8.5 | 7.2 | 7.2 | 8.5 | 12 |
| Group B | 12 | 8.5 | 7.2 | 7.2 | 8.5 | 12 | | |

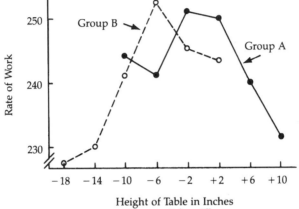

**FIGURE 8-7** The effect of the range of table heights presented on the number of blocks turned during 3-minute trials. The range effect due to this
within-subject design is seen in the superior performance at the middle
heights for each group.
SOURCE: From "Series Effects in Motor Performance Studies," by J. E. Kennedy and J.
Landesman, 1963, *Journal of Applied Psychology, 47,* 202–205. Copyright 1963 by the
American Psychological Association. Reprinted by permission.

why it is called a range effect; people tend to have the highest level of performance in the middle of the range of levels presented because transfer
of learning is highest in the middle of the range. Range effects can result
from a within-subject experiment whenever stimuli or responses can be
put in a consistent order. Poulton (1973) has noted examples of range
effects throughout most areas of experimental psychology.

Although range effects cause Poulton and others to warn against
within-subject experiments, other investigators argue that in many cases
within-subject experiments are preferable. Greenwald (1976), for instance,
has pointed out that a range effect is simply a **context effect.** The participant comes to the experiment with a context already established. In the
table example, for instance, people are already experienced at using certain table heights. He suggests that repeatedly presenting an individual
with only one level of the independent variable, as in a between-subjects
experiment, will not eliminate context. As repeated trials are given at a

single level of the independent variable, a new context develops—the context of the single level. For these reasons, Greenwald claims that context effects cannot be avoided by using either type of design. He suggests that a more important question to ask in choosing a design is to what situation you plan to generalize your results.

For example, in our violent-television experiment, it could be more artificial to repeatedly expose a child to one level of violence (a between-subjects design) than to expose the child to several different levels. Because we would like to generalize the results to a real-life situation having many levels, perhaps we should choose a within-subject design. That is, the range used in the experiment should approximate the range found in the situation to which we are generalizing. As an experimenter, then, although you should be aware that range effects could alter the outcome of your experiment, you should choose the design that allows you to generalize your results to the appropriate situation.

So which are preferable—between-subjects designs, as claimed by Poulton, or within-subject designs, as claimed by Greenwald and some other researchers who do only within-subject designs and single-subject designs? A reasonable position would be that it depends upon the particular experiment you are planning. As we have seen, in some cases,  such as in the study of attitude formation and some areas of memory, it is virtually impossible to use within-subject designs. There are also areas of research in which the most sophisticated counterbalancing schemes may not be successful in correcting order effects such as asymmetrical transfer. In other cases, such as when a therapeutic technique has been found to be successful, it can even be unethical to use within-subject designs that may reverse the beneficial effects of the therapy. On the other hand, using a participant as his or her own control is a powerful experimental procedure, one that reduces variability to such an extent that we can clearly see small but important effects of experimental manipulations. And some areas of research are relatively immune to problems, such as order effects, found in within-subject designs: for example, in memory research the study of retention interval or memory loads, in perception research the study of illusions or sound localization, and in attention research the study of priming. In these cases the most efficient and cleanest experiments use within-subject designs. So as a researcher the best thing you can do is choose a design that best fits the type of research you are doing.

## Matching

One way to gain the advantages of a between-subjects experiment yet avoid some of the problems of individual differences between groups of participants is to use a **matched-groups design.** This simply means that an attempt is made to have the same kinds of participants assigned to each level of your independent variable. In the typical between-subjects experiment, you hope that the individuals assigned to each level are pretty much alike, and you have randomization on your side. Random assignment makes it likely that the groups will be essentially equivalent, and this becomes more likely the larger the groups. However, because this is a random process, occasionally those assigned to each group will be quite different, and you may incorrectly attribute differences in their behavior to the independent variable. That is, your experiment may be confounded by group differences. By matching groups, you can minimize this possibility. On what basis can you match the groups?

MATCHED-GROUPS DESIGN

You must match your groups on a variable that is highly correlated with the dependent variable. In our track-shoe experiment, it would be a waste of time to match the two groups of runners on the basis of IQ scores. Fast minds are not related to fast feet. However, we could have each runner run the 100-yard dash in tennis shoes first and then make up pairs of subjects: the two fastest, the two next fastest, and so on. We could then flip a coin to assign one member of each pair to each of the track-shoe conditions. In this way, we know that the groups are somewhat equivalent in running speed prior to introducing the independent variable. In this experiment, we are assuming a large correlation between tennis-shoe running times and track-shoe running times, because the lower the correlation between the matching variable and the dependent variable, the less we gain by matching.

Through matching, we decrease the probability of being wrong when we say that the independent variable caused a change in behavior. Matching can also provide a statistical advantage, in that when matched groups are used, a statistical test is more likely to say that a given difference in the scores of the dependent variable is due to the independent variable rather than to chance. That is, the tests are more sensitive to any difference associated with the independent variable.

To illustrate this principle, the column on the left of Table 8-6 again lists the randomly chosen men who ran the dash in track shoes with 7-mm spikes (from Table 8-2). In order to match participants, suppose we also had these men run the race in tennis shoes. The tennis-shoe scores are in parentheses. To get a matching group, we now have many more men run the

**TABLE 8-6**
Individual Times to Run the 100-Yard Dash for Two Matched Groups

| Men wearing 7-mm spikes | Time (in seconds) | | Men wearing 13-mm spikes | Time (in seconds) | |
|---|---|---|---|---|---|
| Mike | (12.2) | 11.7 | Vic | (12.2) | 12.2 |
| Homer | (12.8) | 12.2 | Jack | (12.8) | 12.6 |
| Randy | (13.5) | 12.9 | Barry | (13.5) | 13.5 |
| Gordon | (14.0) | 13.2 | Larry | (14.0) | 13.8 |
| John | (14.3) | 13.7 | Jess | (14.3) | 14.2 |
| George | (16.1) | 15.4 | Stuart | (16.1) | 15.8 |
| Harry | (16.7) | 15.8 | Harvey | (16.7) | 16.2 |
| Tim | (17.0) | 16.0 | Sid | (17.0) | 16.6 |
| Bob | (18.7) | 18.2 | Pat | (18.7) | 18.7 |
| Bill | (19.7) | 19.1 | Joe | (19.7) | 19.6 |

Mean for 7-mm men = 14.82 sec.                Mean for 13-mm men = 15.32 sec.
Mean difference = 0.5 sec.

dash in tennis shoes, and we choose as participants those who have the same times as the men in our original group. These new participants are listed in the column on the right, along with their tennis-shoe times in parentheses. Note that we have been able to eliminate any differences in groups for tennis-shoe scores; the scores are exactly the same. Now we have the new group run the race in 13-mm spikes and find that, as in our previous examples, there is an average 0.5-second increase in the mean running time. Would you be more likely to believe that the difference in length of spikes caused the 0.5-second average difference in running times in the original random-groups experiment or in this matched-groups experiment? Statistical tests make decisions in much the same way you do.[13]

One disadvantage in doing matched-groups experiments is that it takes longer to match the groups, so that experiments sometimes require two sessions, one for the pretest and one for the experiment itself. If you are planning to use many participants anyway, the chances of getting large differences between groups using random assignment are small, and the hassle of matching might not be worth the effort.

A final consideration is that the matching process itself may cause some problems. We assumed in the example that the tennis-shoe pretest did not differentially affect the spiked-shoe test. Suppose, however, that the tennis-shoe test taught the runners a smooth-shoe running technique that they could transfer to a later test. We might predict that the smoother the shoes on the later test, the faster the runners will run. Because the shorter spikes

---

[13] Note, though, that the statistical tests used for matched-group designs assume that you have successfully matched on a variable highly correlated with the dependent variable. For this reason, these tests are more conservative in calling a given difference statistically significant. So if you have matched on a variable that is not highly correlated with the dependent variable and use one of these tests, you are less likely to find a statistically significant effect than if you had not matched in the first place.

**TABLE 8-7**

A Summary of the Advantages and Disadvantages of Using Within-Subject and Between-Subjects Designs

| *Within-subject experiments* | |
| --- | --- |
| *Advantages* | *Disadvantages* |
| Fewer participants are required. Experimental time is shorter. Variability between groups is smaller. | Transfer between conditions is possible. ABBA counterbalancing assumes linear confounding effect. All counterbalancing assumes symmetrical transfer. Range effects can cause problems. |
| *Between-subjects experiments* | |
| *Advantages* | *Disadvantages* |
| Transfer effects between conditions are not possible. Counterbalancing is not required. Matching can reduce variability between groups. Random assignment of participants eliminates bias. | Differences between groups are possible. More participants are required. More experimental time is required. Matching takes time and effort and assumes no transfer from matching operation. |

are more like smooth shoes, they will cause faster times. In this case, the pretest would differentially affect the runners' performance at the two levels of the independent variable.

Thus, matched-groups designs can be valuable under certain conditions, but they can also cause more problems than they solve. You should weigh the pros and cons of using a matched-groups design for your own experiment.

Table 8-7 summarizes the advantages and disadvantages of the designs discussed in this chapter. Obviously, you will want to consider these pros and cons within the context of any experiment you are considering doing. When we discuss multiple-variable experiments in Chapter 9, you will find that in many cases a single experiment will have both within-subject variables and between-subjects variables. For example, if we were interested in whether the effect of presenting a warning light on people's reaction time to a tone was dependent upon gender, we might vary "warning light/no warning light" as a within-subject variable and "gender" as a between-subjects variable (obviously!).[14] So for multiple-variable experiments it makes more sense to use the terms *within-subject* and *between-subjects* to refer to variables rather than experiments.

---

[14] The discussion of whether to manipulate a variable within subject or between subjects is a moot point for some variables: gender, species, personality trait, IQ score, and so on.

# Summary

There are two basic ways to assign participants to the levels of the independent variable: You can assign different individuals to each level or assign the same ones to all levels. The first method gives you a **between-subjects experiment** and the second, a **within-subject experiment.** A between-subjects experiment offers an advantage in that participants are exposed to only one level of the independent variable, so the other levels cannot affect the participants' behavior. In addition, experimental sessions can be shorter. The major advantage of a within-subject experiment is that variability due to individual differences is minimized. Some practical advantages of within-subject designs include using fewer participants and minimizing training and instruction time. A disadvantage of within-subjects designs is the necessity to **counterbalance** order effects. An **ABBA counterbalancing** can control for order effects within a participant, but you must be able to assume that the order effect is linear. **Complete counterbalancing** of order across participants is also possible, but you must still make an assumption of **symmetrical transfer** between conditions. In large experiments where complete counterbalancing is not possible, one can use **partial counterbalancing,** random assignment, or randomization within blocks. Even counterbalancing will not overcome **range effects** in experiments where the stimuli or responses may be consistently ordered. Individual differences among the participants assigned to each group representing a level of the independent variable can be reduced by using a **matched-groups procedure.**

# Find It on InfoTrac College Edition

Using InfoTrac College Edition, find two journal articles, one using a between-subjects design and one using a within-subject design. For each article state why you think the experimenter chose to use one type of design over the other. For the within-subject design did the experimenter use some type of counterbalancing? What was it and do you think the counterbalancing scheme was successful?

# 9

# How to Plan Single-Variable, Multiple-Variable, and Converging-Series Experiments

> A carefully conceived and executed design is of no avail if the scientific hypothesis that originally led to the experiment is without merit.
>
> R. E. KIRK (1968)
>
> I have yet to see any problem, however complicated, which, when you looked at it the right way, did not become more complicated.
>
> PAUL ANDERSON

In this chapter we will discuss single-variable experiments, which are the types of experimental designs making up nearly all the examples used in the book to this point; a single variable is manipulated at two or more levels. We will then discuss multiple-variable experiments, in which several independent variables are included in the same experiment and each of these is manipulated at two or more levels. In the psychological literature experiments with this design occur more frequently than any other kind. Finally, we will discuss converging-series designs, in which a number of single-variable or multiple-variable experiments are done in sequence in order to test a hypothesis or theory.

## Single-Variable Experiments

### TWO-LEVEL EXPERIMENTS

In the simplest experiment, there is one independent variable having two levels. Some investigators like to call the groups exposed to these levels the *experimental group* and the *control group*. In some cases it is obvious what the control condition should be: no application of a treatment. For example, if you were interested in the effects of a particular drug on a behavior, the control group would not receive the drug, and the experimental group would.

The control group here would also be valuable just to show that being in the experiment was not causing the observed effect. In other cases, especially where there are several levels of the independent variable, it is not clear which one should be called the control level.[1] For this reason, I will generally stick to the term *level* to describe the independent variable. In any case, we must use at least two levels to have a real experiment. Otherwise, it would be impossible to say that a change in the independent variable caused a change in behavior, because no comparison is possible.

In the early history of experimental psychology the typical experiment reported was a single-variable, two-level experiment. Because our science was young, investigators were more concerned with finding out whether an independent variable had any effect at all than in determining the exact nature of this effect. In addition, they had not yet developed some of the statistical tests required to analyze the more complex experimental designs. In some cases, tests existed but generally were not well known by the average investigator.

Nowadays journal editors usually expect to see more than two levels manipulated in an experiment. Very well-done two-level experiments, particularly when several experiments are reported, are sometimes accepted, but the typical experiment usually has multiple levels. Nevertheless, as a first project a two-level experiment is appropriate. New experimenters need to get their feet wet without drowning, and in some cases two-level experiments can provide valuable results.

## Advantages

Actually, two-level experiments do have several advantages over more complex designs. They offer a way of finding out whether an independent variable is worth studying. If an independent variable has no effect on a person's behavior, you obviously would be wasting your time doing a more complex experiment to determine the exact nature of the effect.

The results of a two-level experiment are also easy to interpret and analyze. The outcome is simply "Yes, the variable did have an effect; the behavior changed in this direction" or "No, the variable had no effect." To determine whether any effect is real or due to chance variation, you usually have to do a statistical test, and tests for two-level experiments are easy to do. They may involve no more than counting pluses and minuses, for example. Once you know which test to use, it should take you only a few minutes of hand calculation (or a few seconds of computer calculation) to statistically analyze your data.

Finally, in some cases you need no more information than a two-level experiment will give you. If the purpose of the experiment is to test two

---

[1] For example, if we decided to vary sex (not how much you get, but which one you are) as the independent variable in an experiment, should we call men or women the control group? Feminists and masculinists could argue for days over this issue, so why not avoid it altogether and assign the groups to Level 1 and Level 2?

competing theories and one theory predicts a difference in behavior for the two levels while the second predicts either no change or an opposite change, then a two-level experiment is adequate to distinguish between the theories. In some types of applied research, a two-level experiment can also provide valuable information. For instance, if you want to pit two pieces of industrial equipment against each other and only two are available that can do the job, a two-level experiment gives you all the information you need. The same principle holds if you are investigating two therapeutic techniques, two educational systems, two training programs, two drugs, two sexes, or two levels of any variable when only two levels are important or available.

### Disadvantages

Although a straight line is the shortest distance between two points, it is not the only line between two points. In other words, you are at a disadvantage in many two-level experiments because they will tell you nothing about the shape of the relationship between the independent and the dependent variables.

Suppose we did an experiment to find out what size of type this book should be printed in so that you would have to spend as little time as possible struggling with my periphrastic prose. We might decide to use a word processor to print several paragraphs. Some of the paragraphs would be printed in 12-point type, and the others in a smaller 10-point type. We could then measure the time it takes people to read the paragraphs printed in each size type. Of course, we would pretest the paragraphs for comprehensibility and counterbalance order and would do all the other good things we have learned in this book.

Figure 9-1 shows fictitious results for this experiment. The arbitrary straight line drawn through the two data points indicates that the smaller

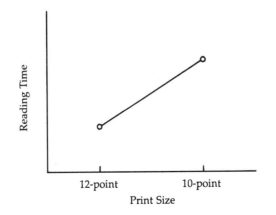

**FIGURE 9-1** Possible results from an experiment measuring the time it takes to read paragraphs printed in 12-point or 10-point type

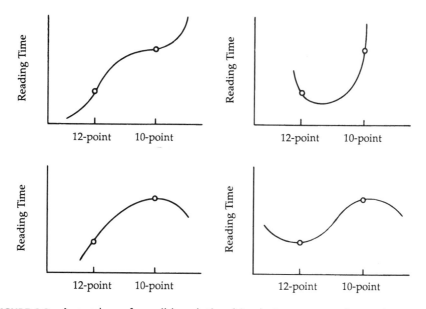

**FIGURE 9-2** A number of possible relationships between type size and reading time. All the functions pass through the same two data points.

the print, the longer the reading time. Thus, the experiment has answered our question: 12-point type makes for speedier reading. However, if we really wanted to know the best print size out of all possible sizes and we chose the two sizes used in the experiment because they were our best guess, then we don't have enough information to make a decision. Our results give no indication whether a straight-line relationship between type size and reading time is true for any sizes other than 12-point and 10-point.

Figure 9-2 shows a number of other relationships that could also be the actual underlying relationship. You can see that not knowing the shape of the relationship makes interpolation questionable.[2] We cannot correctly conclude that a print size halfway between 12-point and 10-point would give a reading time halfway between those sizes.

Extrapolating from two points is even more dangerous than interpolating. Most psychological functions have what are called ceiling and floor effects. A *ceiling effect* occurs when the dependent variable reaches a level that cannot be exceeded. Typical examples of ceiling levels are accuracy of response, 100%; probability of response, 1.0; and confidence in a response, 100%. In each of these cases, it is physically impossible for someone to produce a response exceeding a particular value. (You can't be more accurate than 100%, in other words.) In other cases, although an absolute ceiling does not limit responses, a softer ceiling effectively does. For example, even

[2] Interpolation is an estimate of intermediate values within a known range; extrapolation is an estimate of values beyond a known range.

with practice there is an effective ceiling to the number of items we can hold in short-term memory—about seven. Likewise, within a finite period humans are effectively limited in the amount of information they can process, such as the number of figures they can add up, the number of targets they can find in a display, the number of words they can type, and so forth. The ceiling might not be so hard, but it is still impenetrable.

A *floor effect* is a value below which a response cannot be made. No one can respond in fewer than zero seconds, for example, or give fewer responses than none. Again, the floor need not be absolute. There may be a softer effective floor. For instance, the shortest time to detect a stimulus, although theoretically zero, is effectively about 150 milliseconds. If we take two data points and extrapolate to values above a ceiling or below a floor, we won't be in the attic or basement; we'll be in hot water! And sometimes it is not obvious where a ceiling or floor should be. To avoid these problems, you should make it a rule in a two-level experiment not to interpolate or extrapolate beyond the levels used in the experiment.

INTERPOLATING BETWEEN TWO POINTS IS RISKY.

EXTRAPOLATING BEYOND TWO POINTS IS EVEN MORE DANGEROUS!

Two-level experiments are also sometimes of limited theoretical value. We agreed in Chapters 1–3 that science is built on relationships and that scientists use theories to explain the relationships found in experiments. Each theory competes with other possible theories until an experiment is done that supports one theory to the exclusion of the others. Because many theories predict that a change in an independent variable will cause the dependent variable to change in a particular direction, the outcome of a two-level experiment will often fail to distinguish among competing theories. Other than when opposing theories predict changes in opposite directions, or one predicts a change while the other does not, theory testing usually requires more complex experimental designs.

## MULTILEVEL EXPERIMENTS

**Multilevel experiments** are single-variable experiments presenting three or more levels of the independent variable. They are also called *functional experiments* by some investigators because they allow you to get some idea of the shape of the function relating the independent variable to the dependent variable.

### Advantages

The major advantage of a multilevel experiment is that the results allow us to infer the nature of the experimental relationship. Even if an experiment has only three levels, it still provides us with a much better idea of the relationship than a two-level experiment does.

Suppose we want to know how a student's anxiety level influences test scores. We decide to use two introductory psychology classes[3] and a two-level, between-subjects design. In Class 1 the instructor spends five minutes before each major exam haranguing the students about the importance of grades for success in school. She makes it clear that students with the best grades get the best jobs, that students with college degrees earn a far larger salary, and that the university is a bit overcrowded at the moment.

In Class 2 she also gives a five-minute talk before each exam. In this talk, she reminds the students that making a good grade is not as important as learning the material. She tells them that ten years from now they won't remember what grade they got on this test anyway. We are careful to control as many potential confounding variables as possible, such as grade level, test difficulty, and class instruction. Thus, we decide that the difference in test scores can be attributed to the anxiety produced by the talk. Assuming that the first speech causes a high level of anxiety in the

---

[3] Because here we are using two classes that already exist rather than assigning students to the classes in a random manner, this example is not really an experiment but uses a quasi-experimental design that will be discussed in Chapter 10. I hope you noticed this difference.

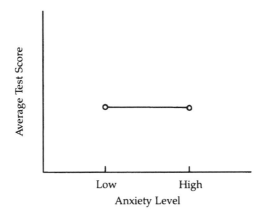

**FIGURE 9-3** Imaginary results from a two-level experiment varying the anxiety level of students and measuring their average test score

students and the second, a lower level, we might get the results shown in Figure 9-3.

At this point the best guess we could make is that there is no relationship between anxiety level and average test score; a straight line drawn through the two points is flat. Suppose, however, that we had decided on a multilevel design and added a third anxiety level, a neutral level in which the instructor gives a five-minute speech simply reminding the students of some procedural details. Figure 9-4 shows imaginary results for this multilevel experiment.

When we graph the third data point, we see that there is, in fact, an important relationship between anxiety level and test scores,[4] although some doubt exists about the exact shape of the function. Any of the three shapes shown in Figure 9-4 seem to be good possibilities; and because most psychological functions do not take sharp turns or change directions rapidly, we know that not many other relationships are possible. As you can see, the third data point allows us to get a much better idea of the shape of the experimental relationship. As we add progressively more levels to our experiment, we can make even better guesses about the true functional relationship between the independent and dependent variables. We can also interpolate and extrapolate from our data points with more confidence. In this example the neutral group that we added could be considered a control group because the teacher was not trying to influence anxiety at all. Another control group, in which the teacher said nothing, could have been added to determine whether saying anything at all affects behavior. Multilevel experiments give this kind of flexibility.

---

[4] If you have had a course in motivation or attention, you may recognize this function as a form of the Yerkes-Dodson law, in which an inverted U describes the relationship between arousal and learning. Good for you!

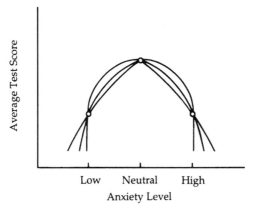

**FIGURE 9-4**  Imaginary results from a three-level experiment varying the anxiety level of students and measuring their average test score

This example also illustrates a second advantage of a multilevel experiment: Generally, the more levels you add, the less critical the range of the independent variable becomes. As you recall from Chapter 7, we determined that although the range should be realistic, it should also be large enough to show a relationship if one exists. Obviously, both of these requirements become easier for us to satisfy as more levels of the independent variable are represented in the experiment.

## Disadvantages

From a practical point of view, the major disadvantage of a multilevel experiment is that it requires more time and effort than a two-level experiment. Recall that every time we add a level to a between-subjects experiment, we increase the number of participants needed. In within-subject experiments, additional levels do not increase the number of participants needed, but they do increase the total time of the experiment and make counterbalancing schemes more ponderous.

The statistical tests required to analyze multilevel experiments are also a bit more difficult to do. They take more time, and it is harder to interpret the data in light of the statistical test.

In weighing the advantages and disadvantages of two-level versus multilevel designs, these slight additional costs of adding levels to the independent variable are usually more than offset by the value of the information gained. This benefit is especially valuable for the first few extra levels added to the design. At some point, of course, adding more levels will do little to increase our knowledge of the experimental relationship.

So far we have been pretending that all experiments have only one independent variable. However, this restriction has been more for the purpose of discussion than it has been a reflection of the real world. Many of the experiments that you will want to do will use more than one independent variable. Here I will discuss some of the general strategies used in designing progressively more complex experiments.

The most frequently used design in experimental psychology is a **factorial design.** To understand the results of most experiments published in psychology journals, you must understand the logic of factorial designs.

## Factorial Designs

The usual way to combine several variables is in a factorial combination that pairs each level of one independent variable with each level of the second and the third and so on. The independent variables in such a design are also called **factors.**[5]

As an example of a factorial experiment, suppose you want to know whether a group with a leader is faster at reaching a consensus than a leaderless group. You need to decide which circumstances you will control and which you will let vary: Should all group members be the same gender or not? Should communication be structured or free? Should you give the group an easy or a hard problem to solve? You may find it unsatisfactory to control or randomize all these factors. For example, you might feel that the effect of a leader on a group's efficiency could depend on the size of the group, in which case you might choose to vary both leadership and group size as factors. Suppose that you choose two levels of leadership—with and without—and four levels of size—3, 6, 10, and 20 members.

Figure 9-5 shows the usual way of representing such a factorial experiment. A *matrix* is formed with one factor on each side. The boxes within the matrix are called *cells.* As with the simpler experiments, participants are assigned to the various cells in a random manner. In the example, the upper left cell would have individuals assigned to groups with three members, one of whom is made the leader. You can see that any row or column by itself forms a simple single-variable experiment. The example we have chosen is called a $2 \times 4$ *design,*[6] because one factor has two levels, and the other has four.

The number of factors represented in a factorial design is limited only by your imagination and the population of the world. Suppose we think that group-decision-making time differs not only with leadership and size but also with the gender of the members. We make gender a third factor having three levels. Three levels? Right—men, women, and mixed (approx-

---

[5] Some investigators also call them **treatments,** which leads to the term *treatment combinations.* In building our science, we emulate the biblical folk building the Tower of Babel; no one can agree on the language. It's enough to make a new investigator a babbling idiot!

[6] The "$\times$" in this expression is read "by," not "times." Thus, an English (rather than algebraic) reading of this design would be a *two-by-four design.*

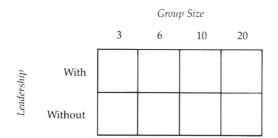

**FIGURE 9-5**  A schematic representation of a 2 x 4 factorial design. One factor, leadership, has two levels: with and without. A second factor, group size, has four levels: 3, 6, 10, and 20 members.

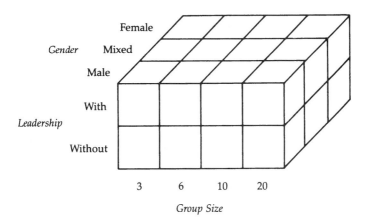

**FIGURE 9-6**  A schematic representation of a 2 x 3 x 4 factorial design. The factors are leadership (with and without), gender (male, mixed, and female), and group size (3, 6, 10, and 20 members).

imately half men and half women). Figure 9-6 shows a schematic of this expanded design,[7] which would be called a 2 × 3 × 4 factorial design.

In Chapter 8 we examined within-subject and between-subjects *experiments,* which was appropriate because we were just considering single-variable experiments. With factorial experiments, the *factors* themselves become within-subject and between-subjects, and both kinds of factors can be included in a single factorial experiment, sometimes called a **mixed factorial design.** In our leadership experiment, for example, we could have assigned a different set of group members to each cell, making both factors into between-subjects factors. Or we could have decided to create a mixed design by having the same members of each group function both with and

[7] Schematically representing more than three factors becomes a bit more difficult. Three-dimensional paper is hard to come by. Experimental designs, however, are not limited by three-dimensional space. They are just difficult to represent in a two-dimensional drawing.

without a leader. In this case, group size would still be a between-subjects factor, but leadership would be a within-subject factor. In deciding whether to make a particular factor within-subject or between-subjects, the advantages and disadvantages of each, as discussed in Chapter 8, would have to be considered. If necessary, appropriate counterbalancing for within-subject factors would also have to be used.

## ADVANTAGES

The major advantage of a factorial experiment is that we can study interactions. An **interaction** occurs when the relationship between one independent variable and the subject's behavior depends on the level of a second independent variable. For example, a group of three may make decisions easily with or without a leader, but as the group gets larger, we may find that leaderless groups take progressively longer to reach a consensus. Thus, the relationship between leadership and decision time depends on the size of the group. Figure 9-7 shows a graph of such an interaction. As you can see, the time to solve a problem is unaffected by whether there is a leader for a group of three people. However, as the groups get larger, having a leader becomes important for minimizing solution time. Two single-variable experiments would not provide us with information about such interactions; they would simply allow us to see the general effect of either leadership or group size. Only a factorial experiment allows us to investigate interactions.

Remember in Chapter 2 when we considered the infinite number of circumstances that could determine behavior? We decided that to do an experiment, we would have to pick one of these circumstances to be our independent variable. The other circumstances would either be controlled or be

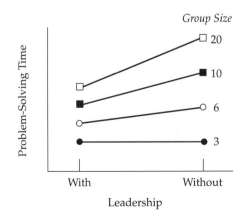

**FIGURE 9-7** These hypothetical results show a possible interaction of leadership with group size. Note that for the smallest group, problem-solving time is independent of leadership but that for larger groups, leadership makes for shorter solution times.

allowed to vary in a random fashion. Once we determined the effect of this circumstance on behavior, we could choose another circumstance to study. The problem with this approach is the naive assumption that once we know the effects of each independent variable, we can simply add them together and account for the behavior. This assumption totally ignores interactive effects among the circumstances. Ignoring interactions when we expect that they exist can lead us to make wrong conclusions.

In designing a single-variable experiment, when you are considering turning any circumstance into a control variable and think that the results could be affected by the level you choose to set it, you are worried about a possible interaction. The words *it might depend* should tip you off. Does having a leader speed up group problem-solving times? *It might depend* on the size of the group. Does print size affect reading speed? *It might depend* on the age of the reader. Does watching violence on TV affect children's aggressiveness? *It might depend* on how much they watch. Whenever you think that the outcome of the experiment you are designing might depend on some other circumstance, you are in some danger of making an error if you make that circumstance into a control variable or a random variable. Taking the experimental results shown in Figure 9-7, suppose that rather than doing a factorial experiment, we had decided that a single-variable experiment was good enough. If we had made group size into a control variable and chosen to use only groups of three, we would have concluded that problem-solving time was unrelated to leadership. On the other hand, if we had chosen groups of 20, we would have concluded that leadership had a large effect on problem-solving time.

The situation is not much better if we turn the *it might depend* circumstance into a random variable. In a leadership experiment having the outcome shown in Figure 9-7, if we had randomly chosen group sizes between 3 and 20, we would simply have underestimated the potentially large effect of leadership. In other words, we would have found a smaller effect of leadership because it would have been averaged across the sizes of our random-sized groups. Suppose that the underlying interactions were of a different form, such as the ones shown in either panel of Figure 9-8. In this case, if group size were a random variable, again we would be averaging across group sizes and would incorrectly conclude that leadership had no effect on problem-solving time. From this discussion you should begin to appreciate why factorial experiments are so widely used in psychology. They are the only experimental designs that allow us to investigate interactions between variables. (For more information on how to interpret interactions, see Chapter 12.)

In Chapter 2 we discovered that whenever a circumstance was made into a random variable, the experimental results increased in generalizability but decreased in precision. On the other hand, choosing to make the circumstance into a control variable increased the precision of the outcome but decreased the generalizability. A factorial experiment gives us a third alternative: we can make the circumstance into another independent

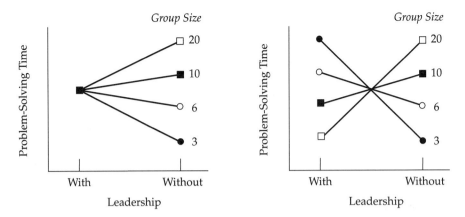

**FIGURE 9-8** Two possible interactions of leadership with group size. In either case, turning group size into a random variable would probably eliminate the effect of leadership.

variable, thereby increasing the precision *and* genera lizability of the result. We can generalize the outcome to a larger set of circumstances, because more circumstances have been made into factors, and we know precisely what the effect is at each level of these factors. Thus, we have the best of all possible worlds, although every time we choose to make another circumstance into a factor, the experiment gets progressively more complex.

A third advantage of factorial experiments is a statistical advantage. Recall from Chapter 8 that most inferential statistical tests compare the size of any difference found between the levels of the independent variable with an estimate of how variable the data are. A difference is more likely to be declared significant by the test if either that difference is large or the variability is small. In a factorial design, when a circumstance that otherwise would add variability to the data is instead made into a factor, the amount of estimated variability in the data decreases. Thus, the more circumstances we can make into factors, the smaller the estimate of variability. The smaller this estimate, the more likely it will be that any difference we find is declared statistically significant.

## DISADVANTAGES

With all these good things going for factorial designs, you know that they must also have some drawbacks. They do. The major disadvantage of a factorial experiment is that it is time-consuming and costly. Suppose that, as in Chapter 2, you are again working for General Nosedive of the Air Force. You are working with a team of engineers designing the cockpit of a new aircraft. Because you are a psychologist and know all about humans, they expect you to tell them how to design the displays and controls and where to place them.

You are aware that some variables might interact with other variables, so you choose a factorial design. For example, you know that the location of the airspeed indicator might affect the best altimeter location. The first factor you select is the length of the pointer on the altimeter. You find that four standard lengths are currently in use, so you assign four levels to this factor. You also have a choice of five possible places to put the altimeter, so you select altimeter location as a second factor and assign it five levels. Your third factor is the size of the airspeed indicator with three levels. Because there are six possible locations for this instrument, you have a fourth factor. The fifth factor is the size of the joystick grip,[8] which has four possible diameters and five possible lengths. We have only started to consider the important variables for cockpit design, and we already have a $4 \times 5 \times 3 \times 6 \times 4 \times 5$ factorial experiment. So far the design has 7200 cells.[9] If we assign ten people to each cell, we will exceed the number of pilots in the Air Force!

As you can see, whenever you add another factor to a factorial experiment, you increase the number of cells in the design by a multiple of the number of levels in that factor. At this rate, the size of factorial designs can get out of hand quickly. Because each additional cell calls for more time and effort, you must be careful not to choose an unrealistic number of factors or levels within each factor.

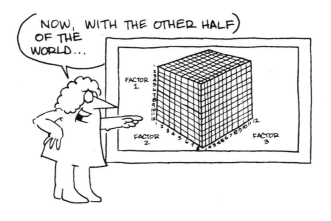

If you do not have the resources to do a large factorial experiment, how do you get an answer for the general? One way is to do several smaller experiments. For instance, in the example you could do $4 \times 5$, $3 \times 6$, and $4 \times 5$ experiments. The problem with this solution is that you are assuming that the independent variables appearing in separate experiments (such

---

[8] Nonfliers can stop snickering now. A joystick is the steering lever on an aircraft.
[9] Although I earlier told you to interpret the $\times$ as *by* so it is a 4 by 5 by 3 by 6 by 4 by 5 factorial experiment, in order to determine the number of cells, the $\times$ can be considered a multiplication sign.

as altimeter location and airspeed indicator size) do not interact. And you have no way of verifying this assumption without combining the variables into one experiment. Nevertheless, this is the way most psychologists who have to find answers to such questions go about doing so in the real world. We will examine a strategy for doing a series of smaller experiments later in this chapter.

There is a second, more sophisticated way of dealing with very large factorial experiments called **response-surface methodology** (Clark & Williges, 1973; Myers, 1971). This method allows you to determine the places within the factorial design where the dependent variable is likely to be at its maximum or minimum without having to fill each cell of the design with data points. In order to do this, one has to assume that some of the most complex interactions will not occur, an assumption that is usually correct. The details about how to use a response-surface methodology are well beyond what the beginning experimenter needs; you should simply realize that such techniques are available should you require them in the future. The references at the end of this chapter will give you a good place to start if you need to use such designs.

A second possible difficulty with factorial experiments is interpreting the results. The statistical procedure used to analyze most factorial experiments and all factorial experiments having more than two factors is **analysis of variance.** This procedure requires you to make certain assumptions about the type of variability in your data. One assumption is that the variability is normally distributed in that familiar bell-shaped curve that approximates many real-world distributions. If the underlying variability in your data does not approximate a normal distribution, an analysis-of-variance statistical test is not appropriate.[10] Unfortunately, you often do not know whether you can meet this assumption until after you have completed your experiment, which is too bad, because other statistical tests presently available for analyzing complex interactions are inadequate. In such cases, you are left with the unpleasant alternative of using a questionable statistical test or doing no statistical analysis at all. Fortunately, most factorial experiments produce distributions that are fair approximations of a normal distribution, thereby allowing you to use analysis of variance. (We will examine analysis of variance in more detail in Appendix A.)

Even when you can satisfy the assumptions of the statistical analysis, interpreting the results of complex factorial experiments is sometimes difficult. The interactions mentioned so far are two-way interactions, in that the relationship between one factor and the dependent variable depends on the level of a second factor. However, you could also have three-way interactions in which the type or size of two-way interaction depends on the level of a third factor. Perhaps the effectiveness of leaders interacts with group size, but only for men. By the time you get into four-way and

---

[10] Bradley (1968), in his book *Distribution-Free Statistical Tests,* has a good discussion of the errors you can make when you fail to satisfy this assumption.

five-way interactions, you will no longer find it obvious how to interpret your results. We will discuss interpreting interactions in more detail in Chapter 12.

We have seen that factorial experiments can offer many advantages over simple single-variable experiments. They allow you to investigate interactions, give you a statistical advantage by decreasing unwanted variability, and permit you to increase the generality of your results without decreasing the precision. However, you pay for these advantages in the time and effort expended and in the difficulty of interpreting the results. Is there a way to get some of the advantages of multiple-variable experiments without these difficulties? Yes. (Read on.)

# Converging-Series Designs

Most journal articles report the results of a series of experiments because many experimenters choose to do a **converging series** of experiments. I use this term to refer to any set of experiments that progressively home in on a solution, rather than tackling a problem in one fell swoop. Most series of experiments are made up of single-variable or small factorial experiments.

In one type of series, we may simply have an applied problem that is too big for a single factorial experiment, like the cockpit-design example. In this case, we might decide to do a series of smaller factorial experiments, because higher-order interactions (three- or four-way interactions or larger) are of little interest. Once we find an optimal level for a particular factor in one experiment, we make the factor into a control variable in subsequent experiments. We then can vary other important factors until we have successively manipulated all the independent variables that might reasonably be expected to affect performance. In this way, we can progressively approach the optimal solution to our overall practical problem.

## CONVERGING OPERATIONS

A more exciting form of converging-series design than those used for practical problems is one that tests psychological theories by converging on a single experimental hypothesis that will explain an observed behavior. This type of experimentation has been called a **converging-operations** approach (Garner, Hake, & Eriksen, 1956). We start out the series with a number of possible hypotheses that could explain the behavior being examined. Each experiment we do will help eliminate one or more of our initial hypotheses until only one remains at the end of the series that can account for the data.

To illustrate a converging-operations technique, let's look at an experiment that investigates whether it takes longer for people to perceive vulgar words than nonvulgar words. Suppose the experimenter presents words using a tachistoscope, an apparatus that exposes visual material for very brief controlled periods. The experimenter presents four words, two vulgar and two nonvulgar, and instructs participants to say the words aloud as soon as they recognize them. The experimenter finds that longer exposures are required for participants to report the vulgar words and concludes that this finding supports the hypothesis that people unconsciously suppress the perception of vulgar material. This perceptual-defense hypothesis maintains that longer exposures are required to overcome this suppression.

Being an outstanding experimenter, you think of a number of other hypotheses that could explain this same finding. First, specific characteristics of the words may have made the nonvulgar words easier to read with short exposures. Second, participants might have perceived all four words equally well but involuntarily suppressed their response on the vulgar words until they could no longer avoid it. Third, participants might have been aware of the words and known what response to make but voluntarily withheld the response until they were positive of being correct. Thus, we have at least four possible hypotheses that can account for the results of the experiment. These are listed in Figure 9-9. We now need to do a series of experiments that will converge on one of these hypotheses and exclude the rest.

The first experiment you might do distinguishes between the word-characteristics hypothesis and the other three. You can repeat the original experiment using two different vulgar and nonvulgar words. If you again find that the vulgar words require longer exposures, you are on your way to eliminating the word-characteristics hypothesis.[11] If longer exposure times were not required to say the vulgar words, your confidence in the word-characteristics hypothesis would increase.[12]

Assuming that the word-characteristics hypothesis has been eliminated, you still must distinguish among the remaining three. In Experiment 2 we might try to determine whether participants perceive the vulgar words at shorter exposures than they report them. We remember that a person's galvanic skin response (GSR) gives an indication of his or her emotional response to stimuli. Thus, we decide to measure participants' GSRs during presentation of the vulgar words to find out how long the words have to be exposed before they are perceived. The GSR can indicate whether

---

[11] Actually, a single experiment seldom eliminates a hypothesis from further consideration. For example, we might have been unlucky and selected two additional vulgar words that were still harder to read than the nonvulgar words. Or we might have failed to consider a subset of this hypothesis. For example, the effect may be due to vulgar words having a lower frequency of usage than nonvulgar words. And we recognize higher-frequency words more quickly. To conclusively exclude a hypothesis, the converging operation must be completely independent of any other possible operation. By changing the specific words, we have not made word frequency completely independent of word vulgarity; therefore, we cannot totally eliminate this hypothesis.

[12] This sentence was carefully worded, because we would not really have provided strong evidence supporting the word-characteristics hypothesis. In experimental psychology we design our experiments to show a difference in the dependent variable due to a manipulation of the independent variable. Showing that an independent variable caused no change in the dependent variable is weak evidence for the proposition that it *cannot* cause a change. There are a number of other reasons for finding no change in behavior. For example, participants may have failed to follow instructions, fallen asleep, or died.

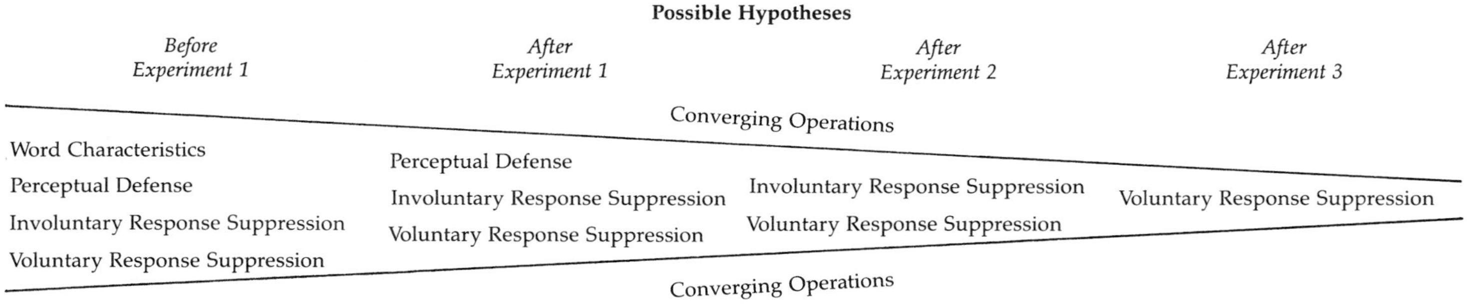

**Possible Hypotheses**

|  |  |  |  |
|---|---|---|---|
| *Before* Experiment 1 | *After* Experiment 1 | *After* Experiment 2 | *After* Experiment 3 |
| Word Characteristics |  |  |  |
| Perceptual Defense | Perceptual Defense |  |  |
| Involuntary Response Suppression | Involuntary Response Suppression | Involuntary Response Suppression |  |
| Voluntary Response Suppression | Voluntary Response Suppression | Voluntary Response Suppression | Voluntary Response Suppression |
|  | Converging Operations | Converging Operations |  |

**FIGURE 9-9** A schematic representation of the hypotheses in contention at each point during the three converging-operations experiments described in the text

participants are perceiving a word, even though they may voluntarily or involuntarily suppress their response.

If you find that the GSR doesn't change until the exposure duration at which the vulgar words are reported, the perceptual-defense hypothesis receives some support. If, however, the GSR shows that the vulgar words are being perceived at the same exposure durations as the nonvulgar words, one of the two remaining hypotheses must be true.

To distinguish between voluntary and involuntary response suppression, you can look for an operation that causes people to voluntarily change the amount of suppression. You might anticipate that when the experimenter is the opposite sex from the participant, more voluntary suppression occurs than when both are the same sex. Thus, in Experiment 3, you attempt to determine if the difference in exposure time for detecting vulgar versus nonvulgar words is less when the experimenter and participant are the same sex. If so, the voluntary-response-suppression hypothesis is supported. If not, involuntary response suppression seems likely.

You can see how the converging operations in this example have allowed us to eliminate all but one hypothesis. The operations we used to zero in on one hypothesis were varied: a stimulus manipulation, a physiological measurement, and an interpersonal-relationship manipulation. We could have chosen other operations, but if the assumptions underlying our operations are correct, these other operations should converge on the same hypothesis. Every time a new operation converges on the hypothesis, we can have increased confidence in that hypothesis.

Actually, this discussion has been a bit idealized. You can seldom sit down before doing a converging series of experiments and detail every possible hypothesis and every operation that will be carried out to distinguish among the hypotheses. If you are like most experimenters, you will work on one experiment at a time. Only after seeing the results of one experiment will you decide on a new operation to get you closer to the true hypothesis.

As you complete more experiments in a series, you may also find that the number of hypotheses is increasing rather than decreasing. Although you can eliminate some old hypotheses, other new ones become obvious as the experimental problem is better understood. At this point it may seem that you are doing a diverging series of experiments rather than a converging series! In fact, you are still converging, but the set of potential hypotheses is simply much larger than you at first imagined it to be.

## ADVANTAGES

Most of the advantages of a converging-series approach are rather obvious from this discussion. You have a great deal more flexibility than you have in a large factorial experiment. In a large factorial experiment, you must decide on the factors and factor levels before starting the experiment, and you are then locked into this predetermined design. One bad choice can destroy a large investment of time and money. A converging series, however, gives you a number of choice points. You can choose new independent variables or levels at each of these points. You can also be much more efficient because you needn't waste time investigating factors and levels that have little effect on the dependent variable.

A converging-series design also has built-in replications. Every time you show an experimental result to be repeatable, it gains prestige in the scientific community. If you had done all three experiments in our vulgar-word example, you would have replicated, or repeated, the basic experimental result of vulgar words requiring longer exposures three times, providing convincing proof of the reliability of this result.

## DISADVANTAGES

There are also some minor disadvantages of converging-series designs. It is difficult and sometimes impossible to determine how variables interact if the variables are manipulated between different experiments. Under certain circumstances, you can combine two experiments from a converging series to analyze them as a single between-subjects factorial experiment. However, if you are really interested in interactive effects, you should do a factorial experiment.

A second disadvantage is that when comparing the results of separate experiments in the series, you are always making a between-subjects comparison with all the accompanying disadvantages of between-subjects designs (see Chapter 8).

Finally, when you use a converging-series design, you must analyze and interpret the results of one experiment before you can begin the next. It often takes several weeks and sometimes months to complete such an analysis. For this reason, many investigators work on more than one series at a time so that they can do an experiment from one series while analyzing an experiment from another series.

Considering the advantages and disadvantages of converging-series designs, it is easy to see why the approach has become so popular in recent years. The converging-series approach offers a highly efficient and flexible way to investigate both applied and basic research problems.

**TABLE 9-1**

A Summary of the Advantages and Disadvantages of Two-Level, Multilevel, Factorial, and Converging-Series Experimental Designs

| Design | Advantages | Disadvantages |
|---|---|---|
| Two-level experiment | It is efficient for determining if a variable has any effect.<br>Results are easy to interpret and analyze.<br>It is adequate for some theory testing.<br>It is useful for applied comparisons. | One cannot infer shape of functions.<br>Interpolation and extrapolation are dangerous.<br>Complex theories are difficult to test. |
| Multilevel experiment | One can infer shape of functions.<br>Range of independent variable is less critical. | It requires more participants or time.<br>Counterbalancing is more ponderous.<br>Statistics are more difficult. |
| Factorial experiment | One can investigate interactions.<br>Adding factors decreases variability, thus increasing statistical sensitivity.<br>It increases generalizability without decreasing precision. | Experiments become large as more factors are added.<br>Statistics are more difficult.<br>Higher-order interactions are sometimes difficult to interpret. |
| Converging-series experiments | They offer more flexibility than large factorial experiments.<br>They have built-in replications. | Interactions are difficult to assess.<br>Between-experiment comparisons are also between-subjects, with associated difficulties.<br>One must analyze prior experiment before doing the next. |

Table 9-1 provides a handy reference summarizing the advantages and disadvantages of all the experimental designs that we have been examining in this chapter.

# Summary

Once you have decided on a research problem worth investigating, you must choose an experimental design. The simplest design you can choose presents only two levels of a single independent variable. This design provides a way to quickly determine if the independent variable has any effect at all on the participant's behavior. Such experiments are also easy to interpret and analyze; for some theoretical and applied problems, they provide all the information necessary. However, these simple experiments can tell you nothing about the shape of the experimental relationship, so both interpolation and extrapolation are risky. Adding more levels to the independent variable will give you a better idea about the functional relationship between the independent and the dependent variables. It also makes choosing a range for the independent variable less critical. A disadvantage of such **multilevel experiments** is that they require more time and effort. They are also a bit harder to interpret and analyze.

The most frequently used multiple-variable experimental design is called a **factorial design.** In this design the independent variables, sometimes called **factors,** are combined so that the levels of each variable occur in combination with the levels of every other variable. If within-subject factors are combined with between-subjects factors, the experiment is said to use a **mixed factorial design.** Factorial designs allow you to investigate **interactions.** Every time you add a factor, the generalizability and precision of the results increase, while the statistical variability decreases. However, large factorial experiments can be time-consuming and costly. The design can become so large that a series of smaller experiments is required or the use of a **response-surface methodology** is necessary. Interpreting the results can also be a problem, particularly when the statistical assumptions of **analysis of variance** cannot be met.

You can use a **converging-series design** in place of a complex factorial design. This design allows you to discover **converging operations,** which progressively eliminate hypotheses until only one remaining hypothesis can account for the data. Converging-series designs offer the advantage of flexibility and also provide built-in replications. However, evaluating interactions between factors varying across experiments is difficult. You must also manipulate these factors in a between-subjects manner, and you must analyze one experiment before beginning the next.

# Find It on InfoTrac College Edition

Chapter 9 discusses single-variable two-level experiments, single-variable multilevel experiments, factorial experiments, and converging-series designs. Try to find examples of each type of design using InfoTrac College Edition. If you search for articles in the various experimental journals, you should find many factorial designs and converging series designs. You may have to look in more applied journals, such as those in the fields of counseling or clinical psychology, to find the simpler single-variable designs.

# 10

# How to Design Nontraditional Research

> The task confronting persons who try to interpret the results from quasi-experiments is basically one of separating the effects of a treatment from those due to the initial noncomparability between the average units in each treatment group.
>
> T. D. COOK & D. T. CAMPBELL (1979)
>
> Instead of studying a thousand rats for one hour each, or a hundred rats for ten hours each, the investigator is likely to study one rat for a thousand hours.
>
> B. F. SKINNER (1966)

Up to this point in the book we have been concentrating on traditional experimental designs. However, it may not always be possible or desirable to design a traditional experiment to answer a particular research question. In this chapter we will discuss three less traditional ways to do research. The first, **quasi-experimentation,** follows many of the rules of experimentation we have learned, but because random assignment of participants to levels of the independent variable is not possible, quasi-experimental designs must be used to minimize possible threats to internal validity that might occur. The second nontraditional designs are **single-subject** and **small-*N* baseline** designs. In this case, because of a limited availability of participants or because showing a clear-cut result of a manipulation on each participant is desired, rules are established that allow effects to be observed without control groups or within-subject counterbalancing. The third nontraditional research discussed is **survey,** or **questionnaire,** research that uses a correlational design rather than an experimental design.

## Quasi-Experiments (and Nonexperimental Designs)

Recall from Chapter 2 that one of the options for assignment of circumstances is to turn them into random variables. In that chapter I also emphasized how important it is for true randomization to take place. If we cannot be sure that a truly random process has been used, a circumstance may vary in a systematic way along with the levels of the independent variable. That is a nice way of saying that we have allowed confounding to raise its ugly head. Whenever we have the possibility of confounding, we must be aware of all the possible threats to internal validity that we discussed in Chapter 2, such as history, maturation, selection, mortality, testing, and statistical regression. Remember those? The purpose of quasi-experimental designs is to minimize each of these threats even though we are not randomizing our groups. In this way we hope to avoid confounding variables.

To illustrate this problem, suppose we wish to determine whether handing out "learning evaluations" (short noncredit quizzes) at the end of each lecture improves class performance on the major tests in a particular college course. We know from our basic experimental model that we must use at least two levels of the independent variable—probably "learning evaluations" versus "no learning evaluations." Some circumstances will become control variables. For example, we would probably teach the same course material to participants whether they were receiving learning evaluations or not. However, we cannot clone students for a between-subjects design, and using a within-subject design is not feasible because we cannot undo having learned the material the first time through. So we will have to make the students assigned to each group into a random variable. Ideally we could put the names of all students in the university who had not taken the course into a hat and draw out 100 students to assign to each of two classes. One class would then be given learning evaluations, and the other would not.

Unfortunately, we would probably not be allowed to force these students to take a particular class; in the real world, students are allowed to choose the classes they wish to take. We might have to use two classes that already exist, perhaps a morning class and an afternoon class, and assign them to the levels of our independent variable. Do you suppose that there are any differences between the types of students who choose to take morning classes and the types who take afternoon classes? Can you imagine dimensions in which these students differ that might be related to class performance?

Suppose the classes were both morning classes, but one met on Monday, Wednesday, and Friday and the other for longer classes on Tuesday and Thursday. Can you imagine dimensions related to days of the week or lecture duration that might affect performance?

An even more likely problem would develop if the instructor taught only one section of this particular course each semester or each year. How many dimensions do you suppose vary between fall and spring students or between students from one year to the next? So while we can avoid turning some circumstances into confounding variables by using control or randomization, we do not have the option of control for participant assignment.

In most applied field settings we do not have the option of making participant assignment a random variable. When random assignment is not possible, it is often possible to use a quasi-experimental design. These quasi-experimental designs allow us to minimize, or in some cases at least assess, the various threats to internal validity we are exposing ourselves to by violating the strict laws of experimentation. Each of the designs that we will examine next has some strengths for countering some threats, but none is able to give us complete assurance that we have eliminated all threats. In discussing quasi-experimentation, it is useful to characterize the different designs using a notation system employed by Cook and Campbell (1979) in their classic book on the topic. In this system an "X" stands for a particular level of the independent variable (also called a treatment). An "O" stands for an observation during which the dependent variable is measured. The subscripts "1" through "n" refer to the order of presenting the treatments $(X_1 \ldots X_n)$ or measuring the observations $(O_1 \ldots O_n)$. A dashed line between experimental groups indicates that they were not randomly chosen.

## NONEXPERIMENTAL DESIGNS

### One-Group Posttest-Only Design

If you measure the behavior of a group that has been exposed to only one level of an independent variable, you are using a **one-group posttest-only design.** Using our notation system, this design looks like this:

$$\overline{\quad\quad\quad} \\ X \quad O$$

When you have no other information to supplement the outcome, this design is essentially useless for determining the impact of the treatment.

For example, suppose a television network airs a program on the Holocaust (X), and you are interested in how the show affected the population's awareness of the event (O). You send out a questionnaire to a group of people and discover that 76% are now aware of what happened during the Holocaust. What do you know about the impact of the telecast? Did it cause an increase in awareness? A decrease? Without knowing what the awareness level was before the show or what the level is for an equivalent group not exposed to the show, your result is useless for answering these questions.

This design is similar to the case-study approach discussed in Chapter 1. However, some important differences generally make case studies more useful. In a case study, the researcher typically knows a great deal about the context in which the behavior is being observed. For this reason, although there may be no direct measure of preobservation behaviors, these can often be inferred. In addition, more than one behavior is usually being observed. These behaviors may form a pattern that provides much more information than is provided by a single dependent variable measured in a more sterile laboratory setting.

### Posttest-Only Design with Nonequivalent Groups

If we add a posttest done on a nonequivalent group to the design we have been discussing, it looks like this:

$$\frac{X \quad O}{\overline{\phantom{--}}\ \overline{\phantom{-}}\ \overline{\phantom{-}}\ \overline{\phantom{-}}}$$

$$\frac{O}{\phantom{XXXX}}$$

By nonequivalent, I mean that the group was chosen using a different selection mechanism than was used to choose the group exposed to the treatment.

In the Holocaust example, suppose we discovered that because a local football team was playing, the telecast was not shown in Miami. We might decide to use a randomly selected sample from Miami as the nonequivalent group and send it the questionnaire. If we now find a difference between groups, can we attribute this difference to the television show? Miami has a large Jewish population. Do you think that being Jewish could affect your awareness of the Holocaust?

The basic problem with a **posttest-only design with nonequivalent groups** is that any observed difference could be due either to the treatment or to selection differences between the groups. The more equivalent the groups, the more convincing the conclusion.

One way of strengthening the conclusion in the absence of a formal pretest is to have informal pretest information by which the two groups can be compared. This pretest information is more useful the more highly correlated it is with the dependent variable. Thus, we might compare our two samples in terms of age, sex, social class, ethnicity, and religion. This comparison could give us an idea of how equivalent the groups are. However, the basic design is still weak, and great care must be taken in interpreting the results of any posttest-only nonequivalent-groups design.

### One-Group Pretest–Posttest Design

Again taking the basic one-group posttest design, consider what would happen if we also gave that group a pretest. This **one-group pretest–posttest design** looks like this:

$$\frac{O_1 \quad X \quad O_2}{\phantom{XXXX}}$$

This design has widespread usage in applied field settings and is an improvement over the nonequivalent-groups design in terms of selection. Obviously, the same participants are selected for both observations. However, we buy this improvement at some cost, because other threats to internal validity can blindside us.

Again, using the Holocaust example, what effect do you think giving a pretest that asks about awareness of this event would have on a posttest assessing awareness of the event? You can see that the threat of testing is a problem in this case. If we decided to minimize the testing problems by giving the pretest well in advance of the treatment—say, one year—we could well run into other threats. History might conspire against us in that some Holocaust-related event besides the telecast, such as the capture of a war criminal, might change the group's awareness. Or, particularly if we were using schoolchildren, maturity could have an effect. If we were using the pretest to select a group, regression could also cause problems. Thus, while the pretest design may solve the selection problem, great care must be taken in interpretation because of the other threats to internal validity.

## QUASI-EXPERIMENTAL DESIGNS

The three designs discussed in the previous section are called **nonexperimental designs** because there is no way to assess many of the threats to internal validity when these designs are used. The designs discussed in this section are called **quasi-experimental designs** because, although they do not meet the strict requirements of the basic experimental model, we can usually assess most of the threats. It is not within the scope of this book to exhaustively cover all quasi-experimental designs. Instead I will mention several that illustrate the two major classes of designs. For more detail, refer to Cook and Campbell's (1979) excellent book.

### Nonequivalent Control Group Design with Pretest and Posttest

The first design uses a nonequivalent control group not exposed to the treatment in addition to a treatment group. Each group is given both a pretest and a posttest. The notation for the design is:

$$
\begin{array}{ccc}
O_1 & X & O_2 \\
\hline
O_1 & & O_2
\end{array}
$$

This design is probably the most widely used in social science field studies. It allows us to assess most of the simple threats to internal validity.

How much we have to worry about certain threats depends to some extent upon the particular experimental outcome. If there is essentially no difference in the pretest scores of the groups, we can have some confidence that the groups are relatively equivalent, and the possibility of a selection or a regression threat is minimized. If the scores of the control group are the same at pretest and posttest, the threats of history and maturation are minimized. Because both groups receive the same tests, differential effects of testing should also be minimal. If the number of participants that drop out of the two groups between pretest and posttest is different, mortality could be a problem. However, the design allows this threat to be assessed. The most serious potential problem when using this design is having a threat that interacts with selection. Again, if the two groups score equivalently at pretest, the threat of a selection interaction is reduced but still possible. For example, while school A is receiving a particular treatment and school B is not, school A may also employ a new principal who requires new standards of the teachers. This history–selection interaction could threaten our conclusions.

We must be even more concerned about interactions with selection when the two groups have very different scores on the pretest. For example, suppose we want to determine whether paying assembly-line workers by the piece increases productivity. We request volunteers who will have their salary lowered but will receive extra money for piecework. At the pretest we discover that the volunteers are more productive, but we figure that we can compare the size of this initial difference with the size of the posttest difference. Sure enough, at posttest the difference is even larger. Both groups improved their productivity, but the piecework group improved more. We conclude that paying by the piece improves productivity. Are we right?

Because there was a pretest difference in productivity, the volunteers in the treatment group not only may have been better at that point but also may have been maturing (learning, becoming more experienced) at a faster rate. Workers are seldom stable, and we know that these workers were not because even the control group improved. When everyone is improving, we should not be surprised that the better workers improve more rapidly. The basic design does not allow us to determine the size of this potential maturation–selection interaction. We might subdivide the treatment group by pretest to get some idea of the effect. That is, we would expect the less able workers from the treatment group to improve more slowly than the more able workers. However, we then have a different design. The point is that even when you use a nonequivalent control group design with both pretests and posttests, your findings may still be subject to threats such as selection interactions.

**Variations.**   Rather than exhaustively detailing each variant of non-equivalent-control-group designs, I will just mention a few possibilities. Sometimes when it is not possible or practical to use the same test for the pretest and posttest, a **proxy pretest** is used. That is, a pretest measure is taken of some variable or variables that should correlate with the posttest. For example, if you wished to evaluate the effects of a new method for teaching algebra, you might expose one class to the new method while a second was taught by the traditional method. Rather than giving a pretest assessing algebra achievement to classes that had yet to learn algebra, you might give them a proxy pretest assessing general mathematical aptitude.

A proxy pretest can be used if it is not possible to give a pretest, such as when the treatment consists of some unpredictable historical event affecting a portion of a population. Alternatively, even when it is possible to give a pretest, testing may be a threat to internal validity, and a proxy test can be used to avoid exposing the participants to the test that will be used as a posttest. In other cases, when novel responses are called for, using the same test as the pretest and posttest could be nonsensical. For example, it would not make much sense to give a final exam for an introductory psychology course to two classes prior to their taking the course.

If testing is a threat, we can use **separate pretest and posttest samples.** Rather than drawing a single sample for each group that will receive both the pretest and the posttest, we draw two samples for each group, one to receive the pretest and one the posttest. For instance, if an educational program is to be given to one class and not the other, the two classes can be randomly subdivided, with half of each given the pretest and the other half given the posttest later. The obvious weakness of this design is that it hinges entirely on the comparability of the pretest and posttest groups. If you believe that the groups might differ along a dimension related to the treatment, the design is considerably weakened.

Another way of strengthening the basic nonequivalent control group design with pretest and posttest is to add **pretest observations at more than one time interval.** Adding one or more pretests can help us assess the effects of two possible threats. Remember when we were discussing how "the able get more able" and how this might cause a maturation–selection interaction? If we had given an even earlier pretest, we could have determined whether the scores on that test fell on the trend line for each group. If they did, we would have a strong case for concluding that a maturation–selection interaction rather than the treatment caused the posttest difference. That is, the two pretests would have established a maturation trend, and the posttest would have been interpreted as nothing more than a continuation of this trend. An additional pretest can also help us assess the effects of statistical regression. If the groups were selected on the basis of the first pretest, regression effects should show up in the scores of the second pretest as well as in the scores of the posttest.

Other variations that are used less frequently include those in which there is a pretest, the treatment is imposed, there is a posttest, the treatment is removed, and there is another posttest. This design can also be expanded by reinstating the treatment, giving another test, ad infinitum (or possibly ad absurdum). These designs are much like the baseline designs we will be discussing later in this chapter. However, unlike quasi-experiments, baseline experiments typically use very few participants, and the data are examined for individuals, usually without the aid of statistical analysis.

In some cases one group can be given a treatment that is expected to change the dependent variable in one direction, and a second group can be given a treatment expected to have the opposite effect. For example, suppose two groups of workers are paid partly by the hour and partly by the piece. We might impose a treatment whereby we paid one group entirely by the hour and the second group entirely by the piece. If we had predicted that paying by the piece would increase productivity, we would expect a decrease for the first group and an increase for the second. An outcome supporting our predictions is strong support for our hypothesis.

**TABLE 10-1**

Procedures for Conducting Various Nonequivalent Control Group Designs with Pretest and Posttest. Note that participants in Groups 1 and 2 were not randomly assigned to the treatment and no-treatment conditions and are therefore considered nonequivalent.

|  | Time 1 | Time 2 | Time 3 | Time 4 |
|---|---|---|---|---|
| Basic nonequivalent control group with pretest and posttest | Test Group 1 | Apply treatment | Test Group 1 | |
|  | Test Group 2 | No treatment | Test Group 2 | |
| With proxy pretest | Proxy Test Group 1 | Apply treatment | Test Group 1 | |
|  | Proxy Test Group 2 | No treatment | Test Group 2 | |
| Separate pretest and posttest samples | Test first half of Group 1 | Apply treatment | Test second half of Group 1 | |
|  | Test first half of Group 2 | No treatment | Test second half of Group 2 | |
| Pretest observations at more than one time interval | Test Group 1 | Test Group 1 | Apply treatment | Test Group 1 |
|  | Test Group 2 | Test Group 2 | No treatment | Test Group 2 |

We have discussed only a few possible variations of the basic nonequivalent control group design. These are also shown in Table 10-1. Others are possible, and you will find information about these in the books listed at the end of the chapter.

### Interrupted Time-Series Designs

The second major class of quasi-experimental designs is called **interrupted time-series designs.** A basic time-series design requires that a single group be observed multiple times prior to treatment and then multiple times after treatment. The notation for one such design looks like this:

$$O_1 \quad O_2 \quad O_3 \quad O_4 \quad O_5 \quad X \quad O_6 \quad O_7 \quad O_8 \quad O_9 \quad O_{10}$$

The outcome easiest to interpret for such a design is an instantaneous, permanent change in the level of an otherwise flat line. For example, if we

INTERRUPTED TIME SERIES

employed a new payoff scheme for workers and found an immediate 10%
increase in productivity and this change was maintained over the course of
the study, we could have considerable confidence that the new payoff
scheme had caused the change. Even given this ideal outcome, however,
we still need to be wary of possible threats such as history or mortality.
Some historical event could have coincided with the introduction of the
treatment. It is also possible but probably unlikely that at exactly the time
the treatment was introduced, some unknown event caused a number of
participants to drop out of the study.

Other potential threats to internal validity can be excluded or assessed
using interrupted time-series designs. For instance, selection and interactions with selections are not problems, because the same group is used
throughout the experiment. Any effects of testing or statistical regression
should have disappeared before the treatment was introduced. Generally,
we should also be able to exclude maturity as a problem, because the effects
of maturity are typically sluggish; hence we would expect to see a trend
line rather than a discontinuous change.

When the change in the dependent variable is delayed, temporary, or
reflected in the slope of an increasing or decreasing trend rather than in the
overall level of a flat line, we usually state our conclusion with less confidence. In this case more sophisticated statistical techniques can sometimes
help tease out treatment effects.

**Variations.**    As with the first type of design, variations of the simple time-series design are possible. One variation that will add considerable strength to a conclusion is the **addition of a nonequivalent no-treatment control group time series.** That is, a second nonequivalent group is measured at each of the observation intervals, but no treatment is given during the series. The control group allows us to assess the effects of history as a threat, because both groups will probably be affected equally by an historical event. If the two groups are selected in a different manner, a history–selection interaction can occur. However, this threat is a problem only in the unlikely event that a unique historical event occurred coincidentally with presentation of the treatment and only for the treatment group.

When treatment effects are expected to be reversible, an **interrupted time series with removed treatment** can be used. After the basic design is completed, the treatment is removed, and another series of observations is taken. This design is really an overlapping combination of two basic time-series designs, one series in which the presence of the treatment is the treatment and the other in which its absence is the treatment. Actually, you may choose to add and delete the treatment as many times as you wish to produce *multiple replications*.[1] Each replication will increase your confidence in the causal effect of the treatment. Again, this design is similar to the baseline designs discussed later in this chapter.

Another way of building in replications is to use nonequivalent groups but introduce the treatment at different points in the series of observations for the two groups. Such a design is called an **interrupted time series with switching replications.** This design offers a way to counter or assess most of the threats to internal validity, such as history and maturity. Also, by having a built-in replication on a sample from a different population, the design enhances the external validity of the experimental conclusion. Table 10-2 summarizes the interrupted time-series designs discussed in this section.

## Statistical Analysis of Quasi-Experiments

Techniques for doing statistical analysis of quasi-experimental data have improved greatly in the past few years. Rather sophisticated statistical tests, which are well beyond the scope of this book, can be found in some of the books listed at the end of this chapter. I am sure you will notice that several of the designs presented here are similar to the baseline designs to be discussed next. However, an important difference between baseline and quasi-experimental designs is that whereas baseline experiments usually have so few participants that statistical analysis is impossible, quasi-experiments can typically be analyzed with the same statistical rigor used for

---

[1] For ethical reasons if the treatment is found to be beneficial, it may be necessary to end the series with the treatment in effect.

**TABLE 10-2**
Procedures for Conducting Various Interrupted Time-Series Designs. Note that participants in Groups 1, 2, and 3 were not randomly assigned to the treatment conditions and are therefore considered nonequivalent.

| Time 1 | Time 2 | Time 3 | Time 4 | Time 5 | Time 6 | Time 7 |
|---|---|---|---|---|---|---|
| *Basic interrupted time-series design* | | | | | | |
| Test Group 1 | Test Group 1 | Test Group 1 | Apply treatment | Test Group 1 | Test Group 1 | Test Group 1 |
| *With addition of a nonequivalent no-treatment control group* | | | | | | |
| Test Group 1 | Test Group 1 | Test Group 1 | Apply treatment | Test Group 1 | Test Group 1 | Test Group 1 |
| Test Group 2 | Test Group 2 | Test Group 2 | No treatment | Test Group 2 | Test Group 2 | Test Group 2 |
| *With removed treatment* | | | | | | |
| Test Group 1 | Test Group 1 | Apply treatment | Test Group 1 | Test Group 1 | Remove treatment | Test Group 1 |
| *With switching replications* | | | | | | |
| Test Group 1 | Apply treatment | Test Group 1 | Test Group 1 | Test Group 1 | Test Group 1 | Test Group 1 |
| Test Group 2 | Test Group 2 | Test Group 2 | Apply treatment | Test Group 2 | Test Group 2 | Test Group 2 |
| Test Group 3 | Test Group 3 | Test Group 3 | Test Group 3 | Test Group 3 | Apply treatment | Test Group 3 |

fully randomized experimental designs. Certainly, it is no longer the case that quasi-experimentation should be avoided because statistical analysis is difficult or impossible.

## Advantages

The biggest advantage of quasi-experiments is that they allow us to do research that was formerly not even possible to do. Quasi-experimentation has provided a new bagful of tools to psychologists who are interested in social issues, clinical evaluation, and educational programs and wish to investigate these issues in the real world. And although care must be taken to determine whether there are threats to internal validity, at least we know what these threats might be, and the designs make it possible to evaluate most of them to see whether they are a problem.

## Disadvantages

Before I wax too ecstatic about quasi-experimentation, let me point out that there are some disadvantages, too. Even if we try our best we may find threats to internal validity. Although it is true that we can usually catch these when they occur, nevertheless finding such a threat pretty much invalidates our results. For example, if we use a basic nonequivalent control group with pretest and posttest design and find a difference in the pretest and posttest for the control group, interpreting any change in the treatment group is problematic at best. A second problem is that these designs are obviously more complex and often require more time and effort to carry out than a more traditional experiment. Measurements have to be taken a number of times rather than just once for each condition. And as I mentioned, statistical tests for quasi-experimental designs, though now possible, are more difficult to do and are not routinely taught in basic courses.

Even given these disadvantages, the behavioral sciences have often been criticized for either doing sound research on simple but unimportant problems or doing unsound research on complex and important problems. The advances in quasi-experimental design have made it possible to do sound research on complex and important problems. Welcome to a new frontier!

# Single-Subject and Small-*N* Baseline Designs

## INDIVIDUAL VERSUS GROUPED DATA

Some investigators contend that the way the majority of psychologists do experiments is at best misleading and at worst pointless. The loudest revolutionary in this group has been Sidman (1960), who claims that the kind of traditional experiments you have been learning about tell us little about an individual's behavior. Sidman points out that experiments usually tell us about the behavior of some imaginary average participant who does not accurately reflect any real individual participant. He claims that most experimenters use groups and pretend that the behavior of individuals in the group resembles the average behavior of the group. He argues that there are times the behavior of an individual in the group may be nothing like the average behavior of the group.

To illustrate this point, consider an experiment designed to find out how quickly a person can learn a simple analogy by being exposed to examples. The first item might be: *edit* is to *tide* as *recap* is to _____. The answer is *pacer,* because *pacer* is *recap* spelled backward. The next item might be: *pets* is to *step* as *tool* is to _____. Again, the answer is *tool* spelled backward, or *loot.* We give each participant three seconds to solve an item before presenting the next item. We might expect learning to occur in an all-or-nothing fashion. That is, we assume that at some point the participant will cry "Aha!" or "Eureka!" and from then on get every item correct.

Figure 10-1 shows fictitious individual results for ten people; Figure 10-2 shows a group curve representing the average person. You can see that the group curve in Figure 10-2 does not represent any of the individual curves in Figure 10-1. The group curve might cause us to conclude that people learn the solution gradually; however, every individual actually appears to have gone from solving none of the items to solving all the items on a single trial.

Because of such discrepancies, Sidman believes, group performance seldom tells us much about how individuals perform. You may recall from Chapter 8 that Poulton (1973) took a very different position on this issue and went so far as to argue that all within-subject designs are basically flawed and only between-subjects manipulations, in which groups are used, can be easily interpreted. Psychologists decided to use groups in the first place because the behavior of individuals is so variable and because an individual participant's variability is likely to be canceled out by others who happen to vary in the opposite direction. Sidman, however, says that variability is not inherent in the participant but is caused by a failure of the experimenter to control all the variables affecting that individual. Once experimenters gain adequate behavioral control, they should no longer find it necessary to use large groups. The way for experimenters to demonstrate that they have gained this control is to do a baseline experiment.

## BASELINE PROCEDURES

To illustrate a Sidmanian **baseline experiment,** let's consider an experiment designed to find out whether punishment can be used to change the behavior of a person with cerebral palsy. Suppose a therapist is working with a client having cerebral palsy who wishes to improve his interview skills.[2]

---

[2] I wish to thank David A. Sachs of Las Cruces, New Mexico, for this particular example. He devised the technique described, although the results I will report are fictitious.

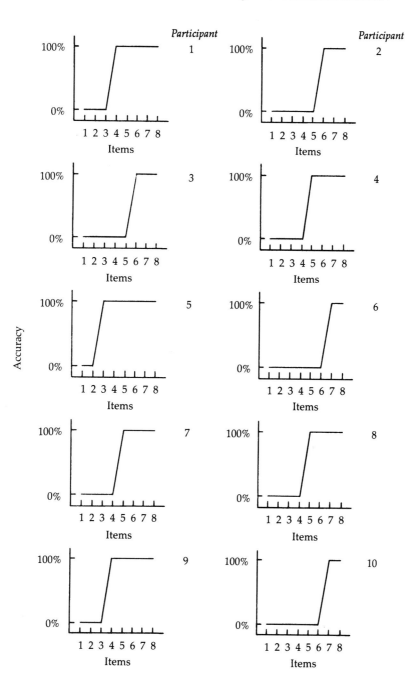

**FIGURE 10-1** Possible individual results for ten participants in an analogy experiment. Once an individual learns the rule for solving this type of problem, that person is correct on all subsequent items.

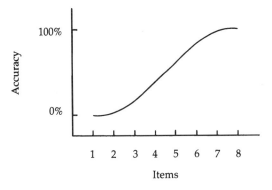

**FIGURE 10-2**  The group curve for the people shown in Figure 10-1. Note that the group curve is a poor representation of any individual.

Individuals with cerebral palsy often have problems controlling their head movements and so tend to lose eye contact. As an attempt to increase the amount of eye contact, which is one aspect of a successful interview, the therapist decides to devise a procedure whereby the client gets a mild electric shock each time eye contact is broken. The client, wishing to improve his social skills, agrees to the shock procedure.[3]

The first step in this type of experiment is to establish a **baseline**—that is, a **steady state** at which the response rate changes very little. One of the nagging problems in baseline experiments is determining how much "very little" is. The methods for determining whether the baseline has reached a steady state vary from a statistical criterion such as "no more than 3% change in the response rate from one session to the next" to a simple visual inspection of the data for obvious fluctuations or trends. Once a baseline has been established, the experimenter begins the experimental manipulation.

In our example, the therapist might have the client report every day for a half-hour simulated interview. During the interview, the therapist

THE FIRST STEP IS TO
ESTABLISH A STEADY STATE...

---

[3] The patient's agreement is a necessary although not always sufficient ethical requirement.

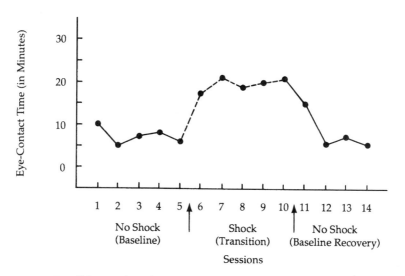

**FIGURE 10-3** Possible results of an experiment in which eye-contact time for a client with cerebral palsy was measured during 30-minute simulated interviews. The first five sessions provided a baseline. Shock was administered on Sessions 6–10, and baseline recovery occurred during Sessions 11–14.

throws a hidden switch whenever the client's eyes do not maintain contact. The switch is connected to a clock so that total time of eye contact during each half-hour session can be determined. After a number of sessions, when the therapist is satisfied that a stable baseline performance has been reached (that is, a fairly consistent time of eye contact per session), the therapist begins the shock procedure. Whenever the client breaks eye contact and the experimenter throws the switch, the client gets a short electrical shock to the forearm. The experimenter then tries to determine whether the amount of eye contact changes from its baseline rate.

Figure 10-3 shows a possible result for this experiment: The therapist decided that a stable baseline had been achieved after Session 5 and began shocks on Session 6. Once the shocks were begun, the client's eye contact increased dramatically. By Session 10, eye contact had reached a stable **transition steady state,**[4] and the experimenter discontinued the shock. By Sessions 12–14, the client had returned to the original baseline behavior.

An experimenter must carry out each of the operations described to have a true baseline experiment: Establish a stable baseline; apply the experimental manipulation, and establish a stable transition steady state; then show **reversibility** by recovering the original baseline when the experimental manipulation is removed.

The logic of the method is that once a baseline has been obtained, an uncontrolled confounding variable is unlikely to suddenly begin to affect

---

[4] The transition steady state is sometimes called the **treatment** or **modification state** in clinical work.

behavior on the same trial in which the experimental manipulation is made. Even if this unlikely event happened, the chances that a confounding variable then ceases to have an effect on the same trial in which the experimental manipulation is discontinued would be extremely small.

To be even more convincing, an experimenter could do an *intrasubject replication,* repeating the procedure with the same individual one or more times. That is, the experimenter might again shock the client on Session 15, continue until a stable transition steady state is achieved, discontinue the shock, and recover the original baseline. Each time the effect can be repeated, our confidence that the change in behavior was caused by the experimental manipulation rather than an uncontrolled confounding variable increases. Even though this is a single-subject design, it would also increase our confidence in the result to do an *intersubject replication*—that is, to repeat the experiment with a few additional individuals. We would still evaluate the results by looking at the data from individuals rather than at grouped data. However, being able to do such intersubject replication strengthens our conclusion.

## ADVANTAGES

The major advantage of a baseline experiment is that it gives us a powerful way of looking at an individual's behavior. For instance, if the results shown in Figure 10-3 were actual data, they would go a long way toward convincing me that eye contact can be controlled by contingent shock. You would be convinced too, wouldn't you?

The results are also easy to interpret. In fact, they are so easy to interpret that baseline experimenters use no statistical tests. Researchers using baseline designs say that if you need a statistical test to convince other investigators that the effect you found is a real effect and not due to chance variation, either the effect is not strong enough to bother with or else you need to refine your techniques to get better control over behavior (eliminate unwanted variability).

In a traditional group experiment, if you use a large number of participants in each group, you may find an effect that is statistically significant but of little practical importance. That is, you may have chosen an independent variable that has an effect on behavior, but the effect may be small compared with other, more important variables. However, a baseline experimental procedure is not sensitive to such unimportant effects. The variability due to the more important independent variables blankets such real but small effects. A baseline procedure, then, guarantees that any effect found is large enough to be of potential importance.

Another advantage of a baseline procedure is the flexibility it allows you in deciding when to impose a level of an independent variable and which level to use. Prior to doing a standard experiment, the investigator must choose the number of trials to present and which levels of the independent variable to use. Because most statistical tests require it, the investigator then needs to collect an equal number of data points for each level of the independent variable. However, investigators who use baseline designs can decide at any point in the experiment to collect more data at the present level or to change to a new level. For instance, in our example, if the therapist had felt the need for more data under the shock condition, the flexibility exists to continue that condition for more sessions before attempting to recover the baseline.

The therapist also could have decided to use an additional level of the independent variable after the experiment was under way. Suppose the change in behavior was not particularly convincing at the specific shock intensity chosen. After recovering baseline and reaching stable performance, the investigator could choose to try a more intense shock on the next block of trials. Thus, the investigator is not required to use predetermined levels of the independent variable.

In addition to the advantages of easy interpretation, the elimination of statistical tests, the guarantee of finding only fairly large effects, and flexibility, baseline experiments can also be used with a single individual. Therapists with only one client with cerebral palsy or experimenters with single participants having unusual disorders, training, or talent could not use a traditional experimental design to study them. However, they could use a baseline procedure.

## DISADVANTAGES

Although baseline experiments offer so many advantages, most experimenters still stick to traditional experimental group designs because they cannot meet the assumptions of baseline experiments. For example, the assumption that experimental effects can be reversed requires that the individual return to the original level of behavior at the end of the experiment. We saw in the previous chapter that many potential sequence and ordering effects require counterbalancing when a within-subject design is used.

SOME PROCESSES ARE
NOT REVERSIBLE.

A baseline experiment is a special kind of within-subject design in which effective counterbalancing is impossible. Thus, any kind of systematically changing confounding variable prevents us from recovering the original baseline. And unless the behavior returns to its former state when the experimental manipulation is removed, we do not know whether to attribute the transition-state behavior to the manipulation or to some confounding variable.

For this reason, many traditional areas of psychology cannot be investigated by baseline procedures. Some obviously inappropriate areas are life span, memory, and some areas of learning. Most of the changes that take place during experiments in these areas cannot be reversed. ("Now forget all the words you have learned.")

A second disadvantage is that baseline designs may not allow us to discover small but important effects. Suppose you work for a telephone company and your job is to find out whether the time it takes a directory-assistance operator to find a number is improved by using a computerized search system rather than a standard telephone book. You decide to use a baseline design, and as each request comes in, you record the length of the call. You have the operator first use the standard telephone book until you achieve a baseline. Then you have the operator switch to a system in which the information is keyed into a computer and the computer provides the numbers. Finally, you have the operator return to the book.

Figure 10-4 shows some possible results. A visual inspection of the figure would probably not convince you or me that there is any difference between using the computerized system and using the standard telephone book. In other words, the transition state does not look any different from the baseline. However, the average call under the computerized system is three seconds shorter than the average call under the book system. If we had done a standard experiment, a statistical test might show such a difference to be significant. But would this be an important effect? Yes, it would be, because each second saved on an average directory-assistance call cumulatively saves telephone companies millions of dollars. That's certainly important to them!

Baseline design proponents may argue that variability is the experimenter's fault, and they may have a point with respect to rats in a sterile laboratory environment. However, I have a difficult time conceiving of how the telephone company scientist could have gained better control of the behavior being measured. In this case the behavior seems to be driven largely by the customer rather than by the operator. In some situations, variability is simply intrinsic to the setting. In this case, small but important effects can be blanketed by this variability, and baseline designs may not be appropriate.

A final disadvantage of baseline experiments is that it is difficult to determine how general any effect we find may be. Because individuals may respond differently to experimental manipulations, our participant may be

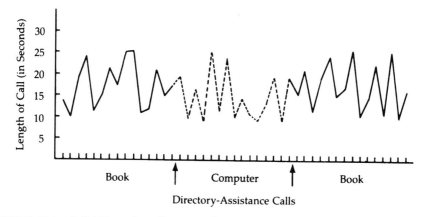

**FIGURE 10-4** A fictitious baseline experiment measuring the length of each directory-assistance call when the operator was alternately using a standard telephone book and a computerized system

an oddball. This criticism can be overcome by redoing the experiment using additional participants. However, the tradition in baseline experiments is to use as few individuals as possible.

Thus, baseline experimental designs can be a valuable tool for some areas of experimental psychology. When the assumptions of the design can be met, a baseline experiment offers a way to convincingly show the effects of important experimental manipulations. Unfortunately, the assumptions are usually so rigorous that baseline designs must be restricted to only a few areas of experimental psychology.

## Survey Research

### WAYS OF DOING SURVEY RESEARCH

Surveys are typically taken to gather information from a sample of people that will be generalized to a larger population. Information about behaviors might be included in a survey; these could also be measured directly. But also included might be information that could not be directly measured, such as opinions, motivations, and even expected future behaviors. In these cases there would seem to be no alternative way of collecting this type of information other than a survey. That is, surveys allow you to ask not only what people do but also why they do it. For this reason surveys are widely used in the social sciences, and when students think of doing a research project, a survey is often one of the first types of research that come to mind.

There are several ways to collect survey information. Perhaps the most widely used method of administration is a **mail survey,** which is mailed directly to the participant. (Survey researchers call those participants who respond to a survey *respondents,* for obvious reasons.) Mail surveys offer several advantages. It is possible to sample people at distant locations at relatively small cost, a task that would be far more difficult and expensive through face-to-face contact. Because anonymity and privacy are easy to maintain, respondents may be more likely to give honest responses. It is also possible to send a mail survey to a representative sample of the population of interest once you have the names and addresses of that population.

However, the big problem with a mail survey is that people are free to toss it in the trash along with their other junk mail. So the response rate may be low, sometimes as low as 20% to 30%. Well, why not just send out four times as many surveys as you need and ignore the nonrespondents? The problem with this solution is that it may produce **nonresponse bias.** We have already discussed nonresponse bias in Chapter 2, but there we called it *selection* as a threat to internal validity. In the case of a survey, you may have carefully chosen a sample that is representative of a larger population and to whom you expect to generalize your findings. But then the composition of that sample changes as participants fail to become respondents. There would be no problem if they became nonrespondents in a random fashion; the sample would still be representative. However, it is difficult to determine why participants fail to respond, and the reasons might systematically bias the sample. Maybe those who fail to respond are busier and busy people happen to be richer or more educated. Or maybe some do not respond because they are uneducated and have difficulty reading surveys. Or perhaps some do not respond because they are politically conservative and believe you are invading their privacy. The problem is that you really do not know how your nonrespondents differ from your respondents and so you do not know how biased your sample has become. Thus, your ability to generalize your findings to the population has become compromised.

The way to minimize nonresponse bias, of course, is to obtain a high response rate. Dillman (1978) suggests a number of ways to improve mail survey response rates. The content of the cover letter included with the survey can make a difference. You should avoid announcing that this is a survey or questionnaire, or pleading for help. It is best to list your institutional affiliation, the date, name and address of the respondent, a statement about why participation is important, a promise of confidentiality, the usefulness of the study, a token reward for participation, where to address questions or comments, a statement of appreciation, your signature in ink, and your title. The letter should give the appearance of being personal rather than a form letter. The token reward might be as small as a quarter or perhaps a pen the respondent can keep after filling out the survey. Research has shown that rewards of this size will increase return rates (Pressley & Tullar, 1977). Another effective strategy is to precontact participants by telephone before the survey is mailed, politely asking them to fill out the survey when it arrives. Finally, follow-up letters also are effective at increasing response rates. Some investigators send out a postcard a week after the original mailing and then a follow-up letter and another copy of the survey several weeks later.

Even with all the efforts mentioned, you should not expect a 100% response rate. The very best mail surveys have response rates on the order of 80%, and a more realistic figure is probably 60%. With these levels of response it is important to assess representativeness of the obtained sample by comparing it with the population. For instance, you probably know something about the distribution of certain demographic variables across the population such as sex, income level, and education. One reason for asking respondents to provide such information on the survey form is so that comparisons can be made with the population. Large deviations of the sample from the population on these demographic variables would be a tip-off that the sample obtained is not representative of the population and so generalization is dangerous.

Another way to collect survey data is by means of a **telephone survey,** in which participants are called on the telephone and asked a standard set of questions. At first this option might strike you as both cheaper and easier than a mail survey. It does have the advantage that it is more personal than a letter and for this reason might elicit more honest and complete responses. However, there are also problems. Getting someone to respond over the phone can be difficult. During the day many families are not home, and in the evenings many homes are deluged with telemarketers trying to sell products and services. Some of these now begin their sales pitches by claiming to be conducting a survey. Lots of folks, understandably, hang up or politely refuse to take any but personal calls. On top of this problem not everyone has a phone, some have two or more (perhaps hooked up only to a computer or fax), and many people have unlisted numbers. Even if you get a participant to respond, some questions are more difficult for the respondent to understand over the phone, particularly with the TV set on and the baby crying in the background. Generally questions have to be shorter and the number of response alternatives limited in order to keep from exceeding the respondent's attention span. Finally, particularly for some sensitive areas, respondents may not be sure that confidentiality will be maintained; they are not really sure you are who you say you are, and there may be other people near the phone who might overhear their responses.

Sometimes it is possible to save time and effort using **group administration** of a survey. In this case the investigator has access to a group of participants and can distribute and collect a written survey in a short time frame. For example, last semester I asked the students in my introductory psychology class to answer a one-page survey on attitudes toward nuclear power generation. Total time to distribute, complete, and collect the survey was about ten minutes. My university requires that class time be used exclusively for educational purposes, so after analyzing the results, I spent part of the next class showing the students the results and using the study to illustrate psychological research methods. Many students at my university also use the introductory psychology student research pool to collect survey information, in this case asking 40 or so students to come to a classroom and fill out a questionnaire. In each of these cases, of course, students can refuse to participate and can fulfill class requirements in alternative ways. Group administration has the advantage of providing large amounts of data rapidly. A disadvantage is that it is hard to ensure complete confidentiality from other respondents sitting close by. It is also often difficult to get a representative sample using such preestablished groups. Do you think students in introductory psychology courses are representative of the general population? Most such groups are selected or self-selected for some purpose other than the research being conducted and are seldom representative samples of populations of interest.

A time-consuming but effective survey technique is the face-to-face **interview.** The respondent meets individually with an interviewer at a location such as a research lab or at the respondent's home or workplace. The interview can be structured, with the interviewer essentially reading questions from a script, or unstructured, in which case the interviewer has the freedom to explore topics as they come up. The structured interview certainly provides more control and makes data analysis easier. On the other hand, the unstructured interview may seem more natural to the participant and may be more likely to elicit deeper and more detailed responses. A strategy used by some investigators is to conduct the first part of the survey as structured and then allow a more unstructured approach toward the end of the session.

We should not overlook the Internet when thinking about survey techniques. An **Internet survey** can be conducted entirely electronically with respondents providing responses over the net. Or the Internet can be used to contact participants or advertise the availability of a survey that would then be mailed to the respondent. For example, a colleague and I just conducted an Internet survey. We belong to a particular professional society and wanted to collect some survey information from a representative sample of members. We took a random sample from the organization's membership directory and, where we could, we used e-mail addresses to send a one-page survey to be filled out electronically and sent back to us. For a few members we had no e-mail addresses or ones that did not work, and for these we used a mail survey. I do not know of any research yet that compares response rates for Internet surveys with those for mail surveys, but I suspect that for short surveys that can be answered electronically, response rates are higher for the Internet. E-mail follow-up reminders are also easy to send. In the future such surveys may be considered a violation of the general rule against unsolicited e-mail, but I believe that is not yet the case.

I also have a colleague who maintains a Web page that he uses to collect survey data. On this page he has asked people to do such things as rate the beauty of computer-generated pictures of faces. He then uses these ratings to determine which facial characteristics are related to beauty. He updates his Web site regularly so that after respondents have made their responses they can find out how their ratings compare with ratings of others. That feedback apparently provides considerable motivation to do the ratings; he has collected thousands of responses in this way. When respondents are self-selected in this way, there are obvious problems with the representativeness of the sample, but for some kinds of research this issue is not a great problem. Do computer geeks surfing the Web have different standards of facial beauty than the rest of the population? Perhaps, but probably not. However, when doing an Internet survey, we should remember that we will always have a biased sample. Not everyone has access to the Internet, and the proportions of Internet users from different demographic groups varies markedly. It is also true that you have to know a lot about setting up a Web site or know someone who does to do this kind of research. However, there are now tutorials available on the Web to help you create surveys. If you think your survey research could be conducted this way, you could use a browser or ask your professor for help in finding such a site.

## SELECTING A SAMPLE

As I have emphasized, in selecting your survey sample you want a group that is representative of the population to whom you want to generalize your conclusions. How do you pick a representative sample? One possibility is to take a **random sample,** a task that is more difficult than you might imagine. If you wanted to generalize to the entire population of the United States, you would first need a list of all U.S. citizens and then you would randomly pick your sample from this list. Putting all these names into a hat and drawing a sample would require a very large hat! In most cases you would have to be content to choose from a smaller population, such as the population of a city, a university, or an introductory psychology class, and hope that population was not too different from the one you were really interested in. Even then, random selection is often not possible. Most departments of psychology get their participants from students taking introductory psychology classes who volunteer to fulfill a course requirement or for extra credit. Some departments pay participants for participation. Either way these people have not been selected at random. I am sure that you can think of many ways that such a sample might differ from a truly random sample. As an example of the impact of nonrandom sampling, in 1993 Ross Perot asked television viewers to send responses to questions printed on a postcard in *TV Guide* and found that 97% favored bigger cuts in government spending. However, the same question put to a random sample showed that only 67% favored such cuts (Tanur, 1994).

When random sampling is not possible, some investigators use a technique called **stratified sampling.** In this case, subpopulations called *strata*[5] are identified, and participants are randomly chosen from within these strata. For example, if the population to be sampled were all U.S. citizens, even though a truly random sample might be impossible to identify, the investigator might want to ensure that economic classes were represented in the proper proportion. In this case, the strata might be incomes up to $20,000, from $20,001 to $40,000, from $40,001 to $60,000, and from $60,000 up. Even if the population were a university's student body, strata might be identified to include the subpopulations of gender, ethnic group, and class rank to ensure that each stratum was proportionally represented in the sample.

## CONSTRUCTING A SURVEY QUESTIONNAIRE

Now that you have chosen a sample, how do you go about making up a survey questionnaire? First of all, you should find out whether you need to make one up at all. If the purpose of your questionnaire is to determine where people fall on a particular personality dimension such as being authoritarian, anxious, internally directed, creative, or some other personal characteristic, a questionnaire has probably already been designed to do this. It is also likely that if this questionnaire has been published, it has already been tested for reliability and validity (see Chapter 7) so you will

---

[5] The everyday meaning of the word *strata* is not too different from this one: layers, such as the layers of rock that you would see where the side of a hill has been cut out for construction. It is easy to picture people of various incomes stacked into such layers. The singular of *strata* is *stratum.*

know whether it is any good. You may find the existence of such a questionnaire when you do your literature search (see Chapter 6), or one of your professors may be able to help you find one. If the questionnaire has been published as part of a journal article, you probably will have little difficulty with copyright restrictions. However, if it is available from a commercial publisher, you will likely have to buy copies of it, and these can be quite expensive. Resist the temptation to plagiarize questions from such a questionnaire. This practice is not only unethical but also, in the case of copyrighted material, illegal.

If your topic of interest is more specific or if you cannot find an existing questionnaire that suits your purpose, you will have to construct one yourself. That seems easy enough. All you have to do is ask questions, right? For example, if you are interested in what people think about the issue of abortion, why not just ask, "What is your opinion about abortion?" That is an example of an **open-ended question** because you have left it open for the respondents to answer any way they wish. Imagine the sentence, paragraph, or book that you will get back as a response to that one open-ended question. Even if you could convince your respondents to take the time to answer this question thoroughly, how could you possibly analyze the reams of data produced? As a first step in constructing your questionnaire, you might wish to ask some people your potential questions in an interview setting. The types of responses people give to such open-ended questions might give you an idea for constructing more restricted **closed-end questions** for your survey. Throughout this process, you should remember that at some point you will have to analyze the data you collect. Ideally, you should be able to convert most of the data into numbers, to make them quantitative. Statisticians tell horror stories about investigators, sometimes students, who walk into their office, plop down a stack of questionnaires, and say: "Here they are. How do I analyze them?"

I do not mean to imply that it is impossible to numerically analyze answers to all open-ended questions. Although it requires extra effort, you can convert answers to well-constructed questions into quantitative data. For example, some survey researchers train independent judges to read answers to open-ended questions and code the answers into predetermined response categories. The responses of individual judges can then be compared to determine how reliable the coding scheme was. The point is that whatever means you use, by the time you finish constructing your questionnaire, you should know exactly what types of data you will end up with and how you will analyze these data.

One way to turn the respondents' answers into numbers is to use closed-ended, **multiple-alternative questions** that restrict the possible responses. Here is an example:

When should a woman be allowed to have an abortion?
_____ Never
_____ Only in the case of rape or incest

_____ Only in the case of rape or incest and with parents' permission for minors

_____ Whenever she decides to do so

The instructions would indicate that a check mark should be put next to only one alternative. With a question item such as this one, we could count up the number of respondents who put check marks next to each alternative. That would give us numbers as data.

Note that although this question will provide quantitative data, even this simple question could be criticized. Some respondents might wonder what the word *allowed* means: Who is doing the allowing? The state? God? Some respondents might not find an alternative that perfectly describes their feelings. For example, some might believe that the fetus's father has some rights or that the age of the fetus is of critical importance. Even the way the question is framed might make a difference. Do you think that the following questions frame the issue in such a way that respondents would feel pressure to answer in a particular way?

"Should the right of a woman to terminate her pregnancy be treated like any other health issue?"

"When should the government limit a woman's right to have an abortion?"

"When should a mother be allowed to take the life of her unborn baby?"

Certain words tend to have particular beliefs and emotions associated with them. In general, people believe that people's *rights* should be protected, that *government limitations* should be minimized, that *women* are independent but that *mothers* have responsibilities, that *fetuses* are not human but *unborn babies* are, and that to *terminate* is not to kill but *to take the life of* is. Most questions would probably not be so blatantly biased as these examples, but smaller forms of bias can creep in even when we try to avoid it. Recently I was writing a questionnaire to find out whether a certain statistics class in my university was adequately preparing our psychology students. I must admit that I did not think that the class was being well taught. Before I caught myself and changed it, the questionnaire I was going to give graduating students contained an item that said, "If you think that this class was taught poorly, which of the following reasons would you give?" I then listed a number of possible problems with the class without listing any possible positive aspects. I was embarrassed when one of my colleagues pointed out the obvious negative bias I had built into the question.

Even small changes in language can result in large apparent changes in opinion. For example, a recent telephone poll found that whereas 53% of people said that the government was spending too much money "on welfare," only 23% said the government was spending too much money "on assistance to the poor."[6] In a similar survey that I mentioned earlier, Ross Perot asked, "Do you believe that for every dollar of tax increase, there should be two dollars in spending cuts with the savings earmarked for deficit and debt reduction?" Sixty-seven percent of a random sample responded positively. However, when the question was rewritten to "Would you favor or oppose a proposal to cut spending by two dollars for every dollar in new taxes, with the savings earmarked for deficit reduction, even if it means cuts in domestic programs like Medicare and education?" only 33% of respondents favored it (Tanur, 1994). You can see that subtle wording changes can make large differences in respondents' opinions.

You should also examine your questions to make sure that all the language is understandable to the respondents in your sample. Because most college students and instructors typically interact with people having some college education, it is easy to forget that the general population has less well-developed reading skills and vocabulary comprehension. So keep your vocabulary appropriate for your sample. You should also make sure that the questions are not so awkwardly stated that they are confusing. For example, questions stated in the negative should typically be avoided: "Does a woman not have the right to an abortion?" The best way to find out if your questions are understandable is to give a draft of your questionnaire to a small sample of people similar to the larger sample you will use in your study and ask for comments.

Another way to force respondents to give responses that can be converted to numbers is to use a **rating scale.** Several types of rating scales provide a graded response. For example, you might ask:

How well do you think Senator Jones has expressed her opinion on the abortion issue?

| Very Poorly | 1 | 2 | 3 | 4 | 5 | 6 | 7 | 8 | 9 | 10 | Very Well |
|---|---|---|---|---|---|---|---|---|---|---|---|

Respondents might be asked to circle a number or place a check mark or an $X$ on the line. Alternatively, the line could be subdivided by putting hash marks on it. In this example verbal labels have been provided at only the ends of the scale: these are called *anchors* because they tie down the meaning of the ends of the continuum. Alternatively, the numbers or hash marks could be given labels as well, such as "poorly," "fairly poorly," "neutral," "fairly well," "well." The number of gradations could also be varied, typically from five to ten. Five gradations is usually considered the minimum because some people avoid the extremes. A five-point scale then becomes a three-point scale with little room remaining to express differences in opinion.

---

[6] From a telephone poll of 600 adult Americans taken for *Time* and CNN on May 18–19, 1994, by Yankelovich Partners, Inc. Reported in *Time*, June 27, 1994, p. 26.

If you are interested in your respondents' attitude about a number of topics, a **Likert scale** might be a good scale to choose. In using a Likert scale, you give your participants a series of statements and ask them to indicate whether they agree or disagree with each statement. The following is an example of one such item:

1. It should be legal for a woman to seek an abortion if her pregnancy results from rape.

| Strongly Agree | Agree | Neutral | Disagree | Strongly Disagree |
|:---:|:---:|:---:|:---:|:---:|
| 1 | 2 | 3 | 4 | 5 |

The respondents are instructed to circle the number of the alternative that best indicates their opinion. Instead of using numbers, a horizontal line can be provided, either subdivided or not, and respondents can put an X or other mark to indicate their attitude. In this case the distance from the end of the line to the mark has to be measured so that the response can be converted into a number. An advantage of a Likert scale is that respondents use the same scale to respond to a variety of items. This internal consistency in formatting minimizes confusion and makes it likely that respondents will use the scale in a consistent manner across items. From a practical point of view, an additional advantage is that the statements can usually be put into a list on the left side of the sheet, with the scale numbers on the right side. The anchors, or descriptors, then need to be printed only once at the top of the page. This formatting saves space and is easy for the respondent to understand. An example is shown in Figure 10-5.

Most researchers also collect demographic information in their surveys, information about the respondent's gender, age, ethnicity, education, income, class rank, religion, grade point average, and so forth. Exactly which information you wish to ask for will depend on the purpose of the survey. For example, if you wanted to determine whether people's attitudes toward abortion were influenced by their religion, you would obviously need to include a question that would allow you to sort the questionnaires according to this factor. As you can see, here again it is important for you to determine, when designing the questionnaire, how you will analyze your data. Not all researchers agree about where in the questionnaire to include demographic items. The most obvious place would be at the beginning, but some researchers have argued that putting demographic items there might lead participants to think the questionnaire is boring, in which case they may be less likely to complete it (Dillman, 1978).

## ADVANTAGES

We have already discussed many of the advantages of surveys and questionnaires. They offer a way of assessing people's opinions, attitudes, motivations, and future behaviors that would not be available to us through

## Opinions on Abortion Issues

Please circle the number on the right that most closely approximates your agreement with each statement.

| | Strongly disagree | Disagree | Neutral | Agree | Strongly agree |
|---|---|---|---|---|---|
| 1. Having an abortion is a sin. | 1 | 2 | 3 | 4 | 5 |
| 2. The government should subsidize abortions for poor women. | 1 | 2 | 3 | 4 | 5 |
| 3. It should be illegal for a woman under 18 years of age to have an abortion without her parents' permission. | 1 | 2 | 3 | 4 | 5 |
| 4. Doctors performing abortions should be required to counsel their patients about alternatives such as adoption. | 1 | 2 | 3 | 4 | 5 |
| 5. The choice to have an abortion should be left entirely up to the pregnant woman. | 1 | 2 | 3 | 4 | 5 |
| 6. "Day-after" abortion pills should be legal. | 1 | 2 | 3 | 4 | 5 |
| 7. People picketing abortion clinics should be arrested. | 1 | 2 | 3 | 4 | 5 |
| 8. Abortion should be available only in cases of pregnancy due to rape or incest. | 1 | 2 | 3 | 4 | 5 |

**FIGURE 10-5** An example of an opinion survey using a Likert scale for responses

standard experimental techniques. In addition, they provide a way to collect large amounts of data relatively inexpensively and quickly.

## DISADVANTAGES

We have also discussed several of the disadvantages of survey research. The large data sets collected can be difficult to analyze, particularly when data analysis has not been planned during the design of the survey. Even then fairly sophisticated statistical techniques may be required to analyze large data sets. In addition, when low response rates are a problem, it becomes difficult to generalize to larger populations because of nonresponse bias.

A third disadvantage is that surveys are really correlational observations rather than experiments. In a survey no independent variable has been manipulated to cause a change in behavior. The data from a survey are essentially multiple dependent measures. For that reason we have to avoid making causal statements from the results. For example, we might want to relate attitudes toward abortion to religious affiliation. Perhaps we discover in a survey that respondents who indicate more fundamental religious beliefs are also more strongly opposed to abortion. We might be tempted to say that the religious beliefs cause negative attitudes toward abortion, but all we can really say is that they are related. I hope you remember the discussions in Chapters 1 and 2 that pointed out the reasons we have to be careful interpreting correlational data.

A final inherent weakness of surveys and questionnaires, even good ones: They do not measure behavior directly but are self-reports. So respondents can tell us anything they want, and we have no way of independently verifying the information. Why would they lie to us? Actually, there are several reasons why their responses might not be truthful. One reason is that they want to protect themselves. Even though the researcher has told them that their responses are anonymous and they do not have to put their names on the form, they may believe that the researcher has somehow coded the forms so that they can be identified. Or if they are filling out the form in a room with other respondents, they may think that somebody else will see their answers. Even if they are convinced that their information will remain confidential, the respondents may have some idea how the information will be used by the researcher and may have some reason for distorting their responses. For example, an individual who smokes marijuana and thinks it ought to be legalized might state falsely that she has never had a bad experience when under the influence of drugs. She probably realizes that if a large number of users report bad experiences, this information could help prevent legalization. Individuals might even lie because they want to bring attention to their group or their cause. For example, if a student thinks that something ought to be done about guns in his high school, he might claim that he has seen more guns in his school than he actually has.

In some cases respondents may not be purposely untruthful but may lie to themselves as well as the researcher. In the case of emotion-laden issues, individuals might not wish to admit their own feelings and attitudes, particularly when these differ from those that are considered socially acceptable. For example, a respondent might strongly deny being a racist, while engaging in behaviors that clearly indicate that he or she is a racist. Because being a racist is not socially acceptable to most members of our society, people have a difficult time admitting to being one even when they are.

In analyzing survey data, then, we should always keep in mind that in the end the data are self-reports. When we discuss the results of surveys, we should remember to qualify our statements in recognition of this fact. We should not say that 27% of high school students have used marijuana if all we know is that 27% have reported using marijuana. As my grandmother used to tell me, "Saying and doing are two different things."

Table 10-3 provides a handy reference summarizing the advantages and disadvantages of the various research techniques we have examined in this chapter.

**TABLE 10-3**
A Summary of the Advantages and Disadvantages of Doing
Quasi-Experiments, Baseline Experiments, and Surveys

| Design | Advantages | Disadvantages |
|---|---|---|
| Quasi-experiments | Allows applied research when experiments are not possible. Threats to internal validity can be assessed. | Threats to internal validity may exist. Designs are more complex than traditional experiments. Statistical analysis can be difficult. |
| Baseline experiments | One individual can provide results that are easy to interpret without statistics. Size and timing of independent-variable manipulation are flexible. One can study infrequently occurring conditions. | Assumptions are difficult to meet (for example, reversibility). One cannot investigate small but important effects. Generalizability is limited. |
| Surveys | One can investigate internal events (for example, attitudes). Large amounts of data can be collected quickly. | Large data sets are sometimes difficult to analyze. Low response rates can cause nonresponse bias. Results are correlational, so causality cannot be inferred. Self-reports may not be truthful. |

# Summary

In applied field settings where random assignment of participants to groups is often not possible, nontraditional designs called **quasi-experimental designs** can sometimes be used. **Nonexperimental designs** are difficult to interpret because of multiple threats to internal validity. These designs include a **one-group posttest-only design,** in which the behavior of only one group is tested after exposure to a treatment; a **posttest-only design with nonequivalent groups,** in which a second group, selected in a different manner, is also tested but not exposed to the treatment; and a **one-group pretest–posttest design,** in which one group is tested before and after exposure to the treatment.

Quasi-experimental designs permit you to eliminate or assess most threats to internal validity. In a **nonequivalent control group design with pretest and posttest,** one group is tested before and after the treatment, and a second group, selected in a different manner, is tested at equivalent times but without being exposed to the treatment. Variations of this basic design include using a **proxy pretest** to measure a variable correlated with the posttest when the use of a pretest is not possible; using **separate pretest and posttest samples** by subdividing the nonequivalent groups and testing half of each group before and half after exposure to the treatment; and making **pretest observations at more than one time interval,** so that each group is tested several times before exposure to the treatment.

The second class of quasi-experimental designs is **interrupted time-series designs,** in which one group is tested multiple times before and after exposure to the treatment. Variations of this design include the **addition of a nonequivalent no-treatment control group time series,** in which a second group, selected in a different manner, is tested at equivalent times but not exposed to the treatment; using an **interrupted time series with removed treatment,** in which a third series of tests is given after the treatment is removed; and using an **interrupted time series with switching replications,** in which two groups selected in different ways are tested at many points in time but are exposed to the treatment at different points in the series.

A second type of nontraditional design is a **baseline experiment** that can show experimental effects using data from only one individual. Baseline experiments are often used to evaluate the effects of treatments or therapeutic interventions. After establishing a **steady-state** rate of responding called a **baseline,** the investigator initiates the experimental manipulation until the rate of responding changes to a new **transition steady state.** The investigator then demonstrates **reversibility** by recovering the original baseline. An advantage of baseline designs is that they offer a convincing way to show important changes in a single individual's behavior. The experimenter can also be flexible in choosing when to manipulate the independent variable and which level to change it to. These results are also easy to interpret. However, some assumptions of baseline experiments, such as reversibility, cannot be met in many areas of psychology. It is also sometimes difficult to show small but important effects and risky to generalize the findings to a larger population.

A third type of nontraditional design is the **survey,** or questionnaire, which can be used to assess the opinions, attitudes, motivations, or future behaviors of a sample of respondents. **Mail surveys** are relatively inexpensive and allow sampling of large geographic areas. However, low response rates can cause problems with **nonresponse bias,** the disproportionate loss of certain segments of the sample, and affect the generalizability of findings from the sample to the larger population. Response rates can be improved with appropriate cover letters, small rewards, precontacts, and follow-up letters. **Telephone surveys** can be done even more quickly and more personally. However, nonresponding is still a problem as well as is the difficulty in getting a representative sample from those with telephones. **Group administration** of surveys can be quite efficient, but the composition of the group is often not representative of the population of interest.

Face-to-face **interviews,** while less efficient than some of the other procedures, allow a more personal interaction with the respondent and the possibility of both structured and unstructured interviewing. A developing survey procedure is the **Internet survey,** in which participation can be solicited on the Internet and responding can be done either electronically or through the mail.

The sample for a survey can be a **random sample,** in which case all members of the population have an equal chance of being selected, or a **stratified sample,** in which case various categories or strata are identified and random sampling occurs within the strata. Survey questionnaires can include **open-ended questions,** which can be difficult to quantify, or **closed-ended questions** with more restricted response options, such as **multiple-alternative questions** or questions using a **rating scale** such as a **Likert scale.** Though surveys offer the opportunity to collect large amounts of data quickly about opinions, attitudes, and future behaviors, the large data sets can be difficult to analyze, low responding can cause nonresponse bias, causality cannot be inferred from correlational data, and self-reports may not be truthful.

## SUGGESTED BOOKS ON QUASI-EXPERIMENTAL STATISTICS

*For the Beginning Student*
Cook, T. D., & Campbell, D. T. (1979). *Quasi-experimentation: Design & analysis issues for field settings.* Chicago: Rand McNally.

*For the Advanced Student*
Box, G. E. P., & Jenkins, G. M. (1976). *Time-series analysis: Forecasting and control.* San Francisco: Holden-Day.
Campbell, D. T., & Stanley, J. C. (1966). *Experimental and quasi-experimental designs for research.* Chicago: Rand McNally.
Kidder, L. H., & Judd, C. M. (1986). *Research methods in social relations,* 5th ed. New York: Holt, Rinehart & Winston.

## SUGGESTED BOOKS ON BASELINE DESIGNS

Hersen, M., & Barlow, D. H. (1984). *Single-case experimental designs: Strategies for studying behavior change.* New York: Pergamon Press.
Robinson, P. W., & Foster, D. F. (1979). *Experimental psychology: A small-N approach.* New York: Harper & Row.

## SUGGESTED BOOK ON SURVEY DESIGNS

Dillman, D. A. (1978). *Mail and telephone surveys: The total design method.* New York: Wiley.

# Find It on InfoTrac College Edition

Using InfoTrac College Edition, search in the educational psychology journals to find an article that uses a quasi-experimental design. Within the context of the experiment you have found, why do you think it was necessary for the researchers to use a quasi-experimental design rather than a more traditional experimental design?

Using InfoTrac College Edition, search in the animal behavior journals to find an experiment using a single-subject or small-$N$ baseline design. Do you think it would have been appropriate to use a more conventional group design to study the problem the author was interested in?

Search journals in social psychology or organizational psychology to find an article describing research using a survey or questionnaire. How was the survey administered (telephone, mail, interview)? Did the survey use open-ended questions, closed-ended questions, or some combination? What was the response rate for this survey? Given this response rate do you think nonresponse bias was a problem?

# 11

## How to Tell When You Are Ready to Begin

An error is a mistake only if repeated.

ANONYMOUS

You should now have all the tools needed for beginning your experiment. However, you may have to ask yourself some questions to determine whether you have considered all the important issues before you can begin collecting data.

When I teach experimental methods, my students have to think up, design, and do an original experiment. Before they are allowed to start collecting data, they are required to present the proposed experiment to the class. It is the job of the class, and my job, to critique the experiment, trying to find flaws and determining whether the student experimenter has considered all necessary details before doing the research. This exercise serves several purposes. It helps develop a critical sense in the students listening to the presentation, an ability that all scientists must have. Preparing

EXPERIMENTAL
REPORTS DUE
TOMORROW AT

HOW TO KNOW WHEN YOU
ARE READY TO BEGIN YOUR
EXPERIMENT

231

A POTENTIALLY CRITICAL GROUP OF PEERS

for the presentation also motivates the student experimenters to try to think about the many assumptions they have made and the small decisions that they may have avoided up to this point. Finally, this exercise allows all of us to help the experimenters by suggesting ways to improve the experiment.

## The Have-a-Nice-Day Society

Before discussing some of the commonly unanswered questions that need to be considered before beginning an experiment, I would like to comment on the emotional response many of my students have to the presentations. Those making the presentations often consider this the most aversive and distressing part of the course. Part of the distress is just the act of making a presentation, any presentation, a skill that is seldom tapped in other college courses. But I suspect that most of the distress is due to having to defend their experiment before a potentially critical group of peers.

The first reaction of the student audience is to keep quiet: "I won't rock your boat if you don't rock mine." Even with my prodding, some students are reluctant to criticize their fellow students' ideas. We live in a have-a-nice-day society where the rules include extreme tolerance of the behaviors and opinions of others. Some people seem to believe that because we all have the right to express our views, the value of one opinion is equal to the value of another. And criticizing other people's opinions is seen as a personal attack on them or on their right of free speech.

Judging from their comments on the student evaluations filled out at the end of the class, some students certainly do perceive my comments at the student presentations as personal and uncalled for. As much as I try to smile, keep my voice down, and project a helpful attitude, these students cannot seem to understand why their nice, friendly teacher has suddenly turned on them.

I hope that the preceding chapters in this book have, at least on an intellectual level, convinced you that within science one opinion is not as good as another. Opinions must be defendable. If the rules of science are violated, the results become suspect or useless. The rules of deductive and inductive logic, discussed in Chapter 3, *are* the basis for arguing that certain results support or refute a theory. The elimination of potential confounding variables, discussed in Chapter 2, *is* required to be able to build a case for causality—that is, to claim that the independent variable caused the change in the dependent variable. The random selection of an experimental sample of participants, discussed in Chapter 2, *is* the basis on which results can be generalized to a larger population.

When the class, the instructor, or colleagues criticize a research proposal, they are attempting to help the proposer follow the rules of science so that after the research is completed, the results can be defended and can be added to the scientific body of knowledge. Although criticism at the proposal stage can be irritating, once the research is completed it is devastating. After-the-fact criticism indicates not only that you made a mistake because you were not thoughtful enough but also that you wasted both your time and the participants' time and perhaps wasted other resources that could have been used to advance the body of knowledge. The message here is not that science is a deadly serious enterprise in which mistakes bring great guilt but that science has certain rules to which you must adhere as a scientist. And you should use whatever resources are available, including the advice of others, to help you follow the rules and do good research.

## Questions before You Begin

The following questions are the ones I most frequently ask my students when they make their research proposals. You may already have answered them. Good for you! If not, be sure that you can before you begin collecting data.

### DOES MY EXPERIMENT SATISFY ETHICAL CONCERNS?

As we saw in Chapter 4, the need to treat research participants ethically raises a number of concerns. Have you considered all these concerns? Will your participants be subjected to any psychological or physical stress? If so, how can it be minimized? Will your participants give informed consent? If you use sign-up sheets, do they give an adequate description of the experiment so that informed consent is possible? Can you document this consent? Are you using deception in your experiment? If so, are you adequately debriefing the participants when the experiment is over? Have you prepared a debriefing statement? Have you prepared a schedule so that you will be able to meet all your participants in a timely way? Have you considered what you will do if your equipment breaks down or if you get sick? Do you know how you are going to ensure that the data you collect remain confidential? Does your experiment have demand characteristics? Are these likely to affect the results? You should ask yourself all these questions before you begin your experiment.

In addition, you should do all the paperwork necessary to get permission from your institutional review board to conduct the study. In some cases, these review boards take several weeks to consider a research proposal, and you cannot begin before they give final approval. So be sure to fill out and submit the paperwork required as soon as you have settled on a design. Following this advice is even more important if your experiment is at all ethically controversial—that is, uses deception, is potentially stressful, involves drugs, and so forth. In this case, the review board will probably take longer, may come back to you to work out some details, or may not even approve the study.

## HOW MANY PARTICIPANTS DO I NEED?

It is often hard to figure out how many participants you will need for your experiment. One of the most frequent mistakes students make is to use too few, so that what appears to be a good result is not statistically significant. Of course, there may be some practical considerations, such as a limited pool of participants, that restrict the number you are allowed to use. If so, you may just have to make do. Assuming that you may use as many participants as you wish, there are statistical ways of determining the power of a statistical test and the approximate number of participants needed. However, these tests are beyond the scope of this book, and in actuality, most experimenters do not use them.

You should also bear in mind that whereas too few participants will not allow you to show statistical significance with a reasonable-sized experimental effect, too many can show statistical significance even with an unimportant effect. In this case, not only is using too many participants inefficient, it may be misleading.

Perhaps the best way to determine how many participants to use is by studying the literature. Certainly, if you are replicating someone else's experiment and a statistically significant effect was reported, you will have a pretty good idea of the numbers needed. Even if you are not doing a direct replication, you will probably be able to find similar experiments that have used the dependent variable you are proposing. The variability found in data generated from particular dependent variables such as reaction times or words recalled from a list tends to be relatively stable. In the unlikely event that you can find no similar experiments, you may have to do a pilot experiment to get some idea of the number of participants you will need.

## SHOULD I RUN PARTICIPANTS INDIVIDUALLY OR IN GROUPS?

Most new experimenters think first of bringing participants in individually for an experiment. Sometimes there's no choice—for example, only one piece of equipment may be available for recording responses. In other cases, some individuals might affect the performance of others in the group, so they must be run individually. However, if you can run participants in groups, you can collect data more efficiently.

When considering your options, you should ask yourself questions like these: Can I give groups a questionnaire rather than ask questions of individuals? Can I collect the necessary data by using slides or an overhead projector to display stimuli to a group, instead of using flip cards or a computer display with individuals? If you are presenting a consistent series of stimuli and recording only the accuracy of responses or the number of responses in a particular category, you can most likely use groups. If the order or timing of stimulus events depends on the responses made or if precise timing of the responses is necessary, then you should probably run participants individually.

## HOW LONG WILL MY EXPERIMENT TAKE?

Calculating the length of the experiment poses questions at several levels. At the grossest level, how many hours, or days, or weeks of collecting data will be necessary? At a finer level, how long will a single experimental session take? If you are going to use individual trials, you cannot answer either of these questions without first determining the length of a trial and the number of trials. To figure out trial length, you must know the sequence of events that will occur during a trial and the time required by each event, including the intertrial interval (the time between trials). Then, by knowing how many trials will be presented, you can determine the total time taken to complete the trials. In some cases the number of trials may have to be estimated, as, for example, when participants must achieve a performance criterion, such as two consecutive trials on which a list of words is correctly recalled.

You should also remember to include the time to do other tasks associated with the experiment. Usually the participants will have to be given some instructions and be allowed to ask questions before starting. A set of practice trials may be included if some learning is anticipated and a relatively stable performance is desired. Rest breaks may be needed to avoid fatigue during long or tedious experiments. A debriefing session at the end of the experiment may be required, particularly if students are serving in the experiment as part of a class requirement and are supposed to be learning about experiments. Finally, some "slop time" should be built in, because people sometimes arrive late. Without this time, consecutive sessions will run progressively later and later. Figure 11-1 shows some of the steps required for determining the time expected for an experimental session.

You will then need to determine how much participant-experimentation time you will be devoting to this experiment. Again, you should anticipate some unplanned time to run extra participants, to replace those who failed to show up, those whose data were eliminated for failure to meet some criterion, or those for whom the equipment malfunctioned. As for the total time needed to complete the experiment, remember that data

*One Trial*

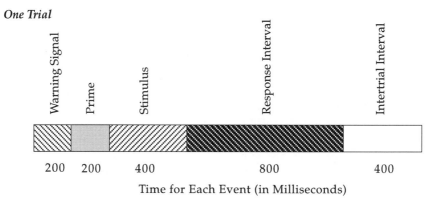

Total time for one trial = 200 + 200 + 400 + 800 + 400 = 2000 ms, or 2 sec

*One Session*

With 20 blocks of 20 trials each, 30-sec rest breaks, 5 minutes for instructions, and 5 minutes for debriefing:

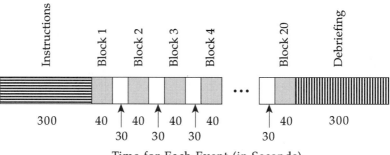

Total time for experiment = 300 sec + (20 blocks × 40 sec) + (19 rest × 30 sec) + 300 sec = 1970 sec, or 32 min 50 sec

Including some flexibility for late arrivals, time to be seated, and so on, this experiment should be scheduled for 40 to 45 minutes.

**FIGURE 11-1** An example of the calculations necessary for determining the time required for an experimental session. In this experiment each trial consists of a 200-millisecond warning signal, a 200-millisecond prime (prestimulus information), a 400-millisecond stimulus, an 800-millisecond response interval, and a 400-millisecond intertrial interval (time between trials).

collection is only part of the job. You will also need time to analyze the data, interpret them, and produce several drafts of the experimental report. And each of these tasks usually takes more time than anticipated.

## DO I NEED TO SET PARTICIPANT RESTRICTIONS?

In general, determining whether to set limitations on who may participate in your experiment depends on the population to which you want to generalize your findings. The limited pool of participants from which you have to draw will probably have already reduced your ability to generalize. For example, if you use college students, you must consider that certain ages are definitely overrepresented and certain ones underrepresented. And you must take into account that compared with the average population of the country, an average group of college students has a higher IQ, is in a higher socioeconomic bracket, has greater reading ability, and is less likely to have health problems. So you cannot legitimately generalize to the entire population.

However, for practical reasons you might wish to exclude some individuals from your experiment even though this further limits the generalizability of your results. For example, if you are studying language performance such as reading ability, identification of words, memory for words, or a number of related language tasks, you might limit your participants to those whose first language is English. If you are studying visual perception, you might use people whose eyesight is corrected to 20/20 or who can pass a test for color blindness. If you are studying motor ability, such as in sports psychology, you might exclude individuals who have physical impairments that would prevent them from contributing useful data. In some cases, you might use only men or only women, whereas in other cases, you might have an equal number of men and women so that you can evaluate the effect of gender on performance. These are only some of the possible restrictions you might wish to consider. Depending on the particular task to be performed in your experiment, other restrictions might be appropriate and should be carefully considered.

## SHOULD I SET ANY A PRIORI CRITERIA FOR ELIMINATING PARTICIPANTS?

As we discussed in Chapter 4, you may wish to set performance criteria before collecting data. For example, I often collect reaction-time data in my experiments. There are sometimes one or two participants whose overall performance level is not comparable to that of the others. So I often set a criterion that data from any individual whose mean reaction time exceeds the mean reaction time of all participants in the experiment by 300 milliseconds will be eliminated from the analysis. Such a criterion, along with the number of participants thus eliminated, should be reported in the results section of the experimental report. And as noted in Chapter 4, participants cannot be eliminated or data thrown out for failure to support a predicted hypothesis.

The general purpose of setting a priori criteria is to eliminate participants who are distinctly different from the others and who therefore add a large amount of variability to the data. They may be different because of motivational factors, personality factors, or personal limitations. Such differences may, certainly, be of interest to psychologists studying individual differences or abnormal behavior. But their behavior is usually not of much interest to most experimental psychologists, whose concern is usually with establishing a science of the behavioral norm.

## CAN I OPERATIONALLY DEFINE ALL MY VARIABLES?

In Chapter 7 I discussed the necessity of being able to operationally define your independent and dependent variables and to state the required operations that need to be carried out to enable you to repeat your experiment. Although you should have determined operational definitions at an early stage of designing your experiment, experimenters sometimes fail to do this.

Because the independent variables are the variables of major interest to the experimenter, great care must be taken in specifying their definition. Suppose that you propose to do the experiment that sets the record for the one most often proposed by my students.[1] You want to know the effects of listening to music on studying. Some variations of this basic experiment are the effects of rock versus classical music, of TV, of noise, and of loud music versus soft music. Suppose the comparison is between rock and classical music. What is rock music? Heavy metal, punk rock, new wave, hip hop, rock and roll? What is classical music? A Strauss waltz, Dvořák's *New World Symphony*, a Beethoven sonata, Tchaikovsky's *1812 Overture*? Even when you use classical music, the outcome of the experiment may be quite different if a quiet string quartet is played rather than a noisy overture complete with rolling timpani and cannons.

Likewise, if the comparison is between loud and soft music, the question is, how loud? An appropriate answer is not "I'll turn it up until it sounds loud" or even "I'll set the volume control of my stereo on 8." Another experimenter would not know what operations to follow to produce the same loudness. Ideally, you would have someone measure the sound with a meter and tell you the average sound-pressure level in decibels.

For the dependent variable, again an operational definition is required. What are you going to measure to see whether the music has an effect on studying? There are a number of possibilities. You could find out how many pages participants were able to read within certain time limits. You could find out how many math problems they completed. You might give them a quiz on the material studied. Or you could ask the participants how difficult they found studying to be under a particular condition. Each of these measures has advantages and drawbacks, but some dependent variable will have to be operationally defined, because no proposal is complete until that is done.

---

[1] This experiment is closely followed in popularity by experiments that test the effects of drug X (for instance, marijuana, alcohol, or cocaine) on the performance of task Y (such as driving, studying, or memorizing). If your instructor requires that you propose an experiment and you want to be impressively original, do not propose either of these experiments!

## HAVE I ARRANGED FOR ANY EQUIPMENT OR MATERIALS NEEDED?

Many experiments require equipment, and nearly all require some sort of materials to be prepared. Fortunately, computers can be used to present stimuli with precise timing and to record and store responses. If you have access to such equipment and know how to use it or can get help from someone who knows how, you will be able to carry out many experiments with a minimum of preparation. However, if computers are not readily available, or if your experiment cannot benefit from computers, you may have to carry out your experiment the old-fashioned way, using whatever equipment is on hand or constructing the equipment and materials yourself. In some cases, you may even have to plan your experiment around the resources that are available.

Among the materials you may have to prepare are a set of instructions, response sheets on which to record data, and a debriefing script. You should generally write the instructions out ahead of time. Later you may well include them in an appendix in the experimental report. In any case, they should certainly be available if someone wanting to replicate your experiment requests them.

It is usually not a good idea simply to hand instructions to your participants and expect them to read them properly. Some people's reading ability leaves a bit to be desired, particularly when the experimenter is hovering over them waiting for them to finish. Experimenters often give written instructions and then also read them aloud—slowly. (After all, it's the first time the participants have heard them, even though the experimenter may have read them many times.) The last sentence of instructions is usually "Do you have any questions?" Even in experiments in which learning should not be a problem, it is often useful to give participants a few practice trials so that they know what to expect once the experiment starts. These practice trials can also be included toward the end of the instructions.

If your experiment is one in which data about individual responses are to be recorded (as opposed to questionnaires, for example), you will probably have to construct data sheets for recording these responses. If you are going to present various types of trials that represent different levels of the independent variable, the response sheets may also include this information. Especially if the trial types are to be randomly presented, you should have determined the random orders ahead of time by using a random number table or some other random device. If you attempt to create a random sequence while the experiment is under way, it will not really be random (see Chapter 2).

Finally, you should write a debriefing script so that you can inform the participants at the end of the experiment about the purpose of the research. When participants serve in an experiment as part of a class requirement, such a debriefing is usually necessary. Even if it is not, the debriefing is a good idea. People will leave the experiment feeling more comfortable and not carry away misconceptions about what they just went through. In addition, they may be able to learn something about psychology from this

experience and, at the very least, will feel better about their experience because somebody has taken the time to explain the purpose of the study and to thank them for their service.

### DO I KNOW HOW I WILL ANALYZE MY DATA?

Chapter 12 deals with how to interpret your experimental results using descriptive and inferential statistics, and Appendix A provides a guide to some commonly used statistical tests. If your experiment is relatively simple and small, these may be sufficient for you to determine how to analyze your data. If your experiment is more complex, you may need some help from your instructor, a statistics book, or a statistical consultant to choose an appropriate way to analyze the results. Regardless of how you determine what is the best way, before you do the experiment you must know how the data will be analyzed. Statistical consultants tell horror stories about people coming to them with reams of data after an experiment is complete only to discover that the data are useless because they are unanalyzable! Don't become a character in one of these stories. Know ahead of time in what form your data will need to be and how they can be analyzed.

### HOW WILL I INTERPRET THE POSSIBLE OUTCOMES OF MY EXPERIMENT?

When you decide to do a particular experiment, you probably have some idea what the results will be. Unlike the starting assumption in statistics, called the *null hypothesis,* that there will be no effect of manipulating the independent variable, you probably actually expect that the differences in the levels of your independent variable will cause a difference in the dependent variable. Scientists are encouraged to be nonpartisan bystanders, not active participants rooting for a particular outcome. In fact, a good deal of the fun of science is predicting the outcome of experiments. Being a good predictor is part of the art of being a good scientist.[2] But be careful that you do not become so enamored of your predictions that you are tempted to lose objectivity and produce a biased experiment.

So be prepared to interpret the results of your experiment regardless of the outcome. Some experiments, because of their design, are considered failures if certain outcomes occur. Scientists sometimes call outcomes such as these that support the null hypothesis a *negative result*. For example, suppose you did the experiment to determine the effects of rock and classical music on a student's ability to study and found that the group listening to rock and the group listening to classical music were not statistically different in their performance. As will be discussed in Chapter 12, because our statistical tests are designed to test for differences, not samenesses, you cannot really say that the performances of the groups were the same, only that you failed to show that they were different. Perhaps it would be interesting to know that rock music affects studying no differently than classical music does, but the failure to find a difference could have been caused by any number of factors aside from the lack of an actual difference—for example, using too few participants or not having proper control of variables, which caused the variability of the data to be high, and so on. In some cases, where a series of experiments using similar experimental conditions produces statistically significant effects, you may be a bit more confident that your negative outcome is meaningful. But generally a negative outcome is uninteresting, except perhaps as a methodological example of what not to do. Regardless of whether the outcome of your experiment is negative or is positive in an unexpected way, you must accept that result and try to explain it. There is a common tendency to want to pass off the result and simply blame it on design or methodological problems. But however strongly you believed in your hypothesis at the beginning of the experiment, once the experiment is over, you must accept whatever result you get and attempt to explain it.

One way to know whether you will be able to interpret the outcome of your experiment is to consider the various possible outcomes and determine whether you could predict each of them. As discussed in Chapter 3, a theory can help you predict. Remember that a theory is simply a statement about the probable relationships among a set of abstract variables—in the case of an experimental theory, between an independent and a dependent variable. It is more general than a statement of the specific outcome of any single experiment. So you may decide that your experiment fits within the context that a particular theory has been proposed to explain; thus, you predict the outcome of your experiment to be that predicted by the theory. You are in an even better situation if two or more theories have been proposed that make differing predictions. If one of these theories supports a positive result and the second a negative result, then interpreting

---

[2] English professors would probably call this statement oxymoronic (but not, I hope, moronic).

your outcome will still be easier if the positive result occurs, for reasons discussed in the previous paragraph. However, the best of all possible worlds is when two theories each predict positive results but in opposite directions. In this case, either outcome can be clearly interpreted.

A second way that a prediction can be made and supported is from prior research. Someone may have done an experiment that is similar to yours in some respects but different in other respects. In this case, you might predict that you will find a similar outcome. If you do, you have shown that the result can be repeated and that it can be generalized to your somewhat different experimental situation, and you are on your way to being able to make a more general theoretical statement. If your outcome is different from that reported in the earlier experiment, you have discovered a limitation of the prior result, and, again, something has been learned.

A third justification for a prediction, particularly when no prior research or theorizing has been done in a particular area, is simply logical argument. For example, you might argue that it is logical for loud and unpredictable music to be distracting because it draws the student's attention away from the studying task. You might also be able to logically predict some other effects from similar reasoning—for example, that the music might help if it masks a loud, even more unpredictable noise or that the more familiar the student is with the music, the less his or her performance will be degraded. Although these predictions are initially based on logic, they could, if supported by experimental outcomes, gain theoretical status.

The reason you want to be able to predict the possible outcomes of your experiment is, basically, so that you will know ahead of time that when the experiment is completed, you will have contributed something important to science. If you cannot defend the various outcomes as supporting anything important, you will have added nothing useful. For example, if the outcome you predict would be expected by all the proposed theories and would eliminate no alternative theories, your work would contribute nothing to the body of knowledge. As discussed in Chapter 3, advances in science are generally made by disconfirming theories, not by confirming theories, and you would not have disconfirmed any. The basic point is that if you believe a particular result could be important for advancing science, you should be able to defend this belief before doing the experiment. Otherwise there is no point in proceeding.

## NOW, AM I READY?

If you have answered all the questions posed here, you are probably ready to begin your experiment. As a final check, you should ask yourself whether you could, at this point, write all the sections of an experimental report except for the results. In fact, you could save yourself considerable time by doing this before collecting data. Graduate students in many experimental psychology programs are required to submit a formal prospectus prior to doing a thesis or dissertation. This document is essentially the final experimental report, except that the results section contains various predicted results rather than actual results and, obviously, contains no statistical analysis. One advantage of doing a prospectus is that most of the writing is completed early. In graduate schools, the procedure also helps protect the student to some extent, because those on the student's faculty committee can indicate before the work is done whether they think the design contains any major flaws. For your purposes, the major advantage of trying to write most of the report is that you would have had to answer the questions in this chapter before writing it. Obviously, you cannot describe an experimental procedure until you have worked out all its details. You cannot write a literature review until you have searched the literature. You cannot predict the outcome of the experiment without knowing the theories that have been proposed or the results previously reported. Writing a prospectus is simply a good way of making sure that you have thoroughly thought through the experiment you are proposing to do.

At this point you should be ready for the excitement of collecting your own data. It can be fun, and a good intellectual exercise, to plan an experiment. Searching the literature requires some discipline and can be interesting. Finding the appropriate statistical tests may thrill some experimenters, but, to be honest, I do statistical tests just because they are part of the experimental process. The creative act of collecting data and testing your theories and predictions is worth the hard work of doing some of the steps that you may find less intrinsically interesting. I do receive satisfaction from moving science along by making a lasting, and potentially immortal, contribution to the body of knowledge. But for me—and I hope for you, too—the most fun of being a scientist is the thrill of discovery, of looking for the first time at data nobody else has seen. And that, by itself, is what makes the whole enterprise worth the effort.

## Summary

Before you are ready to conduct an experiment, there are many practical details to consider. A useful way to determine whether you have anticipated these details is to present your ideas to others—either orally, by means of a presentation, or in writing, through a prospectus. One concern is whether you have satisfied all possible *ethical concerns* and whether the experiment has been approved by an institutional review board. In determining the *number of participants* needed you should find experiments similar to yours that have been reported in the literature and use similar numbers. In addition, you will decide whether to *run participants individually or in groups*. To determine the *experimental time required* to complete the experiment, you will have to determine the time taken for each trial, the number of trials, the time required for other activities, and the number of participants in each condition. In determining whether to set *participant selection restrictions,* you should consider to what population you will generalize your results. In order to avoid including experimental noise in the data, you may also wish to determine *criteria for eliminating participants* from the experiment. To have made adequate *operational definitions of variables* you should be able to specify precisely what operations are required to manipulate the independent variable(s) or measure the dependent variable(s). Arranging for needed *equipment or materials* often includes preparing instructions, response sheets, and debriefing scripts. Finally, you should know how you will statistically *analyze the data* and *interpret the results*. This interpretation will be aided by existing theories, previously reported findings, or logical argument. If all these issues have been considered before you begin your experiment, completing the experiment and reporting the results should run smoothly.

## Find It on InfoTrac College Edition

Using InfoTrac College Edition, find a journal article describing an experiment that had multiple trials and blocks of trials. With all of the elements such as the time for a trial, intertrial intervals, rest periods, instructions, and so forth, can you determine how much time would have been needed for the entire experiment? If the authors mention how much time was required, how does your estimate compare?

# 12

# How to Interpret
# Experimental Results

A well-wrapped statistic is better than Hitler's "big lie"; it misleads, yet it cannot be pinned on you.

D. HUFF (1954)

There are three kinds of lies: lies, damn lies, and statistics.

BENJAMIN DISRAELI

I believe, however, that over the years an overreliance on the impoverished binary conclusions yielded by the hypothesis-testing procedure has subtly seduced our discipline into insidious conceptual cul-de-sacs that have impeded our vision and stymied our potential.

G. R. LOFTUS (1993)

In spite of frequent misuse, statistics can be an elegant and powerful tool for making decisions in the face of uncertainty.

ROGER E. KIRK (1990)

Now you are ready to collect some data. If you are recording responses by hand, it will be necessary to set up response sheets for each participant. Included on this sheet should be such information as the participant's identification number and sex, the condition being presented, and any specific comments you might wish to note about the participant or the experimental session. Obviously, there should also be a place to systematically record the responses. These data are then made into a data set arranged according to independent variables and levels of those variables. If, as is most typical today, the experiment was done on a computer, the program will likely arrange data into a data set for you. If you collected the data by hand, you will need to arrange the data yourself, and if you are using a computer for statistical analysis, you will need to create a data set on the computer. Now that you have a set of numbers, you are still a long way from answering the experimental question: What effect did the independent variable have on the dependent variable? To answer this question, you need to know about several approaches to analyzing data and how to use them.

**TABLE 12-1**
Fictitious Anxiety Scores for Ten Economics Majors and
Ten Psychology Majors

| Economics majors | | Psychology majors | |
| --- | --- | --- | --- |
| Student no. | Score | Student no. | Score |
| 1 | 62 | 11 | 55 |
| 2 | 56 | 12 | 42 |
| 3 | 67 | 13 | 61 |
| 4 | 91 | 14 | 58 |
| 5 | 53 | 15 | 70 |
| 6 | 87 | 16 | 47 |
| 7 | 51 | 17 | 62 |
| 8 | 63 | 18 | 36 |
| 9 | 46 | 19 | 74 |
| 10 | 71 | 20 | 51 |

This chapter should give you an understanding of the logic underlying data analysis. It will not help you do the statistics required to analyze an experiment. If you need to do such calculations, you should first read this chapter and then look for an appropriate statistical operation in Appendix A. That appendix is not meant to be a substitute for a statistics text, but with your instructor's help, it should allow you to analyze most of the simple experimental designs discussed in this book. Neither this chapter nor the appendix will substitute for taking a statistics course. We will be discussing only the basics, enough so that with help in choosing a test, you might be able to analyze a simple experiment. If you wish to do further experimentation, an elementary statistics course is mandatory.

## Plotting Frequency Distributions

Suppose you are interested in whether students who are majoring in psychology differ in anxiety from those majoring in economics. You find a list of majors for your college, randomly pick ten students from the two majors, and convince these students to take a test that has been found to indicate a person's overall anxiety level. The test scores for the two groups are your raw data.[1]

Table 12-1 shows some fictitious scores between 0 and 100. The larger the score, the more anxious the student. Is there a difference between groups? Looking at individual scores in this case is like listening to individual notes from a song; it's difficult to tell what the melody is. You need

---

[1] You will note that this is not really an experiment but a correlational observation, because you are comparing two behaviors: the behavior of choosing a major and the behavior of answering questions on a test. No independent variable has been manipulated in the study.

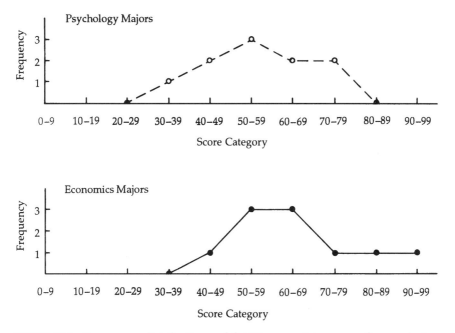

**FIGURE 12-1** Frequency distributions of fictitious anxiety scores for psychology majors and economics majors listed in Table 12-1

some way to rearrange the raw data so that you can interpret them more easily. You can draw a **frequency distribution,** which is simply a plot of how frequently each score appears in the data. You may notice, however, that no score occurred more than one time. Thus, to make the distribution meaningful, you need to put the individual scores into categories. You want several data points in each of the more frequently occurring categories, so you make each category include ten scores (for example, 10 through 19). Figure 12-1 shows such a frequency distribution for each of your two groups. The vertical axis labeled "Frequency" is simply the number of raw data points that fall into each score category.

Plotting a frequency distribution can be a useful first step in finding out whether there is a difference between conditions. Sometimes the experimental effect is strong enough that a visual inspection of the distributions will convince you that there is a difference. In this example, however, the distributions look very much alike.

Statisticians have given names to different types of distributions so that investigators can talk to each other in some common terms without having to show each other a plot of the entire distribution. We have already mentioned the properties of a **normal distribution,** shown in the upper left panel of Figure 12-2. To be normal, a distribution has to fit a complex mathematical formula. For our purposes, however, we can simply say that a distribution approximates a normal distribution if it looks something like the bell-shaped distribution shown in the figure. It is important to know

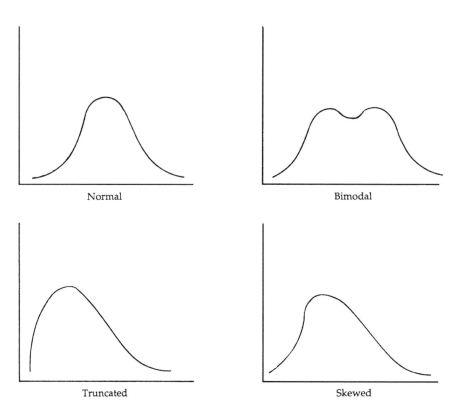

Normal                    Bimodal

Truncated                 Skewed

**FIGURE 12-2**  Four types of frequency distributions

whether your distributions are similar to a normal distribution, because many statistical tests you will wish to use require that the data be approximately normal.

Some other types of distributions are also illustrated in Figure 12-2. A distribution that has two most-frequent categories rather than one is a **bimodal** distribution. The distribution of heights for a group composed of an equal number of men and women would often be bimodal. A distribution is **skewed** if it is asymmetrical through having more scores in one of

A TRUNCATED DISTRIBUTION

the tails. A distribution of IQ scores for Ph.D.'s would be skewed because, generally, few have low IQs. However, if a distribution looks as though one of the tails has been completely chopped off, it is said to be **truncated.** A plot of reaction times would form a truncated distribution because there is a limit to the speed with which a person can respond.[2]

Plotting a frequency distribution allows you to describe your data in a more orderly way than simply listing it in raw form, but it is still a rather cumbersome way to represent the results of an experiment. It would be nice to have a single number that represents how the participants in each group performed. What we need is a way of calculating a descriptive statistic that will describe the data in this manner.

# Statistics for Describing Distributions

Psychologists use two basic kinds of statistics: descriptive statistics and inferential statistics. A **descriptive statistic** is simply a number that allows the experimenter to describe some characteristics of the data rather than having to report every data point. Inferential statistics will be discussed later in the chapter.

### CENTRAL TENDENCY

One of the important things we would like to know about a set of data is the typical behavior of participants under various conditions. Psychologists call a statistic that describes this typical behavior an indication of *central tendency.* One way of comparing the two groups in our example is to calculate a central tendency for the psychology majors and for the economics majors.

There are three common ways to express the central tendency. The **mode** is the easiest statistic to calculate, but it is usually the worst one to use because it ignores lots of data. The mode is simply the most frequently occurring score. In our example there is no mode, because no score occurred

[2] Remember ceiling and floor effects? They usually cause truncated distributions.

PIE À LA MODE

more than once. After the data have been put into categories, a mode can be found. The mode for the psychology majors is the category 50–59, because it occurred with a frequency of 3. Although this category seems to represent the central tendency of this distribution pretty well, note that if only one score were moved, the mode could change dramatically. For example, suppose student 14 scored 71 instead of 58. Now the category mode would be 70–79, because there would be a frequency of 3 in that category. Do you think that this category would represent the central tendency of the distribution well?

The problem is that the mode uses only one property of the data—the most frequently occurring score—to describe typical behavior. It ignores all the other scores. So when you use the mode, you are throwing out lots of information, such as the ordering and size of each number. With small samples, relying on a mode to describe your data can be risky.

The **median** is literally a middle score; it has an equal number of scores above it and below it. To calculate a median, list all the scores in order, and then pick the middle score. If you have an even number of scores, the median falls halfway between the two middle scores. For example, in ordering the ten scores for economics majors, we find that the fifth score is 62 and the sixth is 63, so the median is 62.5. The median for the psychology majors is 56.5. The median does not reflect the size of the differences between scores, because it uses only order as its defining principle. Thus, we can change any score in the distribution without changing the median, as long as the position of the middle score in the list remains the same. Again, we lose some information when we describe our data in terms of a median.

The **mean** is a weighted average of the scores; that is, it is the sum of all individual scores divided by the number of scores that were added. For example, to find the mean for the economics majors, we add the 10 scores for a sum of 647 and then divide by 10, with the result of 64.7 for the mean. The mean for the psychology majors is 55.6. The mean is the center of gravity for the distribution. Thus, because the mean is affected by the size of the scores, it changes whenever any score in the distribution changes.

Which measure of central tendency best describes a distribution? As with most interesting questions, the answer is "It all depends." First, it depends on the shape of the distribution. If you have a normal distribution

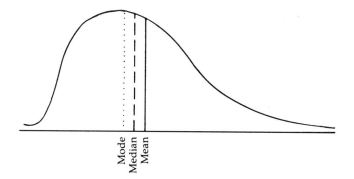

Mode Median Mean

**FIGURE 12-3** The location of the mode, median, and mean for a skewed distribution

or any other unimodal symmetrical distribution, all three measures give you the same number. However, as a distribution becomes more skewed, the three measures get progressively farther apart. Figure 12-3 shows that the mean is most influenced by the size of the extreme scores in the right tail of the distribution. The median is influenced only because there are more scores to the right, while the mode is unaffected by these extreme scores.[3]

You must use your judgment in deciding which measure to use. If you were to plot the incomes for a large group of people, you would probably get a distribution similar to the one in Figure 12-3. In this case a median would probably be the best average, because it would be influenced less than the mean by the few folks who make outlandish salaries. You can probably think of more extreme examples in which a few very large or very small scores can distort the mean. Whenever you must choose a measure to describe an average, you will simply have to examine the shape of the distribution, determine for what purpose the average will be used, and then use your judgment.[4]

## DISPERSION

A measure of central tendency tells you something useful about a distribution, but it describes only one special aspect. A second statistic that helps describe a distribution is a measure of *dispersion*, or how spread out the scores are.

---

[3] Which measure to use is also influenced by the characteristics of the numbers you are using. See Appendix A for a discussion of number scales, and Figure A-1 to see which measure of central tendency is appropriate for each.
[4] I am assuming that you have read Chapter 5 and are trying to be fair with science. The books *How to Lie with Statistics* by Huff (1954) and *Flaws and Fallacies in Statistical Thinking* by Campbell (1974) give many humorous examples of how to make descriptive statistics like the mean into distorting statistics.

One measure of dispersion is the **range,** which we can calculate by subtracting the smallest score from the largest score. In our example for the economics majors, the range is 91 − 46 = 45; for the psychology majors, the range is 74 − 36 = 38. Although the range gives some indication of dispersion, because it is determined by only the smallest and largest scores, it is totally insensitive to scores in between. One extreme score completely changes the range. For this reason, a different measure of dispersion may be more useful.

As an alternative, we can subtract the mean from each score so that we have a number indicating the deviation of each score from the mean. To get a mean deviation, we can then add up these deviations and divide by the number of deviations. However, because the numbers cancel each other out when added, we will get a sum of zero, which doesn't help us much. We could ignore the sign of the deviations, add up the absolute values, and thus get an average deviation. But statisticians feel that a more useful indication of dispersion is found by squaring[5] each deviation (this also gets rid of the plus or minus sign), adding the squares, and then dividing by the number of squared deviations that were added. We then have a measure of dispersion called the **variance.** An even more useful measure is the square root[6] of the variance, a number called the **standard deviation.** Formulas for calculating these measures can be found in Appendix A.

You may find it helpful to view the standard deviation as a way of expressing the extent of error you are making by using the mean to represent the scores in a distribution. In reality, the mean is simply the best estimate you could make about any individual score; thus, the standard deviation indicates, on the average, how good an estimate you have made. If all the scores were the same, the standard deviation would be zero, indicating that the mean would never be in error. As the differences among scores get larger, the standard deviation increases, as does the error you would make by representing a score with the mean.[7]

## Plotting Relationships between Variables

The reason you do an experiment is to find out if there is a relationship between the independent and dependent variables. Although plotting frequency distributions is a good first step in analyzing your data, you will often find it useful to draw a graph to represent the experimental relationship. Graphs are not new to you. They have been cropping up from time to time in earlier chapters. To be complete, however, let's start by looking at basic concepts.

---

[5] Multiplying it times itself.
[6] A number that when multiplied times itself gives us the variance.
[7] Which measure of dispersion to use is also influenced by the characteristics of the numbers you are using. See Appendix A for a discussion of number scales, and Figure A-1 to see which measure is appropriate.

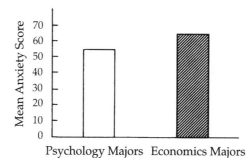

**FIGURE 12-4**   A bar graph showing the mean anxiety scores for the psychology majors and economics majors listed in Table 12-1

## DRAWING GRAPHS

A graph has two axes. The vertical axis (**y-axis**) is called the **ordinate,** and the horizontal axis (**x-axis**), the **abscissa.**[8] When plotting experimental results, you plot the dependent variable on the ordinate and the independent variable on the abscissa. If the levels of the independent variable cannot be represented by numbers, it is usually appropriate to use a **bar graph** to represent the data. Figure 12-4 shows a bar graph for the mean anxiety scores of the psychology and economics majors.

   If the independent variable is continuous, then you can draw a **histogram,** as shown in Figure 12-5. A histogram eliminates spaces between the bars of a bar graph. Figure 12-5 shows fictitious data relating the length of time patients are in therapy to their rating of self-image. Time in therapy is a continuous variable, because we could choose levels anywhere on the continuum of time.

   A more common way of representing data when the independent variable is continuous is to use a **line graph,** or **function.** Figure 12-6 shows the same results as those plotted in Figure 12-5 but is a line graph rather than a histogram. The individual data points are simply plotted and then connected by straight lines. Notice how this way of representing the data emphasizes the trends quite effectively. To use this type of graph, you must

[8] You may find it helpful to remember which term refers to which axis by noticing the shape your mouth takes when saying the first part of each word; "ab_____" is said with a horizontal mouth, and "or_____," with a vertical mouth. That's the way I remember them!

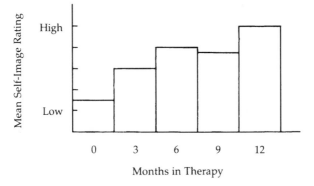

**FIGURE 12-5**  A histogram illustrating the results of a multilevel experiment relating perceived self-image to months spent in therapy (fictitious data)

have data that lie on a continuum. By way of bad example, suppose that on the abscissa of the figure, we had ethnic categories such as Hispanic, African American, and so on, instead of months in therapy. These categories obviously do not lie on a continuum; so the order of listing the categories would be totally arbitrary. Trying to find a trend in such data doesn't make any sense.

Line graphs are also best used to illustrate the results of a functional (multilevel) experiment rather than those of a two-level experiment. The problem with a two-level experiment is that you really do not know whether the relationship is linear, and yet you would be using a straight line to represent it. With a functional experiment, more than two levels of the independent variable are used, and it is possible to get an idea of the shape of the function even though the points are connected with straight-line segments. (For more on constructing figures for an experimental report, see Chapter 13.)

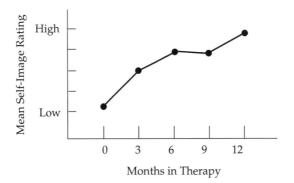

**FIGURE 12-6**  A line graph illustrating the same data as those plotted in the histogram in Figure 12-5

## DESCRIBING FUNCTIONS

Several types of graphed functions are illustrated in Figure 12-7. If changing the independent variable by one unit always causes the dependent variable to change in a given direction by a constant amount, the function is

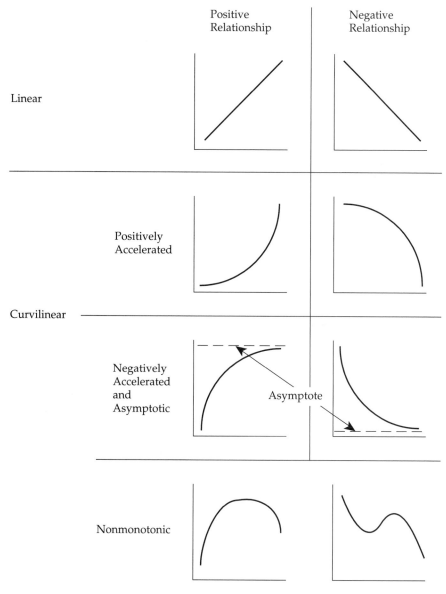

**FIGURE 12-7**  Graphs illustrating some terms used to describe functional
relationships

**linear**; any other relationship is **curvilinear.** If increasing the independent variable causes an increase in the dependent variable, the relationship is **positive**; if it causes a decrease, it is **negative.** A function that never reverses direction (that is, portions of the function are either all positive or all negative) is a **monotonic** function; otherwise, the function is termed **nonmonotonic.** If changes in the dependent variable become increasingly larger as the independent variable increases, the function is **positively accelerated**; if the changes become smaller, it is **negatively accelerated.** A negatively accelerated function eventually approaches a particular level and appears to flatten out. The curve is actually getting closer and closer to a straight line called an **asymptote,** although the curve and asymptote never touch. Such a function is said to be **asymptotic,** or to approach an asymptote.

If you are seeing these terms for the first time, you may feel a bit overwhelmed. However, as you use them to describe psychological relationships, you will find that they become more familiar and allow you to discuss your results more efficiently.

## Describing the Strength of a Relationship

The functions in the previous section either were idealized or were plots of a descriptive statistic rather than individual data points. Rarely, however, will you find every data point falling exactly on a smooth function. If you use raw data to plot an experimental relationship, you will probably find some variability, or spread, around the functions. As we saw in Chapter 1, such a plot is called a **scatterplot.**

### SCATTERPLOTS

Figure 12-8 shows some examples of scatterplots. These plots could result from an experiment, in which case the relationships between independent and dependent variables are plotted, or from a correlational observation (Chapter 1), in which case dependent variables are plotted on both axes. If you observe the spread of the points in a scatterplot, you can get some idea of how strong the relationship is. However, visual observation is a rather crude way of estimating

SCATTERPLOT OF A STRONG RELATIONSHIP?

**FIGURE 12-8**  Four illustrations of scatterplots. Correlation coefficients are shown for three panels. No coefficient is given for the lower right panel because the relationship is curvilinear and a correlation ratio should be used.

this strength. Fortunately, when the relationship is linear,[9] a descriptive statistic called a correlation coefficient can be used for this purpose.

## CORRELATION COEFFICIENTS

A **correlation coefficient** is a number between +1.0 and –1.0, with the sign indicating whether the relationship is positive or negative and the size of the number indicating the strength of the relationship. A correlation of 1.0 (+ or –) indicates a perfect relationship, and 0 indicates no relationship.

Figure 12-8 shows the correlation coefficients for three sets of data. No coefficient is shown for the lower right panel, because the function is obviously curvilinear and simple linear correlation is not appropriate. (There is, however, a way of describing a curvilinear correlation called a *correlation ratio* [Kirk, 1990].) You can find out how to calculate a correlation coefficient by reading Appendix A or by looking in any statistics text.[10]

---

[9] Actually, one form of correlation uses data that can only be ranked or ordered, in which case the term *linear* is meaningless. Such a correlation can be used for any monotonic relationship.

[10] Several statistics texts are listed at the end of the chapter.

Often when a correlation coefficient is reported, a **coefficient of deter-mination,** or proportion of variation explained, is also reported. The coefficient of determination is simply the correlation coefficient squared and represents the proportion of the variability shared by the two variables. So if the reported correlation is +0.5, the coefficient of determination would be +0.25; 25% of the variability is shared between the two variables. Many researchers, including the *Publication Manual of the American Psychological Association* (American Psychological Association, 1994), recommend reporting the coefficient of determination whenever a correlation is reported. However, other researchers claim that the correlation coefficient is a better indication of the effect size for a correlational observation, and that the coefficient of determination seriously underestimates the practical importance of the results (Rosnow & Rosenthal, 1999). If you use these statistics, you should familiarize yourself with these arguments and use these numbers in an informed way.

# Interpreting Results from Factorial Experiments

The results of factorial experiments are more difficult to interpret than those of other types of experiments, because they use more than one independent variable and require you to evaluate interactions. The top graph of Figure 12-9 shows some fictitious results of our earlier experiment in which we measured the time it took students to read paragraphs typed in 12-point or 10-point print. In this case, however, assume that we used 8-year-olds in one group and 12-year-olds in another. Notice that one independent variable (print size) has been plotted on the abscissa, while the other (age) is represented by a point and line code. We can no longer just ask whether the independent variable has had an effect on the dependent variable. We must ask three more specific questions: (1) Is there an effect of print size? (2) Is there an effect of age? (3) Does the effect of one variable depend on the level of the other? The first two questions refer to **main effects,** and the third to an **interaction.**

## MAIN EFFECTS

Because we have two independent variables in this experiment, we have two possible main effects. To discover whether these main effects are significant, we would have to do some statistics. In order to interpret the results of the print size experiment, let's assume that any effect that we can see is statistically significant. To determine whether there is a main effect of print size, we need to ignore any effect of age. Thus, we need to find a point on the graph for each print size that is halfway between the points for each age group. On the graph in Figure 12-9 under the question "Main

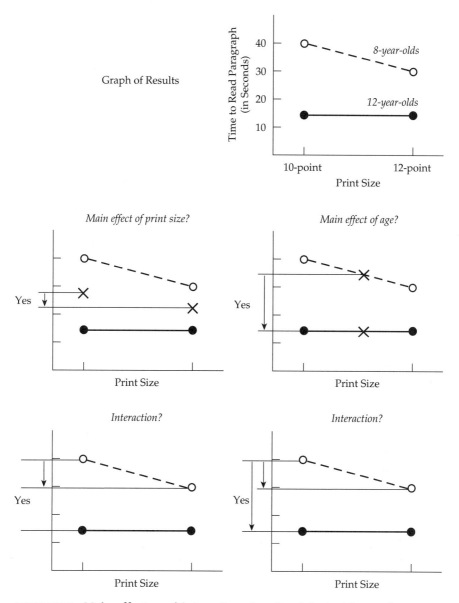

**FIGURE 12-9** Main effects and interactions in a 2 × 2 factorial experiment

effect of print size?" you will see Xs halfway down from each open circle to the corresponding black circle. These Xs represent the effect of print size averaged across the two levels of age, just as if age had never been manipulated. To find out if there is a difference in reading speed for these two Xs, I have drawn a horizontal line across to the ordinate. The arrow shows you that there is a difference between the two Xs that represent the two print sizes. So the answer to our question is yes, there is a main effect of print size. Now follow the same procedure to determine whether there is a main effect of age.

## INTERACTIONS

If you do not remember what an interaction is, you may want to review the discussion on interactions in Chapter 9, where we considered factorial experiments. Remember that an interaction occurs whenever the effect of one variable *depends on* the level of another variable. So in the print size experiment the question is, does the effect of print size depend on the age of the child or, alternatively, does the effect of age depend on the size of print?

In the bottom left graph of Figure 12-9, I have drawn horizontal lines over to the ordinate to discover the effect of going from 10-point to 12-point print size for each age group. Note that for the 8-year-olds there is a decrease in reading time, but for the 12-year-olds there is no change. Thus, the effect of print size does depend on age, and the answer to our question is yes, there is an interaction. In the bottom right graph, I have asked the question the other way: "Does the effect of age on reading time depend on print size?" If you follow the lines on this graph, you will again see that there is a difference. Of course, there is really only one interaction, so the answers to the two questions will always be the same. But checking both ways will give you some additional practice at interpreting interactions.

Figure 12-10 shows some other possible results for this experiment. Using the same procedure we have been discussing, answer the three questions for each graph.

In attempting to determine whether there are main effects and interactions in the graphs you have been viewing, I hope you noticed that when there are only main effects, the interpretation is pretty straightforward. However, when there is an interaction, the interpretation of the main effects is more complex. For example, for the result graphed in Figure 12-9, the main effect of age on reading time is meaningful even though there is an interaction, because the effect exists at both print sizes. However, although there is also a main effect of print size, the interaction makes its interpretation problematic because the effect exists for only one age group. The bottom panel of Figure 12-10 illustrates what is sometimes called a **crossover interaction** in which the lines cross each other. When there are main effects with a crossover interaction, the main effects are difficult to interpret. In fact, they are typically meaningless.

This discussion has been limited to the simplest type of factorial experiment. When each factor has more than two levels, or when more than two factors are used, interpreting interactions becomes even more difficult, although the basic procedures for interpreting your results remain the same.

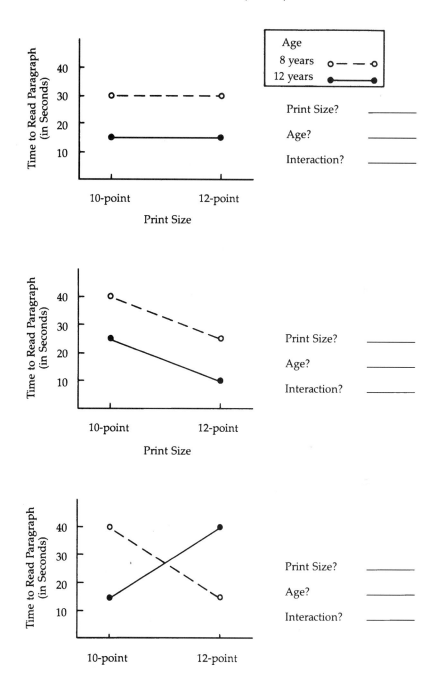

**FIGURE 12-10** Graphs of three possible outcomes for a 2 × 2 factorial experiment. Answer the three questions for each graph. (The answers can be found at the end of the chapter.)

# Inferential Statistics

To discuss the general logic of inferential statistics, let's return to the anxiety test scores for the psychology and economics majors. To find out whether the two groups differed in anxiety level, we plotted frequency distributions and calculated means for each group. We found that the mean for the economics majors was 64.7, and for the psychology majors, 55.6. Is this a real difference? Of course it is, you say: How can a difference not be a difference? And for these two samples you are absolutely correct; any difference between samples is a real difference between samples. However, what a psychologist means by the question is not "Is there a real difference between the scores for the two samples that you happened to choose for this experiment?" but rather "Is it likely that there is a difference in anxiety level between the population of all psychology majors and the population of all economics majors who could have been sampled?" The goal of the experiment is to say something about the two populations that could have been chosen, not just the particular samples that were.

Pretend that you are a bean farmer. You are not doing very well because of bean blight. Bean blight is a mysterious disease that causes many beans to wither and shrivel. To find out whether you can get rid of bean blight, you plant a field with a new type of bean that may resist the blight. After harvesting a blighted field and the new field, you have two bean bins each containing 10 tons of beans. You want to know if both bean bins are blighted.[11] You obviously do not wish to examine every bean in the two bins, so you decide to take a sample of 100 beans from each bin. You find 12 withered beans in the sample from the bin you know to contain blighted beans and 7 in the other sample. Obviously, there is a difference between the samples, but you want to know whether there is a difference between the entire populations of the two bins. An **inferential statistical** test can help you answer this question. The "infer" in "inferential" denotes that the test helps you infer whether there is a difference between the populations.

You, as a psychologist, face the same problem that you would face as a bean farmer. You have chosen a randomly selected sample of data from two potentially different populations (the levels of the independent variable), and you want to know whether the behavior of the populations differs.

## PARAMETRIC VERSUS NONPARAMETRIC TESTS

Many inferential tests are available to help you make this decision. The one you choose depends on your experimental design and what test assumptions your data can meet. (See Appendix A for worked examples of some inferential tests.) The most frequently used tests are called **parametric tests.**

---

[11] Say that quickly three times!

These tests assume that if frequency distributions were plotted for the populations of interest, they would be normal distributions. When this assumption cannot be met, you must use **nonparametric tests.**

Different inferential tests use somewhat different procedures for making inferences about populations. However, all tests that infer whether populations are the same provide a probabilistic statement about the likelihood that two or more samples could have come from the same population. In other words, such tests determine the probability that the observed difference among your data samples is due simply to chance variation. Any time that you randomly choose samples from the same population, it is possible, even though unlikely, that you will observe a large difference. How unlikely must a difference be before you can conclude that the samples come from different populations?

## LEVELS OF SIGNIFICANCE

Although it is probably unfortunate that we adhere to such a strict standard, most psychologists agree that for a result to be significant, the likelihood of obtaining the observed difference in samples due to chance should be less than 1 in 20. Thus, if the samples really came from the same population distribution, you would expect to get a significant difference in only 1 out of 20 (or 5 out of 100) experiments. Some psychologists are even more careful to avoid saying that there is a difference between populations when there isn't. They will not accept a difference as a real difference unless the test indicates that it could be due to chance only 1 time in 100. These strategies are called testing at the .05 **level of significance** or at the .01 level of significance. When these probabilities are reached or exceeded, the result is said to be **statistically significant.**

When reading a journal article, you will see these levels of significance referred to as $p < .05$ or $p < .01$. This means that the test was found to be statistically significant at the .05 or the .01 level, so that you would expect this difference in the levels of the independent variable less than 5 times out of 100 or 1 time out of 100 if they actually came from the same population. Be sure to notice which way the sign is pointing; $p > .05$ means that the test was not found to be significant.

Inferential tests are obviously an important tool for evaluating the results of psychology experiments. In fact, the development of sophisticated statistical tests has been a major influence in making psychology into a respectable science. However, we must realize the limitations of inferential tests.

## MISINTERPRETING STATISTICAL TESTS

Some experimenters believe that when a statistical test fails to show a significant difference in the levels of the independent variable, it has therefore shown that they are significantly the same. This is wrong! To avoid this error, we should keep in mind that inferential tests are designed to say something about the probability of getting a difference if the samples come from the same population; they tell us nothing about getting a sameness if the samples come from different populations. Consequently, negative results (ones that are not statistically significant) are seldom published in psychology journals. Our statistical tests are just not designed to tell us the probability that two samples would be this equivalent if they came from different populations; rather, they tell us how probable it is that samples could come from the same population.[12]

A second mistake some investigators make when using inferential tests is to act as though the .05 and .01 levels are chiseled in stone; they wouldn't be caught dead paying any attention to a .06 level. A more realistic approach to significance levels is to treat them for what they are, a way to help you make a decision. Whenever you make a decision in the face of uncertainty, you have to consider not only the probability of being right or wrong but also the benefits and costs of being right and wrong. In other decisions you do not ignore these factors. For example, if you are deciding whether to fly an airplane, you probably require a

higher probability of fair weather than if you are simply deciding whether to carry an umbrella. The benefits and costs are far different. The .05 and .01 levels ignore such benefits and costs. Thus, you should consider the consequences of being right or wrong when you interpret the results of your experiments and not blindly test at the .05 level.

There is some controversy in psychology about whether the term *significant* should ever be modified—for example, by saying "highly significant." Some argue that the use of such modifiers is wrong because the tradition in psychology is to dichotomize results as *significant* or *nonsignificant* and, more important, that the use of modifiers mistakenly substitutes the size of importance of the effect for the probability of an effect (Harcum, 1989; Levenson, 1990). However, others argue that because probability is a

---

[12] Although my contention that our statistical tests do not test for sameness is true of the vast majority of the psychological literature, technically it is not universally true anymore. Formal statistical tests of equivalence, though largely unfamiliar to psychologists, have been evolving over the past couple of decades. They are beyond the scope of this book, but I would refer those with an interest to read the article "Using Significance Tests to Evaluate Equivalence between Two Experimental Groups," by Rogers, Howard, and Vessey (1993).

continuum, there is nothing wrong with saying that one effect is more significant than another (Kanekar, 1990). Those on both sides of this argument would probably agree that the key is to avoid mistaking the level of statistical significance for practical significance, the issue we have just been considering. For this reason, when reporting a positive result it is best to say that it is *statistically significant* to emphasize that you are not necessarily claiming practical significance. And when reporting a negative result, say that it is *statistically nonsignificant* rather than insignificant. The term *insignificant* certainly does imply unimportant.

When you are trying to avoid confusing statistical significance with practical significance, remember the fine old saying that a difference is a difference only if it makes a difference. Suppose you are an employer, and the owners of the Fast-Finger Speed-Reading School are trying to convince you that you should pay them to teach all your employees how to speed-read. They say that they have experimental evidence showing that people read significantly faster after taking their course. Being a skeptic, you ask how much faster. They admit that the study shows that their students read an average of half a word per minute faster, but they insist that this difference is statistically significant. They could well be correct. By using enough participants and collecting enough data, even tiny differences between populations can be shown to be statistically significant. As an employer, though, you care more about practical significance than statistical significance. As a scientist, you should, too.

In an attempt to encourage experimenters to consider whether their results are important as well as statistically significant and to get away from rigid testing at the .05 level, Geoffrey Loftus (1993, 1996), a former editor of a major psychology journal, says that statistical hypothesis testing is often not really necessary. He encourages experimenters to plot their data in a graph showing means with associated measures of dispersion, such as standard deviations. He believes that more often than not, inspection of such a figure will immediately make apparent the significance of the effect without the necessity of using an inferential statistical test. If this is the case, he discourages the use of such tests.

In the end, evaluating practical significance is a matter of judgment. The tools discussed in this chapter should help you determine when a result is important, but the tools do not establish the importance of the result. You, the experimenter, must do this by using logical arguments to convince other researchers that your differences make a difference.

## Meta-Analysis

Although you will probably not use it if you are doing a simple experiment, you may run across articles that use a statistical technique called **meta-analysis.** You should know something about meta-analysis so that you will understand these articles. In Chapter 6 we discussed how to do a literature search. When you do a search, you will be struck by how many articles there are on a particular subject. Even for relatively narrowly defined areas, hundreds or thousands of articles make up the literature. The typical way in which researchers who write review articles evaluate and integrate these studies is to do a narrative review. The researcher simply reads all the articles, considers some studies important and others minor, tries to keep in mind the results of at least the important ones, and then tries to summarize the major findings. The way researchers carry out this process has been studied and found to be pretty sloppy (Jackson, 1980). In many cases, different researchers come up with completely different conclusions from the same literature. The problem is that such researchers face an almost impossible task, much like being forced to look at the data for 100 participants in an experiment and draw a conclusion without the help of any statistical analysis. What meta-analysis does is to provide a statistical way to integrate the data from many different studies.

You do not have to understand the details of the statistics to understand the results of a meta-analytic study. If you need more detail, see the books on meta-analysis listed at the end of this chapter. Basically, meta-analysis allows you to take the results of an unlimited number of experiments that investigate the same general problem, even if they use different methodologies, and combine them statistically. For example, Lipsey and Wilson (1993) were interested in whether psychological, educational, and behavioral treatments had been found to be effective. They examined a decade and a half's research on this topic, 302 studies. The basic datum for each study in a meta-analytic review is the **mean treatment effect size.** It is very easy to compute this statistic; it is the mean of the control group, subtracted from the mean of the treatment group, divided by the standard deviation of the control group. So in Lipsey and Wilson's review, regardless of how the dependent variable was measured or how the treatment was administered for each study, the mean for the group not undergoing treatment was subtracted from the mean for the group undergoing treatment, and that number was divided by the standard deviation of the first group. Using these mean treatment effects as data, the authors did statistics on them to determine how likely it was that they could have been due to chance. The data can also be reanalyzed in various ways. For example, all the studies using a particular experimental design can be analyzed separately, or those judged to be of high quality can be analyzed separately from those judged to be of low quality. These smaller-scale analyses allow the researcher to evaluate whether the initial grouping of all the studies was appropriate.

Some researchers have been critical of meta-analysis (Wilson, 1985), claiming that the technique is sometimes used to combine the results of many experiments, each of which has serious flaws. In such cases, the outcome of the meta-analysis would be as flawed as the original studies. However, meta-analysis also has its supporters (Mann, 1990), who argue that a sophisticated approach that includes various subanalyses minimizes the possibility of combining flawed studies into a super-flawed result. Meta-analysis certainly seems to be here to stay. When done properly, it can be a valuable tool for integrating the results of an otherwise unwieldy multitude of research.

## Using Computers to Help Interpret Results

Computers are used in many areas of psychological experimentation, such as doing a literature search, presenting stimuli, and recording responses. However, the most widespread use of computers is for statistical data analysis. Computers are particularly valuable for this task because they can quickly store and manipulate large sets of numbers. In recent years the availability of computers has increased, and powerful statistical software now allows most statistical tests to be computed on desktop or laptop machines.

Although the net effect of computers on statistical computation has been overwhelmingly positive, problems can be associated with them. One problem is that because computers take some of the manual effort out of doing statistics, people sometimes act as if they need not devote much mental effort either. Yet it is especially important when you first begin to use statistical tests to understand how they work. Computers allow you to bypass this understanding. If someone shows you the steps necessary for entering data and then the computer gives you back results, it is possible for you to go through the whole process without ever understanding what you did. I require my students to calculate each statistical test once by hand before using a computer, so that they will understand what happens inside that magic little box.

Computers are also so perfect, hardly ever making a mistake, that they lull us into thinking that whatever they tell us is *the truth*. But the adage holds: Garbage in, garbage out. You need to remember the lessons about interpreting results that you have learned in this chapter. Also, you need to know the assumptions and limitations of the various statistics that you may use (see Appendix A). Finally, you should not accept the output from a computer at face value before making some simple checks. Although it is unlikely that the computer made a mistake, you might have made a mistake in setting up and entering the data into the computer. Computers are fast and accurate, but they are exceedingly stupid. The computer does not care in the slightest if you made an error and accidentally told it you were going to enter the data for Condition A before Condition B, and then didn't. The computer will not check to see whether you made such an error; you will have to check.

One way to make a quick check of your statistical results is to look at the descriptive statistics that your computer gives you to see whether they make sense. In our print size experiment, for instance, we expect that the 8-year-olds will read more slowly than the 12-year-olds. We would be wary of the analysis if such logical expectations were not upheld. That could be an indication that we had made a mistake in setting up the data for the computer. We could also calculate some means for a small part of the data by hand to see whether the result agreed with the computerized output. In the print size example we might decide to compute a mean for one age group, for one paragraph, at a particular print size to see whether that mean agreed with the one listed in the output. Several small computations would require only a couple of minutes, but they would greatly increase our confidence that the output was correct.

I hope this general discussion has put the role of computers in perspective. Computers and statistical packages are simply tools that can be used to make data interpretation easier. There is no reason why computers should strike fear in your heart. They are your *friends* and are getting friendlier all the time. But as with all complex tools, care should be taken to make sure that they are being used correctly. These computer friends are not at all flexible and require you to compulsively follow their rules. They believe what you say, even when you are wrong, and they have no common sense for determining when you are wrong. In order to stay out of trouble, you should understand their limitations as well as their capabilities.

## Summary

Once you complete an experiment, you must interpret the data listed on the response sheets. A useful first step is to plot a **frequency distribution** illustrating the number of data points occurring within categories of the dependent variable. Sometimes these distributions are similar to a symmetrical bell-shaped distribution called a **normal distribution.** Others are **bimodal,** with two most frequent categories; **skewed** by having more scores in one tail of the distribution; or **truncated** by having one tail of the distribution missing. Three commonly used statistics describe the central tendency of a distribution: The **mode** is the most frequently occurring category, the **median** is the middle score, and the **mean** is the center of gravity for the distribution. Two statistics are commonly used to describe the dispersion of a distribution: The **range** is the difference between the highest and lowest scores, and the **standard deviation** and sometimes the **variance** describe the dispersion of distributions that are approximately normal.

Graphs illustrate the relationship between the independent and dependent variables. The levels of the independent variable are put on the horizontal axis, the **abscissa,** and the values of the dependent variable are put on the vertical axis, the **ordinate.** A **bar graph** can be used to illustrate data points that represent qualitatively different categories. Either a **histogram** or a **functional line graph** can be used to illustrate continuous variables. In describing functions, you can indicate whether they are **linear** or **curvilinear, positive** or **negative, monotonic** or **nonmonotonic, positively accelerated** or **negatively accelerated,** or **asymptotic.** The strength of an experimental relationship can be illustrated in a **scatterplot,** or if the relationship is linear, you can calculate a **correlation coefficient** and a **coefficient of determination.**

To interpret the results of a factorial experiment, you must determine whether there is a **main effect,** an effect of one factor on the dependent variable at an average value of the other factors. In addition, you must also determine whether the effect of one variable is different depending on the levels of the other variables. Such differences are called **interactions** and, particularly with **crossover interactions,** can make interpretation of main effects difficult.

**Inferential statistics** are used to infer how likely it is that the difference between data samples is due to chance rather than due to a real difference in populations (levels of the independent variable). For an effect to be declared **statistically significant,** the probability that the difference is due to chance usually must be less than .05 or .01. **Parametric tests** assume that population distributions are normal; **nonparametric** tests do not. Researchers sometimes misuse statistical tests by equating nonsignificant results with equivalence of conditions, by overemphasizing the .05 and .01 levels of significance, or by confusing statistical significance with practical significance.

**Meta-analysis** is a statistical technique for combining the results of many experiments. A single statistic called the **mean treatment effect size** is computed for each experiment, and these effect sizes are analyzed to determine how likely it is that such effects could be due to chance.

Computers can often be used to carry out statistical analyses. However, care must be taken to ensure that the assumptions of the statistical tests are met and that the data have been properly entered into the program. The output must be checked for internal consistency and accuracy before it can be accepted.

*Answers to the questions in Figure 12-10:*

| | | |
|---|---|---|
| *Top graph:* | Print size? | *no* |
| | Age? | *yes* |
| | Interaction? | *no* |
| *Middle graph:* | Print size? | *yes* |
| | Age? | *yes* |
| | Interaction? | *no* |
| *Bottom graph:* | Print size? | *no* |
| | Age? | *no* |
| | Interaction? | *yes* |

## SUGGESTED BOOKS ON STATISTICS

*For the Beginning Student*

Hinkle, D. E., Wiersma, W., & Jurs, S. G. (1988). *Applied statistics for the behavioral sciences.* Boston: Houghton Mifflin.

Kirk, R. E. (1990). *Statistics: An introduction.* Fort Worth, TX: Holt, Rinehart & Winston.

*For the Advanced Student*

Keppel, G., & Zeddeck, S. (1989). *Data analysis for research designs: Analysis of variance and multiple regression/correlation approaches.* New York: W. H. Freeman.

Maxwell, S. E., & Delaney, H. D. (1990). *Designing experiments and analyzing data: A model comparison perspective.* Belmont, CA: Wadsworth.

Myers, R. H. (1971). *Response surface methodology.* Boston: Allyn & Bacon.

## SUGGESTED BOOKS ON META-ANALYSIS

Cook, T. D., Cooper, H., Cordray, D. S., Hartmann, H., Hedges, L. V., Light, R. J., Louis, T. A., & Mosteller, F. (Eds.). (1992). *Meta-analysis for explanation: A casebook.* New York: Russell Sage Foundation.

Glass, G. V., McGaw, B., & Smith, M. L. (1981). *Meta-analysis in social research.* Newbury Park, CA: Sage.

Rosenthal, R. (1991). *Meta-analytic procedures for social research* (rev. ed.). Newbury Park, CA: Sage.

# Find It on InfoTrac College Edition

Using InfoTrac College Edition, try to find figures in articles that display graphs illustrating a function. Using the terminology for graphing that we learned—*positive/negative, positively accelerated/negatively accelerated, asymptotic, monotonic/nonmonotonic*—find figures that illustrate these terms.

Find the following articles, which describe the results of a factorial experiment. Examine the graphs noted, and determine whether there are likely to be main effects and interactions. Which graphs show crossover interactions? Read the articles to determine whether these effects were statistically significant.

Williams, H. P., Hutchinson, S., & Wickens, C. D. (1996). A comparison of methods for promoting geographic knowledge in simulated aircraft navigation. *Human Factors, 38,* 50–65. (See Figures 3 and 4.)

Wickens, C. D., & Carswell, C. M. (1995). The proximity compatibility principle: Its psychological foundation and relevance to display design. *Human Factors, 37,* 473–495. (See Figure 1a, b, c, d, and e.)

# 13

# How to Report
# Experimental Results

> The [scientific] writer quite properly reacts to the pressure toward conformity with the writing practices of his group, but he errs if he succumbs abjectly. He needs to qualify and to define exactly, but the danger is that his sentences can become so impossibly larded with subordinate phrases and clauses that even his close associates cannot read them.
>
> G. E. SCHINDLER (1967)

> We are all blind seekers after truth
> Confused by the noisy rabble of words
> Whether we shall ever say what we mean
> Or mean what we say
> We know not,
> And only our doing
> Will teach us in its hour.
>
> B. DECKER (1967)

> As we all know, Ten Commandments were accepted and published. What you may not know is that Moses asked that 34 others be revised and resubmitted; 16 more are still in press as a result of the lengthy publication lag.
>
> PALADINO & HANDELSMAN (1995)

> What appears in print is a sanitized, rationalized account of the research that conforms it to the standard story schema. Although experienced investigators sometimes can guess the probable real story behind the published report by reading between the lines, the written presentation of the research contains none of this.
>
> MADIGAN, JOHNSON, & LINTON (1995)

A classic philosophical debate goes something like this: If a tree falls in the forest and nobody is there to hear it, does it make a sound? The question is whether a person has to hear a sound for the sound to be a sound. What do you think? In reporting research, we can ask a similar question: Is research research if nobody hears about it? The metaphysical answer to either question depends on how you want to define the terms; because we are concerned with a practical answer, we can at least say that unreported research might as well not have been done. The ultimate goal of research is not doing experiments but building a scientific body of knowledge. If other scientists do not know about your experiments, your results cannot be used as building blocks. The experimental report is the way to make your results public so that science can benefit from your research.

Because your experimental report is the product of your research, you should try to make it a high-quality product. Although an elegantly written experimental report cannot save a bad piece of research, a poorly written report can effectively destroy a good piece of research. I know researchers who, if one judges from informal discussions of their research, seem to do well-thought-out experiments on important problems, but their ability to communicate on paper is so poor that their work is unknown. Much good research is probably lost this way.

Even instructors in writing courses have a difficult time teaching people how to write orderly thoughts. I do not have enough room in this chapter to teach you much about writing in general.[1] The most concise instructions I have seen for writing are offered by William Safire (1979):

> Remember to never split an infinitive. The passive voice should never be used. Do not put statements in the negative form. Verbs has to agree with their subjects. Proofread carefully to see if you any words out. If you reread your work, you will find on rereading that a great deal of repetition can be avoided by rereading and editing. A writer must not shift your point of view. And don't start a sentence with a conjunction. Don't overuse exclamation marks!!! Place pronouns as close as possible, especially in long sentences, as of 10 or more words, to their antecedents. Writing carefully, dangling participles must be avoided. If any word is improper at the end of a sentence, a linking verb is. Take the bull by the hand and avoid mixed metaphors. Avoid trendy locutions that sound flaky. Everyone should be careful to use a singular pronoun with singular nouns in their writing. Always pick on the correct idiom. The adverb always follows the verb. Last but not least, avoid cliches like the plague: seek viable alternatives.

The goal of this chapter is quite limited. I will describe the parts of a research report, give you some suggestions for determining whether what you write is readable, and provide an annotated sample report.

Research reports should convey information efficiently by using a consistent format. With this principle in mind, the APA (1994) has compiled a set of rules for writing a research report: the ***Publication Manual of the American Psychological Association.***[2] A well-thumbed copy of this book should sit on every experimental psychologist's desk. This publication

---

[1] If you seem to have a difficult time with your writing, you might find Strunk and White's *Elements of Style* (1979) helpful.

[2] Be sure to use the fourth edition of the *Publication Manual* to write your reports. There were many changes between the third and fourth editions. I was able to incorporate examples of most of these changes into the sample report on pages 268–280, but you will need to refer to the manual to find the many possible variations.

started out in 1929 as a 7-page journal article and has now become a 368-page book. As you can imagine, it is quite a task to try to master all the rules involved in APA-style writing. However, the work you put into this effort will be worthwhile. This style manual is a standard reference and is widely used. For instance, the publisher of the book you are reading asks its authors to use the manual. Unless your instructors in other courses specify a particular style manual to use, you would probably be safe in using the rules from this manual. In your psychology classes, even for a class project, you should follow the general guidelines from the *Publication Manual*. Although I obviously cannot discuss all the topics covered in this tome, I will mention the most important rules and point out where new investigators often make mistakes.[3]

## How APA Style Differs from Other Writing

Before I go into many of the rules from the *Publication Manual,* the rules collectively called APA style, I want to discuss some of the differences between APA style and the writing style of other disciplines. Some of these traditions in psychology may not be immediately obvious to you and, in some cases, are only implied in the *Publication Manual.* Psychology professors sometimes fail to emphasize them because the style becomes so ingrained after reading hundreds of journal articles. It is important for students to be aware of these subtle traditions, because what you learned about writing in some of your other classes might not be acceptable in a psychology class. Much of the information I mention is based on research by Madigan, Johnson, and Linton (1995) that compared the language used in two psychology journals with that used in the *Publication of the Modern Language Association* and the *Journal of American History.*

### LANGUAGE

Research psychologists try to make the language they use transparent. By that I mean that the language you use should not get in the way of the information you are trying to convey. In the humanities, the language and thoughts in written articles are often considered linked in such a way that the words chosen are as important as the thoughts being presented. In psychology the language is expected to be as straightforward and unobtrusive as possible. For example, as I will discuss shortly, much of scientific writing has traditionally been done in a passive voice rather than an active voice; so "the data were analyzed" rather than "I analyzed the data."

---

[3] For students who want to become real experts on APA style, a book entitled *Mastering APA Style: Student's Workbook and Training Guide* is available from the American Psychological Association. For instructors there is also the book *Mastering APA Style: Instructor's Resource Guide.* Send requests to the APA, Order Department, 750 First Street, N.E., Washington, DC 20002-4242.

Though this may seem to be a subtle distinction, it does put the emphasis on the data rather thàn on the investigator. If you try too hard to say things in a creative and unusual way in your scientific writing, other researchers will probably not appreciate your literary efforts, and this writing style may even lead them to question the seriousness of your work.

## CITATIONS

While psychologists cite other people's work nearly as much as historians and far more than literary critics, this citation is typically done in a very different way. Writers in the humanities use many direct quotes; on average historians use a direct quote about every 60 words of text, whereas psychologists on average use a direct quote fewer than once in every 3000 words (Madigan et al., 1995). Rather than directly quoting authors, psychologists paraphrase them. As noted in the previous paragraph, this difference probably reflects a difference in the way language is used. Historians believe that the way something is said is as important as what is being said. Psychologists believe that the data, theories, and logical arguments stand on their own, independent of the specific words used. Students sometimes do not understand why their literature professor lowers their grade for paraphrasing work being cited, whereas their psychology professor lowers their grade for using too many direct quotes. Unfortunately, the world is not always fair, and to be successful you will have to learn these subtle differences. However, let me emphasize that proper citation is as important when another person's ideas are being paraphrased as when a direct quote is used. If you fail to properly cite an author, it is **plagiarism** in either case. The commonly accepted definition of plagiarism is the appropriation (stealing) of the language, ideas, and thoughts of another author. Plagiarism can lead to very serious consequences whether it occurs in an academic setting or in a professional setting.

## SUBHEADINGS

As we will discuss in the next section, APA style requires a specific linear ordering of the sections of a report. Even within those sections psychologists use a lot of subheadings to announce the introduction of new topics. These subheadings minimize the transitional passages required to introduce new topics and allow research reports to be concise. Subheadings are far less common in the humanities. All of this structure imposed on a research report emphasizes what is called a story schema. That means that by telling our research stories within a consistent structure we provide a means of communication between the author and the reader that creates specific expectations about forthcoming information. Again in keeping with a de-emphasis on language, all this structure may produce a less entertaining literary piece, but one that consistently and concisely conveys information.

## FOOTNOTES

Psychologists rarely use footnotes, especially what are called discursive footnotes.[4] The footnotes psychologists use typically clarify a point being made or add some information that may not be of interest to many readers. Historians, on the other hand, use about four or five times as many discursive footnotes as psychologists, and literary critics use double that number (Madigan et al., 1995). By using these footnotes they sometimes establish a parallel text that allows a discussion to take place on several levels at the same time. Psychologists believe that this type of footnote distracts from the clear, concise, linear format expected by the reader.

## DISAGREEMENTS

When historians and literary critics disagree with their colleagues, they sometimes are pretty outspoken about their differences, sometimes to the point that the disagreement becomes personal. One author may accuse another of being "naive" or "failing to fully think an issue through" or even of "willful misinterpretation." Psychologists are encouraged to keep personalities out of disagreements. They are much more likely to couch their differences in terms of the data, the methodology, or the theories rather than to directly criticize another researcher. This tradition of civility to other investigators may come from a recognition that in science we are collectively engaged in an effort to build a coherent body of knowledge. Failure to cooperate could cause the body of knowledge to be poorly constructed or to take longer to be constructed. De-emphasizing the individual helps emphasize the data and theories that make up this body of knowledge.

## HEDGED CONCLUSIONS

Psychologists are much more likely to use hedge words in their academic writing; psychologists on average use more than ten times as many hedge words as historians and literary critics do (Madigan et al., 1995). Here are some typical hedge words and phrases: *is consistent with, lends support to, may be considered, may be related to.* Most of these hedge words are used when psychologists are stating their conclusions. In most cases the researcher is hedging not the data but the theory. As we discussed in Chapter 3, theories are essentially impossible to prove and are difficult, but not impossible, to disprove. For this reason, even the strongest data may be only weakly linked to theory. Psychologists recognizing the weakness of these linkages properly hedge their conclusions. When scientists state their conclusions too dogmatically, their scientific colleagues may accuse them of being naive (but in a civil way!).

---

[4] To emphasize this point I'll use a footnote but not a discursive one. The dictionary says *discursive* means digressive or rambling. A discursive footnote is one that is a bit off the main point of the discussion.

I hope this discussion of some less obvious traditions in APA style will help you understand why psychologists write in a way that is a bit different from what you have learned in other courses. It will still take some time for you to understand fully some of the subtle cultural differences in the way different disciplines use language. This understanding will come with experience in the field, particularly as you read the research literature and begin your own writing.

# Parts of a Report

All experimental reports should contain certain standard sections in proper order. Otherwise we would have to be like the old minister who said of his sermons: "First I tell 'em what I'm gonna tell 'em, then I tell 'em, then I tell 'em what I told 'em." Experimental reports all follow a standard pattern, so we do not need to use much space "telling 'em what we're gonna tell 'em." Not only does the standardized structure improve writing efficiency, but the consistent organization also allows the reader interested in only one section, such as the method or results, to quickly find that information. The parts of a report are listed in the following outline and described in the following sections:

I. Title page
   A. Title
   B. Author(s)
   C. Affiliation(s)
   D. Running head
II. Abstract page
III. Body of report
   A. Introduction
      1. Background
      2. Literature review
      3. Statement of purpose
   B. Method
      1. Participants
      2. Apparatus/materials
      3. Procedure
   C. Results
      1. Verbal statement of results
      2. References to tables and figures
      3. Descriptive and inferential statistics
   D. Discussion
      1. Relationship between stated purpose and results
      2. Theoretical or methodological contribution
      3. Future directions for research
IV. References

## TITLE

During the first two months after publication, about half the research reports in major psychology journals are likely to be read by fewer than 200 psychologists (Garvey & Griffith, 1971). The people who do read a report have probably selected it because of the **title.** Most psychologists regularly scan the title pages of several journals looking for current research that might interest them. Most of the key words used in a literature search (Chapter 6) are also chosen from the title. Thus, in some respects, the title is the most important part of your report; if your title conveys little information or the wrong information, you may lose most readers even before they know what you did.

The two most helpful suggestions for creating a title are contradictory: (1) Put in as much information as possible, and (2) make it as short as possible. Most titles should mention the major independent variables of interest and the dependent variable. You should also identify the general area of research if it is not obvious from the variables. The *Publication Manual* says that titles should be no longer than 10 to 12 words. Most titles should be considerably shorter than this.[5]

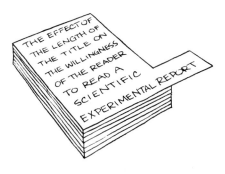

One way to create a title is to start with a long version and then eliminate words until you are absolutely unwilling to shorten it any further. As an example, suppose we needed a title for the print size experiment discussed earlier. As a first step we might start with this: "An Experiment Examining the Effect of the Size of Print on the Time to Read a Standard Paragraph for Children of Various Ages." Now let's shorten it. We can immediately eliminate "An Experiment Examining the Effect of," because these words give the reader no new information. We can also eliminate

---

[5] Although I have no evidence to back it up, it seems to me that in general, the better known the article, the shorter the title. Perhaps this effect is due to the memory span of the reader, or maybe good writers work at creating short titles. Perhaps I should have called this book *Book.*

most of the prepositions (*of, on, to, for*) by rearranging the words. In this case, it is also more efficient to identify the specific levels of the independent variable (8- and 12-year-olds) than to use a general descriptor (children of various ages). After a little work, the title might read: "Print Size and Reading Speed of 8- and 12-Year-Olds." This title contains most of the original information but is certainly much shorter.

The use of a colon in the title can often shorten it and allow words to be eliminated. If you examine the titles in the references at the end of this book, you will find many examples. For example, there is a title by Johnson, "Pupillary Responses during a Short-Term Memory Task: Cognitive Processing, Arousal, or Both?" Without the colon it would be longer—for example, "Are Pupillary Responses during a Short-Term Memory Task an Indication of Cognitive Processing, Arousal, or Both?" There is also an article by Greenwald entitled "Within-Subjects Designs: To Use or Not to Use?" He could have opted for "Should Within-Subjects Designs Be Used or Not?" In this case, the use of a colon does not shorten the title, but it does allow a more interesting, Shakespeareanesque version of the question.

## AUTHOR AND INSTITUTION

After the title, list the **author** or authors, followed by the **institution** where the research was done. It is important to list the institution where the research was done both because that institution should get credit for providing resources and because that institution takes responsibility for maintaining proper ethics and participant care. When there are multiple authors, list only those who have made substantial scientific contributions to the study. People who have simply helped collect or analyze some of the data should be acknowledged in the author note rather than listed as authors. Generally, the person who took primary responsibility for the research will also write the research report and should be listed as first author. Other authors' names should then follow, ordered by the size of their contribution. However, the relative size of a researcher's contribution is not always obvious, and disputes can arise, particularly in the case of student–faculty collaborations. It has been suggested that the best way to avoid these dis-

putes is to discuss the issues early in the research process (Fine & Kurdek, 1993). Among the issues to consider are the nature of professional and non-professional contributions required by the research, the specific abilities of each person, and the duties assigned to each. Although such agreements may need to be renegotiated as the research progresses, having a consensus up front should prevent most serious disputes later.

## ABSTRACT

The **abstract** is the second most important part of the report. Once readers choose your paper because the title is of interest, they will next read the abstract, either in the journal or in *Psychological Abstracts.* Like a door-to-door salesperson, the title may get your foot in the door, but the abstract can get you an invitation into the house.

The abstract should be a condensed version of the complete report. Most investigators wait to write the abstract until the rest of the paper is finished, although it appears immediately after the title in the final report. In the abstract you should introduce the problem, name the variables, briefly present the method, mention the important results, and discuss the implications of the results. To do all of this, you are allowed to use a maximum of only 960 characters, including all letters, spaces, and punctuation (about 100 to 120 words). As you can see, you must cover a lot of information in only a few words. Again, you may find it useful to write a long first draft and then start eliminating unnecessary information and parts of speech. Make sure that the abstract is still comprehensible and contains complete sentences (unlike a title). If the abstract is still too long after this first editing, you will have to make some choices about the relative importance of the remaining information, eliminating the least important material until your abstract meets the length requirement.

Some investigators treat titles and abstracts as afterthoughts. They dash them off after having taken great pains with the body of the paper. In this discussion I have tried to convince you that the title and abstract are the two most important parts of your experimental report. Give them your best effort.

## INTRODUCTION

The **introduction** is used to describe the current state of the body of knowledge. Because it is always the first section of the body of the report, you don't need a heading. You should assume that the reader has some familiarity with your area of research, so you need to mention only the few experiments most relevant to the one you have done. When you cite an experiment, give only the author's name and date of the article in the report body, and give the complete citation in the references section.[6] Describe these key experiments in just enough detail to set the stage for your experiment. A good introduction is a miniature literature review that leaves your readers with the feeling that they know what experiment should be done next—the one you did.

After reviewing the supporting literature, you should state the purpose, or object, of your experiment. This statement should specify the relationship between the independent and dependent variables that you investigated. For example: "The purpose of this experiment was to determine if print size would have the same effect on reading speed for 8-year-olds as for 12-year-olds." If you can predict the outcome of the experiment from the literature review or from a theoretical argument, state that prediction as a hypothesis. You must explain the logic behind your hypothesis, however, because the purpose of predicting an outcome is to make the results easier to interpret later in the report. If your hypothesis is an unsupportable hunch, don't waste the reader's time.

## METHOD

At this point, your readers should know why you did what you did. Now you must tell them what you did. The **method** section should contain enough detail so that the reader could replicate your experiment. However, you must use your judgment about which details are relevant to the experimental outcome. For example, in the print-size experiment, you would not need to specify the exact dimensions of the room in which the paragraphs were read, although you would certainly specify the dimensions of the paper each paragraph was typed on. Because it is impossible to mention each circumstance from the infinite set of circumstances, you should limit yourself to those that could logically have been expected to influence the results.

The method section is usually divided into several subsections. A typical report has three subsections, although you may wish to use additional subsections if your experiment calls for more.

---

[6] A note about how to cite experiments: For one author, just give the author's name and the date of the article: "Jones (1967) found . . ." or "It was found (Jones, 1967) . . ." For two authors, use both last names: "Jones and Smith (1971) found . . . ," or "It was found (Jones & Smith, 1971) that . . ." For more than two authors, use all of the names the first time you cite the research and the first author's name followed by "et al." thereafter: "Johnson et al. (1972) also found . . ."

## Participants

The **participants,** or subjects,[7] subsection should specify who the participants were. Were they students, pilots, children? What gender were they? How many did you use, and how did you select them? (Were they volunteers? Were they satisfying a class requirement? Were they paid?) Be sure to state this information in a way that a reader in Samoa could understand. ("Participants were students from PSY 204 . . ." Eh? What's PSY 204?) If you eliminated data for any participants (see Chapter 5), you should indicate the basis for this decision. For animals, be sure to report their genus, species, supplier, and housing conditions, along with their age and sex.

## Apparatus/Materials

The **apparatus/materials** subsection should describe the equipment or materials you used in your experiment. If you used a standard psychological apparatus, you need only give the general name, the manufacturer, and the model number. ("A Scientific Prototype two-channel tachistoscope, Model 800-F, was used.") Describe any custom-built apparatus in enough detail so that the reader could construct a similar one. ("The slides were back-projected on a Plexiglas panel 15 cm high and 20 cm wide, mounted vertically 30 cm from the participant.")[8] Be sure to make a note of all the measurements at the time you do the experiment. Reconstructing these details after the experiment is often difficult and sometimes impossible.

## Procedure

The **procedure** subsection should specify exactly what happened to each participant during the experiment. When writing this section, imagine that your naive, innocent participant has just walked into the experimental room. What happens from that point on? What instructions did you give? These can usually be paraphrased unless they were a major part of the experimental manipulation. What events happened during a trial, in what order, and with what timing? How many trials were presented? Were they in blocks or sessions? Were trials randomized or counterbalanced? Exactly what was measured, and how was it measured and recorded? What type of experimental design did you use? Why did you choose to use the procedure described?

The procedure section is one of the most difficult sections to write well because you have become intimately familiar with each detail, and the procedure now seems so obvious and straightforward to you. By all means

---

[7] When reading experimental reports published before 1974, you will see the word *subject* abbreviated as *S* and *experimenter* as *E*. These abbreviations are no longer acceptable. In fact, the term *subject* should be avoided if possible and replaced with a more specific term such as students, children, or rats, or if a generic term is necessary, participants, respondents, or individuals.

[8] Report all measurements in metric units. If the object was manufactured in nonmetric units, report them as such but insert the metric equivalents in parentheses. ("The panel was 3 ft [0.91 m] in width.")

have someone who has no idea what you did read the procedure section and then tell you in his or her own words what you did. Then correct any false impressions, and try it with someone else. Eventually the two accounts will correspond, and at that point the procedure section is complete.

## RESULTS

You should typically begin the **results** section of the report by describing your data. Provide raw data only when illustrating a general finding or when showing the results of small-$N$ experiments. Descriptive statistics should be reported first.[9] When you report a measure of central tendency such as a mean or median, you should usually include a measure of dispersion as well, such as a standard deviation. If you have only a few measures to report, you can include them in the text: "The response times for the 1-, 2-, and 3-sec foreperiods were 50, 362, and 391 ms respectively." However, use a table or figure when you must report more than five or six data points.

Investigators typically use tables to show the results of main effects and to give exact values of the dependent variable when these are important. You should type tables on separate pages from the text. The short sample report toward the end of this chapter shows how a table should be organized. For specific problems, refer to the *Publication Manual*.

Use figures sparingly, for they take up journal space and are even more costly to print than are tables.[10] As we saw in Chapter 12, however, figures are a great way to show interactions and to illustrate trends in the data. In most cases, figures are preferable to tables. Readers can generally extract and remember information better from figures than from tables. Here are some general rules to follow in drawing figures:

1. Label the abscissa and ordinate, and specify the units of measurement.[11]
2. Draw the ordinate two-thirds to three-fourths as long as the abscissa.
3. Make 0 the smallest mark on the ordinate. If you must break the ordinate to save space (for example, if you have no response times between 0 and 0.3 sec), indicate the break by a double slashed line at that point.
4. Use point and line codes to indicate those independent variables not listed on the abscissa. Make these codes consistent throughout the report. Do not rely on different colors to make your distinctions. Colors should be used only in coloring books!

---

[9] I have seen many student reports in which the first sentence in the results section was something like "The effect of variable A was significant, $t$ (18) = 4.7, $p < .01$." Reporting the results of an inferential statistical test before describing the data is a little like reporting the results of a ball game by saying that "one of the teams won." Who won? By how much? Or in the experiment: In which direction was the effect? What was the size of the effect?

[10] A figure is any visual representation of data that cannot be set in standard type. Graphs are the most common figures in experimental reports.

[11] New investigators commonly forget this step. To avoid this error, set a rule for yourself that you will never put in a data point until you have labeled the axes.

5. Do not put too many curves on a single figure, usually no more than three or four.
6. Draw your figures on pages separate from the text.

These rules are designed to help you make your results clear and to minimize the possibility of distortion. You may find, however, that you will need to bend them occasionally to keep from distorting your data.

Usually figures submitted to journals for formal publication can now be produced using a computer program and a printer. But be sure, if you do your own figures, that you use a good printer and that the line sizes and letter sizes are appropriate even if the figure must be reduced for publication. To avoid getting parts of the figure too small during a reduction, letter and number sizes should vary by no more than 4 points (for example, from 14-point type to 10-point type).

Once the data have been described, the results of inferential statistical tests can be reported. First tell the reader which test or tests were used and how your variables were mapped onto the test, if this fact is not obvious. The results of these tests are reported in a standard way. For example, if the result of a $t$-test[12] done on two groups of ten subjects was 4.7, which you found to be significant at the .01 level, you would report it as follows: "The difference between groups was found to be significant, $\underline{t}$ (18) = 4.7, $\underline{p}$ < .01."[13] Report other tests in the same way, first stating the symbol for the test statistic (underlined if not a Greek letter), followed by the degrees of freedom in parentheses, an equals sign, the result of the test calculation, a comma, a lowercase $p$ underlined for italic, a < sign (or, for nonsignificant results, a > sign), and finally the testing level. Many journals now require the reporting of the **effect size** as well as standard tests of statistical significance. Reporting an effect size lets the reader determine not only whether any difference you found in your sample was likely to reflect a difference in the population but also whether the difference you found was large enough to be important. You can compute an effect size relatively easily, typically using the values you obtained from your inferential test. You should consult a statistics book or your instructor to find the exact formula to use.

No interpretation of the results, other than information needed for clarification, should be done in the results section. The results section should be used for stating *what* you found; the discussion section is for explaining *why* you think you found what you found, and in the standard format, never the twain should meet. In some cases, if the information can be presented more clearly or efficiently, you may combine the results and discussion sections. If you do that, be sure to clearly use this heading: Results and Discussion Section.

---

[12] A $t$-test is an inferential test that indicates whether the means of two samples are significantly different from each other. The result of a $t$-test is a number. By comparing this number with other numbers listed in a table, you can determine if the means are statistically different at a particular probability level (for example, a probability level of .01, $p$ < .01).

[13] The number in parentheses is the degrees of freedom for the $t$-test. Most statistical tests have a degrees-of-freedom term, either a single number or two numbers. You will find out how to determine this number when you learn those tests.

## DISCUSSION

In your introduction you described what the body of knowledge consisted of and where it needed to be expanded. Your results section then provided a new building block.[14] You now have to describe how the new block fits into the structure and how the new structure differs from the old. Thus, the **discussion** section is the place where you update the body of knowledge with your results.

In most cases the introduction section will have identified competing theories or stated hypotheses predicting the outcome of the experiment. In the discussion section you should briefly review these theories and hypotheses and discuss whether your results support or refute them. If more than one theory or hypothesis can explain your results, you might suggest ways of testing these in future experiments.

This section is also the place to qualify your results, if necessary, and to speculate on the reasons for unpredicted findings (as long as you keep your speculations short and identify them as such). However, you should not waste the reader's time explaining effects that were not statistically significant. Only in rare cases should negative results be interpreted as due to anything other than chance.

Particularly if you are doing applied work, you should use the discussion section to point out the practical value of your results—how and where they can be used and how they might change current applied procedures.

Finally, you can use the discussion section to make suggestions about the direction of future research. Now that you have discussed the new state of the body of knowledge, you may be able to suggest where new expansion should take place.

## REFERENCES

Your **reference** section should list only those references cited in the report and should be ordered alphabetically by the first author's name. The

---

[14] Or, in some cases, your experiment may have blasted away part of the existing structure.

references listed at the end of this book and in the sample report follow the proper style and should provide you with many useful examples. For unusual references, refer to the *Publication Manual*.

## Reducing Language Bias

Without realizing it, most of us at times use language that reflects historical cultural biases. For example, although one of the reasons that the language convention of using *he, him*, and *his* as generic pronouns rather than having to say the longer *he or she, him or her*, and *his or hers* was probably for efficiency, another reason was that, historically, the person being referred to probably was a man. Men did things worth writing about, and women stayed home and raised the kids—or at least that is what the people in control of the language (read that, men) thought. I need not point out to you that the world has changed. Those of us in psychology should certainly acknowledge this change; the majority of psychology graduate students and about three-fourths of the undergraduate psychology majors are now women. We men in psychology should probably consider ourselves lucky that the women are not demanding the use of generic feminine pronouns for a few centuries to even things up.

Bias also creeps into the language when we refer to ethnicity, age, disability, and sexual orientation. In an attempt to minimize it, the APA has included a section in the *Publication Manual* containing guidelines for language usage. Here is my version of these guidelines. I have certainly shortened them and regrouped them, but I believe that I have not distorted them:

1. *Call people what they are.* This first guideline has at least two implications. The first is that we should be specific and refer to groupings of people in as large or as small a group as necessary to be accurate. For instance, do not refer to *man* in a phrase such as *man's search for knowledge* if you mean women as well. Use *men and women* or *human beings* or some other more inclusive term. Do not use *he, him*, or *his* if a woman could be included; use *he or she, him or her*, or *his or hers*, or change the whole sentence to plural—for example, changing "Each participant was asked whether he had . . ." to "Participants were asked whether they had . . ."[15] In this way your language will be more accurate, and nobody will be excluded. On the other hand, avoid using language that refers to too large a group. Do not write *nonwhite* if you mean *African American*. In other words, be as specific as necessary to achieve accuracy.

---

[15] Do not mix singular and plural, such as *"Each participant was told that they could. . . ."* In conversational speech, because it is sometimes difficult to plan sentence structures far enough in advance to match nouns and pronouns and still avoid using *he* or *him* generically, the practice of using a singular noun with a plural pronoun is becoming more common; it is still not correct, but people don't gasp anymore when you do it. However, people will still gasp if you mismatch in a written report. See Foertsch and Gernsbracher (1997) for the practical consequences of such mismatches.

A second implication of this guideline is that terms should be used that refer to people as people, not objects. I have discussed elsewhere in this book the attempt to minimize the use of the term *subject* because it makes the experimental participants sound like objects rather than people. Again, the best terms to use are the most specific: children, students, rats, 8-year-olds, women. If more general terms are needed, *participants, respondents,* or *individuals* are preferable to *subjects.*

2. *Call people what they want to be called.* The way we use language changes over time. Included in these changes are terms that refer to subsets of our population. In some cases the changes occur so rapidly that this book would be out of date in only a couple of years if I tried to give you all of the most up-to-date terminology. In the past 50 years we have gone from *Negro* to *colored* to *Afro-American* to *black* to *African American,* and there is currently some talk of using *people of color.* As this edition goes to print, *Asian American* is preferred to *Oriental,* and *American Indian* or *Native American* is preferred to *Indian.* In referring to sexual orientation (note that the neutral *orientation* is preferred to *choice* because we do not know whether choice is involved), the generally preferred terms are *gay men* and *lesbians.* But in all these cases, you will have to determine what language is preferred at the time you write your report. The best way to do this is to ask your participants what they would like to be called.

3. *People are nouns; their attributes are adjectives.* This guideline acknowledges that people are people, not attributes or conditions. Thus, *people with schizophrenia* are not *schizophrenics;* schizophrenia is a condition, not a person. Likewise *people with disabilities* should not be labeled *the disabled; elderly people* are not *the elderly;* and *gay men* are not *gays.* The same is true for other adjectives such as *male* and *female;* refer to *female participants,* not *females.* The nouns are *men* and *women* or, for high school age and younger, *girls* and *boys.* By the way, be sure to use parallel terms, particularly when nonparallel terms put one group into a subordinate or stereotyped role, such as *men and wives.*

These are guidelines, not rigid rules; in some cases wordiness or clumsy prose might result from following them strictly. They should certainly not be used as an excuse for lessening the accuracy demanded by science. As a final test of the social implications of the language you use, Maggio (1991) suggests imagining that you are a member of the group you are discussing. If you would feel excluded or offended by what you have written, you may need to revise it.

# Writing Style

Experimental reports are not intended to be literary masterpieces or entertaining monologues. Thus, your general writing style should not get in the way of smoothly flowing thoughts, nor should it bring more attention to you than to your research. To meet these requirements, scientific writing has evolved a standard style.

Traditionally, scientific writers have used third-person passive voice rather than first-person active. Instead of writing "I did this experiment to . . . ," the investigator would write "This experiment was done to . . . " Although this style did keep the report from reading like a letter home, it also forced out much of its life. The prose became dull and monotonous and caused the reader more pain than pleasure. Today it is considered proper to use the pronoun *I* to a limited extent—for example, "I thought that . . . ," rather than "It was thought that . . ." You should, however, avoid excessive use of *I* to keep from drawing the reader's attention to you rather than to the research. You should also try to use an active verb form rather than a passive form, especially when there are no pronoun problems—for example, "A previous report described a new method" rather than "In a previous report, a new method was described."[16] Again the general rule is to use words that make the writing come alive without interrupting the smooth flow of thoughts.

The context of a sentence will usually tell you which verb tense to use. Most sentences in the introduction and method sections refer to past actions "Boles (1972) reported . . ." and "The students recalled the words . . . " On the other hand, results "are" and theory "is" even after the experiment is completed. That is, the body of knowledge exists in the present and so should be discussed using present-tense verbs: "These data support an interference theory of forgetting."

Finally, scientific writing should be concise. The limited resources of time and space simply do not allow us the luxury of excess verbiage. For instance, the style I have used in this book would not be appropriate for scientific writing.[17] I have purposely used more words than necessary because I have tried to do more than transfer information; I have tried to convince, cajole, and convert you as well as communicate with you. In scientific writing, you should assume that the reader has already been convinced, cajoled, and converted; your only job, then, is to communicate.

The most common problem new investigators have with report writing is laziness. The investigator is not really lazy, of course, because lazy people do not do experiments, but his or her writing style may be lazy. In writing a report, the most important end of your pencil is the one without the point; the most important key is the delete key. Extremely rare is the person who can write a good, concise report the first time through. Most good scientific writers have to try a number of alternative words and sentence structures before deciding on the best one. Every word must

---

[16] Some writers may object to this form on the grounds that a report cannot describe—an author describes. I suppose writing is largely a matter of personal preference. In this case, I prefer to trade a little accuracy for a lot livelier style.

[17] If I had written the book in scientific style, you would have been bored, I would have been bored, and the publisher would have been bored. My mother would have bought the only copy; she loves me even when I'm boring.

say precisely what you want it to say, and every sentence should flow smoothly into the next. Writing this way is hard work!

When writing a report, most investigators first produce a draft of the best version they are capable of writing. Getting the report to this point may take two or three attempts, because it is often easier to rewrite whole sections than to make corrections on top of corrections. Once you come up with a final draft you are satisfied with, you should give it to several people to read. At least one of these people should be unfamiliar with your experiment, because you are probably so familiar with your own research that you cannot judge how well the report describes it. Because you already know what happened, your mind conveniently fills in all the gaps you leave in the report. An uninformed reader can be a good gap detector.[18]

It is also helpful to give the report to a reader who is familiar with what you did so that he or she can tell you whether you did what you say you did. This person can serve as your error detector. Finally, you should have a reader who is familiar with scientific writing style and is a good writer. This reader can tell you how you might improve the way you say what you did.

AN ENEMY MAKES THE BEST CRITIC.

After getting comments from these readers, you are ready to write a final version of the report. This copy should be neatly typed and proofread before you submit it.

Some of you may find that if you follow the procedure described here, your reports will be more readable; others may find that another procedure works best. Writing is an art; what works for one writer may not work for another. However, the major point we have been discussing is valid for any procedure: the report is the final product of your research and deserves at least the same effort you give to all other aspects of your research.

## A Sample Report

Please ignore the contents of the sample report to follow. Not only is it fictitious, but the writing style suffers because I have attempted to illustrate as many instances of APA style as possible in a short report. The marginal

---

[18] On the death of one of his scientific colleagues, one of my friends remarked to me: "I'm really going to miss him. He was one of my best enemies. Now I don't know whom I'll send my reports to." It is often best to have someone read your report who will be critical without fearing that he or she will break up a social relationship. Friends are often too nice to be good critics.

comments contain shortened versions of some style rules, with an arrow pointing to an example in the report. The definitive word is still the *Publication Manual.*

Your instructor may ask you to violate some of these rules. For example, when a report is not actually going to be submitted to a journal for publication, I prefer to have students incorporate figures and tables into the body of the report. That way the reader has easy access to them while reading the text. Your instructor may have similar preferences.

For a more detailed coverage of APA style you should, obviously, order a copy of the *Publication Manual of the American Psychological Association,* fourth edition (1994).

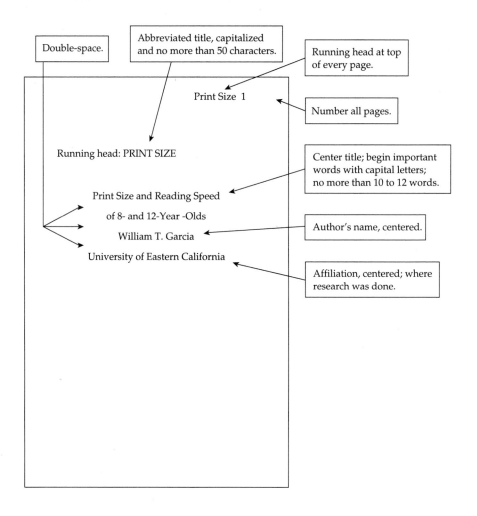

Double-space.

Abbreviated title, capitalized and no more than 50 characters.

Running head at top of every page.

Print Size  1

Number all pages.

Running head: PRINT SIZE

Center title; begin important words with capital letters; no more than 10 to 12 words.

Print Size and Reading Speed

of 8- and 12-Year -Olds

William T. Garcia

Author's name, centered.

University of Eastern California

Affiliation, centered; where research was done.

Do not indent abstract.

Print Size  2

Abstract

The time it took 8- and 12-year-old children to read paragraphs was measured as a function of print size.  Paragraphs were typed in either 12- or 10-point print.  Results indicated that the size of print is an important dimension for the younger children, with the larger print being read 32% faster than the smaller print.  Print size had no effect on reading speed for the older children.  The results are interpreted in the context of the stimulus-impact theory of reading.

Double-space.

No more than 960 characters, including spaces.

No right-margin justification or word breaks.

Margins on all pages on all sides should be 1 inch.

Indent paragraphs five to seven spaces.

Repeat the full title, centered.

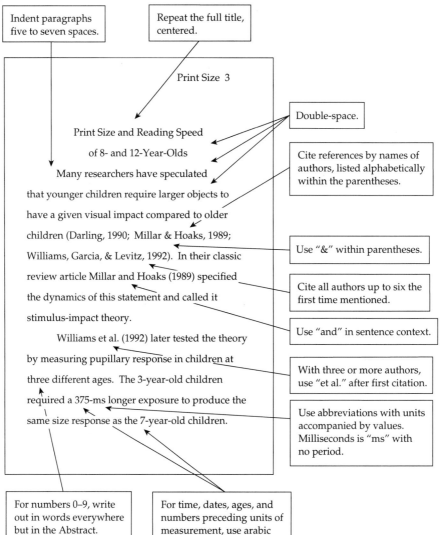

Print Size 3

Double-space.

Print Size and Reading Speed
of 8- and 12-Year-Olds

Many researchers have speculated
that younger children require larger objects to
have a given visual impact compared to older
children (Darling, 1990; Millar & Hoaks, 1989;
Williams, Garcia, & Levitz, 1992). In their classic
review article Millar and Hoaks (1989) specified
the dynamics of this statement and called it
stimulus-impact theory.

Williams et al. (1992) later tested the theory
by measuring pupillary response in children at
three different ages. The 3-year-old children
required a 375-ms longer exposure to produce the
same size response as the 7-year-old children.

Cite references by names of authors, listed alphabetically within the parentheses.

Use "&" within parentheses.

Cite all authors up to six the first time mentioned.

Use "and" in sentence context.

With three or more authors, use "et al." after first citation.

Use abbreviations with units accompanied by values. Milliseconds is "ms" with no period.

For numbers 0–9, write out in words everywhere but in the Abstract.

For time, dates, ages, and numbers preceding units of measurement, use arabic numerals.

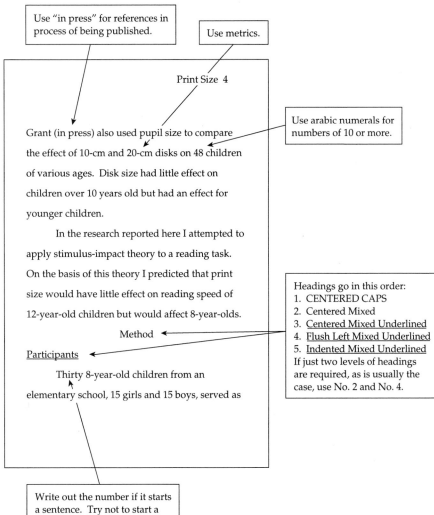

Use "in press" for references in process of being published.

Use metrics.

Print Size  4

Use arabic numerals for numbers of 10 or more.

Grant (in press) also used pupil size to compare the effect of 10-cm and 20-cm disks on 48 children of various ages.  Disk size had little effect on children over 10 years old but had an effect for younger children.

    In the research reported here I attempted to apply stimulus-impact theory to a reading task. On the basis of this theory I predicted that print size would have little effect on reading speed of 12-year-old children but would affect 8-year-olds.

Headings go in this order:
1. CENTERED CAPS
2. Centered Mixed
3. Centered Mixed Underlined
4. Flush Left Mixed Underlined
5. Indented Mixed Underlined
If just two levels of headings are required, as is usually the case, use No. 2 and No. 4.

Method

Participants

    Thirty 8-year-old children from an elementary school, 15 girls and 15 boys, served as

Write out the number if it starts a sentence.  Try not to start a sentence with a number.

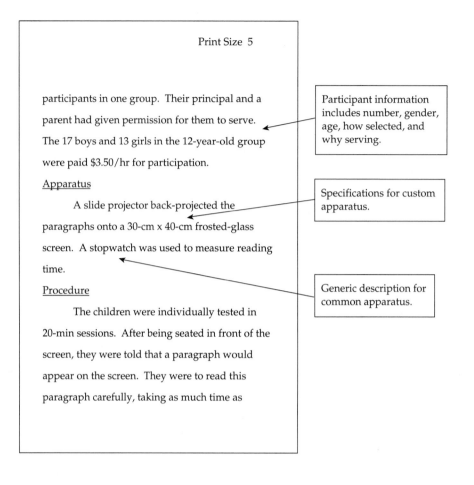

Print Size 5

participants in one group.  Their principal and a parent had given permission for them to serve.  The 17 boys and 13 girls in the 12-year-old group were paid $3.50/hr for participation.

> Participant information includes number, gender, age, how selected, and why serving.

Apparatus

A slide projector back-projected the paragraphs onto a 30-cm x 40-cm frosted-glass screen.  A stopwatch was used to measure reading time.

> Specifications for custom apparatus.

> Generic description for common apparatus.

Procedure

The children were individually tested in 20-min sessions.  After being seated in front of the screen, they were told that a paragraph would appear on the screen.  They were to read this paragraph carefully, taking as much time as

Print Size 6

necessary to understand the material. After
reading a paragraph, each child was asked three
questions, having single-word answers, about the
contents of the paragraph. After the questions
were answered, another paragraph was presented
until each child had read three paragraphs.

Each paragraph had been previously tested
for readability and was at or below an 8-year age
level. The questions had been found to be a good
measure of comprehension.

The experimenter manually timed the
reading latency for each trial using a stopwatch.
Scores were obtained for each of the three trials in

Procedure is in past tense.

Numbers under 10 are
written as words.

Numbers that represent time,
ages, scores, or points on a
scale are written as numerals.

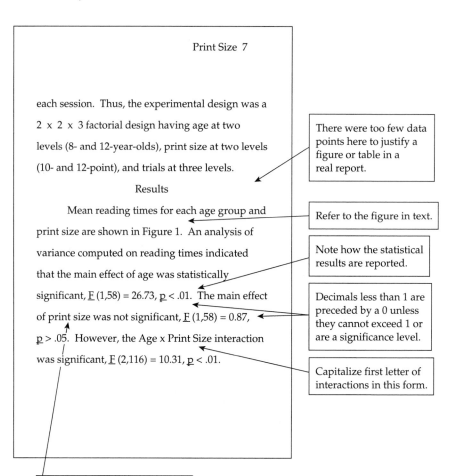

Print Size  7

each session.  Thus, the experimental design was a

2 x 2 x 3 factorial design having age at two

levels (8- and 12-year-olds), print size at two levels

(10- and 12-point), and trials at three levels.

There were too few data points here to justify a figure or table in a real report.

Results

Mean reading times for each age group and

print size are shown in Figure 1.  An analysis of

variance computed on reading times indicated

that the main effect of age was statistically

significant, $\underline{F}$ (1,58) = 26.73, $\underline{p}$ < .01.  The main effect

of print size was not significant, $\underline{F}$ (1,58) = 0.87,

$\underline{p}$ > .05.  However, the Age x Print Size interaction

was significant, $\underline{F}$ (2,116) = 10.31, $\underline{p}$ < .01.

Refer to the figure in text.

Note how the statistical results are reported.

Decimals less than 1 are preceded by a 0 unless they cannot exceed 1 or are a significance level.

Capitalize first letter of interactions in this form.

Main effects are not capitalized.

When reporting means, always include a measure of dispersion, such as a standard deviation.

This table is included only to illustrate the use of tables. In an actual report, using both a table and figure to present equivalent data is redundant.

Print Size 8

Mean reading times and <u>SDs</u> for each of the three trials are shown in Table 1. The main effect of trials failed to reach significance, <u>F</u> (2,24) = 1.53, <u>p</u> > .05.

Check the direction of < and > signs; <u>p</u> > for nonsignificant, <u>p</u> < for significant.

Discussion

The present data are entirely consistent with stimulus-impact theory. No difference in reading time as a function of print size was found for older children. However, for younger children a print size difference caused a significant difference in reading time. An interpretation of these data within the framework of stimulus-impact theory is that even the smaller print size

Report inferential statistics, such as <u>t</u> and <u>F</u>, to two decimals.

Data and interpretations currently exist, so they should be in present tense.

*Data* is a plural word.

Print Size  9

had maximum visual impact on the older children. The younger children required a larger sized print in order to perform at a high level.  As Millar and Hoaks stated in their 1989 article, "High-impact stimuli are necessary for maximal performance in younger children" (p. 346).

> The implication of these results is obvious for publishers of children's reading material. However, before recommendations can be presented to these publishers, additional research is needed to compare reading times for many additional print sizes and for children at many age levels.

For quotations under 40 words, use quotation marks; longer quotations should be put in an indented block, without quotation marks.

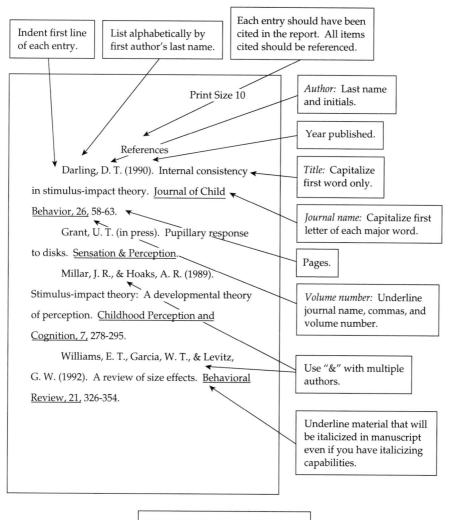

Indent first line of each entry.

List alphabetically by first author's last name.

Each entry should have been cited in the report. All items cited should be referenced.

Print Size 10

*Author:* Last name and initials.

Year published.

References

Darling, D. T. (1990). Internal consistency in stimulus-impact theory. Journal of Child Behavior, 26, 58-63.

*Title:* Capitalize first word only.

*Journal name:* Capitalize first letter of each major word.

Grant, U. T. (in press). Pupillary response to disks. Sensation & Perception.

Pages.

Millar, J. R., & Hoaks, A. R. (1989). Stimulus-impact theory: A developmental theory of perception. Childhood Perception and Cognition, 7, 278-295.

*Volume number:* Underline journal name, commas, and volume number.

Williams, E. T., Garcia, W. T., & Levitz, G. W. (1992). A review of size effects. Behavioral Review, 21, 326-354.

Use "&" with multiple authors.

Underline material that will be italicized in manuscript even if you have italicizing capabilities.

You will find examples of the style for books, magazines, and other references by looking at the References at the end of this book.

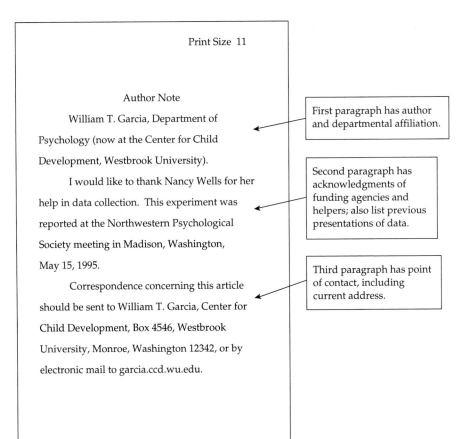

Print Size  11


Author Note

William T. Garcia, Department of
Psychology (now at the Center for Child
Development, Westbrook University).

I would like to thank Nancy Wells for her
help in data collection.  This experiment was
reported at the Northwestern Psychological
Society meeting in Madison, Washington,
May 15, 1995.

Correspondence concerning this article
should be sent to William T. Garcia, Center for
Child Development, Box 4546, Westbrook
University, Monroe, Washington 12342, or by
electronic mail to garcia.ccd.wu.edu.

First paragraph has author
and departmental affiliation.

Second paragraph has
acknowledgments of
funding agencies and
helpers; also list previous
presentations of data.

Third paragraph has point
of contact, including
current address.

Print Size 12

Table 1

Means and Standard Deviations of Paragraph

Reading Times in Seconds as a Function of Age,

Print Size, and Trials

| Print Size | 8-year-olds | | 12-year-olds | |
|---|---|---|---|---|
| | M | SD | M | SD |
| 10-point | | | | |
| Trial 1 | 84.2 | 12.9 | 31.2 | 8.7 |
| Trial 2 | 83.4 | 10.2 | 27.7 | 7.8 |
| Trial 3 | 81.0 | 10.7 | 24.7 | 8.1 |
| 12-point | | | | |
| Trial 1 | 58.2 | 10.1 | 32.3 | 9.2 |
| Trial 2 | 56.1 | 8.2 | 29.1 | 8.3 |
| Trial 3 | 55.9 | 7.7 | 30.8 | 8.5 |

Title in mixed caps, left justified, and underlined.

Use only horizontal rule lines.

When reporting means, always include a measure of dispersion, such as a standard deviation.

Table with title should be understandable standing alone. Title should explain abbreviations used in table.

Use indentation where possible rather than taking a full column.

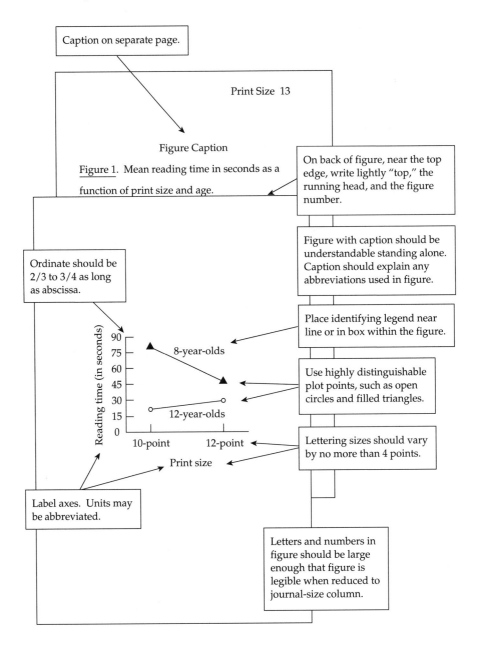

Caption on separate page.

Print Size 13

Figure Caption

Figure 1. Mean reading time in seconds as a

function of print size and age.

On back of figure, near the top edge, write lightly "top," the running head, and the figure number.

Figure with caption should be understandable standing alone. Caption should explain any abbreviations used in figure.

Ordinate should be 2/3 to 3/4 as long as abscissa.

Place identifying legend near line or in box within the figure.

Use highly distinguishable plot points, such as open circles and filled triangles.

Lettering sizes should vary by no more than 4 points.

Label axes. Units may be abbreviated.

Letters and numbers in figure should be large enough that figure is legible when reduced to journal-size column.

# Presentations at Conferences

## ORAL PRESENTATIONS

Although the primary means of reporting research is a written report, most researchers, including many students, also report their results by presenting them at a professional conference. Students have an increasing number of opportunities to present research results in this way. For example, students in my university last year could present their work in a poster session either in the psychology department or in a university-wide research conference, both sponsored by student organizations. They could also present a paper at an undergraduate research conference that drew students from several states or at a conference sponsored by the state psychological association. Some even presented papers or posters at larger regional or national meetings, either in a student session or as a co-author in a regular session. Many students find making presentations exciting, both in telling an audience about their own work and in seeing the broader world of science at work for the first time. However, giving a paper or a poster can be a frightening experience, and other than taking a speech course, most students have little training. Here is a crash course in the art of presenting your research orally.

What does the presentation of a **conference paper** consist of? Although the answer to this question varies depending on the conference, you will generally be expected to stand up in front of a group of 20 to 100 colleagues and present your work within 10 to 20 minutes, leaving some time at the end for questions. Typically, you will have prepared some visual aids such as overheads, slides, or handouts. It is important to realize that presenting your research this way is far different from writing a paper. If you try to read an APA-style research report to your listeners, you will be lucky if they do not walk out on you. The written report is too long, goes into far too much detail, and uses a nonconversational style. You might expect a person reading your written report to fully digest it and carry away many details. We know from research on the human memory that the person listening to your presentation will be able to carry away only a few major points. You want to make sure that those points are easy to grasp and remember.

Ideally, the style of your presentation should be conversational. I remember clearly the first paper I ever gave at a conference. In this case I was speaking to a national group of researchers in an area of study in which I had been working for only five months. I was terrified. But I worked hard at memorizing the presentation so I could give it without notes. I got up, knees shaking, and presented the research without stumbling over very many words. I was pretty proud of myself. But at a reception later, when my adviser asked the conference coordinator, "Didn't David do a good job with his presentation today?" the coordinator said, "No. It sounded as if he was reading the paper, and we don't do that at this conference." I was temporarily crushed, of course, but this was the best advice I could have gotten.

Communication researchers know that conversational speech is quite different from reading a text. In conversational speech we vary our pace according to our mental activity, pausing to think up the next phrase and then unloading the words rather rapidly. The listener uses these pauses and the pacing of the words to follow the thought pattern of the speaker. In reading text, words are paced more regularly without long pauses. This sing-song, monotonous style is a great way to cure a listener's insomnia but a poor way to convey the excitement of the research. As a presenter, you should be thoroughly familiar with what you want to say, but you should not overrehearse to the point that you sound as if you are reading a written report, and are bored by it.

Because you want to try to give the presentation as naturally as possible, it will take you longer to present the material than you expect. If you practice by reading a written version to yourself, even if out loud, you will zoom along because you do not have to slow down to allow something to sink in; you already understand the content. So, you can expect to take at least 20% longer to present the material to an audience. Ideally, you should build in some choice points where you can add material or leave it out as you are giving the presentation to control the length of time you take. If your presentations are like mine, you will end up having to take the shorter route at most of these points.

Think about your audience, and try to tailor your presentation to it. Are the members students, psychologists, experts in your research field, or scientists from many disciplines? Because we are so familiar with our topic by the time we present our research, we tend to forget that not everybody is as familiar with it, or as interested in it, as we are. Try to transport yourself back in time to where you were when you first got the idea for your research. That is probably where your audience will be when you start your presentation.

Judging from many hours of sitting through presentations, I believe that the biggest error presenters make is to zip through the experimental procedure to get on to the important stuff, the results. But unless you make the procedure clear, the results are not important. I have found that the best way to help the listeners understand the procedure is, if possible, to turn them into participants. If I showed a series of visual displays to the participants and then had them make a response, I give the listeners a brief set of instructions, show them a series of overhead transparencies similar to the displays, and have them give the appropriate response. Several representative trials can often take as little time as explaining the procedure in words, and the audience will remember the procedure so much better. Psychologists know that people learn better by doing than by being told. We should take advantage of that principle.

When presenting your paper, go for the big picture. If people really want to know the details of your counterbalancing scheme, the levels of statistical significance at which you tested, or other such details, they can ask you later or ask for a written copy of your paper. Most listeners will never remember these details anyway. Usually, the best way to present results is graphically, using overhead transparencies or slides. I prefer overheads to slides because it is easier to face toward the audience and point to something in the figure (on the transparency not the screen). This is also one reason I prefer overheads to handouts. You cannot point to the thing you are talking about on the listener's handout. Other problems with handouts include the time it takes to distribute the handouts and the loss of control over when the listener is given information (once I have a handout in hand, I tune out the speaker and sneak a look at the results)—to say nothing of the cost, the clutter, and the conservation of trees.

In using an overhead, be sure that you do not block the audience's view of the screen. When you show a graph, remember that this is the first time the audience has seen it. Presenters sometimes flash up a graph and immediately launch into a conclusion: "As you can clearly see, the results confirmed our hypothesis." As a member of the audience I am saying to myself: "Wait a minute. What's on each axis? Is better performance up or down on the graph? Which condition is represented by the solid line, or the dashed line? What would the figure look like if the hypothesis were not supported? What is it about this figure that supports the hypothesis?" The audience should not have to ask all these questions. You should show the figure, pause . . . , explain what is on each axis, explain what the lines or bars represent, and indicate where in the figure the audience should look to find the important information, pointing as you go. Finally, make sure that the figures are big enough and in bold enough print that they can be seen from the back of the room. The figures in your written report will probably have to be redrawn to meet these requirements. A good rule of thumb is that if you can hold a transparency about 6 feet away and can still read it, the audience will probably be able to read it (Estes, 1993). Fortunately, with modern word-processing computers, drawing good figures is an easy task technically; yet I still see illegible figures at many of the conferences I attend.

At the end of your presentation, you should have a transparency or slide that lists your conclusions. This is one final time to give the listener a message to take away. Be conservative. Three to five conclusions are probably all your audience will remember. After giving the conclusions you should be prepared to close decisively. "Uhm . . . I guess that's all I have to say" is not an impressive way to do this! Saying "Thank you for your attention" or "If time permits, I'd be happy to answer questions" will signal your audience that you have finished and let them know that you carefully planned for your presentation to end at this point.

You have just finished your presentation and are ready to sit down, catch your breath, and relax. What a relief! But the chair of your paper session says, "We have time for a few questions." You, of course, have not prepared for any questions because you have answered all possible questions in your lucid presentation. Then some wag in the audience asks: "I don't see how you can claim that your results support Landon's theory. Doesn't the theory of reductivity proposed by Wagner last year predict your findings?" You, of course, have never heard of Wagner. How do you respond?

I have no pat answers to give you for such a question.[19] My point is that you should prepare yourself as best you can to field questions. After you have exhausted all the potential questions you can think up, you should ask others to pose questions for you. In fact, the best way to prepare for presenting a paper is to make a trial presentation to a group of colleagues, perhaps your classmates or other students and faculty members in your department. Strongly encourage them to ask you hard questions. Try to answer those questions when they are asked, and think about the questions again later when you have time to prepare better answers. Some of these questions may reappear at the conference. Be prepared.

## POSTERS

Most conferences now include **poster** sessions as well as paper presentations. Picture a large room full of free-standing bulletin boards lined up in rows. People presenting posters stand in front of the bulletin boards, and behind them the posters are thumbtacked to the cork boards. Crowds are milling about, some people drifting by the posters reading titles and others talking with the presenters. Typically at such a poster session presenters are given an hour or so to stand in front of their poster, explain their research, and discuss anything the ever-changing audience wants to discuss.

The advantage of giving a poster rather than a paper is that you can have truly interactive conversations, usually with people who have an interest in what you have done. This format works particularly well for simply designed research having straightforward results that can be easily captured in a few graphs. The disadvantage of a poster is that the first person comes up, asks you what you did, and you are two minutes into the explanation when a second person asks you the same thing. If you start over, the first person will get bored. If you continue, the second person may have trouble following you. This pattern is repeated often throughout the poster session, and when you have finished, you may feel that you never had the opportunity to explain your work fully to anyone. This disadvantage is particularly serious when your research is complex or uses an unusual complicated methodology or involves testing highly detailed and unfamiliar theories. In these cases you may simply not have the time to tell the elaborate story required to do your research justice.

As a general strategy in preparing for a poster session, you should try to put together several mini-presentations. One less than a minute should

---

[19] I believe that honesty is the best policy in these situations, but I have heard people try to bluff their way out. There are several categories of retorts: 1. I'm pressed for time—"You may be right, but the issue is much too complex to discuss here. Why don't you see me afterward?" "I've thought about that, but I rejected it for a number of reasons too detailed to discuss in the time I have for questions." "I don't think that his theory directly applies in this case, but I would be happy to discuss it with you later." 2. Tell me more—"In what way do you think that his theory applies to my findings?" "Could you be more specific?" "I would be interested in hearing your thoughts on that issue." 3. It's not my fault—"My co-author would be happy to answer that question."

quickly capsulize your work. This one you might give to the casual member of the audience who wants only a brief overview. You might prepare another "less mini" presentation lasting perhaps several minutes, that you give to someone who shows considerable interest in your work. You should also be prepared to discuss your work more fully with the few researchers who might come by who also work in your area of research. You should also devote a lot of effort to making the poster self-explanatory. The better job your poster does at explaining what you did, the easier it will be for you to spend your time interacting with your audience rather than rehashing the basics. What should be in this poster?

When your poster is accepted for presentation, you will be sent information telling you details of the setup. Typically you will be provided with a cork board measuring 4 by 8 feet and thumbtacks (take your own tacks anyway to be sure). You will mount your materials on this board. Above all do not simply take a manuscript copy of your paper with you and tack it to the board! The printing is too small, the detail is too great, and no one will take the time to read it. Remember that your audience will have only a few minutes at most to spend trying to understand what you did. You want to convey as much information in those few minutes as you can. In this case a picture really is worth a thousand words.

Figure 13-1 shows a sample poster arrangement. The information is put on panels about the size of standard sheets of paper. You will notice that much of the material is figures. As a general strategy you should present as little text as possible. Where you do have text, try putting it into figure captions. A second general principle is that information flow should start

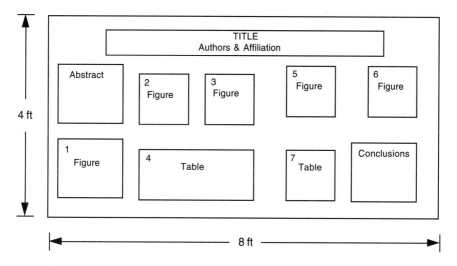

**FIGURE 13-1** A sample poster arrangement. The title and author lettering should be at least 1 inch high, other lettering at least .33 inch. Information should flow from upper left to lower right in columns. Maximize graphics. Minimize text.

in the upper left and move to the lower right. However, unlike English text, it should not be arranged in left-to-right rows. The members of your audience will fall all over one another if you force them to walk back and forth as they follow your panels. Instead put the information into columns. Numbering the panels as shown in the figure is helpful, or in some cases it might be appropriate to use arrows to help guide the audience.

At the top of the board should be a title and a list of the authors. The lettering for these should be at least 1 inch (72 points) high. Remember that the poster will be viewed from a distance of a meter or more. The title should be large enough to be read over the heads of the people talking to the presenter. Many people circulating will simply read the title, not be interested, and move on. Under the names of the authors should be their affiliations, such as their universities or colleges. This print as well as all the rest of the lettering can be smaller, but still at least 1/3 of an inch (24 points) high. Figures, drawings, charts, or illustrations should be similar to those used in slides or overheads, with simple heavy lines. One of the organizations I belong to suggests checking the readability of your materials using the "Toe Test" (Human Factors and Ergonomics Society, 1995). Have a friend or two stand above your poster materials, which have been placed on the floor next to their feet. Can they read them? If not, have them toe the materials into a trash can and try again!

The abstract should be simple and concise. Take out all unnecessary details. The research methods used should be explained using as few words as possible and using pictures for illustration. Depending on your study, the pictures might show stimulus materials for your various conditions, or perhaps sample items from your survey, or perhaps a schematic of your experimental design. Results should be graphed with easily readable symbols and lettering. If possible, put your statistical results in the figure caption. Generally you should not list raw data or statistical tables. Finally, include a conclusions section in which you briefly summarize your results. List no more than five or so items. The audience will not be taking notes and will be looking at a lot of other posters, so you want to emphasize only a few points that they might remember later. Also pitch your materials to your audience. For example, if it is made up of scientists from many fields rather than just psychologists, you should be particularly careful to avoid psychological jargon and to relate the conclusions to real-world applications.

For esthetic reasons some people use colored paper to border their panels, but you should not be too fancy. Scientists are more impressed by pretty data than by pretty graphics. If possible, the panels, or even the whole set of panels, can be dry-mounted on a stiff board or, if you are traveling, the entire poster can be duplicated onto one or two large sheets that can be rolled up in a tube. That way you do not have to worry about getting the panels straight and evenly spaced at the start of a session when you are already a little flustered and nervous. Finally, proofread the poster! Perhaps because the lettering is so large that it is more difficult to read normally, posters seem to have a large number of typos. I have seen world-renowned researchers using professionally produced posters with errors that they have had to correct with a ballpoint pen. These researchers are embarrassed, and you would be too.

As is the case with papers, you should try giving your poster presentation to some colleagues. Have them ask questions. When you are done, ask them how they think the poster or presentation could be improved. Finally, if possible, have copies of a complete written report available to hand out. People will be likely to request these.

Regardless of how you present your research, you should take pride in presenting it and do a quality job. Remember that this is the product of all the work you have done up to this point. All that effort could go to waste if you present your work in an unclear or uninteresting way.

## Summary

Because research is worthless unless other scientists know about it, experimenters must make their results known by writing a high-quality experimental report. This report should follow the guidelines recommended by the APA in its *Publication Manual.* Psychological writing differs from the writing found in other disciplines such as history and literary criticism. For instance, the language is more straightforward, few direct-quote citations are used, subheadings are used more liberally, discursive footnotes are infrequent, intellectual disagreements seldom turn personal, and conclusions are often hedged. A report has standardized sections. Because many readers will decide whether to read a report on the basis of its **title,** your title should be short but convey enough information to help them make this decision. The **authors** and the **institution** where the research was done follow the title. The **abstract,** a short (960-character) version of the complete report, ends the preliminaries.

In the body of the report, the **introduction** should review enough literature to give the reader an idea of the current body of knowledge and should state the purpose of the experiment. The **method** section provides the information necessary to replicate the experiment. It is typically divided into three subsections: **participants,** which describes their type and number and how they were recruited; **apparatus/materials,** which gives others the information necessary to order or build the equipment and materials similar to those used; and **procedure,** which should give a detailed account of what happened to each participant. The **results** section summarizes the findings of the experiment. Descriptive statistics are reported, including measures of central tendency and dispersion, either in the text or in tables or figures. The results of inferential statistical tests are then reported, usually including the **effect size.** The report writer then relates results back to the body of knowledge in the **discussion** section. The report concludes with an alphabetical list of the **references** cited in the paper.

To convey information as efficiently as possible while keeping the general writing style lively, it is no longer necessary to write experimental reports exclusively in third-person passive voice. Active verbs are now considered preferable, and occasional use of first person is acceptable. The introduction and method sections are typically written in the past tense, but the present tense is appropriate for the results and discussion sections. Because the report should be as concise as possible, you should avoid lazy writing and should use the comments of other readers to make the report a high-quality product.

Because it is important to avoid language bias and be accurate in research reports, three guidelines should be followed: Call people what they are; avoid generic masculine terms when referring to both genders (*man* for *human beings, he* for *he or she*), and use *participant* rather than *subject.* Call people what they want to be called; ask your ethnic participants what the correct terminology is. People are nouns, and their attributes are adjectives. *People with disabilities* are not *the disabled; female participants* are *women,* not *females.*

Research can also be reported at professional meetings in the form of a **conference paper** or **poster.** A paper is usually presented to a group of 20 to 100 colleagues in 10 to 20 minutes. It should be given in a conversational manner, leaving out many details from the written report. Visual aids such as overhead transparencies should be carefully prepared so that they can be easily read. The procedure and results sections, in particular, should be prepared with the level of the listener in mind. Presenters should be ready for questions. Posters are given in a more interactive way. A poster containing a title and 6 to 8 panels is prepared, and short presentations are given to colleagues who circulate through the room asking questions. The poster should be formatted carefully with large print, readable figures, and not too much detail. Both papers and posters should be practiced with friendly colleagues before the conference.

## Find It on InfoTrac College Edition

Using InfoTrac College Edition, look through a number of articles in psychology journals for titles that you think could be improved. Choose three that you think are particularly poor and try to rewrite them to make them better. In each case explain why your title is better.

Read the method sections of several psychology journal articles you find in a search of InfoTrac College Edition. Suppose you want to replicate each of these experiments. Do you think all of the information required for replication is included in each method section? Note any missing information.

Look at the graphs in the results sections of the psychology journal articles. Do any graphs violate the general rules listed in Chapter 13? Note how these graphs should be redrawn to conform to the rules.

Reading through the psychology journal articles, find three instances in which the rules for language bias have been violated.

# Epilogue

We shall not cease from exploration
And the end of all our exploring
Will be to arrive where we started
And know the place for the first time.

T. S. ELIOT

Congratulations on having wended your way through my thoughts on doing psychology experiments. May my words and pictures have helped to hold your interest rather than obstruct your progress. There is a delicate balance between informality and precision, a balance that varies from one reader to another. I hope my prose was not too unbalanced for you.

Obviously, this book has not instantly transformed you into a full-blown experimental psychologist, but I trust it has given you enough information so that you can attempt some simple experiments on your own. You will find that doing experiments is a lot more fun than reading about doing experiments. So now go have some fun!

# APPENDIX A
# How to Do Basic Statistics

If you are a calculatophobic (see Chapter 3), this appendix is written for you. You should be able to use this simplified "cookbook" version of statistics if you have learned only basic algebra. In the preface to the first edition, I said that this book was not a statistics book, and the minor concession I am making in this appendix does not contradict that statement. Some teachers and students who used the first edition felt the need for a brief description of basic descriptive statistics and inferential statistical tests. Here I will tell you how to do a few of these. I will not tell you why you are doing what you are doing, however, and generally I will tell you only a little bit about the conditions for choosing what to do.

It has been my observation that writing words about numbers usually confuses things. Instead, I have attempted to show you what to do with the numbers by means of a worked example. If you arrange the numbers from your data the way the numbers are arranged in the example and follow the same steps, you should have few problems.

I will first mention some characteristics of numbers. Then I will give you a short glossary of statistical symbols. Finally, I will provide you with worked examples of each statistical operation.

## Characteristics of Numbers

Numbers can be used in a variety of ways. Some ways convey a lot of information (it is 28 miles to the fair) and some only a little (the first baseman is number 28). Some statements and statistical operations are possible with some numbers (the theater, which is 14 miles away, is half as far as the fair). These same statements are ludicrous with others (the second baseman is number 14; for this reason he is only half the first baseman). So, before you can do a statistical operation on numbers, you must determine whether that operation makes sense for the type of numbers you are using.

### NOMINAL SCALE

Numbers that are simply used to name something are said to be on a **nominal scale.** Nominal scale data have no quantitative properties. The only legitimate statistical operation you can do with nominal data is to count the number of instances that each number occurs: How many players are there with the number 28?

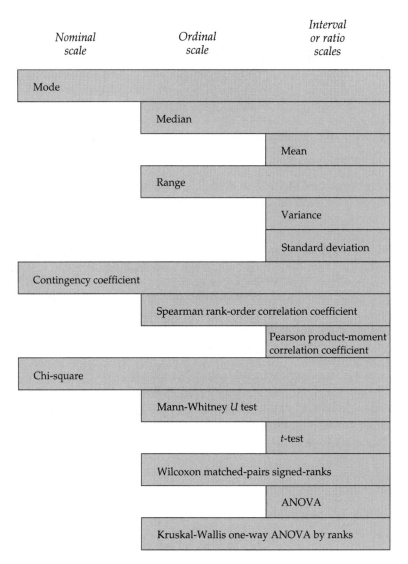

**FIGURE A-1**  Statistical operations and the number scales they require

## ORDINAL SCALE

Numbers that can be ordered, or ranked, are said to lie on an **ordinal scale.** The race car driver who was champion the previous year is allowed to put the number 1 on his or her car. The driver who was second in the point standings is number 2, and so on. We know from these ordinal scale numbers that driver 1 performed better than driver 2, but we do not know by how much. Drivers 1 and 2 might have been 500 points apart, whereas drivers 2 and 3 might have been only 2 points apart.

## INTERVAL SCALE

If the intervals between numbers are meaningful, the numbers lie on an **interval scale.** Temperature measured on a Fahrenheit scale is interval. It is 10° between 50° and 60°. It is also 10° between 60° and 70°.

## RATIO SCALE

If you can make a ratio out of two numbers and that ratio is meaningful, you have a **ratio scale.** Thus, although you cannot say that a temperature of 20° is twice as hot as 10°, you can say that 20 miles is twice as far as 10 miles. The big difference between an interval and a ratio scale is that the latter has an absolute zero point. On the Fahrenheit scale, "zero degrees" has no particular meaning other than the fact it is 32 arbitrary degrees below the freezing point of water. For quantities like distance, weight, and volume, zero units is a meaningful concept.

One question you must answer before you perform a statistical operation is "What number scale am I dealing with?" Figure A-1 lists the operations we will be discussing in this appendix and the scales they require.

Operations that can be carried out on numbers from lower order scales such as nominal can also be used with numbers from higher order scales such as ratio. For this reason, the shaded area in the figure indicates that all the operations can legitimately be performed with interval or ratio data, but only three of them can be used with nominal data.

# Symbols Used in Statistical Formulas

$$
\begin{aligned}
X &= \text{a datum or score} \\
N &= \text{the total number of scores} \\
\Sigma &= \text{sum, or add, the scores} \\
X^2 &= \text{square } X \text{ (multiply it by itself)} \\
X^3 &= \text{cube } X \text{ (multiply it by itself twice)} \\
\sqrt{X} &= \text{square root of } X \text{ (What number multiplied by itself equals } X\text{?)} \\
|x| &= \text{absolute value of } X \text{ (the number disregarding its sign)}
\end{aligned}
$$

# Descriptive Statistics

## MEASURES OF CENTRAL TENDENCY

### Mode

The mode is the most frequently occurring score. Count the number of times each score occurs, and pick the score with the most occurrences. The mode in the example in the next section is 2, because this number occurs twice.

## Median

The median is the middle score. The scores should first be ordered by size. For an odd number of scores, the median is the middle one. For an even number of scores, the median lies halfway between the two middle scores. In the following example the median is 2.5, because the middle two scores are 2 and 3.

## Mean

$$\text{Mean} = M = \overline{X} = \frac{\Sigma X}{N}$$

*Example*

| X |
|---|
| 1 |
| 2 |
| 2 |
| 3 |
| 4 |
| 5 |

$\Sigma X = 17$
$N = 6$

$\overline{X} = \dfrac{17}{6} = 2.8$

## MEASURES OF DISPERSION

### Range

The range is the largest score minus the smallest score. In the previous example

$$\text{Range} = 5 - 1 = 4$$

### Variance

$$\text{Variance} = S^2 = \frac{\Sigma(X - \overline{X})^2}{N}$$

*Example*

| | X | $\overline{X}$* | $X - \overline{X}$ | $(X - \overline{X})^2$ |
|---|---|---|---|---|
| | 1 | 3 | −2 | 4 |
| 6 scores | 2 | 3 | −1 | 1 |
| so | 3 | 3 | 0 | 0 |
| N = 6 | 3 | 3 | 0 | 0 |
| | 4 | 3 | 1 | 1 |
| | 5 | 3 | 2 | 4 |
| | $\Sigma X = 18$ | | | $\Sigma(X - \overline{X})^2 = 10$ |

*Mean $= \overline{X} = \dfrac{18}{6} = 3$.

$$\frac{\Sigma(X - \overline{X})^2}{N} = \frac{10}{6} = 1.67$$

## Standard Deviation

$$\text{Standard deviation} = SD = \sigma = \sqrt{S^2} = \sqrt{\frac{\Sigma(X - \overline{X})^2}{N}}$$

In the previous example

$$SD = \sqrt{1.67} = 1.29$$

## MEASURES OF ASSOCIATION

### Contingency Coefficient

The **contingency coefficient** (C) is a measure of the strength of association between two sets of numbers when nominal scale data are being considered. A chi-square ($\chi^2$) test must first be done (see p. 319). Suppose that a chi-square test has been conducted on a two-variable experiment, and you wish to know the strength of association between these two nominal-scale variables. Also suppose that $\chi^2$ was found to be 15, with a total number of observations of $N = 100$. Then the contingency coefficient is:

$$C = \sqrt{\frac{\chi^2}{N + \chi^2}} = \sqrt{\frac{15}{100 + 15}} = \sqrt{.130} = .36$$

No further testing for the statistical significance of the association is necessary, as the chi-square test has already been computed to test for significance.

### Spearman Rank-Order Correlation Coefficient

A **Spearman rank-order correlation coefficient** (*rho*) is used to measure the strength of association between two ordinal scale variables. In this case, two scores, or ranks, are obtained for each participant, and the difference *d* is determined.

### *Example*

| Participant | Rank on first measure | Rank on second measure | d | $d^2$ | |
|---|---|---|---|---|---|
| Bill | 4 | 4 | 0 | 0 | |
| Jane | 1 | 2 | −1 | 1 | |
| Bob | 5 | 5 | 0 | 0 | |
| Pete | 2 | 3 | −1 | 1 | $N = 5$ |
| Mary | 3 | 1 | +2 | 4 | |
| | | | | $\Sigma d^2 = 6$ | |

$$rho = 1 - \frac{6\Sigma d^2}{N^3 - N} = 1 - \frac{6(6)}{125 - 5} = 1 - \frac{36}{120}$$
$$= 1 - .3 = .7$$

To determine whether the obtained *rho* is likely to have occurred because of chance variation rather than an actual association, we must consult the table of critical values for *rho* in Appendix B (Table B-1). We see that with $N$ of 5, *rho* must equal 1 to be significant. It does not. We can also see from the table that the larger the number of participants, the better our chances of finding a statistically significant effect, given that there is an association present.

## Pearson Product-Moment Correlation Coefficient

A **Pearson product-moment correlation coefficient** ($r$) can be used to measure the strength of association between two interval or ratio scale variables. In the following example, $X$ represents the score on one variable, and $Y$ the score on a second variable.

### Example

| Participant | X | X² | Y | Y² | XY | |
|---|---|---|---|---|---|---|
| Tom | 9 | 81 | 8 | 64 | 72 | |
| Sue | 4 | 16 | 4 | 16 | 16 | |
| Jill | 4 | 16 | 6 | 36 | 24 | |
| Dave | 2 | 4 | 4 | 16 | 8 | $N = 8$ |
| Ken | 1 | 1 | 3 | 9 | 3 | |
| Jo | 3 | 9 | 2 | 4 | 6 | |
| Juan | 7 | 49 | 8 | 64 | 56 | |
| Al | 5 | 25 | 5 | 25 | 25 | |
| | $\Sigma X = 35$ | $\Sigma X^2 = 201$ | $\Sigma Y = 40$ | $\Sigma Y^2 = 234$ | $\Sigma XY = 210$ | |

$$r = \frac{N\Sigma XY - \Sigma X \Sigma Y}{\sqrt{N\Sigma X^2 - (\Sigma X)^2}\sqrt{N\Sigma Y^2 - (\Sigma Y)^2}} = \frac{8(210) - (35)(40)}{\sqrt{8(201) - 35^2}\sqrt{8(234) - 40^2}}$$

$$= \frac{1680 - 1400}{\sqrt{1680 - 1225}\sqrt{1872 - 1600}} = \frac{280}{\sqrt{383}\sqrt{272}} = \frac{280}{(19.57)(16.49)}$$

$$= \frac{280}{322.7} = .868$$

To test whether an $r$ of this size is statistically significant with eight pairs of scores, refer to Table B-2 in Appendix B, listing critical values of $r$. To use this table, you must determine a quantity called the *degrees of freedom* ($df$). For this test the degrees of freedom is $N - 2$. So in the example $df = 6$. Because $r$ of .868 exceeds the listed value of .834, it is statistically significant at the $p < .01$ level. That is, we would expect this strength of association to occur in a sample less than 1 time in 100 due to chance selection from a single population.

# Inferential Statistical Tests

## CHI-SQUARE

The **chi-square ($\chi 2$) test** is used to determine whether the observed frequency of occurrence of scores is statistically different from the expected frequency.

### Example

| | Number of participants predicting heads after a string of tails | Number of participants predicting tails after a string of tails |
|---|---|---|
| Observed | 60 | 40 |
| Expected | 50 | 50 |
| $O - E$ | +10 | −10 |
| $(O - E)^2$ | 100 | 100 |
| $\dfrac{(O - E)^2}{E}$ | 2 | 2 |

$$\chi^2 = \Sigma \frac{(O - E)^2}{E} = 2 + 2 = 4$$

The expected frequency can be the frequency based either on a set of previous observations or on a theoretical prediction. Usually, the theoretical prediction is that the observed frequency will be that expected by chance. For instance, in the example the expectation is that the participants' predictions will show no bias (no gambler's fallacy); half of the time heads will be predicted, and half of the time, tails.

The final step in doing an inferential statistical test is to compare the final result of your computation with a table of critical values. You will find a table for chi-square values in Appendix B (Table B-3). To find the appropriate number in the table, you must first determine the number of degrees of freedom as follows:

$df$ = The number of $O - E$ being considered, minus 1, which in this case equals $2 - 1 = 1$

In the table we find that with $df = 1$, $\chi^2$ must exceed 3.84 to be significant at the $p < .05$ level of significance. Thus, the data in our example are statistically different from chance at the .05 level. If we had been testing at the $p < .01$ level, $\chi^2 = 4$ would not have exceeded 6.64, and the test would have failed to reach significance.

## *t*-TEST FOR UNCORRELATED MEASURES

There are two forms of the ***t*-test,** one for uncorrelated and one for correlated measures. The *t*-test for uncorrelated measures is used to determine the probability that an observed difference between two independent groups of participants occurred by chance. The underlying distributions are assumed to be normal.

### Example

| | | Group 1 | |
|---|---|---|---|
| $X_1$ | $\overline{X}_1$ | $X_1 - \overline{X}_1$ | $(X_1 - \overline{X}_1)^2$ |
| 9 | 7 | 2 | 4 |
| 8 | 7 | 1 | 1 |
| 7 | 7 | 0 | 0 |
| 7 | 7 | 0 | 0 |
| 4 | 7 | −3 | 9 |
| $\Sigma X_1 = 35$ | | | $\Sigma(X_1 - \overline{X}_1)^2 = 14$ |

$$N_1 = 5$$

$$M_1 = \overline{X}_1 = \frac{\Sigma X_1}{N_1} = \frac{35}{5} = 7$$

$$\sigma_1 = \sqrt{\frac{\Sigma(X_1 - \overline{X}_1)^2}{N_1}} = \sqrt{\frac{14}{5}} = \sqrt{2.8} = 1.67$$

| | | Group 2 | |
|---|---|---|---|
| $X_2$ | $\overline{X}_2$ | $X_2 - \overline{X}_2$ | $(X_2 - \overline{X}_2)^2$ |
| 5 | 3 | 2 | 4 |
| 4 | 3 | 1 | 1 |
| 3 | 3 | 0 | 0 |
| 2 | 3 | −1 | 1 |
| 1 | 3 | −2 | 4 |
| $\Sigma X_2 = 15$ | | | $\Sigma(X_2 - \overline{X}_2)^2 = 10$ |

$$N_2 = 5$$

$$M_2 = \overline{X}_2 = \frac{\Sigma X_2}{N_2} = \frac{15}{5} = 3$$

$$\sigma_2 = \sqrt{\frac{\Sigma(X_2 - \overline{X}_2)^2}{N_2}} = \sqrt{\frac{10}{5}} = \sqrt{2} = 1.41$$

$$t = \frac{M_1 - M_2}{\sqrt{\left(\frac{\sigma_1}{\sqrt{N_1 - 1}}\right)^2 + \left(\frac{\sigma_2}{\sqrt{N_2 - 1}}\right)^2}} = \frac{7 - 3}{\sqrt{\left(\frac{1.67}{\sqrt{5 - 1}}\right)^2 + \left(\frac{1.41}{\sqrt{5 - 1}}\right)^2}}$$

$$= \frac{4}{\sqrt{\left(\frac{1.67}{2}\right)^2 + \left(\frac{1.41}{2}\right)^2}} = \frac{4}{\sqrt{.697 + .497}} = \frac{4}{\sqrt{1.194}} = \frac{4}{1.09} = 3.67$$

The degrees of freedom for an uncorrelated $t$-test is:

$$df = N_1 + N_2 - 2$$
$$= 5 + 5 - 2 = 8$$

Table B-4 in Appendix B indicates that, with 8 $df$, $t$ must exceed 3.355 for the difference to be significant at $p < .01$. Thus, our value of 3.67 is significant at that level.

## $t$-TEST FOR CORRELATED MEASURES

The $t$-test for correlated measures is used to determine the probability that an observed difference ($D$) between two conditions for the same or matched participants occurred by chance.

$$t = \frac{\overline{X}_D}{\dfrac{\sigma_D}{\sqrt{N-1}}}$$

### Example

| Participant | Condition 1 | Condition 2 | Difference (D) | $\overline{X}_D{}^*$ | $X_D - \overline{X}_D$ | $(X_D - \overline{X}_D)^2$ |
|---|---|---|---|---|---|---|
| 1 | 9 | 6 | 3 | 3 | 0 | 0 |
| 2 | 8 | 5 | 3 | 3 | 0 | 0 |
| 3 | 7 | 5 | 2 | 3 | −1 | 1 |
| 4 | 8 | 4 | 4 | 3 | 1 | 1 |
| 5 | 8 | 5 | 3 | 3 | 0 | 0 |
| $N = 5$ | $\Sigma X_1 = 40$ | $\Sigma X_2 = 25$ | $\Sigma D = 15$ | | | $\Sigma(X_D - \overline{X}_D)^2 = 2$ |

$$^*M_D = \overline{X}_D = \frac{\Sigma D}{N} = \frac{15}{5} = 3$$

$$\sigma_D = \sqrt{\frac{\Sigma(X_D - \overline{X}_D)^2}{N}} = \sqrt{\frac{2}{5}} = \sqrt{.4} = .632$$

$$t = \frac{\overline{X}_D}{\dfrac{\sigma_D}{\sqrt{N-1}}} = \frac{3}{\dfrac{.632}{\sqrt{5-1}}} = \frac{3}{\dfrac{.632}{2}} = \frac{3}{.316} = 9.49$$

The degrees of freedom for correlated measures is

$$df = N - 1 = 5 - 1 = 4$$

Table B-4 is used for either form of the $t$-test. In this example, $t$ must exceed 4.604 to be significant at the $p < .01$ level. It does, so it is.

## MANN–WHITNEY $U$ TEST

The **Mann–Whitney $U$ test** is used under the same general conditions as an uncorrelated $t$-test but only when the assumptions of normal distributions or an interval scale cannot be met.

$$U = N_1N_2 + \frac{N_1(N_1 + 1)}{2} - R_1$$

or  whichever is smaller

$$U = N_1N_2 + \frac{N_2(N_2 + 1)}{2} - R_2$$

where

$N_1$ = the number of participants in the smaller group
$N_2$ = the number of participants in the larger group
$R_1$ = the sum of the ranks for the smaller group
$R_2$ = the sum of the ranks for the larger group

*Example*

| | Group 1 | | Group 2 | |
|---|---|---|---|---|
| | $X_1$ | Rank | $X_2$ | Rank |
| | 1 | 1 | 2 | 2 |
| | 3 | 3.5 | 4 | 5 |
| | 3 | 3.5 | 7 | 8 |
| | 5 | 6 | 8 | 9.5 |
| $N_1 = 10$ | 6 | 7 | 10 | 13.5 |
| | 8 | 9.5 | 13 | 16 |
| | 9 | 11.5 | 15 | 17 |
| | 9 | 11.5 | 16 | 18 |
| | 10 | 13.5 | 17 | 19 |
| | 12 | 15 | 18 | 20 |
| | | $R_1 = 82$ | | $R_2 = 128$ |

The rankings were determined by ordering all scores regardless of which group they came from. Where there were ties in rankings, an average was used.

$$U = N_1N_2 + \frac{N_1(N_1 + 1)}{2} - R_1 = (10)(10) + \frac{10(10 + 1)}{2} - 82$$

$$= 100 + \frac{110}{2} - 82 = 73$$

or

$$U = (10)(10) + \frac{10(10 + 1)}{2} - 128 = 27$$

Because 27 is smaller, $U = 27$.

Two tables for determining the critical values of $U$ can be found in Appendix B. If we wished to test for significance at the $p < .05$ level, we would use Table B-5. The value for $U$ when $N_1 = 10$ and $N_2 = 10$ is 23. To be significant, our value must be equal to or *smaller than* this critical value. Because 27 is not, it is not statistically significant at this level.

Note that the Mann–Whitney $U$ test is different from the other tests in that to be significant the value must be smaller rather than larger than the value in the table. To find a table for values of $N_1$ smaller than 7, you will have to use a more advanced text than this one. For values of $N_2$ larger than 20, $U$ must be converted to a $z$ score using this formula:

$$z = \frac{U - \dfrac{N_1 N_2}{2}}{\sqrt{\dfrac{(N_1)(N_2)(N_1 + N_2 + 1)}{12}}}$$

The $z$ score can then be compared with the critical values listed in Table B-7 in Appendix B.

## WILCOXON MATCHED-PAIRS SIGNED-RANKS TEST

The **Wilcoxon matched-pairs signed-ranks test** is used to determine the probability that an observed difference ($D$) between two conditions for the same or matched participants occurred by chance. It differs from the $t$-test for correlated measures in that it can be used with ordinal data and the underlying distributions need not be normal

$$\left. \begin{array}{l} T = \Sigma\, R_+ \\ T = |\Sigma\, R_-| \end{array} \right\} \text{ whichever is smaller}$$

where

$R_+$ is a rank having a positive difference.
$R_-$ is a rank having a negative difference.

*Example*

| Pair | Condition 1 | Condition 2 | Difference (D) | Rank of D ignoring sign | Rank having a positive D | Rank having a negative D |
|------|-------------|-------------|----------------|-------------------------|--------------------------|--------------------------|
| 1 | 54 | 50 | 4 | 3 | 3 | |
| 2 | 47 | 32 | 15 | 9 | 9 | |
| 3 | 39 | 33 | 6 | 4 | 4 | |
| 4 | 42 | 45 | −3 | 2.5 | | −2.5 |
| 5 | 51 | 38 | 13 | 7 | 7 | |
| 6 | 46 | 39 | 7 | 5 | 5 | |
| 7 | 42 | 44 | −2 | 1 | | −1 |
| 8 | 54 | 46 | 8 | 6 | 6 | |
| 9 | 42 | 39 | 3 | 2.5 | 2.5 | |
| 10 | 47 | 33 | 14 | 8 | 8 | |
| | | | | | $\Sigma\, R_+ = \overline{45.5}$ | $|\Sigma\, R_-| = \overline{3.5}$ |

The smaller of 45.5 and 3.5 is 3.5; thus:

$$T = |\Sigma\ R_-| = 3.5$$

To test for statistical significance, look at Table B-8 in Appendix B. To reach significance, $T$ must be equal to or smaller than the number listed. In the example there are ten pairs of scores, so $n = 10$, and assuming that we did not predict the direction of the difference between conditions, a two-tailed test is appropriate. We see, then, that 3.5 is smaller than 5 but not 3, so $p < .02$.

## ANALYSIS OF VARIANCE

**Analysis of variance** (ANOVA) can be used for interval or ratio data when the underlying distributions are approximately normal. ANOVA tests are available for either within-subject (repeated measures) or between-subjects (separate groups) designs and for designs with multiple independent variables. In this appendix, however, we will limit our consideration to a between-subjects design with one independent variable. In the following example the independent variable has three levels. However, the formulas given can also be used for designs having more than three groups.

Although the calculations for ANOVA appear to be complicated, the rationale behind the test is really relatively simple. Suppose you conduct an experiment in which you collect data from three groups. The experimental question is whether the three samples come from the same population and differ only by chance variation, or whether the samples come from different populations and differ due to the independent variable as well as to chance variation. ANOVA allows you to partition the variance found in the distribution containing all the scores you sampled. Part of the variance in this distribution is due to differences between groups, including variance due to the independent variable. A second part is due to chance variation among participants within groups.

The final number calculated when doing ANOVA is called an *F value*. It is a ratio of the variance between groups to the variance within groups. If the groups sampled come from the same population and the independent variable has no effect, we would expect the ratio to be close to 1. That is, the between-group variance should be about the same size as the within-group variance. However, if the independent variable has an effect and the groups come from different populations, we would expect the between-group variance to be larger than the within-group variance. The $F$ value would then be greater than 1. As the value of $F$ gets larger, we would become increasingly confident that the differences among groups were due to the effects of the independent variable rather than to chance variation.

In the following example, we first calculate a quantity called the *total sum of squares* ($SS_{TOT}$) followed by a *sum of squares between groups* ($SS_{bg}$) and *within groups* ($SS_{wg}$). $SS_{bg}$ and $SS_{wg}$ are then divided by their appropriate degrees of freedom to get the mean squares between groups ($MS_{bg}$) and within groups ($MS_{wg}$). $MS_{bg}$ is then divided by $MS_{wg}$ to find the value of $F$.

You should be able to follow the example, but if you get into trouble, the following definitions might help:

$T$  is the total sum of all scores for all groups.
$T_j$  is the total sum of scores in group $j$.
$N$  is the number of scores in all groups.
$n_j$  is the number of scores in group $j$.
$\sum\limits_{j=1}^{k}$  means to sum for all groups from 1 to $k$.
$k$  is the number of groups.

### Example

| Group 1 | | Group 2 | | Group 3 | |
|---|---|---|---|---|---|
| $X_1$ | $X_1^2$ | $X_2$ | $X_2^2$ | $X_3$ | $X_3^2$ |
| 3 | 9 | 9 | 81 | 10 | 100 |
| 5 | 25 | 6 | 36 | 8 | 64 |
| 4 | 16 | 5 | 25 | 11 | 121 |
| 3 | 9 | 8 | 64 | 10 | 100 |
| 1 | 1 | 7 | 49 | 9 | 81 |
| 2 | 4 | 7 | 49 | 10 | 100 |
| 5 | 25 | 6 | 36 | 11 | 121 |
| 2 | 4 | 4 | 16 | 12 | 144 |
| 3 | 9 | 8 | 64 | 10 | 100 |
| 1 | 1 | 7 | 49 | 9 | 81 |
| $T_1 = 29$ | 103 | $T_2 = 67$ | 469 | $T_3 = 100$ | 1012 |
| $n_1 = 10$ | | $n_2 = 10$ | | $n_3 = 10$ | |

$N = 10 + 10 + 10 = 30$
$T = 29 + 67 + 100 = 196$
$k = 3$

$$SS_{TOT} = \Sigma X^2 - \frac{T^2}{N} = (103 + 469 + 1012) - \frac{(196)^2}{30}$$

$$= 1584 - \frac{38416}{30} = 1584 - 1281 = 303$$

$$SS_{bg} = \sum_{j=1}^{k} \frac{T_j^2}{n_j} - \frac{T^2}{N} = \frac{29^2}{10} + \frac{67^2}{10} + \frac{100^2}{10} - \frac{(196)^2}{30}$$

$$= \frac{841}{10} + \frac{4489}{10} + \frac{10000}{10} - 1281$$

$$= 84.1 + 448.9 + 1000 - 1281 = 1533 - 1281 = 252$$

$$SS_{wg} = SS_{TOT} - SS_{bg} = 303 - 252 = 51$$

$$df_{bg} = k - 1 = 3 - 1 = 2$$

$$df_{wg} = N - k = 30 - 3 = 27$$

$$MS_{bg} = \frac{SS_{bg}}{df_{bg}} = \frac{252}{2} = 126$$

$$MS_{wg} = \frac{SS_{wg}}{df_{wg}} = \frac{51}{27} = 1.89$$

$$F = \frac{MS_{bg}}{MS_{wg}} = \frac{126}{1.89} = 66.7$$

We can now compare this number with the critical values for $F$ listed in Table B-9 in Appendix B. With 2 $df$ in the numerator and 27 $df$ in the denominator, $F$ must equal or exceed 3.38 to be significant at $p < .05$ and equal or exceed 5.57 to be significant at $p < .01$. Because 66.7 far exceeds these critical values, the difference between the groups is highly significant. Note that the test could reach statistical significance owing to a difference between any two groups. To determine which means are statistically different from one another, further tests would have to be conducted. These tests are beyond the scope of this book. They can be found in the recommended texts at the end of Chapter 12.

## KRUSKAL–WALLIS ONE-WAY ANOVA BY RANKS

If the assumptions of an interval or ratio scale or normal distributions cannot be met, a Kruskal–Wallis ANOVA can be used to test for differences between two or more independent groups. Only an ordinal scale is necessary.

In the following example:

$K$ = the number of groups
$n_j$ = the number of scores per group
$N$ = the total number of scores
$R_j$ = the sum of ranks for group $j$
$t$ = the the number of ties for each score

### Example

| Group 1 | | Group 2 | | Group 3 | |
|---|---|---|---|---|---|
| $X_1$ | Rank | $X_2$ | Rank | $X_3$ | Rank |
| 8 | 15 | 2 | 2.5 | 6 | 11 |
| 4 | 5.5 | 5 | 8.5 | 5 | 8.5 |
| 7 | 13 | 2 | 2.5 | 4 | 5.5 |
| 5 | 8.5 | 3 | 4 | 5 | 8.5 |
| 7 | 13 | 1 | 1 | 7 | 13 |
| | $R_1 = 55.0$ | | $R_2 = 18.5$ | | $R_3 = 46.5$ |

$K = 3$
$n_j = 5$
$N = 15$

Rank all the scores to get the ranks for each group.

| Score | Rank | Average for ties | t |
|---|---|---|---|
| 1 | 1 | 1 | |
| 2 | 2 | 2.5 | 2 |
| 2 | 3 | | |
| 3 | 4 | 4 | |
| 4 | 5 | 5.5 | 2 |
| 4 | 6 | | |
| 5 | 7 | | |
| 5 | 8 | 8.5 | 4 |
| 5 | 9 | | |
| 5 | 10 | | |
| 6 | 11 | 11 | |
| 7 | 12 | | |
| 7 | 13 | 13 | 3 |
| 7 | 14 | | |
| 8 | 15 | 15 | |

Now place the ranks from this table next to the individual scores for each group in the previous table, and sum them to get $R_1$, $R_2$, $R_3$.

$$H = \frac{12}{N(N + 1)} \sum_{j=1}^{k} \frac{R_j^2}{n_j} - 3(N + 1)$$

$$= \frac{12}{15(15 + 1)} \left[ \frac{(55)^2}{5} + \frac{(18.5)^2}{5} + \frac{(46.5)^2}{5} \right] - 3(15 + 1)$$

$$= \frac{12}{15(16)} \left[ \frac{3025}{5} + \frac{342.25}{5} + \frac{2162.25}{5} \right] - 3(16)$$

$$= \frac{12}{240} \left[ \frac{5529.5}{5} \right] - 48$$

$$= .05(1105.9) - 48 = 55.295 - 48 = 7.295$$

The correction for ties is to divide $H$ by $1 - \frac{\Sigma(t^3 - t)}{N^3 - N}$.

$$1 - \frac{(2^3 - 2) + (2^3 - 2) + (4^3 - 4) + (3^3 - 3)}{15^3 - 15}$$

$$1 - \frac{(8 - 2) + (8 - 2) + (64 - 4) + (27 - 3)}{3375 - 15}$$

$$1 - \frac{96}{3360} = 1 - .029 = .971$$

$$H = \frac{7.295}{.971} = 7.51$$

According to Table B-10 in Appendix B, for group sizes of 5, 5, and 5, the probability of having an $H$ as large as 7.51 is less than .049. Thus, the difference between groups is statistically significant at the $p < .05$ level. Because this value is smaller than the 7.98 required for the $p < .01$ level, the difference is not significant at that level.

If the groups contain more than five participants, $H$ is distributed like chi-square. To determine the critical value in that case, refer to Table B-3 with $k - 1$ degrees of freedom.

## Conclusion

This appendix should allow you to compute some very basic statistical operations. However, if you go much beyond a basic course in experimentation, you will need to do at least three additional things. First, you will need to learn to use more complex tests for designs having multiple independent variables and mixtures of within-subject and between-subjects variables. Second, you will need to learn to use packaged computer programs to save time and effort. Third, and probably most important, you must go beyond a cookbook approach to statistics. As a researcher you should understand why you do what you do.

An understanding of the concepts underlying statistical operations not only allows you to choose the most powerful way to analyze your data but also allows you to design research so that the data can be effectively analyzed. Statistical consultants tell horror stories about inexperienced researchers who dump volumes of data on their desks and ask, "How do I analyze this?" In some cases the data defy analysis.

The point is that design and statistical analysis are integrally linked. If you plan to design your research, you should also understand the concepts underlying the statistical operations that should be used to analyze the outcome.

# APPENDIX B
# Statistical Tables

**TABLE B-1**

Critical Values of *rho* (Spearman Rank-Order Correlation Coefficient)

| N | p = .0500 | p = .0100 |
|---|-----------|-----------|
| 5 | 1.000 | — |
| 6 | .886 | 1.000 |
| 7 | .786 | .929 |
| 8 | .738 | .881 |
| 9 | .683 | .833 |
| 10 | .648 | .794 |
| 12 | .591 | .777 |
| 14 | .544 | .715 |
| 16 | .506 | .665 |
| 18 | .475 | .625 |
| 20 | .450 | .591 |
| 22 | .428 | .562 |
| 24 | .409 | .537 |
| 26 | .392 | .515 |
| 28 | .377 | .496 |
| 30 | .364 | .478 |

SOURCE: Computed from Olds, E. G., Distribution of the sum of squares of rank differences for small numbers of individuals, *Annals of Mathematical Statistics*, 1938, 9, 133–148, and the 5% significance levels for sums of squares of rank differences and a correction, *Annals of Mathematical Statistics*, 1949, *20*, 117–118. Table B-1 is taken from *Elementary Statistics*, Underwood et al., Appleton-Century-Crofts.

**TABLE B-2**

Critical Values of *r* (Pearson Product-
Moment Correlation Coefficient)

| df | Levels of significance for two-tailed test | | |
|---|---|---|---|
| | .10 | .05 | .01 |
| 1 | .988 | .997 | .9999 |
| 2 | .900 | .950 | .990 |
| 3 | .805 | .878 | .959 |
| 4 | .729 | .811 | .917 |
| 5 | .669 | .754 | .874 |
| 6 | .622 | .707 | .834 |
| 7 | .582 | .666 | .798 |
| 8 | .549 | .632 | .765 |
| 9 | .521 | .602 | .735 |
| 10 | .497 | .576 | .708 |
| 11 | .476 | .553 | .684 |
| 12 | .458 | .532 | .661 |
| 13 | .441 | .514 | .641 |
| 14 | .426 | .497 | .623 |
| 15 | .412 | .482 | .606 |
| 16 | .400 | .468 | .590 |
| 17 | .389 | .456 | .575 |
| 18 | .378 | .444 | .561 |
| 19 | .369 | .433 | .549 |
| 20 | .360 | .423 | .537 |
| 25 | .323 | .381 | .487 |
| 30 | .296 | .349 | .449 |
| 35 | .275 | .325 | .418 |
| 40 | .257 | .304 | .393 |
| 45 | .243 | .288 | .372 |
| 50 | .231 | .273 | .354 |
| 60 | .211 | .250 | .325 |
| 70 | .195 | .232 | .303 |
| 80 | .183 | .217 | .283 |
| 90 | .173 | .205 | .267 |
| 100 | .164 | .195 | .254 |

SOURCE: Adapted from R. A. Fisher, *Statistical
Methods for Research Workers*, 14th Edition.
Copyright 1973, Hafner Press.

**TABLE B-3**
Critical Values of Chi-Square

| df | $p = .05$ | $p = .01$ |
|----|-----------|-----------|
| 1  | 3.84  | 6.64  |
| 2  | 5.99  | 9.21  |
| 3  | 7.82  | 11.34 |
| 4  | 9.49  | 13.28 |
| 5  | 11.07 | 15.09 |
| 6  | 12.59 | 16.81 |
| 7  | 14.07 | 18.48 |
| 8  | 15.51 | 20.09 |
| 9  | 16.92 | 21.67 |
| 10 | 18.31 | 23.21 |
| 11 | 19.68 | 24.72 |
| 12 | 21.03 | 26.22 |
| 13 | 22.36 | 27.69 |
| 14 | 23.68 | 29.14 |
| 15 | 25.00 | 30.58 |
| 16 | 26.30 | 32.00 |
| 17 | 27.59 | 33.41 |
| 18 | 28.87 | 34.80 |
| 19 | 30.14 | 36.19 |
| 20 | 31.41 | 37.57 |
| 21 | 32.67 | 38.93 |
| 22 | 33.92 | 40.29 |
| 23 | 35.17 | 41.64 |
| 24 | 36.42 | 42.98 |
| 25 | 37.65 | 44.31 |
| 26 | 38.88 | 45.64 |
| 27 | 40.11 | 46.96 |
| 28 | 41.34 | 48.28 |
| 29 | 42.56 | 49.59 |
| 30 | 43.77 | 50.89 |

SOURCE: From Table 4 of Fisher & Yates, *Statistical Tables for Biological, Agricultural and Medical Research,* published by Longman Group Ltd., London (previously published by Oliver and Boyd Ltd., Edinburgh). By permission of the authors and publishers.

**TABLE B-4**
Critical Values of $t$

| $df$ | $p = .10$ | $p = .05$ | $p = .02$ | $p = .01$ |
|---|---|---|---|---|
| 1 | 6.314 | 12.706 | 31.821 | 63.657 |
| 2 | 2.920 | 4.303 | 6.965 | 9.925 |
| 3 | 2.353 | 3.182 | 4.541 | 5.841 |
| 4 | 2.132 | 2.776 | 3.747 | 4.604 |
| 5 | 2.015 | 2.571 | 3.365 | 4.032 |
| 6 | 1.943 | 2.447 | 3.143 | 3.707 |
| 7 | 1.895 | 2.365 | 2.998 | 3.499 |
| 8 | 1.860 | 2.306 | 2.896 | 3.355 |
| 9 | 1.833 | 2.262 | 2.821 | 3.250 |
| 10 | 1.812 | 2.228 | 2.764 | 3.169 |
| 11 | 1.796 | 2.201 | 2.718 | 3.106 |
| 12 | 1.782 | 2.179 | 2.681 | 3.055 |
| 13 | 1.771 | 2.160 | 2.650 | 3.012 |
| 14 | 1.761 | 2.145 | 2.624 | 2.977 |
| 15 | 1.753 | 2.131 | 2.602 | 2.947 |
| 16 | 1.746 | 2.120 | 2.583 | 2.921 |
| 17 | 1.740 | 2.110 | 2.567 | 2.898 |
| 18 | 1.734 | 2.101 | 2.552 | 2.878 |
| 19 | 1.729 | 2.093 | 2.539 | 2.861 |
| 20 | 1.725 | 2.086 | 2.528 | 2.845 |
| 21 | 1.721 | 2.080 | 2.518 | 2.831 |
| 22 | 1.717 | 2.074 | 2.508 | 2.819 |
| 23 | 1.714 | 2.069 | 2.500 | 2.807 |
| 24 | 1.711 | 2.064 | 2.492 | 2.797 |
| 25 | 1.708 | 2.060 | 2.485 | 2.787 |
| 26 | 1.706 | 2.056 | 2.479 | 2.779 |
| 27 | 1.703 | 2.052 | 2.473 | 2.771 |
| 28 | 1.701 | 2.048 | 2.467 | 2.763 |
| 29 | 1.699 | 2.045 | 2.462 | 2.756 |
| 30 | 1.697 | 2.042 | 2.457 | 2.750 |
| 60 | 1.671 | 2.000 | 2.390 | 2.660 |
| ∞ | 1.645 | 1.960 | 2.326 | 2.576 |

SOURCE: From Table 3 of Fisher & Yates, *Statistical Tables for Biological, Agricultural and Medical Research,* published by Longman Group Ltd., London (previously published by Oliver and Boyd Ltd., Edinburgh). By permission of the authors and publishers.

**TABLE B-5**

Critical Values of the Mann–Whitney $U$ Test at the $p < .05$ Level

| $N_2$ | $N_1$ | | | | | | | | | | | | | |
|---|---|---|---|---|---|---|---|---|---|---|---|---|---|---|
| | 7 | 8 | 9 | 10 | 11 | 12 | 13 | 14 | 15 | 16 | 17 | 18 | 19 | 20 |
| 3 | 1 | 2 | 2 | 3 | 3 | 4 | 4 | 5 | 5 | 6 | 6 | 7 | 7 | 8 |
| 4 | 3 | 4 | 4 | 5 | 6 | 7 | 8 | 9 | 10 | 11 | 11 | 12 | 13 | 13 |
| 5 | 5 | 6 | 7 | 8 | 9 | 11 | 12 | 13 | 14 | 15 | 17 | 18 | 19 | 20 |
| 6 | 6 | 8 | 10 | 11 | 13 | 14 | 16 | 17 | 19 | 21 | 22 | 24 | 25 | 27 |
| 7 | 8 | 10 | 12 | 14 | 16 | 18 | 20 | 22 | 24 | 26 | 28 | 30 | 32 | 34 |
| 8 | 10 | 13 | 15 | 17 | 19 | 22 | 24 | 26 | 29 | 31 | 34 | 36 | 38 | 41 |
| 9 | 12 | 15 | 17 | 20 | 23 | 26 | 28 | 31 | 34 | 37 | 39 | 42 | 45 | 48 |
| 10 | 14 | 17 | 20 | 23 | 26 | 29 | 33 | 36 | 39 | 42 | 45 | 48 | 52 | 55 |
| 11 | 16 | 19 | 23 | 26 | 30 | 33 | 37 | 40 | 44 | 47 | 51 | 55 | 58 | 62 |
| 12 | 18 | 22 | 26 | 29 | 33 | 37 | 41 | 45 | 49 | 53 | 57 | 61 | 65 | 69 |
| 13 | 20 | 24 | 28 | 33 | 37 | 41 | 45 | 50 | 54 | 59 | 63 | 67 | 72 | 76 |
| 14 | 22 | 26 | 31 | 36 | 40 | 45 | 50 | 55 | 59 | 64 | 67 | 74 | 78 | 83 |
| 15 | 24 | 29 | 34 | 39 | 44 | 49 | 54 | 59 | 64 | 70 | 75 | 80 | 85 | 90 |
| 16 | 26 | 31 | 37 | 42 | 47 | 53 | 59 | 64 | 70 | 75 | 81 | 86 | 92 | 98 |
| 17 | 28 | 34 | 39 | 45 | 51 | 57 | 63 | 67 | 75 | 81 | 87 | 93 | 99 | 105 |
| 18 | 30 | 36 | 42 | 48 | 55 | 61 | 67 | 74 | 80 | 86 | 93 | 99 | 106 | 112 |
| 19 | 32 | 38 | 45 | 52 | 58 | 65 | 72 | 78 | 85 | 92 | 99 | 106 | 113 | 119 |
| 20 | 34 | 41 | 48 | 55 | 62 | 69 | 76 | 83 | 90 | 98 | 105 | 112 | 119 | 127 |

SOURCE: Adapted and abridged from Tables 1, 3, 5, and 7 of Auble, D., Extended tables for the Mann–Whitney statistics, *Bulletin of the Institute of Educational Research at Indiana University*, 1953, *1*(2).

**TABLE B-6**
Critical Values of the Mann–Whitney *U* Test at the *p* < .01 Level

| $N_2$ | 7 | 8 | 9 | 10 | 11 | 12 | 13 | 14 | 15 | 16 | 17 | 18 | 19 | 20 |
|---|---|---|---|---|---|---|---|---|---|---|---|---|---|---|
| 3 | — | — | 0 | 0 | 0 | 1 | 1 | 1 | 2 | 2 | 2 | 2 | 3 | 3 |
| 4 | 0 | 1 | 1 | 2 | 2 | 3 | 3 | 4 | 5 | 5 | 6 | 6 | 7 | 8 |
| 5 | 1 | 2 | 3 | 4 | 5 | 6 | 7 | 7 | 8 | 9 | 10 | 11 | 12 | 13 |
| 6 | 3 | 4 | 5 | 6 | 7 | 9 | 10 | 11 | 12 | 13 | 15 | 16 | 17 | 18 |
| 7 | 4 | 6 | 7 | 9 | 10 | 12 | 13 | 15 | 16 | 18 | 19 | 21 | 22 | 24 |
| 8 | 6 | 7 | 9 | 11 | 13 | 15 | 17 | 18 | 20 | 22 | 24 | 26 | 28 | 30 |
| 9 | 7 | 9 | 11 | 13 | 16 | 18 | 20 | 22 | 24 | 27 | 29 | 31 | 33 | 36 |
| 10 | 9 | 11 | 13 | 16 | 18 | 21 | 24 | 26 | 29 | 31 | 34 | 37 | 39 | 42 |
| 11 | 10 | 13 | 16 | 18 | 21 | 24 | 27 | 30 | 33 | 36 | 39 | 42 | 45 | 48 |
| 12 | 12 | 15 | 18 | 21 | 24 | 27 | 31 | 34 | 37 | 41 | 44 | 47 | 51 | 54 |
| 13 | 13 | 17 | 20 | 24 | 27 | 31 | 34 | 38 | 42 | 45 | 49 | 53 | 56 | 60 |
| 14 | 15 | 18 | 22 | 26 | 30 | 34 | 38 | 42 | 46 | 50 | 54 | 58 | 63 | 67 |
| 15 | 16 | 20 | 24 | 29 | 33 | 37 | 42 | 46 | 51 | 55 | 60 | 64 | 69 | 73 |
| 16 | 18 | 22 | 27 | 31 | 36 | 41 | 45 | 50 | 55 | 60 | 65 | 70 | 74 | 79 |
| 17 | 19 | 24 | 29 | 34 | 39 | 44 | 49 | 54 | 60 | 65 | 70 | 75 | 81 | 86 |
| 18 | 21 | 26 | 31 | 37 | 42 | 47 | 53 | 58 | 64 | 70 | 75 | 81 | 87 | 92 |
| 19 | 22 | 28 | 33 | 39 | 45 | 51 | 56 | 63 | 69 | 74 | 81 | 87 | 93 | 99 |
| 20 | 24 | 30 | 36 | 42 | 48 | 54 | 60 | 67 | 73 | 79 | 86 | 92 | 99 | 105 |

The column group spanning 7–20 is headed $N_1$.

SOURCE: Adapted and abridged from Tables 1, 3, 5, and 7 of Auble, D., Extended tables for the Mann–Whitney statistics, *Bulletin of the Institute of Educational Research at Indiana University*, 1953, *1*(2).

**TABLE B-7**

Probabilities Associated with Various z-Scores. The body of the table gives one-tailed probabilities under $H_o$ of z. The left marginal column gives various values of z to one decimal place. The top row gives various values to the second decimal place. Thus, for example, the one-tailed p of $z \geq .11$ or $z \leq -.11$ is $p = .4562$.

| z | .00 | .01 | .02 | .03 | .04 | .05 | .06 | .07 | .08 | .09 |
|---|---|---|---|---|---|---|---|---|---|---|
| .0 | .5000 | .4960 | .4920 | .4880 | .4840 | .4801 | .4761 | .4721 | .4681 | .4641 |
| .1 | .4602 | .4562 | .4522 | .4483 | .4443 | .4404 | .4364 | .4325 | .4286 | .4247 |
| .2 | .4207 | .4168 | .4129 | .4090 | .4052 | .4013 | .3974 | .3936 | .3897 | .3859 |
| .3 | .3821 | .3783 | .3745 | .3707 | .3669 | .3632 | .3594 | .3557 | .3520 | .3483 |
| .4 | .3446 | .3409 | .3372 | .3336 | .3300 | .3264 | .3228 | .3192 | .3156 | .3121 |
| .5 | .3085 | .3050 | .3015 | .2981 | .2946 | .2912 | .2877 | .2843 | .2810 | .2776 |
| .6 | .2743 | .2709 | .2676 | .2643 | .2611 | .2578 | .2546 | .2514 | .2483 | .2451 |
| .7 | .2420 | .2389 | .2358 | .2327 | .2296 | .2266 | .2236 | .2206 | .2177 | .2148 |
| .8 | .2119 | .2090 | .2061 | .2033 | .2005 | .1977 | .1949 | .1922 | .1894 | .1867 |
| .9 | .1841 | .1814 | .1788 | .1762 | .1736 | .1711 | .1685 | .1660 | .1635 | .1611 |
| 1.0 | .1587 | .1562 | .1539 | .1515 | .1492 | .1469 | .1446 | .1423 | .1401 | .1379 |
| 1.1 | .1357 | .1335 | .1314 | .1292 | .1271 | .1251 | .1230 | .1210 | .1190 | .1170 |
| 1.2 | .1151 | .1131 | .1112 | .1093 | .1075 | .1056 | .1038 | .1020 | .1003 | .0985 |
| 1.3 | .0968 | .0951 | .0934 | .0918 | .0901 | .0885 | .0869 | .0853 | .0838 | .0823 |
| 1.4 | .0808 | .0793 | .0778 | .0764 | .0749 | .0735 | .0721 | .0708 | .0694 | .0681 |
| 1.5 | .0668 | .0655 | .0643 | .0630 | .0618 | .0606 | .0594 | .0582 | .0571 | .0559 |
| 1.6 | .0548 | .0537 | .0526 | .0516 | .0505 | .0495 | .0485 | .0475 | .0465 | .0455 |
| 1.7 | .0446 | .0436 | .0427 | .0418 | .0409 | .0401 | .0392 | .0384 | .0375 | .0367 |
| 1.8 | .0359 | .0351 | .0344 | .0336 | .0329 | .0322 | .0314 | .0307 | .0301 | .0294 |
| 1.9 | .0287 | .0281 | .0274 | .0268 | .0262 | .0256 | .0250 | .0244 | .0239 | .0233 |
| 2.0 | .0228 | .0222 | .0217 | .0212 | .0207 | .0202 | .0197 | .0192 | .0188 | .0183 |
| 2.1 | .0179 | .0174 | .0170 | .0166 | .0162 | .0158 | .0154 | .0150 | .0146 | .0143 |
| 2.2 | .0139 | .0136 | .0132 | .0129 | .0125 | .0122 | .0119 | .0116 | .0113 | .0110 |
| 2.3 | .0107 | .0104 | .0102 | .0099 | .0096 | .0094 | .0091 | .0089 | .0087 | .0084 |
| 2.4 | .0082 | .0080 | .0078 | .0075 | .0073 | .0071 | .0069 | .0068 | .0066 | .0064 |
| 2.5 | .0062 | .0060 | .0059 | .0057 | .0055 | .0054 | .0052 | .0051 | .0049 | .0048 |
| 2.6 | .0047 | .0045 | .0044 | .0043 | .0041 | .0040 | .0039 | .0038 | .0037 | .0036 |
| 2.7 | .0035 | .0034 | .0033 | .0032 | .0031 | .0030 | .0029 | .0028 | .0027 | .0026 |
| 2.8 | .0026 | .0025 | .0024 | .0023 | .0023 | .0022 | .0021 | .0021 | .0020 | .0019 |
| 2.9 | .0019 | .0018 | .0018 | .0017 | .0016 | .0016 | .0015 | .0015 | .0014 | .0014 |
| 3.0 | .0013 | .0013 | .0013 | .0012 | .0012 | .0011 | .0011 | .0011 | .0010 | .0010 |
| 3.1 | .0010 | .0009 | .0009 | .0009 | .0008 | .0008 | .0008 | .0008 | .0007 | .0007 |
| 3.2 | .0007 | | | | | | | | | |
| 3.3 | .0005 | | | | | | | | | |
| 3.4 | .0003 | | | | | | | | | |
| 3.5 | .00023 | | | | | | | | | |
| 3.6 | .00016 | | | | | | | | | |
| 3.7 | .00011 | | | | | | | | | |
| 3.8 | .00007 | | | | | | | | | |
| 3.9 | .00005 | | | | | | | | | |
| 4.0 | .00003 | | | | | | | | | |

SOURCE: Reproduced by permission from Siegel, S., *Nonparametric Statistics for the Behavioral Sciences*. New York: McGraw-Hill Book Company, Inc., 1956 (p. 247).

**TABLE B-8**

Critical Values of the Wilcoxon $T$. The $T$ is the smaller of the sum of ranks having differences that are all of the same sign. For a given number of differences $n$, the $T$ is significant at a particular level if it is equal to or less than the value shown.

| | Level of significance for a one-tailed test | | | | | Level of significance for a one-tailed test | | | |
|---|---|---|---|---|---|---|---|---|---|
| | .05 | .025 | .01 | .005 | | .05 | .025 | .01 | .005 |
| | Level of significance for a two-tailed test | | | | | Level of significance for a two-tailed test | | | |
| $n$ | .10 | .05 | .02 | .01 | $n$ | .10 | .05 | .02 | .01 |
| 5 | 0 | — | — | — | 28 | 130 | 116 | 101 | 91 |
| 6 | 2 | 0 | — | — | 29 | 140 | 126 | 110 | 100 |
| 7 | 3 | 2 | 0 | — | 30 | 151 | 137 | 120 | 109 |
| 8 | 5 | 3 | 1 | 0 | 31 | 163 | 147 | 130 | 118 |
| 9 | 8 | 5 | 3 | 1 | 32 | 175 | 159 | 140 | 128 |
| 10 | 10 | 8 | 5 | 3 | 33 | 187 | 170 | 151 | 138 |
| 11 | 13 | 10 | 7 | 5 | 34 | 200 | 182 | 162 | 148 |
| 12 | 17 | 13 | 9 | 7 | 35 | 213 | 195 | 173 | 159 |
| 13 | 21 | 17 | 12 | 9 | 36 | 227 | 208 | 185 | 171 |
| 14 | 25 | 21 | 15 | 12 | 37 | 241 | 221 | 198 | 182 |
| 15 | 30 | 25 | 19 | 15 | 38 | 256 | 235 | 211 | 194 |
| 16 | 35 | 29 | 23 | 19 | 39 | 271 | 249 | 224 | 207 |
| 17 | 41 | 34 | 27 | 23 | 40 | 286 | 264 | 238 | 220 |
| 18 | 47 | 40 | 32 | 27 | 41 | 302 | 279 | 252 | 233 |
| 19 | 53 | 46 | 37 | 32 | 42 | 319 | 294 | 266 | 247 |
| 20 | 60 | 52 | 43 | 37 | 43 | 336 | 310 | 281 | 261 |
| 21 | 67 | 58 | 49 | 42 | 44 | 353 | 327 | 296 | 276 |
| 22 | 75 | 65 | 55 | 48 | 45 | 371 | 343 | 312 | 291 |
| 23 | 83 | 73 | 62 | 54 | 46 | 389 | 361 | 328 | 307 |
| 24 | 91 | 81 | 69 | 61 | 47 | 407 | 378 | 345 | 322 |
| 25 | 100 | 89 | 76 | 68 | 48 | 426 | 396 | 362 | 339 |
| 26 | 110 | 98 | 84 | 75 | 49 | 446 | 415 | 379 | 355 |
| 27 | 119 | 107 | 92 | 83 | 50 | 466 | 434 | 397 | 373 |

SOURCE: From Roger E. Kirk, *Elementary Statistics* (2nd ed.). Pacific Grove, CA: Brooks/Cole, 1984.

**TABLE B-9**

Critical Values of *F.* The top number in each cell is for testing at the .05 level; the bottom number is for testing at the .01 level.

| | | | | Degrees of freedom for numerator | | | | | | |
|---|---|---|---|---|---|---|---|---|---|---|
| | 1 | 2 | 3 | 4 | 5 | 6 | 8 | 12 | 24 | ∞ |
| 1 | 161.45 | 199.50 | 215.72 | 224.57 | 230.17 | 233.97 | 238.89 | 243.91 | 249.04 | 254.32 |
| | 4032.10 | 4999.03 | 5403.49 | 5625.14 | 5764.08 | 5859.39 | 5981.34 | 6105.83 | 6234.16 | 6366.48 |
| 2 | 18.51 | 19.00 | 19.16 | 19.25 | 19.30 | 19.33 | 19.37 | 19.41 | 19.45 | 19.50 |
| | 98.49 | 99.01 | 99.17 | 99.25 | 99.30 | 99.33 | 99.36 | 99.42 | 99.46 | 99.50 |
| 3 | 10.13 | 9.55 | 9.28 | 9.12 | 9.01 | 8.94 | 8.84 | 8.74 | 8.64 | 8.53 |
| | 34.12 | 30.81 | 29.46 | 28.71 | 28.24 | 27.91 | 27.49 | 27.05 | 26.60 | 26.12 |
| 4 | 7.71 | 6.94 | 6.59 | 6.39 | 6.26 | 6.16 | 6.04 | 5.91 | 5.77 | 5.63 |
| | 21.20 | 18.00 | 16.69 | 15.98 | 15.52 | 15.21 | 14.80 | 14.37 | 13.93 | 13.46 |
| 5 | 6.61 | 5.79 | 5.41 | 5.19 | 5.05 | 4.95 | 4.82 | 4.68 | 4.53 | 4.36 |
| | 16.26 | 13.27 | 12.06 | 11.39 | 10.97 | 10.67 | 10.27 | 9.89 | 9.47 | 9.02 |
| 6 | 5.99 | 5.14 | 4.76 | 4.53 | 4.39 | 4.28 | 4.15 | 4.00 | 3.84 | 3.67 |
| | 13.74 | 10.92 | 9.78 | 9.15 | 8.75 | 8.47 | 8.10 | 7.72 | 7.31 | 6.88 |
| 7 | 5.59 | 4.74 | 4.35 | 4.12 | 3.97 | 3.87 | 3.73 | 3.57 | 3.41 | 3.23 |
| | 12.25 | 9.55 | 8.45 | 7.85 | 7.46 | 7.19 | 6.84 | 6.47 | 6.07 | 5.65 |
| 8 | 5.32 | 4.46 | 4.07 | 3.84 | 3.69 | 3.58 | 3.44 | 3.28 | 3.12 | 2.93 |
| | 11.26 | 8.65 | 7.59 | 7.01 | 6.63 | 6.37 | 6.03 | 5.67 | 5.28 | 4.86 |
| 9 | 5.12 | 4.26 | 3.86 | 3.63 | 3.48 | 3.37 | 3.23 | 3.07 | 2.90 | 2.71 |
| | 10.56 | 8.02 | 6.99 | 6.42 | 6.06 | 5.80 | 5.47 | 5.11 | 4.73 | 4.31 |
| 10 | 4.96 | 4.10 | 3.71 | 3.48 | 3.33 | 3.22 | 3.07 | 2.91 | 2.74 | 2.54 |
| | 10.04 | 7.56 | 6.55 | 5.99 | 5.64 | 5.39 | 5.06 | 4.71 | 4.33 | 3.91 |
| 11 | 4.84 | 3.98 | 3.59 | 3.36 | 3.20 | 3.09 | 2.95 | 2.79 | 2.61 | 2.40 |
| | 9.65 | 7.20 | 6.22 | 5.67 | 5.32 | 5.07 | 4.74 | 4.40 | 4.02 | 3.60 |
| 12 | 4.75 | 3.88 | 3.49 | 3.26 | 3.11 | 3.00 | 2.85 | 2.69 | 2.50 | 2.30 |
| | 9.33 | 6.93 | 5.93 | 5.41 | 5.06 | 4.82 | 4.50 | 4.16 | 3.78 | 3.36 |
| 14 | 4.60 | 3.74 | 3.34 | 3.11 | 2.96 | 2.85 | 2.70 | 2.53 | 2.35 | 2.13 |
| | 8.86 | 6.51 | 5.56 | 5.03 | 4.69 | 4.46 | 4.14 | 3.80 | 3.43 | 3.00 |
| 16 | 4.49 | 3.63 | 3.24 | 3.01 | 2.85 | 2.74 | 2.59 | 2.42 | 2.24 | 2.01 |
| | 8.53 | 6.23 | 5.29 | 4.77 | 4.44 | 4.20 | 3.89 | 3.55 | 3.18 | 2.75 |
| 18 | 4.41 | 3.55 | 3.16 | 2.93 | 2.77 | 2.66 | 2.51 | 2.34 | 2.15 | 1.92 |
| | 8.28 | 6.01 | 5.09 | 4.58 | 4.25 | 4.01 | 3.71 | 3.37 | 3.01 | 2.57 |
| 20 | 4.35 | 3.49 | 3.10 | 2.87 | 2.71 | 2.60 | 2.45 | 2.28 | 2.08 | 1.84 |
| | 8.10 | 5.85 | 4.94 | 4.43 | 4.10 | 3.87 | 3.56 | 3.23 | 2.86 | 2.42 |
| 25 | 4.24 | 3.38 | 2.99 | 2.76 | 2.60 | 2.49 | 2.34 | 2.16 | 1.96 | 1.71 |
| | 7.77 | 5.57 | 4.68 | 4.18 | 3.86 | 3.63 | 3.32 | 2.99 | 2.62 | 2.17 |
| 30 | 4.17 | 3.32 | 2.92 | 2.69 | 2.53 | 2.42 | 2.27 | 2.09 | 1.89 | 1.62 |
| | 7.56 | 5.39 | 4.51 | 4.02 | 3.70 | 3.47 | 3.17 | 2.84 | 2.47 | 2.01 |

*Degrees of freedom for denominator*

*(continued)*

**TABLE B-9**    *(continued)*

| | | | | Degrees of freedom for numerator | | | | | | |
|---|---|---|---|---|---|---|---|---|---|---|
| | 1 | 2 | 3 | 4 | 5 | 6 | 8 | 12 | 24 | ∞ |
| 40 | 4.08 | 3.23 | 2.84 | 2.61 | 2.45 | 2.34 | 2.18 | 2.00 | 1.79 | 1.52 |
| | 7.31 | 5.18 | 4.31 | 3.83 | 3.51 | 3.29 | 2.99 | 2.66 | 2.29 | 1.82 |
| 50 | 4.03 | 3.18 | 2.79 | 2.56 | 2.40 | 2.29 | 2.13 | 1.95 | 1.74 | 1.44 |
| | 7.17 | 5.06 | 4.20 | 3.72 | 3.41 | 3.19 | 2.89 | 2.56 | 2.18 | 1.68 |
| 60 | 4.00 | 3.15 | 2.76 | 2.52 | 2.37 | 2.25 | 2.10 | 1.92 | 1.70 | 1.39 |
| | 7.08 | 4.98 | 4.13 | 3.65 | 3.34 | 3.12 | 2.82 | 2.50 | 2.12 | 1.60 |
| 70 | 3.98 | 3.13 | 2.74 | 2.50 | 2.35 | 2.23 | 2.07 | 1.89 | 1.67 | 1.35 |
| | 7.01 | 4.92 | 4.07 | 3.60 | 3.29 | 3.07 | 2.78 | 2.45 | 2.07 | 1.53 |
| 80 | 3.96 | 3.11 | 2.72 | 2.49 | 2.33 | 2.21 | 2.06 | 1.88 | 1.65 | 1.31 |
| | 6.98 | 4.88 | 4.04 | 3.56 | 3.26 | 3.04 | 2.74 | 2.42 | 2.03 | 1.47 |
| 90 | 3.95 | 3.10 | 2.71 | 2.47 | 2.32 | 2.20 | 2.04 | 1.86 | 1.64 | 1.28 |
| | 6.92 | 4.85 | 4.01 | 3.53 | 3.23 | 3.01 | 2.72 | 2.39 | 2.00 | 1.43 |
| 100 | 3.94 | 3.09 | 2.70 | 2.46 | 2.30 | 2.19 | 2.03 | 1.85 | 1.63 | 1.26 |
| | 6.90 | 4.82 | 3.98 | 3.51 | 3.21 | 2.99 | 2.69 | 2.37 | 1.98 | 1.39 |
| 200 | 3.89 | 3.04 | 2.65 | 2.42 | 2.26 | 2.14 | 1.98 | 1.80 | 1.57 | 1.14 |
| | 6.97 | 4.71 | 3.88 | 3.41 | 3.11 | 2.89 | 2.60 | 2.28 | 1.88 | 1.21 |
| ∞ | 3.84 | 2.99 | 2.60 | 2.37 | 2.21 | 2.09 | 1.94 | 1.75 | 1.52 | |
| | 6.64 | 4.60 | 3.78 | 3.32 | 3.02 | 2.80 | 2.51 | 2.18 | 1.79 | |

*Degrees of freedom for denominator* (left-side vertical label)

SOURCE: Adapted from Table F of H. E. Garrett, *Statistics in Psychology and Education*, 5th Edition, Copyright 1958, David McKay Co., Inc.

**TABLE B-10**
Critical Values for *H* (Kruskal–Wallis One-Way ANOVA by Ranks)

| $n_1$ | $n_2$ | $n_3$ | *H* | *p* | $n_1$ | $n_2$ | $n_3$ | *H* | *p* |
|---|---|---|---|---|---|---|---|---|---|
| 2 | 1 | 1 | 2.7000 | .500 | 4 | 3 | 2 | 6.4444 | .008 |
| 2 | 2 | 1 | 3.6000 | .200 | | | | 6.3000 | .011 |
| 2 | 2 | 2 | 4.5714 | .067 | | | | 5.4444 | .046 |
| | | | 3.7143 | .200 | | | | 5.4000 | .051 |
| 3 | 1 | 1 | 3.2000 | .300 | | | | 4.5111 | .098 |
| | | | | | | | | 4.4444 | .102 |
| 3 | 2 | 1 | 4.2857 | .100 | 4 | 3 | 3 | 6.7455 | .010 |
| | | | 3.8571 | .133 | | | | 6.7091 | .013 |
| 3 | 2 | 2 | 5.3572 | .029 | | | | 5.7909 | .046 |
| | | | 4.7143 | .048 | | | | 5.7273 | .050 |
| | | | 4.5000 | .067 | | | | 4.7091 | .092 |
| | | | 4.4643 | .105 | | | | 4.7000 | .101 |
| 3 | 3 | 1 | 5.1429 | .043 | 4 | 4 | 1 | 6.6667 | .010 |
| | | | 4.5714 | .100 | | | | 6.1667 | .022 |
| | | | 4.0000 | .129 | | | | 4.9667 | .048 |
| 3 | 3 | 2 | 6.2500 | .011 | | | | 4.8667 | .054 |
| | | | 5.3611 | .032 | | | | 4.1667 | .082 |
| | | | 5.1389 | .061 | | | | 4.0667 | .102 |
| | | | 4.5556 | .100 | 4 | 4 | 2 | 7.0364 | .006 |
| | | | 4.2500 | .121 | | | | 6.8727 | .011 |
| 3 | 3 | 3 | 7.2000 | .004 | | | | 5.4545 | .046 |
| | | | 6.4889 | .011 | | | | 5.2364 | .052 |
| | | | 5.6889 | .029 | | | | 4.5545 | .098 |
| | | | 5.6000 | .050 | | | | 4.4455 | .103 |
| | | | 5.0667 | .086 | 4 | 4 | 3 | 7.1439 | .010 |
| | | | 4.6222 | .100 | | | | 7.1364 | .011 |
| 4 | 1 | 1 | 3.5714 | .200 | | | | 5.5985 | .049 |
| 4 | 2 | 1 | 4.8214 | .057 | | | | 5.5758 | .051 |
| | | | 4.5000 | .076 | | | | 4.5455 | .099 |
| | | | 4.0179 | .114 | | | | 4.4773 | .102 |
| 4 | 2 | 2 | 6.0000 | .014 | 4 | 4 | 4 | 7.6538 | .008 |
| | | | 5.3333 | .033 | | | | 7.5385 | .011 |
| | | | 5.1250 | .052 | | | | 5.6923 | .049 |
| | | | 4.4583 | .100 | | | | 5.6538 | .054 |
| | | | 4.1667 | .105 | | | | 4.6539 | .097 |
| 4 | 3 | 1 | 5.8333 | .021 | | | | 4.5001 | .104 |
| | | | 5.2083 | .050 | 5 | 1 | 1 | 3.8571 | .143 |
| | | | 5.0000 | .057 | 5 | 2 | 1 | 5.2500 | .036 |
| | | | 4.0556 | .093 | | | | 5.0000 | .048 |
| | | | 3.8889 | .129 | | | | 4.4500 | .071 |
| | | | | | | | | 4.2000 | .095 |
| | | | | | | | | 4.0500 | .119 |

*(continued)*

**TABLE B-10** *(continued)*

| Sample sizes | | | | | Sample sizes | | | | |
|---|---|---|---|---|---|---|---|---|---|
| $n_1$ | $n_2$ | $n_3$ | $H$ | $p$ | $n_1$ | $n_2$ | $n_3$ | $H$ | $p$ |
| 5 | 2 | 2 | 6.5333 | .008 | 5 | 4 | 4 | 7.7604 | .009 |
|   |   |   | 6.1333 | .013 |   |   |   | 7.7440 | .011 |
|   |   |   | 5.1600 | .034 |   |   |   | 5.6571 | .049 |
|   |   |   | 5.0400 | .056 |   |   |   | 5.6176 | .050 |
|   |   |   | 4.3733 | .090 |   |   |   | 4.6187 | .100 |
|   |   |   | 4.2933 | .122 |   |   |   | 4.5527 | .102 |
| 5 | 3 | 1 | 6.4000 | .012 | 5 | 5 | 1 | 7.3091 | .009 |
|   |   |   | 4.9600 | .048 |   |   |   | 6.8364 | .011 |
|   |   |   | 4.8711 | .052 |   |   |   | 5.1273 | .046 |
|   |   |   | 4.0178 | .095 |   |   |   | 4.9091 | .053 |
|   |   |   | 3.8400 | .123 |   |   |   | 4.1091 | .086 |
| 5 | 3 | 2 | 6.9091 | .009 |   |   |   | 4.0364 | .105 |
|   |   |   | 6.8218 | .010 | 5 | 5 | 2 | 7.3385 | .010 |
|   |   |   | 5.2509 | .049 |   |   |   | 7.2692 | .010 |
|   |   |   | 5.1055 | .052 |   |   |   | 5.3385 | .047 |
|   |   |   | 4.6509 | .091 |   |   |   | 5.2462 | .051 |
|   |   |   | 4.4945 | .101 |   |   |   | 4.6231 | .097 |
| 5 | 3 | 3 | 7.0788 | .009 |   |   |   | 4.5077 | .100 |
|   |   |   | 6.9818 | .011 | 5 | 5 | 3 | 7.5780 | .010 |
|   |   |   | 5.6485 | .049 |   |   |   | 7.5429 | .010 |
|   |   |   | 5.5152 | .051 |   |   |   | 5.7055 | .046 |
|   |   |   | 4.5333 | .097 |   |   |   | 5.6264 | .051 |
|   |   |   | 4.4121 | .109 |   |   |   | 4.5451 | .100 |
| 5 | 4 | 1 | 6.9545 | .008 |   |   |   | 4.5363 | .102 |
|   |   |   | 6.8400 | .011 | 5 | 5 | 4 | 7.8229 | .010 |
|   |   |   | 4.9855 | .044 |   |   |   | 7.7914 | .010 |
|   |   |   | 4.8600 | .056 |   |   |   | 5.6657 | .049 |
|   |   |   | 3.9873 | .098 |   |   |   | 5.6429 | .050 |
|   |   |   | 3.9600 | .102 |   |   |   | 4.5229 | .099 |
| 5 | 4 | 2 | 7.2045 | .009 |   |   |   | 4.5200 | .101 |
|   |   |   | 7.1182 | .010 | 5 | 5 | 5 | 8.0000 | .009 |
|   |   |   | 5.2727 | .049 |   |   |   | 7.9800 | .010 |
|   |   |   | 5.2682 | .050 |   |   |   | 5.7800 | .049 |
|   |   |   | 4.5409 | .098 |   |   |   | 5.6600 | .051 |
|   |   |   | 4.5182 | .101 |   |   |   | 4.5600 | .100 |
| 5 | 4 | 3 | 7.4449 | .010 |   |   |   | 4.5000 | .102 |
|   |   |   | 7.3949 | .011 |   |   |   |   |   |
|   |   |   | 5.6564 | .049 |   |   |   |   |   |
|   |   |   | 5.6308 | .050 |   |   |   |   |   |
|   |   |   | 4.5487 | .099 |   |   |   |   |   |
|   |   |   | 4.5231 | .103 |   |   |   |   |   |

SOURCE: Adapted and abridged from Kruskal, W. H., and Wallis, W. A., Use of ranks in one-criterion variance analysis, *Journal of American Statistical Association*, 1952, *47*, 614–617, with the kind permission of the authors and the publisher. (The corrections to this table given by the authors in Errata, *Journal of the American Statistical Association*, 1953, *48*, 910, have been incorporated.)

# APPENDIX C
# Table of Random Numbers

| Col. (1) | (2) | (3) | (4) | (5) | (6) | (7) | (8) | (9) | (10) | (11) | (12) | (13) | (14) |
|------|------|------|------|------|------|------|------|------|------|------|------|------|------|
| **Line** | | | | | | | | | | | | | |
| 1 | 10480 | 15011 | 01536 | 02011 | 81647 | 91646 | 69179 | 14194 | 62590 | 36207 | 20969 | 99570 | 91291 | 90700 |
| 2 | 22368 | 46573 | 25595 | 85393 | 30995 | 89198 | 27982 | 53402 | 93965 | 34095 | 52666 | 19174 | 39615 | 99505 |
| 3 | 24130 | 48360 | 22527 | 97265 | 76393 | 64809 | 15179 | 24830 | 49340 | 32081 | 30680 | 19655 | 63348 | 58629 |
| 4 | 42167 | 93093 | 06243 | 61680 | 07856 | 16376 | 39440 | 53537 | 71341 | 57004 | 00849 | 74917 | 97758 | 16379 |
| 5 | 37570 | 39975 | 81837 | 16656 | 06121 | 91782 | 60468 | 81305 | 49684 | 60672 | 14110 | 06927 | 01263 | 54613 |
| 6 | 77921 | 06907 | 11008 | 42751 | 27756 | 53498 | 18602 | 70659 | 90655 | 15053 | 21916 | 81825 | 44394 | 42880 |
| 7 | 99562 | 72905 | 56420 | 69994 | 98872 | 31016 | 71194 | 18738 | 44013 | 48840 | 63213 | 21069 | 10634 | 12952 |
| 8 | 96301 | 91977 | 05463 | 07972 | 18876 | 20922 | 94595 | 56869 | 69014 | 60045 | 18425 | 84903 | 42508 | 32307 |
| 9 | 89579 | 14342 | 63661 | 10281 | 17453 | 18103 | 57740 | 84378 | 25331 | 12566 | 58678 | 44947 | 05585 | 56941 |
| 10 | 85475 | 36857 | 43342 | 53988 | 53060 | 59533 | 38867 | 62300 | 08158 | 17983 | 16439 | 11458 | 18593 | 64952 |
| 11 | 28918 | 69578 | 88231 | 33276 | 70997 | 79936 | 56865 | 05859 | 90106 | 31595 | 01547 | 85590 | 91610 | 78188 |
| 12 | 63553 | 40961 | 48235 | 03427 | 49626 | 69445 | 18663 | 72695 | 52180 | 20847 | 12234 | 90511 | 33703 | 90322 |
| 13 | 09429 | 93969 | 52636 | 92737 | 88974 | 33488 | 36320 | 17617 | 30015 | 08272 | 84115 | 27156 | 30613 | 74952 |
| 14 | 10365 | 61129 | 87529 | 85689 | 48237 | 52267 | 67689 | 93394 | 01511 | 26358 | 85104 | 20285 | 29975 | 89868 |
| 15 | 07119 | 97336 | 71048 | 08178 | 77233 | 13916 | 47564 | 81056 | 97735 | 85977 | 29372 | 74461 | 28551 | 90707 |
| 16 | 51085 | 12765 | 51821 | 51259 | 77452 | 16308 | 60756 | 92144 | 49442 | 53900 | 70960 | 63990 | 75601 | 40719 |
| 17 | 02368 | 21382 | 52404 | 60268 | 89368 | 19885 | 55322 | 44819 | 01188 | 65255 | 64835 | 44919 | 05944 | 55157 |
| 18 | 01011 | 54092 | 33362 | 94904 | 31273 | 04146 | 18594 | 29852 | 71585 | 85030 | 51132 | 01915 | 92747 | 64951 |
| 19 | 52162 | 53916 | 46369 | 58586 | 23216 | 14513 | 83149 | 98736 | 23495 | 64350 | 94738 | 17752 | 35156 | 35749 |
| 20 | 07056 | 97628 | 33787 | 09998 | 42698 | 06691 | 76988 | 13602 | 51851 | 46104 | 88916 | 19509 | 25625 | 58104 |
| 21 | 48663 | 91245 | 85828 | 14346 | 09172 | 30168 | 90229 | 04734 | 59193 | 22178 | 30421 | 61666 | 99904 | 32812 |
| 22 | 54164 | 58492 | 22421 | 74103 | 47070 | 25306 | 76468 | 26384 | 58151 | 06646 | 21524 | 15227 | 96909 | 44592 |
| 23 | 32639 | 32363 | 05597 | 24200 | 13363 | 38005 | 94342 | 28728 | 35806 | 06912 | 17012 | 64161 | 18296 | 22851 |
| 24 | 29334 | 27001 | 87637 | 87308 | 58731 | 00256 | 45834 | 15398 | 46557 | 41135 | 10367 | 07684 | 36188 | 18510 |
| 25 | 02488 | 33062 | 28834 | 07351 | 19731 | 92420 | 60952 | 61280 | 50001 | 67658 | 32586 | 86679 | 50720 | 94953 |
| 26 | 81525 | 72295 | 04839 | 96423 | 24878 | 82651 | 66566 | 14778 | 76797 | 14780 | 13300 | 87074 | 79666 | 95725 |
| 27 | 29676 | 20591 | 68086 | 26432 | 46901 | 20849 | 89768 | 81536 | 86645 | 12659 | 92259 | 57102 | 80428 | 25280 |
| 28 | 00742 | 57392 | 39064 | 66432 | 84673 | 40027 | 32832 | 61362 | 98947 | 96067 | 64760 | 64584 | 96096 | 98253 |
| 29 | 05366 | 04213 | 25669 | 26422 | 44407 | 44048 | 37937 | 63904 | 45766 | 66134 | 75470 | 66520 | 34693 | 90449 |
| 30 | 91921 | 26418 | 64117 | 94305 | 26766 | 25940 | 39972 | 22209 | 71500 | 64568 | 91402 | 42416 | 07844 | 69618 |
| 31 | 00582 | 04711 | 87917 | 77341 | 42206 | 35126 | 74087 | 99547 | 81817 | 42607 | 43808 | 76655 | 62028 | 76630 |
| 32 | 00725 | 69884 | 62797 | 56170 | 86324 | 88072 | 76222 | 36086 | 84637 | 93161 | 76038 | 65855 | 77919 | 88006 |
| 33 | 69011 | 65797 | 95876 | 55293 | 18988 | 27354 | 26575 | 08625 | 40801 | 59920 | 29841 | 80150 | 12777 | 48501 |
| 34 | 25976 | 57948 | 29888 | 88604 | 67917 | 48708 | 18912 | 82271 | 65424 | 69774 | 33611 | 54262 | 85963 | 03547 |
| 35 | 09763 | 83473 | 73577 | 12908 | 30883 | 18317 | 28290 | 35797 | 05998 | 41688 | 34952 | 37888 | 38917 | 88050 |

*(continued)*

## Table of Random Numbers *(continued)*

| Col. (1) Line | (2) | (3) | (4) | (5) | (6) | (7) | (8) | (9) | (10) | (11) | (12) | (13) | (14) |
|---|---|---|---|---|---|---|---|---|---|---|---|---|---|
| 36  91567 | 42595 | 27958 | 30134 | 04024 | 86385 | 29880 | 99730 | 55536 | 84855 | 29080 | 09250 | 79656 | 73211 |
| 37  17955 | 56349 | 90999 | 49127 | 20044 | 59931 | 06115 | 20542 | 18059 | 02008 | 73708 | 83317 | 36103 | 42791 |
| 38  46503 | 18584 | 18845 | 49618 | 02304 | 51038 | 20655 | 58727 | 28168 | 15475 | 56942 | 53389 | 20562 | 87338 |
| 39  92157 | 89634 | 94824 | 78171 | 84610 | 82834 | 09922 | 25417 | 44137 | 48413 | 25555 | 21246 | 35509 | 20468 |
| 40  14577 | 62765 | 35605 | 81263 | 39667 | 47358 | 56873 | 56307 | 61607 | 49518 | 89656 | 20103 | 77490 | 18062 |
| 41  98427 | 07523 | 33362 | 64270 | 01638 | 92477 | 66969 | 98420 | 04880 | 45585 | 46565 | 04102 | 46880 | 45709 |
| 42  34914 | 63976 | 88720 | 82765 | 34476 | 17032 | 87589 | 40836 | 32427 | 70002 | 70663 | 88863 | 77775 | 69348 |
| 43  70060 | 28277 | 39475 | 46473 | 23219 | 53416 | 94970 | 25832 | 69975 | 94884 | 19661 | 72828 | 00102 | 66794 |
| 44  53976 | 54914 | 06990 | 67245 | 68350 | 82948 | 11398 | 42878 | 80287 | 88267 | 47363 | 46634 | 06541 | 97809 |
| 45  76072 | 29515 | 40980 | 07391 | 58745 | 25774 | 22987 | 80059 | 39911 | 96189 | 41151 | 14222 | 60697 | 59583 |
| 46  90725 | 52210 | 83974 | 29992 | 65831 | 38857 | 50490 | 83765 | 55657 | 14361 | 31720 | 57375 | 56228 | 41546 |
| 47  64364 | 67412 | 33339 | 31926 | 14883 | 24413 | 59744 | 92351 | 97473 | 89286 | 35931 | 04110 | 23726 | 51900 |
| 48  08962 | 00358 | 31662 | 25388 | 61642 | 34072 | 81249 | 35648 | 56891 | 69352 | 48373 | 45578 | 78547 | 81788 |
| 49  95012 | 68379 | 93526 | 70765 | 10593 | 04542 | 76463 | 54328 | 02349 | 17247 | 28865 | 14777 | 62730 | 92277 |
| 50  15664 | 10493 | 20492 | 38391 | 91132 | 21999 | 59516 | 81652 | 27195 | 48223 | 46751 | 22923 | 32261 | 85653 |

SOURCE: *Table of 105,000 Random Decimal Digits,* Statement no. 4914, File no. 261-A-1, Interstate Commerce Commission, Washington, D.C., May 1949.

# GLOSSARY

**ABBA counterbalancing** A technique for minimizing the effect of a linear confounding variable in an experiment having one independent variable with two levels, A and B. Level A is presented first, followed by two presentations of level B and a final presentation of A.

**Abscissa** The horizontal axis (see *x-axis*) of a graph, upon which the levels of an independent variable are often represented.

**Abstract** A short (960 characters at most) summary of a research report.

**Alternative-form reliability** A means of determining a test's reliability by giving a second test, having items similar to the first, to the same group and calculating a correlation coefficient on the two sets of scores.

**Analogical theory** A theory that explains how psychological relationships work by drawing an analogy to a physical model.

**Analysis of variance** A parametric test of statistical inference used for analyzing data from a factorial experiment or a multilevel single-variable experiment.

**Applied research** Research having as its primary purpose the solution of a specific problem.

**Archival research** A type of study in which existing public or private records are examined, organized, and interpreted.

**Asymptote** The imaginary line that a negatively accelerated function approaches as it flattens out.

**Bar graph** A means of illustrating the frequency of qualitative data using spaced vertical bars. Qualitative class intervals are plotted on the abscissa, with frequency represented on the ordinate and the frequency of each class represented by the height of the bar over that class interval.

**Baseline experiment** A type of single-variable experiment that can show effects using data from a single participant. A steady-state baseline rate of responding is established, following which an experimental manipulation is made and a transition state established. Finally, the manipulation is removed and the baseline recovered.

**Basic research** Study aimed at understanding the basic mechanisms of science. Although such research can lead to the solution of applied problems, the goal is simply to enhance the body of knowledge.

**Between-subjects design** An experimental research strategy in which each research participant provides data for only one level of the independent variable (or variables).

**Bimodal distribution** A frequency distribution having two humps, each of which has a maximum value.

**Blind experiment** An experiment in which participants are unaware of the levels of the independent variable to which they are being exposed.

**Case history** A nonexperimental means of collecting data that contains detailed accounts of the behaviors of a single person or event.

**Ceiling effect**   The truncation of data at the top of a distribution due to a limit on the highest score possible.

**Chi-square test**   A nonparametric test of statistical inference that is used to determine whether the observed frequency of occurrence of scores is statistically different from the expected frequency.

**Choice reaction time**   The time taken to give one of several responses to one of several stimuli.

**Closed-ended question**   A survey question that requires respondents to answer within an imposed structure.

**Coefficient of determination**   A statistic computed by squaring the correlation coefficient that specifies the proportion of variation explained.

**Complete counterbalancing**   An experimental design in which the order of the levels of the independent variable is such that across participants every level of the independent variable occurs an equal number of times and also follows every other level an equal number of times.

**Composite dependent variable**   A measure of behavior that combines the results of several dependent variables into one measure of overall performance.

**Concurrent validity**   A means of establishing a test's validity by determining whether it successfully predicts some specific criterion when the test and the criterion measurements are taken at the same time.

**Conference paper**   An oral presentation of a research project to a meeting of researchers.

**Confounding variable**   A variable whose levels are correlated with the levels of the independent variable such that any change in behavior could be due either to the levels of

the independent variable or those of the confounding variable.

**Construct validity**   The strength of the link between the term used to refer to a class of behaviors (aggression) and the behavior being manipulated or measured (number of threatening statements).

**Content validity**   A means of establishing a test's validity by carefully analyzing the subject matter purportedly covered in the test and then constructing the test so that it contains a representative set of items.

**Context effect**   The influence on participants' behavior of exposure to the levels of variables that they bring with them to an experiment and those that they develop during the experiment.

**Contingency coefficient**   A measure of the strength of association between two sets of nominal-scale numbers.

**Control group**   In a between-subjects design, the participants who are treated in a way comparable to those in the experimental group (or groups) except for not being exposed to the experimental manipulation.

**Control variable**   A circumstance of the experiment that the experimenter sets at a particular level and prevents from varying.

**Converging-series design**   A sequence of experiments conducted in order to progressively eliminate competing theoretical hypotheses.

**Correlation**   A relationship between two variables that is of a particular direction and a particular strength.

**Correlational observation**   A research design in which the researcher attempts to determine whether two or more variables are related without attempting to manipulate the variables or draw causal conclusions.

**Correlation coefficient**   A number between +1.0 and −1.0 that expresses the strength and direction of a relationship between two variables.

**Counterbalancing**  A way of ordering the presentation of levels of the independent variable in order to minimize or eliminate the effects of sequential confounding variables.

**Critical incident**  In applied research, a single instance that is considered to be diagnostic of a possible relationship between independent and dependent variables.

**Crossover interaction**  An interaction from the results of a factorial experiment in which the graphed lines representing the independent variables cross each other.

**Curvilinear function**  A function that departs from a straight line and contains components that can be fit by various mathematical formulas for curved lines.

**Deduction**  A means of reaching a logical conclusion from a set of premises; this conclusion contains no more information than the premises taken collectively (for example, *A* is a *B*; *B* is a *C*; therefore, *A* is a *C*).

**Demand characteristics**  Attributes of an experiment that lead a participant to behave in a certain way, usually in support of the experimental hypothesis, independent of the levels of the independent variable.

**Dependent variable**  The behavior the experimenter chooses to measure; this behavior may be dependent upon the levels of the independent variable.

**Descriptive statistics**  Ways of reducing data sets so that only certain properties are described (for example, central tendency or dispersion of a distribution).

**Descriptive theory**  A theory that simply attaches names to events without necessarily explaining why or how the events have occurred.

**Double-blind experiment**  An experiment in which neither the participant nor the experimenter knows the particular level of the independent variable being presented.

**Dual-task methodology**  A way of indirectly inferring the processing requirements of a task by measuring performance on a second task performed simultaneously.

**Electronic publishing**  The publication of information in electronic form, such as on the Internet, rather than in paper form.

**Ethnography**  A qualitative research design that describes a culture in detail.

**Experimental group**  Those participants in a between-subjects experiment exposed to the treatment condition.

**Experimental method**  A research technique in which an independent variable is manipulated and a dependent variable is measured. The experimental method allows a causal inference to be made: Any change in the dependent variable was caused by the manipulation of the independent variable.

**External validity**  The generalizability of an experimental result to a particular real-world population, situation, or setting different from that represented in the experiment.

**Fabrication of results**  A type of scientific fraud in which false data are constructed.

**Face validity**  The weakest form of establishing a test's validity; the test is simply examined to determine whether, on the surface, it looks as if it is measuring what it is supposed to measure.

**Factorial design**  An experimental design containing more than one independent variable in which every level of each independent variable is combined with every other level.

**Floor effect**   The truncation of data at the bottom of a distribution due to a limit on the lowest score possible.

**Frequency distribution**   A plot of the number of scores occurring for each score value or for two or more limited ranges of score values.

**Function**   A line or curve illustrating the relationship of one variable to another.

**Functional experiment**   An experiment having three or more levels of an independent variable such that a functional relationship between the independent and dependent variables can be shown.

**Group administration of surveys**   The collection of survey data through simultaneous administration to a group of respondents.

**Hawthorne effect**   A change in behavior due simply to the experimenter's paying attention to the participants rather than to the effects of the independent variable.

**Histogram**   A means of illustrating the frequency of quantitative data using contiguous vertical bars. Quantitative class intervals are plotted on the abscissa, with frequency represented on the ordinate and the frequency of each class represented by the height of the bar over that class interval.

**History as a threat to internal validity**   A change in the dependent variable due to the occurrence of an event between the testing of levels of the independent variable.

**Hypothesis**   A statement about a predicted relationship between two or more variables.

**Independent variable**   A circumstance having two or more levels manipulated by the experimenter so that effects on the dependent variable can be observed.

**Induction**   A logical process in which the conclusion contains more information than the observations on which it is based.

**Inferential statistic**   A statistical test that allows one to infer the likelihood that an observed result is due to chance alone.

**Informed consent**   A procedure ensuring that research participants have been given all important information about the study and have formally agreed to participate.

**Institutional review board**   A committee at a research-oriented institution constituted to ensure that all research is conducted in an ethical manner.

**Interaction in a factorial design**   The effect of the nonadditive combination of multiple independent variables on a dependent variable.

**Internal validity**   The certainty of the assertion that it was the manipulation of the independent variable that caused the change in the dependent variable.

**Internet survey**   A survey administered electronically over the Internet.

**Interrupted time-series design**   A quasi-experimental design in which a single group is observed multiple times before an experimental manipulation and then multiple times after the manipulation.

**Interval scale**   Measurements in which the intervals between numbers are a constant unit; $1 = n - (n - 1)$ (for example, Fahrenheit temperature).

**Interview**   The structured or unstructured collection of survey data by means of direct face-to-face contact of an interviewer with a respondent.

**Kruskal–Wallis one-way ANOVA by ranks**   An inferential statistical test appropriate for ordinal data that tests for differences between two or more independent groups.

**Latin Square**   A type of counterbalancing that assures that each level of the independent variable appears in every ordered position equally often.

**Level of significance**    The statistical probability required by scientists to say it is unlikely that an observed characteristic of a sample is due to chance rather than being true of the underlying population. This probability is usually $p < .05$ or $p < .01$.

**Likert scale**    A rating scale that allows a researcher to investigate respondents' attitudes about topics by indicating their level of agreement with a statement.

**Linear function**    A function that forms a straight line.

**Line graph**    A means of illustrating the relationship of two variables using a continuous line or curve.

**Literature search**    The process of examining the formal scientific body of knowledge for written material relevant to a particular area of research.

**Mail survey**    A survey administered by sending it through the mail.

**Main effect**    In a factorial design, the relationship between the levels of one independent variable and a dependent variable averaged across the levels of other independent variables.

**Mann–Whitney *U* test**    A nonparametric test of statistical inference used for testing the difference between two groups using rank-order information.

**Matched-groups design**    A method of assigning participants in between-subjects designs whereby sets of participants are first formed by matching them on a variable that is highly correlated to the dependent variable; then participants from each set are randomly assigned to groups.

**Maturation as a threat to internal validity**    A change in the dependent variable due to participants' aging between the testing of levels of the independent variable.

**Mean**    A measure of central tendency of a distribution that is calculated by adding all of the scores and then dividing the total by the number of scores.

**Mean treatment effect size**    A statistic for representing the size of the effect of an experimental manipulation on behavior; it is the mean of the control group, subtracted from the mean of the treatment group, divided by the standard deviation of the control group.

**Median**    A measure of central tendency of a distribution that is calculated by ordering all scores and selecting the middle score.

**Meta-analysis**    A technique for estimating the cumulative size of an experimental effect across multiple experiments.

**Mixed factorial design**    A factorial design having at least one within-subject and one between-subjects independent variable.

**Mode**    A measure of central tendency of a distribution that is the most frequent score.

**Monotonic function**    A function that increases throughout its range or decreases throughout its range.

**Mortality as a threat to internal validity**    A difference in the dependent variable due to differential participant attrition from groups exposed to different levels of the independent variable.

**Multiple-alternative question**    A question written such that the possible response alternatives are restricted.

**Naturalistic observation**    A type of research in which behavior is studied within its natural setting.

**Negative function**    A relationship in which increasing values of one variable are associated with decreasing values of a second variable.

**Negatively accelerated function**   A function in which the rate of increase or decrease of one variable decreases as a second variable increases. Such functions are characterized by steep initial slopes that become progressively flatter.

**Nominal scale**   A measurement scale without quantitative properties in which numbers are used as names (for example, a runner with the number 342 pinned to her shirt).

**Nondifferential transfer**   (See *Symmetrical transfer.*) In an experiment in which the two levels of the independent variable are A and B, the effect on behavior of having B follow A is the same as having A follow B.

**Nonequivalent control group design**   A quasi-experimental design that uses a control group constituted in a manner different from the experimental group.

**Nonexperimental design**   A research design not having protection from the threats to internal validity provided by experimental or quasi-experimental designs. For this reason, the results of such research are impossible to defend.

**Nonexperiment control group**   A group of participants used to assess the demand characteristics of an experiment that is not actually exposed to the levels of the independent variable but is told of the experimental conditions and asked how they would respond.

**Nonmonotonic function**   A function that changes from negative to positive slope or positive to negative slope in at least one place.

**Nonparametric test**   A test of statistical inference that does not require any assumptions about the underlying population distributions, such as that they are normally distributed.

**Nonresponse bias**   The distortion of survey results due to the differential rate of responding by various subgroups.

**Normal distribution**   A frequency distribution, defined by a particular mathematical function, that is bell-shaped, is unimodal, is symmetrical, and has the same mean, median, and mode.

**One-group posttest-only design**   A nonexperimental design in which a single group is exposed to only one level of an independent variable.

**One-group pretest–posttest design**   A nonexperimental design in which a single group is tested, exposed to only one level of an independent variable, and then retested.

**Open-ended question**   A survey question that allows respondents to freely structure their answers.

**Operational definition**   The definition of a concept by means of specifying the operations required to manipulate or measure the concept.

**Order effect**   In a within-subject design, the dependence of the behavior measured on the presentation order of the levels of the independent variable.

**Ordinal scale**   A measurement scale in which the order of the numbers is meaningful but intervals between or ratios of the numbers are not (for example, 9 is greater than 8).

**Ordinate**   The vertical axis (see *y-axis*) of a graph, upon which the levels of a dependent variable are usually represented.

**Parametric test**   A test of statistical inference in which assumptions are made about the underlying population distributions, usually that they are normally distributed.

**Partial counterbalancing**   A way of ordering the presentation of levels of the independent variable in order to minimize some of the effects of sequential confounding variables.

**Participants**   The humans or animals whose behavior the researcher is investigating (formerly called subjects).

**Pearson product-moment correlation coefficient**   A statistic used to measure the strength of association between two interval or ratio scale variables.

**Percent savings**   A composite dependent variable in which the number of trials to relearn a task is subtracted from the number of trials to originally learn the task, divided by the number of trials to originally learn, and multiplied by 100 to determine the percent of trials saved by having learned the task previously.

**Pilot experiment**   A small-scale experiment that might not satisfy all of the requirements of experimentation conducted for the purpose of pretesting the levels and procedures to be used in the final experiment.

**Placebo**   In drug research, a nonactive substance administered in the same manner that the active drug is administered; sometimes the placebo can cause a change in behavior even though it is physiologically nonactive.

**Positive function**   A relationship in which increasing values of one variable are associated with increasing values of a second variable.

**Positively accelerated function**   A function in which the rate of increase or decrease of one variable increases as a second variable increases. Such functions are characterized by shallow initial slopes that become progressively steeper.

**Poster presentation**   The presentation of a research project by means of the posting of a series of panels representing the research.

**Posttest-only design with nonequivalent groups**   A nonexperimental design in which one group is exposed to one level of an independent variable and a second group chosen using a different selection mechanism is exposed to a second level.

**Predictive validity**   A means of establishing a test's validity by determining whether it successfully predicts some specific criterion.

**Proxy pretest**   A test whose results are correlated with the posttest and used in quasi-experimental designs having nonequivalent groups for the purpose of demonstrating partial equivalence of the groups.

**Psychohistory**   Psychobiographies, usually of well-known individuals, that attempt to explain behavior patterns by examining critical events in their lives.

**Pure research**   (See *Basic research.*) Research aimed at understanding the basic mechanisms of science. Although such research can lead to the solution of applied problems, the goal is simply to enhance the body of knowledge.

**Qualitative design**   Research designs that use descriptive data such as written descriptions of people, including opinions and attitudes, and of events and environments.

**Quantitative designs**   Research designs in which events can be quantified so that the final data are numerical (for example, an experiment).

**Quantitative theory**   A theory that states relationships in mathematical terms.

**Quasi-experimental designs**   Research designs that do not satisfy the participant randomization requirements of experimentation but that allow many of the threats to internal validity to be assessed.

**Questionnaire**   A written survey administered individually or in groups.

**Randomization**   A method of selection that operates by chance such that every item has an equal chance of being selected.

**Randomization within blocks**   A method of selection in which conditions are randomly assigned to trials within the constraint that each condition occur an equal number of times within each block of trials.

**Randomization within constraints**   A method of selection in which items are randomly chosen within the bounds of some selection rule or rules (for example, conditions are randomly chosen within the constraint that they be represented an equal number of times).

**Random sample**   A subgroup of a population selected by some random process.

**Random variable**   A circumstance in an experiment whose level is determined by chance rather than being controlled by the experimenter.

**Range**   The difference between the smallest value of a set of numbers and the largest value.

**Range effect**   In within-subject designs in which the stimuli or responses can be put into a consistent order, the tendency for the best performance to occur in the middle positions due to high transfer of learning.

**Rating scale**   A response technique that allows a respondent to give a graded response indicating the respondent's rating (for example, from "strongly agree" to "strongly disagree").

**Ratio scale**   A measurement scale in which the ratios of the numbers are meaningful (for example, 4 cm is twice as long as 2 cm).

**Reliability**   The degree to which a measurement can be successfully repeated.

**Repeated measures design**   (See *Within-subject design.*) An experimental design in which the same group of participants is exposed to all levels of the independent variable (or variables).

**Response-surface methodology**   A technique used to estimate the effects of a combination of many independent variables without having to conduct a complete factorial experiment combining all levels of all variables.

**Scatterplot**   A means of graphing data points in which the position of each point is determined by its value corresponding to the variables on each axis.

**Selection as a threat to internal validity**   A difference in the dependent variable due to any difference in the composition of participant groups exposed to different levels of the independent variable.

**Separate groups design**   (See *Between-subjects design.*) An experimental design in which each group is exposed to only one level of an independent variable.

**Simulation control group**   In order to assess demand characteristics of an experiment, participants are asked to pretend that they have been exposed to an experimental manipulation and to simulate the expected behavior.

**Skewed distribution**   An asymmetrical distribution whose tail extends farther in one direction than the other.

**Small-*N* baseline design**   (See *Baseline experiment.*) A type of single-variable experiment that can show effects using data from a small number of participants. A steady-state baseline rate of responding is established, following which an experimental manipulation is made and a transition state established. Finally, the manipulation is removed and the baseline recovered.

**Spearman rank-order correlation coefficient**    A statistic used to measure the strength of association between two ordinal scale variables.

**Split-half reliability**    A means of determining a test's reliability by statistically splitting a single test into halves and correlating their scores.

**Standard deviation**    A measure of the dispersion of a frequency distribution in which each score is subtracted from the mean, squared, and summed. The sum is then divided by the number of scores, and the square root is taken.

**Statistical conclusion validity**    The degree to which a statistically significant relationship between the independent and dependent variables indicates that there is a real relationship.

**Statistical regression as a threat to internal validity**    During repeated testing, the movement of participants' extreme scores toward the group mean.

**Statistical significance**    A result is said to be statistically significant if the statistical probability required by scientists to say that it is unlikely an observed characteristic of a sample is due to chance, rather than being true of the underlying population, has been reached. This probability is usually $p < .05$ or $p < .01$.

**Stratified sampling**    A process by which a sample of a population is selected such that appropriate representation is given to subpopulations, or strata (such as income levels or ethnic groups).

**Survey**    The collection of data by means of asking people about their opinions or behaviors.

**Symmetrical transfer**    In an experiment in which the two levels of the independent variable are A and B, the effect on behavior of having B follow A is the same as having A follow B.

**Telephone survey**    A survey administered by telephone interviews.

**Testing as a threat to internal validity**    A change in the dependent variable due to participants' prior exposure to the testing instrument or situation.

**Test–retest reliability**    A means of determining a test's reliability by repeating the test on the same group a second time and calculating a correlation coefficient on the two sets of scores.

**Theory**    A statement about the probable relationships among a set of abstract variables.

**Treatment**    The application of an experimental manipulation by the experimenter, usually as contrasted to the control condition, or group in which no treatment is given.

**Treatment × Subject design**    See *Within-subject design.*

**Truncated distribution**    A limitation on the range of a particular variable that results in a bounded frequency distribution (for example, a ceiling or floor effect).

**t-test**    A parametric test of statistical inference used for determining the probability that an observed difference between data samples representing two different levels of an independent variable occurred by chance.

**Validity**    The degree to which something (a measuring device, a concept) corresponds to a standard.

**Variance**    A measure of the dispersion of a frequency distribution in which each score is subtracted from the mean, squared, and summed. The sum is then divided by the number of scores.

**Wilcoxon matched-pairs signed-ranks test**    An inferential statistical test appropriate for ordinal data used to determine the probability that an observed difference between conditions for the same or matched participants occurred by chance.

**Within-subject design**    An experimental design in which each participant is exposed to all levels of the independent variable (or variables).

***x*-axis**    (See *Abscissa.*) The horizontal axis of a graph, upon which the levels of an independent variable are often represented.

***y*-axis**    (See *Ordinate.*) The vertical axis of a graph, upon which the levels of a dependent variable are usually represented.

# REFERENCES

AAU statement on preventing and probing research fraud. (1983). *Chronicle of Higher Education, 26,* 8.

Adair, J. G. (1973). *The human subject.* Boston: Little, Brown.

Adair, J. G., & Epstein, J. (1968). Verbal cues in the mediation of experimenter bias. *Psychological Reports, 22,* 1045–1053.

Adams, J. A. (1972). Research and the future of engineering psychology. *American Psychologist, 27,* 615–622.

Aldridge, J. W. (1978). Levels of processing in speech perception. *Journal of Experimental Psychology: Human Perception and Performance, 4,* 164–177.

American Medical Association. (1989, April). *AMA surveys of physician and public opinion on health care issues: 1989.* Chicago: Author.

American Psychological Association. (1982). *Ethical principles in the conduct of research with human participants.* Washington, DC: Author.

American Psychological Association. (1986). Guidelines for ethical conduct in the care and use of animals. *Journal of the Experimental Analysis of Behavior, 45,* 127–132.

American Psychological Association. (1992). Ethical principles of psychologists and code of conduct. *American Psychologist, 47,* 1597–1611.

American Psychological Association. (1994). *Publication manual of the American Psychological Association* (4th ed.). Washington, DC: Author.

American Psychological Association. (1997). Animal rights activity increases: Threats made against behavioral scientists. *Science Agenda, 10,* 1, 4.

Arnoult, M. D. (1972). *Fundamentals of scientific method in psychology.* Dubuque, IA: William C. Brown.

Associated Press. (1985). [Data available from POLL computer database]. Storrs, CT: Roper Center for Public Opinion.

Barber, B. (1976). The ethics of experimentation with human subjects. *Scientific American, 234,* 25–31.

Barber, T. X. (1976). *Pitfalls in human research.* New York: Pergamon Press.

Barber, T. X., & Silver, J. J. (1968). Fact, fiction, and the experimenter bias effect. *Psychological Bulletin Monograph Supplement, 70,* 1–29.

Boyce, J. R. (1989). Use of animals in research: Can we find a middle ground? *Journal of the Veterinary Medicine Association, 194,* 24–25.

Bradley, J. V. (1968). *Distribution-free statistical tests.* Englewood Cliffs, NJ: Prentice-Hall.

Bryant, F. B., & Wortmen, P. M. (1978). Secondary analysis: The case for data archives. *American Psychologist, 33,* 381–387.

Burd, S. (1993). Report finds animal-rights activists have stepped up attacks. *The Chronicle of Higher Education, 40,* A31.

Campbell, S. K. (1974). *Flaws and fallacies in statistical thinking.* Englewood Cliffs, NJ: Prentice-Hall.

Christensen, L. (1988). Deception in psychological research: When is its use justified? *Personality and Social Psychology Bulletin, 14,* 664–675.

Clark, C., & Williges, R. C. (1973). Response surface methodology central-composite design modifications for human performance research. *Human Factors, 15,* 295–310.

Coke-Pepsi slugfest. (1976, July 26). *Time,* pp. 64–65.

Cook, T. D., & Campbell, D. T. (1979). *Quasi-experimentation: Design & analysis issues for field settings.* Chicago: Rand McNally.

Cordes, C. (1990). U. S. enters lawsuit accusing scientist, institutions of fraud. *The Chronicle of Higher Education, 37,* A1, A24, A25.

Coren, S., & Halpern, D. F. (1991). Left-handedness: A marker for decreased survival fitness. *Psychological Bulletin, 109,* 90–106.

Coren, S., & Porac, C. (1977). Fifty centuries of right-handedness: The historical record. *Science, 198,* 631–632.

Daly, M., & Wilson, M. (1988). *Homicide.* New York: Aldine de Gruyter.

Decker, B. (1967). Words about words: I. Pessimistic. *Journal of Creative Behavior, 1,* 34.

Dewsbury, D. A. (1990). Early interactions between animal psychologists and animal activists and the founding of the APA committee on precautions in animal experimentation. *American Psychologist, 45,* 315–327.

Dillman, D. A. (1978). *Mail and telephone surveys: The total design method.* New York: Wiley.

Doyle, A. C. (1989). A scandal in Bohemia. In *The adventures of Sherlock Holmes.* New York: Tom Dougherty Associates. (Original work published 1891)

Dunlap, K. (1920). *Mysticism, Freudianism, and Scientific Psychology.* St. Louis: C. V. Mosby.

Erickson, F. (1973). What makes school ethnography "ethnographic"? *Anthropology and Education Quarterly, 4,* 10–19.

Estes, W. K. (1993). How to present visual information. *APS Observer, 6,* 6–9.

Feeney, D. M. (1987). Human rights and animal welfare. *American Psychologist, 42,* 593–599.

Fine, M. A., & Kurdek, L. A. (1993). Reflections on determining authorship credit and authorship order on faculty-student collaborations. *American Psychologist, 48,* 1141–1147.

Fisher, R. A. (1936). Has Mendel's work been rediscovered? *Annals of Science, 1,* 115.

Foertsch, J., & Gernsbacher, M. A. (1997). In search of gender neutrality: Is singular *they* a cognitively efficient substitute for generic *he*? *Psychological Research, 8,* 106–111.

Gallup, G. G., & Suarez, S. D. (1985). Alternatives to the use of animals in psychological research. *American Psychologist, 40,* 1104–1111.

Gantt, W. H. (1928). Ivan P. Pavlov: A biographical sketch. In W. H. Gantt (Ed.), *I. P. Pavlov's lectures on conditioned reflexes* (pp. 11–31). New York: Liveright.

Garner, W. R., Hake, H. W., & Eriksen, C. W. (1956). Operationalism and the concept of perception. *Psychological Review, 63,* 149–159.

Garvey, W. D., & Griffith, B. C. (1971). Scientific communication: Its role in the conduct of research and creation of knowledge. *American Psychologist, 26,* 349–362.

Glass, G. V., McGaw, B., & Smith, M. L. (1981). *Meta-analysis in social research.* Newbury Park, CA: Sage.

Glinski, R. J., Glinski, B. C., & Slatin, P. T. (1970). Nonnaivety contamination in conformity experiments: Sources, effects, and implications for control. *Journal of Personality and Social Psychology, 16,* 478–485.

Gosling, C., Knight, N., & McKenney, L. S. (Eds.). (1989). *Search PsycINFO: Student Workbook.* Washington, DC: American Psychological Association.

Gould, S. J. (1981). *The mismeasure of man*. New York: Norton.

Greenberg, M. S. (1967). Role playing: An alternative to deception? *Journal of Personality and Social Psychology, 7*, 152–157.

Greenwald, A. G. (1976). Within-subjects designs: To use or not to use? *Psychological Bulletin, 83*, 314–320.

Grobe, R. P., Pettibone, T. J., & Martin, D. W. (1973). Effectiveness of lecture pace on noise level in a university classroom. *Journal of Educational Research, 67*, 73–75.

Gross, A. E., & Flemming, I. (1982). Twenty years of deception in social psychology. *Personality and Social Psychology Bulletin, 8*, 402–408.

Hadaway, C. K., & Marler, P. L. (1998). Did you really go to church this week? Behind the poll data. *The Christian Century, 115*, 472–476.

Halpern, D. F., & Coren, S. (1993). Left-handedness and life span: A reply to Harris. *Psychological Bulletin, 114*, 235–241.

Harcum, E. R. (1989). The highly inappropriate calibrations of statistical significance. *American Psychologist, 44*, 964.

Harlow, H. F. (1958). The nature of love. *American Psychologist, 13*, 673–685.

Harris, L. J. (1993a). Do left-handers die sooner than right-handers? Commentary on Coren and Halpern's (1991) "Left-handedness: A marker for decreased survival fitness." *Psychological Bulletin, 114*, 203–234.

Harris, L. J. (1993b). Reply to Halpern and Coren. *Psychological Bulletin, 114*, 242–247.

Havemann, J. (1989, July 13). Proposals on animal research rattle cages. *Albuquerque Journal*, p. E4.

Hayakawa, S. I. (1978, June–July). *Change*, 6.

Herzog, H. A. (1995). Has public interest in animal rights peaked? *American Psychologist, 50*, 945–947.

Hostetler, A. J. (1988, June). Indictment: Congress sends message on fraud. *APA Monitor*, p. 5.

Huff, D. (1954). *How to lie with statistics*. New York: Norton.

Human Factors and Ergonomics Society. (1995). *Instructions and guidelines for poster presenters: Guidelines for preparing and arranging posters*. Santa Monica, CA: Author.

Infeld, L. (1950). *Albert Einstein*. New York: Scribner's.

Jackson, G. B. (1980). Methods for integrative reviews. *Review of Educational Research, 50*, 438–460.

Jacobson, J. W., Mulick, J. A., & Schwartz, A. A. (1995). A history of facilitated communication: Science, pseudoscience, and antiscience. *American Psychologist, 50*, 760.

Jaschik, S. (1991). Agriculture Dept. issues final rules on care of research animals. *The Chronicle of Higher Education, 37*, A25–A31.

Jensen, A. R. (1978). Sir Cyril Burt in perspective. *American Psychologist, 33*, 499–503.

Johnson, D. A. (1971). Pupillary responses during a short-term memory task: Cognitive processing, arousal, or both? *Journal of Experimental Psychology, 90*, 311–318.

Jung, J. (1969). Current practices and problems in use of college students for psychological research. *Canadian Psychologist, 10*, 280–290.

Justice Department and Department of Agriculture release report on animal rights extremism activities. (1993, September). *Federation News*, p. 6.

Kanekar, S. (1990). Statistical significance as a continuum. *American Psychologist, 45*, 296.

Kennedy, J. E., & Landesman, J. (1963). Series effects in motor performance studies. *Journal of Applied Psychology, 47*, 202–205.

Kenrick, D. T., & Keefe, R. C. (1992). Age preferences in mates reflect sex differences in reproductive strategies. *Behavioral and Brain Sciences, 15,* 75–133.

Kihlstrom, J. F. (1995) From the subject's point of view: The experiment as conversation and collaboration between investigator and subject. American Psychological Society Annual Convention, June 27, 1995.

Kimmel, A. J. (1996). *Ethical issues in behavioral research: A survey.* Cambridge, MA: Blackwell.

Kirk, R. E. (1968). *Experimental designs: Procedures for the behavioral sciences.* Pacific Grove, CA: Brooks/Cole.

Kirk, R. E. (1990). *Statistics: An introduction.* Fort Worth, TX: Holt, Rinehart & Winston.

Krasner, L. (1958). Studies of the conditioning of verbal behavior. *Psychological Bulletin, 55,* 148–170.

Kuhn, T. S. (1970). *The structure of scientific revolutions* (2nd ed.). Chicago: University of Chicago Press.

LeCompte, M. D., & Preissle, J. (1993). *Ethnography and qualitative design in educational research.* San Diego, CA: Academic Press.

Lerner, I. M. (1968). *Heredity, evolution, and society.* San Francisco: W. H. Freeman.

Levenson, R. L., Jr. (1990). Comment on Harcum. *American Psychologist, 45,* 295–296.

Ley, W. (1955). *Salamanders and other wonders.* New York: Viking Press.

Lipsey, M. W., & Wilson, D. B. (1993). The efficacy of psychological, educational, and behavioral treatment: Confirmation from meta-analysis. *American Psychologist, 48,* 1181–1209.

Loftus, G. R. (1993). Editorial comment. *Memory & Cognition, 21,* 1–3.

Loftus, G. R. (1996). Psychology will be a much better science when we change the way we analyze data. *Current Directions in Psychological Science, 5,* 161–171.

Madigan, R. M., Johnson, S., & Linton, P. (1995). The language of psychol-ogy: APA style as epistemology. *American Psychologist, 50,* 428–436.

Maggio, R. (1991). *The bias-free word finder: A dictionary of nondiscriminatory language.* Boston: Beacon Press.

Mangan, K. S. (1990). Universities beef up security at laboratories to protect researchers threatened by animal-rights activists. *The Chronicle of Higher Education, 37,* A16–A19.

Mann, C. (1990). Meta-analysis in the breech. *Science, 249,* 476–480.

Martin, D. W., & Kelly, R. T. (1974). Secondary task performance during directed forgetting. *Journal of Experimental Psychology, 103,* 1074–1079.

Masling, J. (1966). Role-related behavior of the subject and psychologist and its effects upon psychological data. In D. Levine (Ed.), *Nebraska symposium on motivation.* Lincoln: University of Nebraska Press.

McAskie, M. (1978). Carelessness or fraud in Sir Cyril Burt's kinship data? A critique of Jensen's analysis. *American Psychologist, 33,* 496–498.

McDonald, K. (1983). Fraud in scientific research: Is it the work of "psychopaths"? *Chronicle of Higher Education, 26,* 7.

Medvedev, Z. A. (1969). *The rise and fall of T. D. Lysenko* (I. M. Lerner, trans.). New York: Columbia University Press.

Meyers, C. (1990). Association fights restrictions on use of animals in research, drawing praise from scientists and anger from its critics. *The Chronicle of Higher Education, 37,* A25–A27.

Meyers, R. H. (1971). *Response surface methodology.* Boston: Allyn & Bacon.

Milgram, S. (1963). Behavioral study of obedience. *Journal of Abnormal and Social Psychology, 67,* 371–378.

Miller, N. E. (1985). The value of behavioral research on animals. *American Psychologist, 40,* 423–440.

Mitchell, D. B., & Richman, C. L. (1980). Confirmed reservations: Mental travel. *Journal of Experimental Psychology: Human Perception and Performance, 6,* 58–66.

Monte, C. F. (1975). *Psychology's scientific endeavor.* New York: Praeger.

Navon, D., & Gopher, D. (1979). On the economy of the human processing system. *Psychological Review, 86,* 214–255.

Nelson, N., Rosenthal, R., & Rosnow, R. L. (1986). Interpretation of significance levels and effect sizes by psychological researchers. *American Psychologist, 41,* 1299–1301.

Nicks, S. D., Korn, J. H., & Mainieri, T. (1997). The rise and fall of deception in social psychology and personality research, 1921 to 1994. *Ethics and Behavior, 7,* 69–77.

Olson, P. O. (1989). Motorcycle conspicuity revisited. *Human Factors, 31,* 141–146.

Orne, M. T. (1962). On the social psychology of the psychological experiment: With particular reference to demand characteristics and their implications. *American Psychologist, 17,* 776–783.

Orne, M. T. (1970). Hypnosis, motivation and the ecological validity of the psychological experiment. In W. J. Arnold & M. M. Page (Eds.), *Nebraska symposium on motivation.* Lincoln: University of Nebraska Press.

Orne, M. T., & Evans, F. J. (1965). Social control in the psychological experiment: Antisocial behavior and hypnosis. *Journal of Personality & Social Psychology, 1,* 189–200.

Ortmann, A., & Hertwig, R. (1997). Is deception acceptable? *American Psychologist, 52,* 746–747.

Palladino, J. J., & Handelsman, M. M. (1995). On the light side: The history of APA format and style. *Psy Chi Newsletter, 21,* 6.

Parsons, H. J. (1974). What happened at Hawthorne? *Science, 183,* 922–932.

Pifer, L., Shimizu, K., & Pifer, R. (1994). Public attitudes toward animal research: Some international comparisons. *Society and Animals, 2,* 95–113.

Pirsig, R. M. (1975). *Zen and the art of motorcycle maintenance.* New York: Bantam.

Plous, S. (1996a). Attitudes toward the use of animals in psychological research and education: Results from a national survey of psychologists. *American Psychologist, 51,* 1167–1180.

Plous, S. (1996b). Attitudes toward the use of animals in psychological research and education: Results from a national survey of psychology majors. *Psychological Science, 7,* 352–358.

Popper, K. R. (1968). *The logic of scientific discovery* (rev. ed.). New York: Basic Books.

Porac, C., & Coren, S. (1981). *Lateral preferences and human behavior.* New York: Springer-Verlag.

Position statement on the use of animals in research. (1993.) *NIH Guide, 22,* 2–3.

Poulton, E. C. (1973). Unwanted range effects from using within-subject experimental designs. *Psychological Bulletin, 80,* 113–121.

Poulton, E. C. (1979). Composite model for human performance in continuous noise. *Psychological Review, 86,* 361–375.

Poulton, E. C., & Freeman, P. R. (1966). Unwanted asymmetrical transfer effects with balanced experimental designs. *Psychological Bulletin, 66,* 1–8.

Pressley, M. M., & Tullar, W. L. (1977). A factor interactive investigation of mall survey response rates from a commercial sample. *Journal of Marketing Research, 14,* 108–111.

Reed, J. G., & Baxter, P. M. (1992). *Library use: A handbook for psychology* (2nd ed.). Washington, DC: American Psychological Association.

Roethlisberger, F. J. (1977). *The elusive phenomena: An autobiographical account of my work in the field of organized behavior at the Harvard Business School.* Cambridge, MA: Division of Research, Graduate School of Business Administration (distributed by Harvard University Press).

Rogers, J. L., Howard, K. I., & Vessey, J. T. (1993). Using significance test to evaluate equivalence between two experimental groups. *Psychological Bulletin, 113,* 553–565.

Roscoe, S. M. (1980). *Aviation psychology.* Ames: Iowa State University Press.

Rosenberg, M. J. (1969). The conditions and consequences of evaluation apprehension. In T. Rosenthal & T. L. Rosnow (Eds.), *Artifact in behavioral research.* New York: Academic Press.

Rosenthal, R., & Fode, K. L. (1973). The effect of experimental bias on the performance of the albino rat. *Behavioral Science, 8,* 183–189.

Rosenzweig, S. E. G. (1970). Boring and the Zeitgeist: Eruditone gesta beavit. *Journal of Psychology, 75,* 59–71.

Rosnow, R. L., & Rosenthal, R. (1999). *Beginning behavioral research: A conceptual primer* (3rd ed.). Upper Saddle River, NJ: Prentice Hall.

Rowland, L. W. (1939). Will hypnotized persons try to harm themselves or others? *Journal of Abnormal and Social Psychology, 34,* 114–117.

Ryder, R. D. (1979). The struggle against speciesism. In D. Paterson & R. D. Ryder (Eds.), *Animal rights—a symposium* (p. 14). London: Centaur Press.

Safire, W. (1979, November 4). *New York Times Magazine,* pp. 16–18.

Schindler, G. E. (1967). Why engineers and scientists write as they do: Twelve characteristics of their prose. *IEEE Transactions on Engineering Writing and Speech, EWS–10,* 32.

Schultz, D. P. (1969). The human subject in psychological research. *Psychological Bulletin, 72,* 214–228.

Segal, E. (1982). Editorial. *Journal of the Experimental Analysis of Behavior, 38,* 115.

Seligman, M. E. P. (1988). President's comments. *American Psychological Association Monitor, 29,* 2.

Sidman, M. (1960). *Tactics of scientific research.* New York: Basic Books.

Singer, P. (1976). *Animal liberation.* London: Jonathan Cape.

Singer, P. (1985). *In defense of animals.* New York: Basil Blackwell.

Skinner, B. F. (1950). Are theories of learning necessary? *Psychological Review, 57,* 193–216.

Skinner, B. F. (1953). *Science and human behavior.* New York: Free Press.

Skinner, B. F. (1959). A case history in scientific method. In S. Koch (Ed.), *Psychology: A study of a science.* New York: McGraw-Hill.

Skinner, B. F. (1966). Operant behavior. In W. K. Honig (Ed.), *Operant behavior: Areas of research and application* (p. 21). New York: Appleton-Century-Crofts.

Smart, R. (1966). Subject selection bias in psychological research. *Canadian Psychologist, 7,* 115–121.

Staff (1983). *Chronicle of Higher Education, 29,* 7.

Staff. (1994, June 27). *Time,* p. 26.

Strunk, W., Jr., & White, E. B. (1979). *The elements of style* (3rd ed.). New York: Macmillan.

Tanur, J. M. (1994). The trustworthiness of survey research. *The Chronicle of Higher Education, 40,* B1–B3.

Van Orden, G. C., & Paap, K. R. (1997). Functional neural images fail to discover pieces of mind in parts of the brain. *Philosophy of Science Journal, 64,* 885–994.

Weber, S. J., & Cook, T. D. (1972). Subject effects in laboratory research:

An examination of subject roles, demand characteristics, and valid inference. *Psychological Bulletin, 77,* 273–295.

Westfall, R. S. (1973). Newton and the fudge factor. *Science, 179,* 751–758.

Wickens, C. D. (1984). Processing resources in attention. In R. Parasuraman & D. R. Davies (Eds.), *Varieties of attention.* New York: Academic Press.

Wilson, G. T. (1985). Limitations of meta-analysis in the evaluation of the effects of psychological therapy. *Clinical Psychology Review, 5,* 35–47.

Wolins, L. (1962). Responsibility for raw data. *American Psychologist, 17,* 657–658.

Woodworth, R. S. (1940). *Psychology* (4th ed.). New York: Holt.

# INDEX

TO THE OWNER OF THIS BOOK:

I hope that you have found *Doing Psychology Experiments*, 5th Edition by David Martin useful. So that this book can be improved in a future edition, would you take the time to complete this sheet and return it? Thank you.

School and address: _____

Department: _____ Instructor's name: _____

The name of the course in which I used this book is: _____

   1. What I like most about this book is: _____

     _____

   2. What I like least about this book is: _____

     _____

   3. Were all of the chapters of the book assigned for you to read? Yes _____ No _____

   4. If not, which were omitted? _____

   5. Did you receive a free subscription to InfoTrac with this text?

     If yes, did you use it? Yes _____ No _____

   6. Did you find InfoTrac to be a useful tool? Yes _____ No _____

   7. Was InfoTrac easy to use? _____

   8. Did you utilize the Website (see web address on the back of this book)?

     Yes _____ No _____

   9. In what ways did you utilize the Website? Please explain: _____

     _____

  10. Was this the only book you used in this course? If not, please explain: _____

     _____

  11. In the space below, or on a separate sheet of paper, please write specific suggestions for improving this book and anything else you'd care to share about your experience in using this book.

     _____

     _____

     _____

     _____

     _____

  12. What is your major course of study? _____

  13. Do you plan to keep this text? Yes _____ No _____

  14. Do you plan to keep this text? Yes _____ No _____

  15. Do you access the World Wide Web from your own computer or a computer at school?

     Own computer _____ Computer at school _____

Optional:

Your name: _____ Date: _____

May Wadsworth quote you, either in promotion for *Doing Psychology Experiments*, Fifth Edition, or in future publishing ventures?

Yes: _____ No: _____

Sincerely,

*David Martin*

FOLD HERE

BUSINESS REPLY MAIL

FIRST CLASS     PERMIT NO. 358     PACIFIC GROVE, CA

POSTAGE WILL BE PAID BY ADDRESSEE

ATTN: *David Martin*

WADSWORTH PUBLISHING COMPANY
511 FOREST LODGE ROAD
PACIFIC GROVE, CA     93950-9968

FOLD HERE